The At-one-ment
BETWEEN
God and Man

STUDIES
IN THE
SCRIPTURES

"The Path of the Just is as the Shining Light, Which Shineth More and More Unto the Perfect Day."

SERIES V

The At-one-ment
BETWEEN
God and Man

"There is One God, and One Mediator Between God and Man, the Man Christ Jesus; Who Gave Himself a Ransom for All, to be Testified in Due Time." "We Also Joy in God Through our Lord Jesus Christ, by Whom We Have Now Received the Atonement."—I Timothy 2:5, 6; Romans 5:11

DAWN BIBLE STUDENTS ASSOCIATION
East Rutherford, N. J. 07073

(Originally Published in 1899)

TO THE KING OF KINGS AND LORD OF LORDS

IN THE INTEREST OF

HIS CONSECRATED "SAINTS."

WAITING FOR THE ADOPTION,

— AND OF —

"ALL THAT IN EVERY PLACE CALL UPON THE LORD,"

"THE HOUSEHOLD OF FAITH."

— AND OF —

THE GROANING CREATION, TRAVAILING AND WAITING FOR THE MANIFESTATION OF THE SONS OF GOD,

THIS WORK IS DEDICATED

"To make all see what is the fellowship of the mystery which from the beginning of the world hath been hid in God." "Wherein He hath abounded toward us in all wisdom and prudence, having made known unto us the mystery of His will, according to His good pleasure which He hath purposed in Himself; that in the dispensation of the fullness of the times He might gather together in one all things, under Christ."
Eph. 3:4, 5, 9; 1:8-10

PRINTED IN U. S. A.

PUBLISHERS' FOREWORD

In the republishing of this book, THE ATONEMENT BETWEEN GOD AND MAN, the publishers are convinced that they are making available for students of the Bible a veritable treasure-house of knowledge on the various phases of the atonement doctrine of the Bible. At a time when the Biblical doctrine of a "ransom for all" is being challenged by higher critics, evolutionists, and even by former believers, it is particularly appropriate that this bulwark of the "faith once delivered unto the saints" should again be placed in circulation.

In serving as the republishing agents of the volume, we are happy to acknowledge the co-operation of its many friends throughout the world, and to thank them for helping to make possible the undertaking.

The Publishers

The At-one-ment Between God and Man

The Author's Foreword

THE FIRST EDITION of this Volume was published in 1899. It is now in the hands of large numbers of God's people in various languages throughout the civilized world. Numerous letters tell us of great help received from its pages in the elucidation of Divine Truth—in the explanation of the Bible. Some have found special help along one line, some along another; and some along all lines. The chapter entitled, "The Undefiled One," relating to our Lord's assuming earthly conditions when born the babe at Bethlehem, has attracted special attention, and has been declared by many to reflect a great light upon a variety of Scriptural and scientific subjects.

With a system of theology which acknowledges its own fallibility, and asks and expects Divine guidance and enlightenment to the end of the Church's journey, it seems remarkable that this Volume, written 19 years ago, requires little correction, in order to be in full line with the latest thought of Bible students respecting the teachings of the Divine Word.

The keynote of this Volume is the Ransom-price. Apparently this doctrine, from which radiate all other doctrines connected with our salvation, has been in a great measure lost sight of, obscured, from the time the apostles fell asleep in death until now. Bible students have found the Ransom to be the key which unlocks the entire Bible—which decides at once what is Truth and what is error.

It is not surprising that, appreciating the subject and studying it so carefully, our views respecting it have become more and more clear. The Bible statements respecting the Ransom have not in any wise changed, nor has our confidence in them changed; but they are more luminous; we understand them better. We hold that the Bible statements on the sub-

Author's Foreword

ject are infallible, and that it is because we are not infallible that our views are capable of expansion as we search the Scriptures and are guided into the understanding of them as promised, by the Holy Spirit. We are not demurring against the Divine Plan of gradual unfoldment, but rejoicing in it. We have nothing to apologize for. The Ransom looms before us more grandly with every fresh ray of Divine Light.

Now we see that our Lord Jesus left the Heavenly glory that He might accomplish a ransoming work for Adam and his race. We see that His change of nature from a spirit to a human being was with a view to enabling Him to be the Ransom-price—a perfect man for a perfect man—**Anti-lutron**—a corresponding price. We now see that Jesus gave Himself to be a Ransom-price for all at the time of His consecration at thirty years of age at Jordan. He continued in giving the Ransom-price, that is, in laying down His life, which in due time would constitute the Ransom-price for Father Adam and his race. He finished this work of laying down His life, surrendering it, sacrificing it, permitting it to be taken from Him, when He on the cross cried: "It is finished!" Nothing more could be laid down than was there laid down—a Ransom, a corresponding price, for Father Adam. But it was not paid over as a price in settlement of Adam's account, else Adam and the entire sinner race would then and there have been turned over to Jesus. The price was merely laid in the hands of Divine Justice as a deposit, to the credit of the One who had died, that He might apply it later in harmony with the Divine Plan. Our Lord Jesus was raised from the dead a spirit being of the Divine nature, as a reward for His faithfulness and loyalty to God in surrendering His earthly life sacrificially. "Him hath God highly exalted and given a name above every name."

Jesus could not make any use of the Ransom-price while still on earth. He could not even bring His dis-

Author's Foreword

ciples into fellowship with the Father. Hence He declared: "I ascend to My God and to your God, to My Father and to your Father." He also declared: "Except I go away, the Holy Spirit will not come." Ten days after our Lord ascended, His followers, having met according to His direction in the upper room, received the Pentecostal blessing—the evidence that they had been accepted of the Father through the merit of Jesus' sacrifice. Jesus had used as an **imputation** the Ransom merit which He had deposited in the Father's hands; but He did not give it to His disciples. It was not for them as a possession, but for the world—"a Ransom for all." All of Jesus' disciples renounced their share in the Ransom blessings that are coming to the world at the Second Advent of our Lord, that they may have a share with the Redeemer in a still greater blessing—honor and immortality. The Ransom-price is designed to bring to Adam and his race the earthly life and earthly rights and honors which were lost by Father Adam, when by disobedience he became a sinner, the loss being entailed upon all of his family, the entire human race. The time for giving the results of the Ransom, viz., Restitution to Adam and his race, is after our Lord's Second Advent, when He shall set up His Kingdom, designed for the very purpose of bringing back the rebellious race into full fellowship with the Father and to eternal life—as many as will.

The Call of the Church is not to give an additional Ransom-price, nor to add to that which Jesus gave; for His is sufficient. The Church's invitation is to demonstrate that they have the same spirit, disposition, that Jesus had, to do the Father's will at any cost—even unto death; and those demonstrating this may be accepted of the Father as members of a Royal Priesthood, of which Jesus is the Head; as a Bride class, Jesus being the glorious Heavenly Bridegroom. It is required that these come back to God under a Covenant the same as Jesus made, "Gather My saints to-

Author's Foreword

gether unto Me, those that have made a Covenant with Me by sacrifice."—Psalm 50:5

Not until these shall have been called and chosen and found faithful and been glorified, will the time come for Christ and His Bride class to take control of the world for their uplift; and not until then will it be proper for the Savior to transfer to Divine Justice the merit of His death, which He placed in the Father's hands as a deposit when dying, with the words: "Father, into Thy hands I commit My spirit" —My life and all of its rights. When this Ransom-price shall have been formally delivered over to Justice in the end of this Age, it will no longer be a deposit at the command of the Savior but will have been exchanged for Adam and his race, all of whom will be immediately transferred by the Father to the Son, that His Millennial Kingdom may begin and all the families of the earth be subjected to the Redeemer, that He may uplift them out of sin and death conditions to all that was lost in Adam—to all for which Jesus died to regain for man.

But the Church class, in process of selection for nearly nineteen centuries, could not be acceptable sacrifices to God as was their Redeemer, Jesus, because He alone was holy, harmless, undefiled—we are imperfect, sinners, and God does not accept imperfect, blemished, sinful sacrifices. What, then, could be done to make us acceptable sacrifices and to permit us to be associated with Jesus on the spirit plane? The proper thing was done—an imputation of the merit of Jesus was granted by Divine Justice on behalf of all who would enter into a Covenant of Sacrifice, and for whom Jesus would become Advocate, or Surety. This imputation of the merit of His sacrifice to the Church by Jesus might be likened to a mortgage, or an encumbrance, upon the Ransom-sacrifice, which would hinder it from being applied to the world until its application to the Church shall be completed.

Author's Foreword

The Church's Covenant is to sacrifice all their earthly life and rights, that they may become New Creatures in Christ and joint-heirs with Him on the spirit plane.

It was on the basis of this imputation of our coming Restitution blessings, and our own personal consecration to the Lord, that our Redeemer, acting as our great High Priest and Advocate, brought us into that relationship with the Father's Plan which permitted us to receive the begetting of the Holy Spirit, and to cease to be of the human family and become members of the spiritual family, of which Jesus is the Head. All of the Church, therefore, are sharers with Jesus in a work of self-sacrifice, in that we tender ourselves to the Lord and He, as God's High Priest, offers us up as a part of His own sacrifice. Thus we "fill up that which is behind of the afflictions of Christ." Thus we suffer with Him that we may also reign with Him. Not until all of the spirit-begotten ones shall have passed into death will the merit of Christ, placed on deposit in the hands of Justice when He died, and mortgaged in the interest of the Church, be released from that mortgage and be ready for full application in the purchase of Adam and his race under the terms of the New Covenant.

If we were writing this Volume again, we would here and there make very minor differences of expression in harmony with what we have here presented. We ask our readers to have this in mind. The differences are not of a kind that will permit us to say that the expressions in the book are wrong—merely they are not as full and clear as they might have been if the writing were to be done now.

For some up-to-date comments on the New Covenant, we request the new readers to note the author's foreword to "Studies," Volume VI.

Your servant in the Lord,
Charles T. Russell

October 1, 1916.
Brooklyn, N. Y.

CONTENTS

STUDY I

THE FACT AND PHILOSOPHY

It Lies at the Foundation of Christian Doctrine from the Bible Standpoint—Three Views of the Subject—The "Orthodox View," the "Heterodox View"; the Bible View, which Unites and Harmonizes Both—Evolution Theory Antagonistic to the Truth on this Subject—Reconciliation of Divine Justice Accomplished—Reconciliation of the Church in Progress—Reconciliation of the World Future—The Grand Final Results when the Mediatorial Throne and Kingdom will be Vacated. 15

STUDY II

THE AUTHOR OF THE ATONEMENT

The Almighty, Jehovah—The Savior of Sinners, Through Christ—"Worthy is the Lamb"—"The Self-Existing One"—The I Am—A False Tradition—Based on Forgery—The Unity of Father and Son Scripturally Shown—The Scriptural Usage of the Word Jehovah and the Title Lord—The word God in the Old Testament—In the New Testament—The Harmonious Bible Testimony—"He that Hath Seen Me Hath Seen the Father"—He Thought it not Robbery to be Equal. 33

STUDY III

THE MEDIATOR OF THE ATONEMENT

THE ONLY BEGOTTEN ONE

"Who Is He?"—The Logos, a God—The Only Begotten of Jehovah—The Bible's Testimony—"He Who Was Rich"—"Before Abraham Was I Am"—"The First and the Last"—"Jehovah Possessed Me in the Beginning"—The Logos Made Flesh—Not Incarnated—He Humbled Himself—"He Who Was Rich for Our Sakes Became Poor"—No Hypocrisy in this Testimony—Our Lord's Conduct not Deceptive—The Holy, Harmless, Undefiled, Separate from Sinners. . . 83

STUDY IV

THE MEDIATOR OF THE ATONEMENT

THE UNDEFILED ONE

Seemingly Conflicting Scriptures Reconciled—The Roman Catholic Doctrine of Mary's Immaculate Conception Not Sustained—The Birth of Jesus Separate from Sinners Essential to the Divine Arrangement—Otherwise no Ransom Possible—The Latest Deductions of Science in re the Union of Life and Protoplasm—The Logos Made Flesh—Born of a Woman yet Undefiled—How the Imperfect Mother Could and Did Bring Forth the Undefiled One—This Same Principle Operating in Other Features of the Divine Plan, as Testified by the Scriptures. 97

STUDY V

THE MEDIATOR OF THE ATONEMENT

"MADE LIKE UNTO HIS BRETHREN"

AND

"TOUCHED WITH A FEELING OF OUR INFIRMITIES"

Who "His Brethren" are—In What the Likeness Consisted—How He was Tempted in all Points, Like as We are Tempted, Yet Without Sin—The Wilderness Temptations—Their Resemblance to Ours—Some of which would "Deceive if it were Possbible the Very Elect"—In What Sense our Lord was Made Perfect Through Sufferings—Though a Son, yet Learned He Obedience—How He was Made in the Likeness of Sinful Fesh, Yet Without Sin—"Himself took our Infirmities"—How He was "Touched." 107

STUDY VI

THE MEDIATOR OF THE ATONEMENT

DAVID'S SON AND DAVID'S LORD

How David's Son—Joseph's Genealogy Through Solomon—Mary's Genealogy Through Nathan—Abase the High, Exalt the Low—Whence Christ's Title to be David's Lord—How He was Both Root and Branch of David—Meaning of His Title, "The Everlasting Father"—How Secured and How to be Applicable—Who are Children of Christ—The Church His "Brethren"—Children of the God and Father of our Lord Jesus Christ. 129

STUDY VII

THE MEDIATOR OF THE ATONEMENT
"THE SON OF MAN"

What this Title Does not Mean—What It Does Mean—Its Honors Indisputable, Can be Claimed by None Other—The Son of Man as Seen by the World—Pilate's View, Rousseau's View, Napoleon's View—Significance of Statements, "No Beauty in Him that we Should Desire Him"; and "His Visage Was so Marred"—"The Chiefest Among Ten Thousand"—"Yea, He is Altogether Lovely." 149

STUDY VIII

THE CHANNEL OF THE ATONEMENT
THE HOLY SPIRIT OF GOD

The Operation of the Holy Spirit—Now and in the Millennium—Various Descriptive Names of the Holy Spirit, "Spirit of Love," "Spirit of Truth," etc.—In Contrast, the Unholy Spirit, "Spirit of Error," "Spirit of Fear," etc.—Personal Pronouns Applied—The Significance of the Word Spirit—"God is a Spirit"—"The Holy Spirit Was not yet Given"—Gifts of the Spirit—The Transforming Power of the Holy Spirit—The Spirit by Measure and Without Measure—"The Spirit of the World," Antichrist—The Battle Between this and the Holy Spirit—Spirit Fightings Without and Within the Saints—The Spirit that Lusteth to Envy—Taught of the Spirit—the Parakletos, the Comforter—He Shall Guide You into all Truth and into Full Atonement—The Spirit's Supervision None the Less Since the Miraculous Gifts Were Discontinued. 163

STUDY IX

THE BAPTISM, WITNESS AND SEAL
OF THE
SPIRIT OF AT-ONE-MENT

Spirit Baptism, One Only—In Three Parts—The Significance of this Baptism—"The Keys of the Kingdom of Heaven"—Another Baptism of the Spirit Promised "Upon all Flesh"—Its Significance—Prayer for the Spirit—The Witness of the Spirit—Its Importance—No Peace With God Without It—Few Know Whether They Have It or Not—"'Tis a Point I Long to Know"—How to Recognize the Spirit's Witness—Differences of Administration—The Spirit's Testimony—"Sanctified by the Spirit"—"Filled With the Spirit"—The Seal of the Spirit—"The Promise" which it Seals—Unto the Day of Deliverance—The Highest Attainment to be Sought—and Retained. 209

STUDY X

THE SPIRIT OF A SOUND MIND

The Spirit of God in His People Casts Out the Spirit of Fear—Mankind in General Unsound Mentally and Physically—The Sense in Which the Holy Spirit is the Spirit of a Sound Mind—The Operations Producing this Result—The Evidences of the Spirit of a Sound Mind. 249

STUDY XI

THE HOLY SPIRIT OF AT-ONE-MENT

SUPPOSED OBJECTIONS CONSIDERED

Apparently Contradictory Scriptures Examined—Quench not the Spirit—Grieve not the Holy Spirit—The Spirit of Truth—The Comforter—Filled with the Holy Spirit—Lying to the Holy Spirit—Tempting the Spirit of the Lord—Sin Against the Holy Spirit—"The Spirit Said"—"It Seemed Good to the Holy Spirit"—"Forbidden of the Holy Ghost"—"The Holy Ghost Witnesseth"—"The Holy Ghost hath Made You Overseers"—The Holy Spirit a Teacher—"An Unction from the Holy One"—The Spirit Maketh Intercessions with Groanings—How the Spirit Reproves the World—"Hereby Know Ye the Spirit of God" from "the Spirit of Antichrist. 263

STUDY XII

THE SUBJECT OF THE ATONEMENT—MAN

What is Man?—The "Orthodox" Answer—The Scientific Answer—The Bible Answer—Man's Body—The Spirit of Man—The Human Soul—Confusion Through Mistranslation—The Propagation of Souls—What is "Sheol," "Hades," to which all Souls Go, in the Interim Between Death and Resurrection?—The Scriptural Statements Severally Considered. 301

STUDY XIII

HOPES FOR LIFE EVERLASTING AND IMMORTALITY SECURED BY THE ATONEMENT

The Earnest Expectations or Hopes of the Groaning Creation—Are not Proofs—The Promises and the Outworking of Atonement, as Proofs—A Distinction and a Difference—Is the Human Soul Immortal, or has it a Hope of Becoming Immortal?—Are Angels Immortal?—Is Satan Immortal?—The Life and Immortality Brought to Light Through the Gospel—The Greek Words Rendered Immortal and Immortality in the Scriptures—Wherein the Hope of the Church and the Hope for the Saved World Differ. 383

STUDY XIV

THE NECESSITY FOR THE ATONEMENT—THE CURSE

The "Curse" a Present and Not a Future Evil—Where and Why the Blight Came Upon All—When this "Wrath" of God Against Sin Will Cease—"Escape" Now and in the Future—Atonement Necessary, Because of the Plan adopted by God—Man an Example for Angels and for Future Creations. 405

STUDY XV

"A RANSOM FOR ALL"
THE ONLY BASIS FOR AT-ONE-MENT

At-one-ment Impossible Without a Ransom—Secured but not Compelled—To be the Ransomer Became a Favor—The Significance of Ransom and Redeem—What Ransom was Paid for Man?—Justification by Faith thus Secured—"Ye are Bought with a Price."—By Whom?—Of whom?—For what Purpose?—How Love Co-operated with Justice—The "Ransom for All" was not Taken Back—Fatherhood Rights of the First Adam Purchased by the Second Adam—Ransom not Pardon—Man's Death not a Ransom—False Reasoning of Universalist Theories—Justice not Obligated by the Ransom—The Only Name—The Mediator's Method Typed in Moses—Ransom, Substitution—Was a Different Plan Possible? 421

STUDY XVI

THE MINISTRY OF RECONCILIATION
OR AT-ONE-MENT

This Ministry Committed to the Royal Priesthood—Anointed to Preach of the At-one-ment—Why the Joyful News is not Appreciated—The Results of this Ministry—Persecution and Glory—How it Tests Fidelity—Only the Faithful may Share the Atonement Work Future. **487**

THE FACT AND PHILOSOPHY
—OF—
THE ATONEMENT

STUDY I

It Lies at the Foundation of Christian Doctrine from the Bible Standpoint—Three Views of the Subject—The "Orthodox View," the "Heterodox View"; the Bible View, which Unites and Harmonizes Both—Evolution Theory Antagonistic to the Truth on this Subject—Reconciliation of Divine Justice Accomplished—Reconciliation of the Church in Progress—Reconciliation of the World Future—The Grand Final Results when the Mediatorial Throne and Kingdom will be Vacated.

THE doctrine of the Atonement lies at the very foundation of the Christian religion. Having thus the most important place in theology, a clear understanding of this subject is very essential, and this is generally conceded amongst Christian people. Nevertheless, the Atonement, though believed in, is little understood; the various ideas and theories respecting it are disconnected as well as vague; and faith built upon these disconnected and vague views of the foundation doctrine must, of necessity, be proportionately unstable, weak and vague. On the contrary, if this important subject be clearly seen, in all the grandeur of the proportions accorded it in the Word of God, as the foundation of the divine plan of salvation, it not only will firmly establish faith, rooting and grounding it upon correct principles, but it will serve as a guide in discriminating between truth and error in connection with all the minutiae of faith. When the foundation is well established and clearly discerned, and every item of faith built upon it is kept in exact alignment with the foundation, the entire faith superstructure will be perfect. As we shall show later, every doctrine and theory may be brought in contact with this touchstone, and have its proportion of gold or of dross quickly determined thereby.

There are two general views of the Atonement:—

(1) What is known as the orthodox view, namely, that man, as a transgressor of the divine law, came under divine condemnation—"under wrath"; and that God, while hindered by Justice from exonerating the sinner, has provided a just redemption for him, and thus provided for the forgiveness of his sins, through the sacrifice of Christ. This entire work of satisfying the claims of Justice and making the sinner acceptable to God, is denominated the work of Atonement.

(2) What is known as the unorthodox view of the Atonement (at one time represented chiefly by Unitarians and Universalists, but which has recently been spreading rapidly and generally in every quarter of Christendom), approaches the subject from the opposite side: it presupposes no requirement on the part of divine justice of a sacrifice for the sinner's transgression; it ignores the wrath of God as represented in any special sentence of death; it ignores "the curse." It holds that God seeks and waits for man's approach, placing no hindrance in the way, requiring no atonement for man's sin, but requiring merely that man shall abandon sin and seek righteousness, and thus come into harmony with God—be **at-one with** God. Hence this view is generally styled **At-one-ment**, and is understood to signify harmony with righteousness regardless of the methods by which mankind may be brought into this state: atonement for sin being considered from the standpoint of expiation by the sinner himself, or else as unconditional forgiveness by God. From this standpoint our Lord Jesus and all his followers have part in the at-one-ment, in the sense that they have taught and exhorted mankind to turn from sin to righteousness, and in no sin-offering or ransom sense.

(3) The view which we accept as the Scriptural one, but which has been overlooked very generally by theologians, embraces and combines both of the foregoing views. The Bible doctrine of the Atonement, as we shall endeavor to show, teaches clearly:

(a) That man was created perfect, in the image of God, but fell therefrom, through wilful disobedience, and came under the sentence of wrath, "the curse," and thus the entire race became "children of wrath."—Eph. 2:3

(b) While God justly executed against his disobedient creature the sentence of his law, death, and that without mercy, for over four thousand years, yet, nevertheless, blended with this justice and fidelity to principles of righteousness was the spirit of love and compassion, which designed an ultimate substitutional arrangement or plan of salvation, by which God might still be just and carry out his just laws against sinners, and yet be the justifier of all who believe in Jesus. (Rom. 3:26) By this plan all the condemned ones might be relieved from the sentence without any violation of Justice, and with such a display of divine love and wisdom and power as would honor the Almighty, and prove a blessing to all his creatures, human and angelic—by revealing to all, more fully than ever before seen, the much diversified wisdom and grace of God.—Eph. 3:10—Diaglott

(c) It was in the carrying out of this program of Atonement to the divine law for its transgression by father Adam, that our dear Redeemer died, "a ransom for all, to be testified in due time."—1 Tim. 2:6

(d) But the sacrifice for sins does not complete the work of Atonement, except so far as the satisfaction of the claim of Justice is concerned. By virtue of the ransom paid to Justice, a transfer of man's account has been made, and his case, his indebtedness, etc., is wholly transferred to the account of the Lord Jesus Christ, who paid to Justice the full satisfaction of its claims against Adam, and his race. Thus Jesus, by reason of this "purchase" with his own precious blood, is now in consequence the owner, master, "Lord, of all."—Rom. 14:9

(e) One object in this arrangement for Adam and his race was the annulment of their **death sentence**, which, so long as it remained, estopped Love from any efforts to recover the condemned, whose privileges of future life under any circumstances were wholly abrogated—destroyed.

(f) Another object was the placing of the fallen race beyond the reach of divine Justice, and under the special supervision of Jesus, who as the representative of the Father's plan proposes not only to satisfy the claims of Justice, but also undertakes the instruction, correction and restitution of so many of the fallen race as shall show their desire for harmony with Justice. Such he will ultimately turn over to the Justice of the divine law, but then so perfected as to be able to endure its perfect requirements.

(g) Though originally the only separating influence between God and man was the divine **sentence**, now, after six thousand years of falling, degradation and alienation from God through wicked works—and because of ignorance, superstition, and the wiles of the Adversary—and because the divine character and plan have been misrepresented to men, we find the message of grace and forgiveness unheeded. Although God freely declares, since the ransom was accepted, that he is now ready to receive sinners back into harmony with himself and to eternal life, through the merit of Christ's sacrifice, nevertheless the majority of mankind are slow to believe the good tidings, and correspondingly slow to accept their conditions. Some have become so deluded by the sophistries of Satan, by which he has deceived all nations (Rev. 20:3), that they do not believe that there is a God; others believe in him as a great and powerful adversary, without love or sympathy, ready and anxious to torment them to all eternity; others are confused by the Babel of conflicting reports that have

The Fact and Philosophy

reached them, concerning the divine character, and know not what to believe; and, seeking to draw near unto God, are hindered by their fears and by their ignorance. Consequently, as a matter of fact, the number who have yet availed themselves of the opportunity of drawing nigh unto God through Christ is a comparatively small one—"a little flock."

(h) Nevertheless, the sacrifice for sins was not for the few, but for the "many," "for all." And it is a part of the divine program that he who redeemed all with his own precious blood shall ultimately make known to all men, "to every creature," the good tidings of their privilege under divine grace, to return to at-one-ment with their Creator.

(i) Thus far only the Church has been benefited by the Atonement, except indirectly; but the teaching of the Scriptures is that this Church shall constitute a priestly Kingdom, or "royal priesthood," with Christ the Royal Chief Priest, and that during the Millennial age this Heavenly Kingdom class, this royal priesthood, shall fully and completely accomplish for mankind the work of removing the blindness which Satan and error and degradation brought upon them, and shall bring back to full at-one-ment with God whosoever wills, of all the families of the earth.

(j) In harmony with this is the apostle's statement that we, believers, the Church, **have received** the Atonement. The Atonement was made, so far as God was concerned, eighteen centuries ago, and that for all; but only believers have received it in the sense of accepting the opportunity which the grace of God has thus provided—and the rest of mankind are blinded. "The god of this world hath blinded the minds of them which believe not, lest the light of the glorious gospel of Christ, who is the image of God, should shine unto them."—2 Cor. 4:4

(k) In harmony with this thought also is the statement of Scripture, that the first work of Christ in connection with his Millennial reign, will be to bind, or restrain, Satan, that he shall deceive the nations no more for the thousand years (Rev. 20:3), also the numerous statements of the prophets, to the effect that when the Kingdom of God shall be established in the earth, the knowledge of the Lord shall fill the whole earth, as the waters cover the great deep, and none shall need to say to his neighbor, "Know thou the Lord" (Heb. 8:11), also the petition of the Lord's prayer, "Thy Kingdom come, thy will be done on earth"—because this implies what the apostle expressly declares, that God desires all men to be saved and **come to a knowledge of the truth.** —1 Tim. 2:4

(l) The Atonement, in both of its phases—the satisfaction of Justice, and the bringing back into harmony or at-one-ment with God of so many of his creatures as, under full light and knowledge, shall avail themselves of the privileges and opportunities of the New Covenant—will be completed with the close of the Millennial age, when all who shall wilfully and intelligently reject divine favor, offered through Christ, "shall be destroyed from among the people," with "an everlasting destruction from the presence of the Lord, and from the glory of his power"—with a destruction from which there will be no hope of recovery by future resurrection.—Acts 3:23; 2 Thess. 1:9

(m) Then the great work of the Atonement will be completed, and all things in heaven and in earth will be found in harmony with God, praising him for all his munificence and grace through Christ; and there shall be no more dying and no more sighing, no more pain there, because the former things shall have passed away—as the result of the work of the Atonement, commenced by the propitiation of Justice by our Redeemer's sacrifice, concluded by the full reconciliation of all found worthy of eternal life.

However the word Atonement may be viewed, it must be conceded that its use at all, as between God and man, implies a difficulty, a difference, an opposition, existing between the Creator and the creature —otherwise they would be at one, and there would be no need of a work of atonement, from either standpoint. And here particularly we discern the deadly conflict that exists between the Bible and the modern doctrine of Evolution, which, for the past thirty years in particular, has been permeating the faith of Christian people of all denominations, and which shows itself most markedly in theological schools and in the principal pulpits of Christendom.

The Evolution theory denies the fall of man; denies that he ever was in the image and likeness of God; denies that he was ever in a fit condition to be on trial before the bar of exact Justice; denies that he ever sinned in such a trial, and that he ever was sentenced to death. It claims that death, so far from being a penalty is but another step in the process of evolution; it holds that man, instead of falling from the image and likeness of God into sin and degradation, has been rising from the condition of a monkey into more and more of the image and likeness of God. The logical further steps of the theory would evidently be, to deny that there could be any justice on God's part in condemning man for rising from a lower to a higher plane, and denying, consequently, that Justice could accept a sin-offering for man, when there had been no sin on man's part to require such an offering. Consistently with this thought, it claims that Christ was not a sin-offering, not a sacrifice for sins—except in the same sense, they would say, that any patriot might be a sacrifice for his country; namely, that he laid down his life in helping to lift the race forward into greater liberties and privileges.

But we find that the Word of God most absolutely contradicts this entire theory, so that no harmony is possible between the Scripture teaching and the teaching of Evolution—science falsely so-called. Whoever believes in the Evolution theory, to that extent disbelieves the Scripture theory; and yet we find a very large number of Christian people vainly struggling and attempting to harmonize these antagonizing teachings. To whatever extent they hold the theory of Evolution, to that extent they are off the only foundation for faith which God has provided; to that extent they are prepared for further errors, which the Adversary will be sure to bring forward to their attention, errors presented so forcibly from the worldly-wise standpoint that they would, if it were possible, deceive the very elect. But the very elect will have "the faith once delivered to the saints"; the very elect will hold to the doctrine of the Atonement, as presented in the Scriptures; the very elect will thus be guarded against every item and feature of the Evolution theory: for the very elect will be taught of God, especially upon this doctrine of the Atonement, which lies at the very foundation of revealed religion and Christian faith.

The Scriptures unequivocally testify that God created man in his own image and likeness—mental and moral; that man, an earthly being, was the moral and intellectual image or likeness of his Creator, a spirit being. They declare his communion with his Creator in the beginning; they declare that his Creator approved him as his workmanship, and pronounced him very "good," very acceptable, very pleasing; they show that the proposition of life or death was set before the perfect Adam, and that when he became a transgressor it was an intelligent and wilful act, inasmuch as it is declared that Adam "was not deceived." They declare the beginning of the execution of the death penalty. They record the progress for centuries of the death sentence upon the race. They point out how God revealed to faithful Abraham his purpose, his intention, not at once, but later on, to bring in a blessing to the race, which he declared he had cursed with the sentence of death.—Gen. 1:31; 2:17; 3:23; 1 Tim. 2:14; Gen. 12:3; 18:18; 3:17

Since the curse or penalty of sin was death, the blessings promised implied life from the dead, life more abundant: and the promise to Abraham was that in some unexplained way the Savior who would accomplish this work of blessing the world should come through Abraham's posterity. The same prom--

The Fact and Philosophy

ises were, with more or less clearness, reiterated to Isaac, to Jacob and to the children of Israel. The prophets also declared that the Messiah coming should be a Lamb slain, a sin-offering, one who should "pour out his soul unto death," for our sins, and not for his own. And they portrayed also the result of his sacrifice for sins, in the glory and blessing that should follow; telling how ultimately his Kingdom shall prevail, and, as the Sun of Righteousness, he shall bring into the world the new day of blessing and life and joy, which shall dispel the darkness and gloom and the sorrow of the night of weeping, which now prevails as the result of original sin and the fall, and inherited evil tendencies.—Isa. 53:10-12; 35; 60; 61

The Apostle Peter, speaking under the inspiration of the Holy Spirit, so far from telling us that man had been created on the plane of a monkey, and had risen to his present degree of development, and would ultimately attain perfection by the same process of evolution, points, on the contrary, a reverse lesson, telling us that Christ died for our sins, and that, as a consequence of the redemption accomplished by his sacrifice, there shall ultimately come to mankind, at the second advent of our Lord, great times of refreshing—times of restitution of all things, which, he declares, "God hath spoken by the mouth of all his holy prophets since the world began." (Acts 3:19-21) Whoever may think the Apostle Peter was preaching a doctrine of evolution, when preaching the gospel of restitution, must have closed his eyes and stopped the operation of his reasoning faculties; for if the original condition of man was that of a monkey, or if it was anything whatever inferior to our present condition, the apostle would have been the veriest fool to hold out, as a grand hope and prospect, **times of restitution**, for restitution means a restoration of that condition which previously existed.

On the contrary, the apostle's words are thoroughly out of harmony with and antagonistic to the theory of evolution, and in strictest harmony with the doctrine of the Atonement, reconciliation and restitution—in strictest harmony with the Scriptural teaching that mankind were sold under sin, and became the slaves of sin, and suffered the degradation of sin, as the result of father Adam's original disobedience and its death-penalty. Restitution, the good tidings which Peter preached, implies that something good and grand and valuable was lost, and that it has been **redeemed** by the precious blood of Christ, and that it shall be **restored**, as the result of this redemption, at the second advent of Christ. And the apostle's reference to the prophets, declaring that these restitution times were mentioned by all of them who were holy, distinctly implies that the hope of restitution is the only hope held out before the world of mankind by divine inspiration.

All the apostles similarly pointed backward to the fall from divine favor, and to the cross of Christ as the point of reconciliation as respects divine Justice, and forward to the Millennial age as the time for the blessing of all the world of mankind with opportunities of knowledge and help in **their reconciliation to God.** They all point out the present age as the time for the gathering out of the elect Church to be associates with Messiah (his "royal priesthood" and "peculiar people") to co-operate with him as his "bride," his "body," in the work of conferring upon the world the blessings of restitution secured for them by the sacrifice finished at Calvary.

Mark the words of the Apostle Paul along this line: "By one man's disobedience sin **entered into the world**—and death as a result of sin; and so death passed upon all men, for [by reason of inherited sin and sinful dispositions] all are sinners. The Apostle Paul quite evidently was no more an Evolutionist than the Apostle Peter and the prophets. Mark the hope which he points out as the very essence of the Gospel, saying: "God commendeth his love toward us, in that while we were yet sinners Christ **died for us**; much more then, being now **justified by his blood**, we shall be saved from wrath through him." (Rom. 5:8, 9) Here is a specific declaration that the race was under divine wrath; that the saving power was the blood of Christ, the sacrifice that he gave on our behalf; and that this sacrifice was an expression of divine love and grace. The apostle proceeds to show the work of Atonement, and the restitution which will follow as a result, saying: "As through one offense [Adam's disobedience] sentence came upon all men to condemnation [the death sentence]; so also through one righteous act the free gift [the reversal of the sentence] came on all men unto justification of life. For as through the disobedience of one man [Adam] many were made sinners [all who were in him] so by the obedience of one [Jesus] many [all who ultimately shall avail themselves of the privileges and opportunities of the New Covenant] shall be constituted righteous."—Rom. 5:12, 18, 19

The same apostle, in many other of his masterly and logical discourses, presents the thought that the Atonement, so far as God is concerned, is a thing of the past—finished when **"we were reconciled to God** through the death of his Son," while we were yet sinners. (Rom. 5:10) In this he evidently did not refer to a work accomplished in the sinner, reconciling the sinner to God, because he states it in the reverse manner, and declares that it was accomplished, not in us, but by Christ for us, **and while we were sinners.** Note also that in various of his learned and logical discourses he points out a work of blessing to the world, to be accomplished through the glorified Church, under Christ, her divinely appointed Head, showing that it will consist in bringing the world to a knowledge of God's grace in Christ, and that **thus** so many of the redeemed world as may be willing can return to at-one-ment with their Creator during the Millennial Kingdom—a restitution of the divine favor lost in Eden.

As an illustration of this point note the argument of Rom. 8:17-24. Here the apostle distinctly marks a separate salvation of the Church and the subsequent salvation or deliverance of the world, the "groaning creation." He calls attention to the Church as the prospective joint-heir with Christ, who, if faithful in suffering with him in this present time, shall ultimately share his glory in his Kingdom. He assures us that these sufferings of this present time are unworthy of comparison with the glory that shall be revealed in us by and by. And then he proceeds to say that this glory to be revealed in the Church after its sufferings are all complete, is the basis for all the earnest expectations of the groaning creation, —whose longings and hopes necessarily await fruition in the time when the sons of God shall be revealed or manifested.

Now the sons of God are unrevealed; the world knows them not, even as it knew not their Master; and though the world, indeed, looks forward with a vague hope to a golden age of blessing, the apostle points out that all their earnest expectations must wait for the time when the Church, the sons of God, shall be glorified and shall be manifested as the kings and priests of God's appointment, who shall reign over the earth during the Millennial age, for the blessing of all the families of the earth, according to the riches of divine grace as revealed by God in his promise to Abraham, saying: "In thy seed shall all the families of the earth be blessed."—Gal. 3:8, 16, 29

The apostle proceeds to show that mankind in general, the intelligent earthly creation, was subjected to **frailty** ("vanity") by heredity, by the transgression of father Adam, according to divine providence, and yet is not left without hope; because under divine arrangement also, a sacrifice for sins has been provided, and provision made that ultimately mankind in general may be emancipated, set free, from slavery of sin, and from its penalty, death, and may attain the glorious freedom (from sickness, pain, trouble, sorrow) which is the liberty of all who are the sons of God. It was from this plane of sonship and such "liberty" that mankind fell through disobedience, and to the same plane of human sonship they will be privileged to return, as a result of the great sin-offering at Calvary, and of the completion of the work of Atonement in them, reconciling them to the divine law by the Redeemer, as the Great Prophet, the antitype of Moses. (Acts 3:22, 23) The apostle also points out that the Church, which already has received the Atonement (accepted the divine arrangement) and come into harmony with God, and has been made possessor of the first-fruits of the spirit, nevertheless, by reason of the surroundings, groans also, and waits for her share of the completed work of the Atonement, in her complete reception to divine favor, the deliverance of the body of Christ, the Church, in the first resurrection.—Rom. 8:23-25

These two features of the Atonement, (1) the righting of the wrong, and (2) the bringing of the separated ones into accord, are shown in the divine proposition of a New Covenant, whose mediator is Christ Jesus our Lord. When father Adam was perfect, in complete harmony with his Creator, and obedient to all of his commands, a covenant between them was implied, though not formally expressed; the fact that life in its perfection had been given to father Adam, and that additionally he had been given dominion over all the beasts and fish and fowl, and over all the earth as the territory of his dominion, and the additional fact that it was declared that if he would violate his faithfulness to the Great King, Jehovah, by disobedience, he would forfeit his life, and vitiate all those rights and blessings which had been conferred upon him—this implied, we say, a covenant or agreement on God's part with his creature that his life was everlasting, unless he should alter the matter by disobedience, and bring upon himself a sentence of death.

The disobedience of Adam, and its death penalty, left him utterly helpless, except as the Almighty provided for the recovery of the race through the New Covenant, and the New Covenant, as the apostle points out, has a mediator—God, on the one part deals with the mediator, and not with the sinner; the sinner, on the other part, deals with the mediator and not with God. But before our Lord Jesus could become the Mediator he must do for mankind a work which, in this figure, is represented as **sealing** the New Covenant with his own precious blood— "The blood of the New Covenant." (Matt. 26:28; Mark 14:24; Heb. 7:22; 9:15-20) That is to say, God, in justice, cannot receive nor deal with the sinner, either directly, or indirectly through a mediator, so as to give the sinner a release from the sentence of death, and reconciliation to God, with its accompanying blessing, the gift of eternal life—except first divine Justice be remembered and satisfied. Hence it was that our Lord Jesus, in paying our penalty by his death, made possible the sealing of the New Covenant between God and man, under the terms of which all who come unto God by him, the mediator, are acceptable.

Reconciliation with God, at-one-ment with him, was impossible until, first, the redemption had been secured with the precious blood, that the one seeking at-one-ment might approach God, through the mediator of the New Covenant: "I am the Way, the Truth and the Life; no man cometh unto the Father but by me." (John 14:6) It is for this reason that the highest privilege of the most favored of mankind, previous to the commencement of Christ's sacrifice, was that of "servants" and "friends" of God—none could be accorded the high privilege of sonship (with all that this implies of divine favor and eternal life), and none were thus recognized. (John 1:12; Matt. 11:11) Thus it will be seen that those who ignore the sin-offering and Justice-appeasement features of the Atonement are ignoring important and indispensable parts—primary and fundamental features. But not less do others err, who, while recognizing the sacrifice of Christ as the sacrifice of the Atonement for sealing the New Covenant, ignore a work of reconciliation **toward men, by which men are to be** brought, through the operation of the New Covenant, back into harmony with God.

Nor can this work of Atonement, so far as mankind is concerned, be accomplished instantaneously and by faith. It may begin in an instant and by faith, and **at-one-ment** may be reckonedly accomplished between the sinner and the Almighty through faith; but the scope of the At-one-ment which God purposes is grander and higher than this. His arrangement is that those of the human race who desire to return to at-one-ment with him (and his righteous law) shall be reckonedly accepted through their Mediator, but shall not be fully and completely received (by the Father) while they are actually imperfect. Hence, while it is the work of the Mediator (Head and "body") to proclaim to mankind the fact that God has provided a sin-offering, whereby he can be just and yet receive the sinner back into harmony with himself, and that he is now willing to confer the blessing of sonship and its eternal life and freedom from corruption, it is additionally his work to make clear to all mankind that this offer of salvation is a great boon and should be promptly accepted and that its terms are but a reasonable service; and additionally to this, it is the Mediator's work, as the Father's representative, to actually restore—to mentally, morally, and physically restitute mankind—so many of them as will receive his ministry and obey him. Thus eventually the Mediator's work will result in an **actual at-one-ment** between God and those whom the Mediator shall restore to perfection.

This great work of the Mediator has appropriated to it the entire Millennial age; it is for this purpose that Messiah's Kingdom shall be established in the earth, with all power and authority: it is for this purpose that he must reign, that he may put down every evil influence which would hinder the world of mankind from coming to a knowledge of this gracious truth of divine love and mercy—this provision under the New Covenant, that "whosoever will" may return to God. But while the great Mediator shall thus receive, bless and restore, under the terms of the New Covenant, all who desire fellowship with God through him, he shall destroy from among the people, with an everlasting destruction, all who, under the favorable opportunities of that Millennial Kingdom, refuse the divine offer of reconciliation.—Acts 3:23; Matt. 25:41, 46; Rev. 20:9, 14, 15; Prov. 2:21, 22

The close of the Millennial age will come after it shall have accomplished all the work of mediation for which it was designed and appointed. And there the mediatorial office of Christ will cease because there will be no more rebels, no more sinners. All desirous of harmony with God will then have attained it in perfection; and all wilful sinners will by that time have been cut off from life. Then will be fulfilled our Lord's prophecy that all things in heaven and earth will be found praising God; and then will be realized the divine promise that there shall be no more dying, no more sighing and no more crying, because the former things (conditions) will have passed away.—Rev. 21:4; Psa. 67

When the great Mediator-King shall resign his completed work to the Father, delivering up his office and kingdom as the apostle explains (1 Cor. 15:24-28), what lasting results may we expect the great Mediator's redemptive work toward mankind to show?

It will have accomplished:—

(1) The sealing of the New Covenant with his own precious blood; making its gracious provisions possible to all mankind.

(2) The reconciling or bringing back into harmony with God of a "little flock," a "royal priesthood," zealous of good works—willing to lay down their lives in God's service; who, because thus copies of their Savior, shall by divine arrangement be privileged to be his joint-heirs in the Millennial Kingdom and partakers of his divine nature.— 1 Pet. 2:9, 10; Titus 2:14; Rom. 8:29

(3) The reconciliation, the full restitution, of an earth full of perfect, happy human beings—all of mankind found desirous of divine favor upon the di-

The Fact and Philosophy

vine terms: these the Mediator turns over to the Father, not only fully restored but fully instructed in **righteousness and self-control and full of the spirit of** loyalty to God, the spirit of holiness and possessed of its blessed fruits—meekness, patience, kindness, godliness—love. In this condition they shall indeed be blameless and irreproachable, and capable of standing every test.

(4) The destruction of all others of the race, as unworthy of further favor—the cumberers of the **ground, whose influence could not be beneficial to** others, and whose continued existence would not glorify their Creator.

Thus, at the close of the Millennial age, the world will be fully back in divine favor, fully at-one with God, as mankind was representatively in harmony, at-one with God, in the person of Adam, before transgression entered the world: but additionally they will possess a most valuable experience with evil; for by it they will have learned a lesson of the sinfulness of sin, and the wisdom, profit and desirableness of righteousness. Additionally, also, they will possess an increase of knowledge and the wider exercise of the various talents and abilities which were man's originally in creation, but in an undeveloped state. And this lesson will be profitable, not to man alone, but also to the holy angels, who will have witnessed an illustration of the equilibrium of divine Justice, Love, Wisdom, and Power in a measure which they could not otherwise have conceived possible. And the lesson fully learned by all, we may presume, will stand for all time, applicable to other races yet uncreated on other planets of the wide universe.

And what will be the center of that story as it shall be told throughout eternity? It will be the story of the great **ransom** finished at Calvary and of the atonement based upon that giving of the corresponding price, which demonstrated that God's Love and Justice are exactly equal.

In view of the great importance of this subject of the Atonement, and in view also of the fact that it is so imperfectly comprehended by the Lord's people, and in view, additionally, of the fact that errors held upon other subjects hinder a proper view of this important subject, we propose, in its discussion in this volume, to cover a wide range, and to inquire:—

(1) Concerning Jehovah, the Author of the plan of the Atonement.

(2) Concerning the Mediator, by whom the Atonement sacrifice was made, and through whose instrumentality all of its gracious provisions are to be applied to fallen man.

(3) Concerning the Holy Spirit, the channel or medium through which the blessings of reconciliation to God are brought to mankind.

(4) Respecting mankind, on whose behalf this great plan of Atonement was devised.

(5) Respecting the ransom, the center or pivotal point of the Atonement.

Taking these subjects up in this, which we believe to be their proper and logical order, we hope to find the divine statement respecting these various subjects so clear, so forceful, so satisfactory, as to remove from our minds much of the mist, mystery and misconception which have hitherto beclouded this most important subject of the Atonement. But to attain these desirable results we must not come to these subjects hampered by human creeds or opinions. We must come to them untrammeled by prejudice, ready, willing, nay anxious, to be taught of God—anxious to unlearn whatever we have hitherto received merely through our own conjectures or through the suggestions of others, that is not in harmony with the Word of the Lord; anxious also to have the whole counsel of God upon every feature of this subject. To all who thus come, who thus seek, who thus knock, the great Teacher opens the way, and "they shall all be taught of God."—Isa. 54:13

STUDY II

THE AUTHOR OF THE ATONEMENT

The Almighty, Jehovah—The Savior of Sinners, Through Christ—"Worthy is the Lamb"—"The Self-Existing One"—The I Am—A False Tradition—Based on Forgery—The Unity of Father and Son Scripturally Shown—The Scriptural Usage of the Word Jehovah and the Title Lord—The word God in the Old Testament—In the New Testament—The Harmonious Bible Testimony—"He that Hath Seen Me Hath Seen the Father"—He Thought it not Robbery to be Equal.

"To Us there is One God, The Father, and One Lord, Jesus Christ."

JEHOVAH God claims for himself the authorship of the great plan of Atonement, which we have just seen is in progress of development—which began at Calvary and will not be complete until the close of the Millennial age, when the Lord Jesus Christ, the mediator of the Atonement, shall deliver up the dominion of earth, restored and in full subordination to the Father. In harmony with this are numerous statements of the Scriptures; for instance, "I am Jehovah thy God, the Holy One of Israel, thy Savior." Again, "I am Jehovah, and beside me there is no Savior." Again, "I Jehovah am thy Savior and thy Redeemer, the Holy One of Jacob." And again, "I am Jehovah thy God from the land of Egypt, and thou shalt know no God but me: for there is no Savior beside me." Again, "To the only wise God, our Savior, be glory and majesty, dominion and power, both now and ever, amen." Again, "We trust in the living God, who is the Savior of all men, especially of those that believe."—Isa. 43:3, 11; 60:16; Hos. 13:4; Jude 25; 1 Tim. 4:10; Titus 1:3; 2:10

If this thought were fully received—that the Almighty Jehovah, himself, is the Savior, the Author of the great plan of Salvation, and the executor of it, through his willing agents and representatives—it would deliver many from false conceptions of the relationship between the heavenly Father and his heavenly Son, in respect to the salvation of mankind. It would leave no room for the almost blasphemous view of the matter, held by a considerable number of professing Christians; viz., that the heavenly Father stood in wrath, seeking to slay or to torture the human sinner, and that the heavenly Son, our Lord Jesus, full of love and mercy (which according to this theory the Father lacked), interposed, and satisfied the heavenly Father's malice and anger by receiving the blow of wrath in man's stead: and that now Jehovah is placated, merely because, being just, he cannot require at the hands of the sinner, again, that which has already been paid through the precious blood of Christ. The sooner this terrible erroneous view of the Atonement is gotten rid of by those who hold it, the better will be the prospect for their progress in spiritual things—in the knowledge, in the grace, and in the love of the true God.

The proper view of the matter shows us the heavenly Father perfect in all the attributes of nobility of character: perfect in his justice, so that the just sentence of his righteous law cannot be infracted, even by himself; perfect in wisdom, so that his plan and arrangement, not only with respect to man's creation, but also with respect to man's salvation, the Atonement, etc., were all so complete that no contingency or failure could arise, nor any necessity for change of the divine plan; as it is written, "I am the same, I change not, saith the Lord," and, "Known unto the Lord are all his works, from the foundation of the world:" perfect also in his love, than which there could be no greater love possible, and yet that love in full balance and accord with the other divine attributes, so that it could spare the sinner only in harmony with the just program marked out by divine wisdom: perfect also in power, so that all his good purposes, and good intentions, and just program, and loving designs, fully co-ordinated, shall be executed, and bring the originally designed result; as it is written, "My word that goeth forth out of my mouth shall not return unto me void; it shall accomplish that which I please, and it shall prosper in the thing whereto I sent it."—Isa. 55:11; Mal. 3:6; Acts 15:18

When we thus see, from the Scriptural standpoint, that the great Jehovah himself is the Author of the salvation brought unto us by our Lord Jesus, it leads us to more fully and more properly honor and love our Almighty God, while it does not detract from the honor, love and esteem in which we properly hold and reverence our Lord and Savior, Jesus Christ. For we see in the Heavenly Son the Heavenly Father's image, and recognize him as the "Messenger of the Covenant," through whom all the covenanted blessings of Jehovah are to be brought to mankind, and without whom none of the divine blessings are obtainable. In harmony with this thought, that our Lord Jesus in all matters acts as the **representative** of the Father, Jehovah, in the work of salvation, note the following statements of the Scriptures:—

"The kindness and love of **God our Savior** toward man appeared. . . . He saved us by the washing of regeneration and renewing of the Holy Spirit; which he shed on us abundantly **through** Jesus Christ our Savior."—Tit. 3:4-6

"Him hath God exalted with his right hand to be a Prince and a Savior, for to give repentance to Israel, and forgiveness of sin."—Acts 5:31

"We have seen and do testify that the **Father sent the Son** to be the Savior of the world."—1 John 4:14

"Paul, an apostle of Jesus Christ, according to an appointment of **God our Savior** and of Jesus Christ our hope."—1 Tim. 1:1

"This is good and acceptable in the sight of **God our Savior**. . . . For there is one God and one Mediator between God and men, the man Christ Jesus."—1 Tim. 2:3, 5

Note also our Lord Jesus' own words on this subject:—"The Father sent not the Son into the world to condemn the world, but that the world through him might be saved."—John 3:17

"I can of mine own self do nothing; as I hear I judge."—John 5:30

"As the Father hath sent me, so likewise I send you [disciples]."—John 20:21

"Of that day and hour [when the heavenly Kingdom should be set up] knoweth no man, no not the angels in heaven, **neither the Son**, but my Father only."—Mark 13:32

"The times and seasons the Father hath put in his own power."—Acts 1:7

"The works which I do in my Father's name bear witness."—John 10:25

"I send the promise of my Father upon you."—Luke 24:49

"I am come in my Father's name."—John 5:43

"Whatsoever I speak, therefore, even as the Father said unto me, so I speak."—John 12:50

"My Father is greater than I."—John 14:28

"I ascend unto my Father and your Father, and to my God and your God."—John 20:17

"WORTHY THE LAMB THAT WAS SLAIN"

Our Lord Jesus himself has furnished us, in the last book of the Bible, "The Revelation of Jesus Christ, **which God gave unto him,** to show unto his servants" (Rev. 1:1), a most beautiful picture of this subject of the Atonement, illustrating the general plan of man's redemption from sin and its curse. This is found in Rev. 5. There the Heavenly Father, the Ancient of Days, is shown seated on the heavenly throne, and in his hand a scroll written inside and outside, sealed with seven seals. That scroll, representing the divine plan, known only to the Father, Jehovah himself, was kept in his own power—in his own hand— until some one should be **proved** worthy to know it, and become its executor as Jehovah's honored agent and representative. The symbolic picture proceeds to show that up to the time our Lord Jesus suffered for us at Calvary, "the just for the unjust, that he might bring us to God," no one had ever been found (proved) worthy to take up the divine plan and even understand its contents.

But when our Lord Jesus had **proven** his loyalty to the Heavenly Father by his obedience, not only in humbling himself to take man's estate for the suffering of death, but also in his obedience "even unto death," and still further, "even unto the [ignominious] death of the cross," then and thereby he did prove himself worthy of every confidence and trust. As the apostle declares, "**Wherefore** him hath God highly exalted and given him a name that is above every name, that at the name of Jesus every knee should bow, both of things in heaven and things on earth." (Phil. 2:9-11) It is at this point that the picture we are considering (Rev. 5:9-13) shows our Lord Jesus as the Lamb that had been slain, before whom obeisance was made, and who was proclaimed, Worthy the Lamb! "Thou art worthy to take the scroll and to open the seals thereof, because thou wast slain, and hast redeemed us to God by thy blood out of every kindred and tongue and people and nation." Thus is pictured to us the high exaltation of the Heavenly Father's representative, the "Messenger [servant] of the Covenant." Because of his humility and complete submission and obedience to the Father's will he is proclaimed thenceforth the sharer of the Father's throne, and, by the Father's own arrangement, the proclamation was made throughout the heavenly hosts, "Worthy is the Lamb that was slain, **to receive** power, and riches, and wisdom, and strength, and honor, and glory, and blessing"; and finally "every creature" shall catch the thought that Jehovah has very highly exalted his Only Begotten Son, even to association with himself in the Kingdom, and shout their approval, saying, "The blessing, and the honor, and the glory, and the power be unto Him that sitteth upon the throne [of the universe—Jehovah] and unto the Lamb—for ever and ever!" No wonder, then, that we are instructed that thence forth all men shall honor the exalted Son even as they honor the Father who thus highly exalted him.—John 5:23

The apostle declares that this glorification of Jesus furnishes an illustration of divine law, that "He that humbleth himself shall be exalted." But let us also notice in this symbolic picture (vs. 13) that the exaltation of our Lord Jesus Christ to glory and honor and power and dominion does not imply that the Heavenly Father abdicates the throne of heaven in his favor, nor that the Father and the Son are one in person, for both persons are recognized, the Father, as always, being given the first place in praise and honor. And this again reminds us of our Lord's words, "As the Father hath appointed unto me a Kingdom, so I appoint also unto you [my disciples] a kingdom." (Luke 22:29) And again he says to his faithful followers, "He that overcometh will I grant to sit with me in my throne, even as I also overcame, and am set down with my Father in his throne."—Rev. 3:21

As a further evidence that the entire work of redemption is of the Father though through the Son, note the apostle's declaration, that God "in these last days hath spoken unto us by his Son, whom he hath appointed heir of all things [promised], by whom also he made the worlds, who . . . when he had by himself purged our sins, sat down at the right hand of the Majesty on High [Jehovah], being made so much better than the angels." And again he declares of him: "We have such an High Priest, who is set on the right hand of the throne of the Majesty of the Heavens [Jehovah], a servant of holy things, and of the true tabernacle, which the Lord [Jehovah] pitched, and not man." And again the same apostle declares, "This man [our Lord Jesus] after he had offered one sacrifice for sins forever, sat down on the right hand of God." (Heb. 1:2-4; 8:1; 10:12) Again he exhorts us to continue "looking unto Jesus, the Author [starter] and finisher of our faith, who for the joy that was set before him endured the cross, despising the shame, and is set down at the right hand of the throne of God." Again he exhorts us to consider **"the God of our Lord Jesus Christ, the Father of glory,"** and "what is the exceeding greatness of his power to usward who believe, according to the operation of the might of his power, **which he wrought in Christ**, when he raised him from the dead, and set him at his own right hand in the heavenlies, far above all principality, and power, and might, and dominion, and every name that is named, not only in this world but also in that which is to come, and hath put all things under his feet." (Heb. 12:2; Eph. 1:17-22) Again the Apostle Peter declares of our Lord Jesus that he "is gone into heaven, and is at the right hand of God; angels and authorities and powers **being made subject** unto him [by the Father]."—1 Pet. 3:22

All these various Scriptures indicate most clearly the very high exaltation of our Lord Jesus Christ, as the **Father's reward** for his wonderful obedience and manifestation of the Father's spirit of love, in the sacrifice of himself on behalf of sinners; but they neither indicate that the Lord Jesus was the Father, nor that he has been exalted to take the Father's place upon the heavenly throne, or in the affection and worship of his intelligent creatures. On the contrary, they expressly show the Heavenly Father as the superior in honor and power, as the Benefactor who thus glorified and exalted the Son, and set him at his own right hand, or place of chief favor, and made him a sharer in the throne or dominion of the heavenly kingdom, angels and all the hosts of heaven being subjected to him. Indeed, so strong is the language sometimes used in respect to the high exaltation of our Lord Jesus, and the plenitude of power bestowed upon him by the Father, that in one instance the inspired writer deemed it very proper to call attention to the fact that none of these statements of his high exaltation implied either that he was the equal of the Father or his superior: hence he says, speaking of the Millennial reign of Christ, "He [Christ] must reign till he hath put all enemies under his feet. The last enemy that shall be destroyed is death. For he [the Father] hath put all things under his [the Son's] feet. But when he [the Father] saith, 'All things are put under him [the Son],' **it is manifest that he [the Father] is excepted, which did put all things under him [the Son]**. And when all things [earthly] shall be subdued under him [the Son], then shall the Son himself be subject unto him [the Father] that put all things under him [the Son], that God [the Father] may be all in all."—1 Cor. 15:25-28

"THE SELF-EXISTING ONE"

The Almighty God has appropriated to himself and declared his name to be Jehovah, which signifies the "Self-Existing One" or "The Immortal One." Thus we read his declaration to Moses, saying: "I appeared unto Abraham, unto Isaac, and unto Jacob by the name of God Almighty [the superior or most mighty God], but by my name Jehovah was I not known to them." (Exod. 6:3) By this name, Jehovah, God was thereafter recognized amongst his people. The name is used hundreds of times throughout the Old Testament, but is covered, in a large degree, from the English reader, through an error of the translators, who have rendered it "Lord." It can, however, be recognized readily, being always printed in small capitals when used to translate this sacred name, Jehovah.

Thus in the first Commandment given to Israel the Lord said, "I am Jehovah, thy God . . . thou shalt have no other gods [mighty ones] before me [my equals] . . . for I Jehovah thy God am a jealous God."—Exod. 20:2-5

Again Moses declares, "Hear, O Israel, Jehovah our God is one—Jehovah; and thou shalt love Jehovah thy God with all thine heart and with all thy soul and with all thy might." (Deut. 6:4, 5) And this is the very passage of Scripture which our Lord Jesus himself commended as the very essence of truth. When inquired of respecting the greatest commandment, he said, quoting this Scripture, "Thou shalt love the Lord [Jehovah] thy God with all thy heart, and with all thy soul, and with all thy mind; this is the primary and great commandment." (Matt. 22:38) Again we read, "I am Jehovah; that is my name: and my glory [honor] will I not give to another." (Isa. 42:8) And let not the context escape our notice, for this positive declaration that the name Jehovah is exclusively that of "the Father of Lights with whom is no variableness" immediately follows his prophetic proclamation of Messiah as Jehovah's honored and elect Son-servant, saying:—

"Behold my servant, whom I uphold; mine elect in whom my soul delighteth: I have put my spirit upon him. He shall bring forth judgment to the Gentiles. . . . He shall not fail nor be discouraged until he have set judgment in the earth: and the isles shall wait for his law. Thus saith God, Jehovah, I Jehovah have called thee in righteousness and will hold thine hand and will keep thee, and will give thee for a covenant of the people, for a light of the Gentiles; to open the blind eyes, to bring out the prisoners from the prison [death], and them that sit in darkness out of the prison house. I am Jehovah: that is my name."—Isa. 42:1-8

THE NAME OF JEHOVAH APPLIED ONLY TO THE FATHER OF GLORY

The claim is sometimes made that the name Jehovah is applied in Scripture to our Lord Jesus and hence that it is not the distinctive and special name of the Heavenly Father. This is a mistake; but for the benefit of all we will here examine the passages supposed by some to support this claim. We will show that they do not contradict the foregoing Scriptures which declare it to be the proper and special name of the great "I AM."

(1) The text chiefly relied on to prove that Jehovah may properly be considered the name of Christ Jesus reads, "I will raise unto David a righteous Branch, and a King shall reign and prosper, and shall execute judgment and justice in the earth. . . . And this is the name whereby he shall be called, **the Lord our righteousness."**—Jer. 23:5, 6

Evidently our Lord Jesus and his Millennial reign are referred to; and the name in the Hebrew is **Jehovah-Tsidkenu.** What is the explanation? Merely this: the translators, in their zeal to find a place where the name Jehovah was associated with Jesus as a name, have given us a poor translation. No difficulty would appear if it had been translated—"This is the name with which he shall be called, **Our Righteousness of Jehovah."** And how appropriate is this name to the work and office of our Lord Jesus. Did he not stand as the representative of God's righteousness and suffer the penalty of Justice as man's ransom—that God might be just and yet be the justifier of him that believeth in Jesus? Surely no name could be more appropriate.

It should not be overlooked, that this same name precisely, **Jehovah-Tsidkenu,** occurs again in the writings of the same Prophet. But our friends never call attention to it, and the translators, although rendering it by the same English words, do not put those words in large capital letters as in the other case. Why? Because the connections show that **Jehovah-Tsidkenu** will be the name of the entire Church, the New Jerusalem—"And this is the name wherewith she shall be called **[Jehovah-Tsidkenu],** our Righteousness of Jehovah."—Jer. 33:16

And that this name will be appropriate to the glorified Church all can readily see: she not only shares her Lord's sufferings for righteousness "filling up that which is behind of the afflictions of Christ" (Col. 1:24; 1 Pet. 5:9), but is also promised a share in all the glories of her Lord, as a wife shares her husband's honors and **name:** just as the Church bears

The Author of the Atonement

the name of Christ as members of the body of Christ. – Rev. 3:12; 19:7, 21:9

Nor are these the only instances of the name Jehovah being used to compound **another** name. Note that the mount upon which Abraham offered Isaac and where God provided him a ram for sacrifice as a substitute for Isaac, was called by him, Mount of Jehovah's Providence—**Jehovah-Jireh.** (Gen. 22:14) Moses named an altar which he built **Jehovah-Nissi** or Banner of Jehovah. (Exod. 17:15) Gideon built an altar and called its name **Jehovah-Shalom**—The Peace of Jehovah. (Judges 6:23, 24) Ezekiel prophesied of a city to come, whose name shall be **Jehovah-Shammah**—The Wonder of Jehovah.—Ezek. 48:35

(2) It is suggested that when it is recorded that Jehovah appeared to Abraham (Gen. 18:1), and again to Moses (Exod. 3:3-15), it must have been Christ **Jesus in his prehuman condition; and hence that** the name would be his. We answer that such reasoning is unwarranted: that if the name were applied to another it would merely indicate that such servant was highly esteemed of Jehovah and really treated for the occasion as a steward or representative—commissioned to exercise divine power as well. In Exodus 3:2, we are distinctly informed that the one representing Jehovah and using his most distinguished name, " I am," was "the **angel** [messenger] of Jehovah." That this honored **messenger** was "the **Word"** of John 1:1, **our Lord Jesus in his prehuman** estate. we do not for a moment question. But the highest and most honored messenger should not be confounded with the one whom he represents and in whose name he speaks and whose power he exercised and bestowed upon Moses.

(3) Isaiah 40:3 refers to John the Baptist's mission, "Prepare ye the way of **Jehovah**"; and we are asked to consider this a proof that Jesus is but another name for Jehovah. But again we answer. Not so! Jesus was indeed the honored servant of Jehovah, and his **representative** among men in the fullest sense; but he himself declares, "The Father hath **sent me**"; "As I hear I judge"; "Of mine own self I can

do nothing"; "The Father is greater than I." And we must believe the messenger. The fact is, as we have already shown,* that John the Baptist but foreshadowed a greater Messenger, even the entire Christian Church in the flesh; which in turn will usher in the Christ, head and body, in spiritual glory, and the work of that glorified Christ will still be a further step in the same great work of preparing the way of Jehovah and making the place of his feet glorious. And this work, when closed at the end of the Millennium, will be the full accomplishment of this prophecy.—See 1 Cor. 15:24-28; John 6:57; 5:30; 10:28

(4) Our Lord Jesus is spoken of by the apostle as "the Lord of Glory" (1 Cor. 2:8), and we are asked to consider this a proof that he is the Father, Jehovah, because the latter in Psa. 24:7-10 is styled the "King of glory." We answer that such flimsy arguments as this prove only the weakness of the theory they are advanced to support. Our Lord Jesus will indeed be majestic, a King of Glory, when during the Millennial age he shall wield the scepter of earth in Jehovah's name and power: but the same inspired apostle shows clearly, in the same epistle in which he declares Jesus "the Lord of glory," that when his Kingdom shall reach its highest degree of glory it will be delivered over to the Father "who did put all things under him [the Son] that he [the Father] may be all in all."

(5) In two of the prophetic pen-pictures of Christ's Millennial Kingdom it is declared, "In the last days it shall come to pass, that the mountain [kingdom] of the house of **Jehovah** shall be established in the top of the mountains [overruling other kingdoms] ... and many people shall say, Come ye, let us go up to the mountain [kingdom] of **Jehovah** . . . and he will teach us of his ways and we will walk in his paths. . . . And he shall judge among the nations."—Isa. 2:2-4; Micah 4:1-3

It is held that since Christ is to reign and judge and possess the Kingdom during the Millennium,

---

*Vol. II. Chap. 8.

the name Jehovah here should be considered as the name of Christ. We answer, Not so! It must not be forgotten that all blessings are **of** the Father though all are **by** the Son. (1 Cor. 8:6) And so our Lord Jesus taught us in his model prayer to say, "Our Father which art in heaven ... **Thy Kingdom** come, **thy will** be done on earth as in heaven." (Matt. 6:10) This is shown also in the connections (Micah 4:8) where the Christ ("head" and "body"—the New Jerusalem) is referred to as the "Tower of the flock" to whom shall come the first dominion—lost by Adam in Eden, redeemed by Jesus at Calvary.

(6) "Bethlehem Ephratah ... out of thee shall he come forth unto me that is to be ruler in Israel; whose goings forth have been **of old, from everlasting.**" (Micah 5:2) These words we are asked to accept as proofs that Jesus was Jehovah—from everlasting to everlasting—because Moses declared, "Jehovah ... from everlasting to everlasting, thou art God."—Psa. 90:1, 2.

We reply that this is asking that an unreasonable inference should be drawn—contradictory not only of the hundreds of instances of the use of the name Jehovah in other Scriptures, but contradictory also of the connections in which these words are found. Reading onward to Micah 5:4, we find it stated of Messiah: "He shall stand and feed [Jehovah's flock—Psa. 23:1] in the strength of Jehovah; **in the majesty of the name of Jehovah, his God.**

Nothing could be more explicit on the subject. What then is meant by the words of Micah 5:2? We answer that they can be well understood thus— "Whose goings forth have been [foretold] from of old, from everlasting [his coming and Messiahship were purposed and provided for in the divine plan]."

(7) We are referred to the prophecy of the Millennial Kingdom in Isaiah 25:6-9, and asked to consider this a proof that the name **Jehovah** is applicable to our Lord Jesus: because it is there stated that—"In **this mountain** [kingdom] shall **Jehovah** of hosts make **unto all people** a feast of fat things. . . . He will

swallow up death in victory; and the Lord Jehovah will wipe away tears from off all faces."

No, we reply. This is far from being a proof of that. We must notice indeed that our Lord, the glorified Christ, is represented as the speaker, and his work of the Millennial age is briefly summed up in the first verse of this chapter—"O Jehovah my God; I will exalt [honor] thee, I will praise thy name." This will be the result of the Millennial reign, and at its close all things will be back in subjection to Jehovah whose power it is, working in the Christ, that shall put all things under him. Messiah comes **to earth as Jehovah's mighty servant and vicegerent,** Immanuel, "God with us." This view is corroborated absolutely by the Apostle Paul, who after quoting from this prophecy and pointing to its fulfilment in the destroying of Adamic death during the Millennium says—"Thanks be unto **God who giveth us the victory** [deliverance—triumph] through our Lord Jesus Christ."—1 Cor. 15:57

(8) We are asked to consider as a proof that the name Jehovah properly belongs to our Lord Jesus. the fact that he is named—Wonderful, Counselor [or guide, or miraculous pattern], Mighty God, Everlasting Father, Prince of Peace.—Isa. 9:6

We will examine the full meaning of this Scripture later on, merely remarking under this head that nothing in it justifies us in applying the name Jehovah to our adorable Lord and Master, Jesus. Note, however, that if such had been the thought, no better place than this could have been found for adding the name Jehovah among the other titles. But, on the contrary, the very next verse declares. "The zeal of Jehovah of hosts will accomplish this [prophecy]."—Verse 7

(9) "Say unto the cities of Judah, Behold your God! Behold my Lord [adonai] Jehovah will come with strong hand; and his arm shall rule for him. ... He shall feed his flock like a shepherd."—Isa. 40: 9, 10, 11

We are told that here surely is one passage in which our Redeemer is called by the great name

The Author of the Atonement

Jehovah. But we answer, No—he is here called the **"arm"** of Jehovah as in other places: the mighty Arm of Jehovah "shall **rule for** him," until he shall have put down all authority and power opposed to Jehovah and his righteous law—until he shall have brought forth judgment unto victory; until he shall have made the place of Jehovah's feet (the earth his footstool) glorious—and shall have delivered up the Kingdom to God, even the Father.—1 Cor. 15:24-28; Matt. 12:20

Other instances in which our Lord Jesus is prophetically represented as the "right arm" or strength of Jehovah are:—

"Who hath believed our report [preaching]? And to whom is the **Arm** of Jehovah revealed? [Few recognize the Lord's Arm during this age—"not many great," etc.]. . . . He is despised and rejected of men."—Isa. 53; John 12:38

"The isles shall wait upon me, and on mine **Arm** shall they trust."—Isa. 51:5-9

"Jehovah hath made bare his holy **Arm** in the eyes of all nations [at the setting up of his Kingdom]; and all the ends of the earth shall see the salvation of our God."—Isa. 52:10

"His [Jehovah's] **Arm** brought salvation for him. . . . And the Redeemer shall come to Zion, and unto them that turn from ungodliness in Jacob, saith Jehovah."—Isa. 59:15-20

(10) In John 12:41 we read, "These things said Esaias [Greek for Isaiah], when he saw his glory and spoke of him." We are asked to concede that this probably applies to Isaiah 6:1. We reply that we believe it does: but notice that the Hebrew word rendered **Lord** in that verse is not **Jehovah** but **Adonai**: our present contention is that the name Jehovah does not properly apply to any one except the Heavenly Father—although it may be applied to his special messengers while they are speaking or acting for him representatively in his name.

Nor do we dispute that **Adonai** is sometimes used as one of the many titles of the Heavenly Father. We claim that in this text it does not apply to the Father but to the Son. Similarly the same word **Adonai** is used in referring to Christ and his Millennial kingdom in the second Psalm (4-9): "The Lord [**Adonai**] shall have them in derision. Then shall he speak to them in his wrath and trouble them in his sore displeasure. . . . The Lord [**Jehovah**] hath said unto me, Thou art my Son; this day have I begotten thee."

But some one may perhaps claim that **Adonai** of Isa. 6:1 must refer to the same person as **Jehovah** of verses 3 and 5. We answer, Not so: the "Messenger of the Covenant," the representative of Jehovah, might well be saluted with praise in the name of the Father whom he represented. Note again that in verse 8 it is not **Jehovah** who gives the message, nor who pronounces the judgment, but **Adonai;** for the Father "hath committed all judgment unto the Son." —Matt. 23:34, 36, 38; John 5:22, 27

Other instances of references to our Lord Jesus in **close connection with** the name **Jehovah,** and yet another word used in the Hebrew, but translated also **Lord** in our Common Version Bibles, might be cited. Note Malachi's statement, "Behold I will send my messenger, and he shall prepare the way before me; and the Lord [**Adon** from the same root as **Adonai**] whom ye seek shall suddenly come to his temple, even the Messenger of the Covenant, whom ye delight in: behold, he shall come, saith the Lord [**Jehovah**] of hosts. . . . He shall purify the sons of Levi, and purge them as gold and silver, that they may offer unto the Lord [**Jehovah**] an offering of righteousness."—Mal. 3:1-4

Another familiar reference of this kind is found in the noble Messianic Psalm which declares, "Thou art fairer than the children of men; grace is poured upon thy lips: therefore God hath blessed thee forever. . . . Thy throne, O God, is forever and ever: the sceptre of thy kingdom is a right sceptre. Thou lovest righteousness and hatest wickedness: therefore God, **thy God,** hath anointed thee with the oil of gladness above thy fellows." Then the Church is referred to as the daughter of the Father, and as the bride, the Lamb's wife, and she is exhorted to reverence the King's Son as her Lord—"So shall the King greatly desire thy beauty: for he is thy **Lord** [**Adon**—not Jehovah] and worship thou him."—Psa. 45:2-11; Heb. 1:8, 9; 1 Cor. 11:3; Eph. 5:23; John 5:23

(11) We are asked to consider Isaiah's statement (8:13, 14) a proof that the name Jehovah is properly applicable to our Lord Jesus. It reads: "Sanctify Jehovah of hosts himself; and let him be your fear, and let him be your dread." The stress is laid upon the next verse, which without specifying who, declares, "He shall be for a stone of stumbling and for a rock of offense to both the houses of Israel." We cannot admit this as proof; for quite to the contrary, the context shows a third party (besides Jehovah and the Prophet), even our Lord Jesus, who says, "Bind up the testimony, seal the law among my disciples. And I will wait upon **Jehovah**. . . . Behold I and the children whom **Jehovah** hath given me."—Isa. 8:16-18; compare Heb. 2:13

(12) Psalm 110 is referred to as proof that our Lord Jesus is in Scripture called **Jehovah**. We reply that no argument could be farther fetched or more untrue. On the contrary, it proves the reverse. "**Jehovah** said unto **Adon**, Sit thou at my right hand, until I make thine enemies thy footstool. . . . **Adonai** at thy [Jehovah's] right hand shall strike," etc. Again, "**Jehovah** hath sworn and will not repent, Thou art a priest forever after the order of Melchizedek."—Psa. 110:1, 4, 5

Whoever cannot see that the one referred to is exalted to Jehovah's right hand or position of chief favor, and made a priest of a new Order, is surely **blinded** by his prejudice. We refer such, however, to our Lord's own interpretation and application of these words to himself; showing himself to be the **Adon**, David's Lord, exalted by his Lord, Jehovah.—Matt. 22:44, 45

The Apostle Peter, speaking under the influence of the Holy Spirit at Pentecost, made the same application of these words. And the Apostle Paul also refers to them with similar import.—Acts 2:34; Heb. 1:13; 10:12, 13

(13) Since our Lord Jesus is acknowledged to be the Great Teacher, it is claimed that he fulfilled the prediction—"All thy children shall be taught of Jehovah." (Isa. 54:13) In answer and contradiction we refer to our Lord Jesus' own words. He quoted these very words of the Prophet in his discourse, and clearly showed that he was not and did not claim to be the Jehovah of this prophecy. His words were, "It is written in the prophets, And they shall be all taught of God. Every man, therefore, that hath heard, and hath **learned of the Father**, cometh unto me."—John 6:45

The Father himself, the great Jehovah, is not only the great law-giver but also the Great Teacher of his own law. His own great plan for human salvation will yet be seen by all of his intelligent sons to contain the grandest possible exemplifications of Justice, Love and Wisdom in combination, and yet each perfect, inviolate.

Our Lord Jesus was and still is the Great Teacher of men by the appointment of the Heavenly Father, the great Master Teacher above all. And this is precisely what our dear Redeemer claimed and taught. Did he not publicly declare that his teachings were of things he had already learned of the Father?— saying, "I speak that which I have seen with my Father." "My doctrine [teaching] is not mine, but his that sent me. If any man will do his will, he shall know of the doctrine, whether it be of God, or whether I speak of myself. . . . He that seeketh the glory **of him that sent him** the same is true." "The word which ye hear is not mine, but the Father's which **sent me**." "I have given them **thy** word." "They have kept **thy** word." Sanctify them through **thy** truth: **thy** word is truth."—John 7:16-18; 8:38; 14:24; 17:6, 14, 17

Likewise our Lord appointed special teachers under him, the apostles; and still others in the church to be teachers and under-shepherds of the Lord's flock, instructing them, "Feed my sheep"; "feed my lambs." "Take heed to yourselves and to all the flock, over which the Holy Spirit hath made you overseers. to feed the Church of God which he hath purchased

The Author of the Atonement

with blood of his own [Beloved son]." (Acts 20:28) Yet none of these teachers were to teach doctrines of **their own,** which could be only "wisdom of this world." The people of God were to be taught of **Jehovah,** and none can be true teachers save as they present to men the words and plan and character of Jehovah as the standards of truth and excellence. In doing this they necessarily call attention to "the doctrines of Christ" and "the apostles' doctrines," all of which were but expressions and inculcations of the Father's grand and eternal law.

Unlike some who style themselves teachers today, neither our Lord Jesus nor his apostles attempted or claimed **originality.** Mark the humble words of our Lord Jesus, than which nothing could be more beautiful—"I do nothing of myself, but **as my Father hath taught me,** I speak these things." (John 8:28) Can we wonder that one found so humble and so loyal to Jehovah could be and was entrusted with so great honor and power—so highly exalted to the Father's right hand? And that the lessons thus **taught** our Lord Jesus were well **learned** by him we have the inspired testimony—"Though he were a Son, yet learned he obedience by the things which he suffered."—Heb. 5:8; Phil. 2:8

Moreover, the Lord showed through the prophets that Jesus, the Great Teacher appointed by the Master Teacher, Jehovah, would be himself taught of Jehovah; and in order that he might become "a merciful and faithful High Priest" to humanity, and be proved worthy to be "the Captain of our salvation," it was needful that he be **perfected in experiences** through things which he suffered. (Heb. 2:9, 10) Note how clearly the following prophecies declared long before that our Lord would be **taught** of Jehovah, and would learn well the lessons, and manifest love for the law and obedience to the Law-giver:

"My Lord Jehovah [**Adonai Jehovah**] hath given me the tongue of the learned [instructed], that I should know how to speak a word in season to him that is weary: he wakeneth morning by morning, he wakeneth mine ear to hear as the learned [instructed]. My Lord Jehovah [**Adonai Jehovah**] hath opened mine ear, and I was not rebellious, neither turned away back [from his teachings]. I gave my back to the smiters, and my cheeks to them that plucked off the hair: I hid not my face from shame and spitting."—Isa. 50:4-10; Matt. 26:67; 27:26, 30; Isa. 53:11

Hear further on this subject the word of the Lord's testimony respecting the preparation of our Lord Jesus for the grand office of Royal High Priest for mankind:—

"The spirit of Jehovah shall rest upon him—the spirit of wisdom and understanding, the spirit of counsel and of might, the spirit of knowledge and of the fear [reverence] of Jehovah; and shall make him of quick understanding in the fear [reverence] of Jehovah: so that he shall not judge after the sight of his eyes"—for he has been touched with a feeling of our infirmities and is therefore the better able to succor all who come unto God by him—his Church now, and by and by the world, during his Millennial Kingdom.—Isa. 11:1-10; Heb. 2:18

Again prophetically Messiah is represented as saying: "Thou wilt **show me** [cause me to have knowledge of] the path of life." "I will bless **Jehovah**, who hath given me counsel." These expressions occur in connections quoted by the apostles as applicable to our Savior, "the man Christ Jesus." (Psa. 16:7-11) Thus is confirmed by prophecy the statement of the Evangelist, "And the child [Jesus] grew, and waxed strong in spirit [mind], **filled with wisdom**; and the grace [blessing] of God was upon him. . . . Jesus **increased in wisdom** and in stature and in favor with God and man."—Luke 2:40, 52

Having examined the strongest Bible texts presented on the subject, we are confident that the Scriptures do not authorize the use of the great name Jehovah as the appellative for any other being than our Heavenly Father: we are confident that they restrict its use and forbid its application to another.

All can see the propriety of the Almighty's decision that he shall be recognized as the center of authority, wisdom, justice, love, and power; because this is the truth, and anything else would be untruth and to that extent evil, injurious. And we have seen from the foregoing quotations from our Lord's own words, and from the words of the apostles, whom he specially instructed by word of mouth, and inspired after Pentecost with the Holy Spirit, that none of them ever intimated either that the Heavenly Father and the Heavenly Son were one in **person,** nor that they are equal in glory and in power—as is, without divine authority, declared in the creeds and catechisms of men.

Nevertheless, the Heavenly Father has manifested no jealousy of the greatness of his great Chief Servant, the "Messenger of the Covenant whom ye delight in:" on the contrary he has highly exalted him to be next to himself in dignity and in power. Hearken to the words of our Lord Jesus himself: "The Son can do nothing of himself, but what he seeth the Father do: for what things soever he [the Father] doeth, these also doeth the Son likewise. For the Father loveth the Son, and showeth him all things that himself doeth: and he will show him greater works than these, that ye may marvel. For as the Father raiseth up and makes alive the dead, so also the Son makes alive whom he pleases. For the Father judgeth no man, but hath committed all judgment unto the Son: that all men should honor the Son, **even as they honor the Father.** He that honoreth not the Son honoreth not the Father which hath sent him."—John 5:19-23

It is only as we get clearly in mind the Scriptural declaration respecting the great Author of the plan of Atonement, Jehovah, and see the distinction between him and his honored Servant, "The Only Begotten of the Father," his "Beloved Son," in the work of the Atonement, that we are properly prepared to understand the philosophy of the Atonement. It is in great measure because of the confusion of thought respecting the Father and the Son that very many Christian people are thoroughly confused respecting the Atonement, and therefore in danger of letting slip their faith in this fundamental and most important doctrine of divine revelation.

The Apostle Paul presents the matter of the relationship between the Father and the Son in respect to our redemption most clearly and most forcefully, saying: "There is no other God but One . . . To us there is but One God, the Father, of whom are all things, and we in him; and one Lord, Jesus Christ, by whom are all things, and we by him." (1 Cor. 8: 4, 6) That is to say, there is only the one eternal and Almighty God, the Author and Source of all things, to whom we belong, and there is only the one Lord, Jesus Christ, through whom the Heavenly Father operates in respect to all the various features of his plan, and by and through whom alone we have had remission of sins, through faith in his blood, and access to the Father, and to the grace wherein we stand, rejoicing in hope of the glory of God.—Rom. 5:1

A TRADITION OF THE FATHERS SUPPORTED BY A FORGERY—AN INTERPOLATION

We are leaving to following chapters for consideration the greatness and worthiness of our Lord Jesus Christ, through whom the entire work of Atonement has been and will be accomplished—and the great honor bestowed upon him, not only since he redeemed the world, but also the great honor and dignity which were his before he became the world's Redeemer. We are now seeking to distinguish clearly something respecting the great Author of the plan: but inasmuch as the general thought of Christendom is greatly perplexed by what is known as "The doctrine of the Trinity," a doctrine which its most pronounced advocates admit they do not understand and cannot comprehend or explain, therefore it is appropriate that we here examine those texts of Scripture which are supposed to give some color or support to this confusing doctrine of men, for which no authority can be found in the Word of God. We have already called attention to various Scriptures which emphatically state that there is but one Almighty God—not two, nor three, nor more. We now call attention to the fact that the word "Trinity" does not occur in the Scriptures: nor does any word occur there of equivalent meaning; nor is any statement made which even unreasonably could be interpreted to signify any such thing. Indeed, those who hold to the doctrine of the Trinity, in attempting to explain their own thought, hopelessly entangle themselves, as well as their hearers. They declare in one breath that there is only **one** God (because the Scriptures so positively emphasize this point that it cannot be ignored), yet in the same breath they declare that there are three Gods (because to this theory they are committed by "traditions of the fathers" handed down from earliest Papacy).

But how could there be **three** Gods and yet only one God? If there are three Gods, **"equal** in power and in glory," as the catechisms declare, then it is untrue to say there is only **one** God. If there is only "One God, the Father, of whom are all things," as St. Paul asserts; and if, as Jesus declared, the Father is **greater** than his honored Son; and if the Father raised his Beloved Son from the dead, and **exalted him on high**, honored him, and has appointed for him a Kingdom; and if ultimately the Son will deliver up the Kingdom again to the Father, that the Father may be all in all; then it cannot be true that there are **several Gods of equal power.** Nevertheless, we shall show conclusively in the succeeding chapter that our Lord Jesus Christ is **a God**, but that, while he is to be honored even as the Father is honored, and that in honoring him we honor the Father who exalted him, still the united voice of the Scriptures most emphatically assert there is but one Almighty God, the Father of all. As the apostle declares, "The **head** of the woman is the man, the **head** of man is Christ, and the **head** of Christ is God."—1 Cor. 11:3

There is one statement found in the Scriptures, and only one, which seems in the slightest degree to even imply the doctrine of a Trinity of Gods; and that passage is now admitted by all scholars to be spurious— an interpolation. It is therefore omitted from the Revised Version of the New Testament, although the translators of that Revised Version, so far as we are aware, were every one of them Trinitarians. While they would have liked to retain this passage, as the only Scripture support (and then very imperfect in statement), they could not retain it conscientiously.

Nor were the translators of our Common Version of the Bible blameworthy for inserting this interpolation, because at the time of that translation it was impossible to know of its spurious character. Since its translation hundreds of old Greek manuscripts have been found, but none of these of earlier date than the seventh century contains this clause, which favors the Trinity. It is therefore not denied by scholars, without respect to denominational proclivities, that the spurious words were inserted to give support to the doctrine of the Trinity, at a time when the discussion of that doctrine was rife in the Church, and when the advocates of the doctrine of the Trinity were perplexed before their opponents, because they had no Scriptural evidence to bring in substantiation of their theory. The spurious words were no doubt interpolated by some over-zealous monk, who felt sure of the doctrine himself, and thought that the Holy Spirit had blundered in not stating the matter in the Scriptures: his intention, no doubt, was to help God and the truth out of a difficulty by perpetrating a fraud. But all such suggestions, to the effect that God has not given us a complete revelation, "sufficient that the man of God may be thoroughly furnished," and that it needs adding to, are of the Adversary, as was this suggestion that it would be proper to commit a wrong, a forgery, for the sake of doing good, and rectifying the mistake of the Almighty. The monk-scribe or priest who committed this forgery, apparently about the beginning of the seventh century, has much to answer for, in his addition to the Word of God, and the evil influence which it has exerted over God's people, who, seeking for the truth on this subject, were misled by his forgery.

The spurious interpolation is found in 1 John 5:7, and consists of the words, **"in heaven the Father, the Word and the Holy Spirit, and these three are one. And there are three that bear witness in earth."** These words, omitted from the text, leave it simple

The Author of the Atonement

and easy to be understood, and fully in accord with all the remainder of the Scriptures; but with these words in the text, as they have stood for centuries, confusion is produced; for nonsense is asserted. For instance, with these words remaining in the text, the sense would be that the Father and the Son and the Holy Spirit agreed in bearing one testimony in heaven, namely that Jesus is the Christ. How absurd! Who is there in heaven ignorant of the fact that Jesus is the Christ? To whom, therefore, would it be necessary for the Father, the Son and the Holy Spirit to bear this record or testimony? None. But it was a convenient place for the Adversary to get in his work of corruption of the truth, and he found a servant willing to serve him.

Not only does the Revised Version omit this verse, but so also do all modern translations—the Emphatic Diaglott, Young's Bible translation, the American Bible Union translation, the Improved Version. The latter says:—

"This text concerning the Heavenly Witnesses is not contained in any Greek MS which was written earlier than the fifth century. It is not cited by any of the Greek ecclesiastical writers; nor by any of the early Latin fathers, even when the subjects upon which they treated would naturally have led them to appeal to its authority: it is, therefore, evidently spurious."

Lang's Critical Commentary, referring to this spurious passage, says:—

"Said words are wanting in all the Greek codices; also in the Codex Sinaiticus [the oldest known Greek MS], and in all the ancient versions, including the Latin, as late as the eighth century; and [in MSS written] since that time they are found in three variations. Notwithstanding the Trinitarian controversies, they are not referred to by a single Greek Father, or by any of the old Latin Church Fathers."

Hudson's Greek and English Concordance says:—

"The words are found in no Greek MS before the 15th or 16th century, and in no early version."

The passage is pronounced an interpolation by the following Bible scholars of recognized ability:—Sir

Isaac Newton, Benson, Clark, Horne, Griesbach, Tischendorf, Tregelles, Lachman and Alford. The latter says:—

"Unless pure caprice is to be followed in the criticism of the sacred text, there is no shadow of reason for supposing them genuine."

Dr. Constantine Tischendorf says:—

"That this spurious addition should continue to be published as a part of the Epistle I regard as an impiety."

Prof. T. B. Wolsey inquires:—

"Do not truth and honesty require that such a passage should be struck out of our English Bibles—a passage which Luther would not express in his translation, and which did not creep into the German Bible until nearly fifty years after his death?"

Dr. Adam Clarke commenting on this passage says:

"It is likely this verse is not genuine. It is wanting in every MS of this epistle written before the invention of printing, one excepted—the Codex Montfortii, in Trinity College, Dublin. The others which omit this verse amount to one hundred and twelve. It is wanting in both the Syriac, all the Arabic, Ethiopic, Coptic, Sahadic, Arminian, Slavonic, etc.; in a word, in all the ancient versions but the Vulgate; and even of this version, many of the most ancient and correct copies have it not. It is wanting also in all the ancient Greek Fathers, and in most even of the Latin."

John Wesley, the founder of Methodism, endeavored to support the doctrine of the Trinity, yet in one of his sermons from this text he quoted the words of Servetus:—"I scruple using the words 'trinity' and 'persons' because I do not find those terms in the Bible"—and to this quotation Wesley added, "I would insist only on the direct words, unexplained, as they lie in the text." He labored to prove the doctrine of the Trinity, because he believed this spurious passage was genuine, positive information from the ancient MSS of the Bible being of recent acquisition. For instance, at the time of the preparation of our King James or Common Version Bible (A. D. 1611), the translators had the advantage of but eight Greek MSS. and none of those of earlier date than the tenth century. Now, however, there are about seven hundred MSS, some of which, especially the Sinaitic MS and the Vatican MS No 1209, are very old, reaching back to about A. D. 350.

THE SCRIPTURE TEACHING RESPECTING THE FATHER AND THE SON AND THEIR UNITY

A sharp distinction should be drawn between a confession of faith in a Trinity, and a confession of faith in the Unity of the heavenly Father, Jehovah, and the heavenly Son, our Lord Jesus Christ, and the Holy Spirit. The doctrine of the Trinity holds that the Father, the Son and the Holy Spirit "are one in person, equal in glory and in power," as stated in the Church creeds. The Bible, while showing the absolute **Unity** between the Father and the Son and Holy Spirit in the various steps of the great plan of salvation, most positively contradicts the thought that the Father and Son are one in person, denies that they are equal in majesty and in power, except as before shown, that the Father has glorified the Son, has highly exalted him and given him a name above all others except his own, making him his agent and representative in the exercise of "all power in heaven and in earth." All the various Scriptures agree in their statements to the effect that the Father **sent the Son** into the world; and that the Son, for the joy set before him by the Father, endured the cross, and despised the shame; and that he was the heavenly Father's first and only begotten Son; and that after he shall have accomplished the work which the Father has given him to do, he shall deliver up the Kingdom of earth, at the close of the Millennial age, to the Father; and the additional statements already called to attention, in which the Son cheerfully and fully acknowledges that he "came forth from the Father," that he "came not to do his own will" but the Father's will; and that the power he used was not his own power, but the Father's power; also his statement, "The Father is greater than I," and the declaration of the prophecy, that he is the Messenger or servant of the Covenant, and not the Maker of the Covenant;

together with the repeated declarations of the New Testament Scriptures, that he is the Mediator of the New Covenant—the one Mediator **between** God and men, the man Christ Jesus, who gave himself a ransom for all." These various Scriptures all consistently and harmoniously teach a distinction of person and glory and power as between the heavenly Father and the heavenly Son; but a most absolute and profound unity of plan, will, purpose: for the Son was **worthy** to be the executor of the great plan of Jehovah, **because** he had no will of his own, but renounced his own will that **he** might be filled with the Father's spirit and do his will in every particular.—John 6:38, 39

Moreover, the very words "Father" and "Son" imply a difference, and contradict the thoughts of the Trinity and oneness of person, because the word "father" signifies **life-giver**, while the word "son" signifies **the one who has received life** from another. The heavenly Father received life from no one; he is the fountain, the source of life, not only to our Lord Jesus, his **only begotten** Son, but through him the source of life to all others of his creatures. And all this is fully in accord with the Scripture which stands at the head of this chapter, in which the apostle plainly denies that the Father and the Son are one in person or in power, saying, "To us there is one God, the Father, **of** whom are all things . . . and one Lord, Jesus Christ **by** whom are all things."

The thoughtful **reader** will at once recognize the Scriptural harmony and simplicity of the view herein presented, while all will admit that the doctrine of the Trinity is impossible of reasonable understanding or explanation. Its most earnest advocates admit this, and instead of endeavoring to do the impossible thing of explaining it, they avoid discussion, claiming that it's "a great mystery," unexplainable. But, strange to say, this doctrine of three Gods in one God, which not only has no Scriptural support, but is opposed by the Scriptures from Genesis to Revelation, both directly and indirectly and which is so opposed to reason as to be unreasonable, is nevertheless a strongly entrenched doctrine amongst Christians, even amongst Protestants—those who profess faith in the Bible and to protest against any teachings not found therein. Why is this? We answer, that it is one of the **dark mysteries** by which Satan, through the Papacy, has beclouded the Word and character and plan of God. As it is written, "The god of this world hath blinded the minds of them that believe not, lest the light of the glorious gospel of Christ, who is the image of God, should shine unto them." (2 Cor. 4:4) He has put upon the poor world utter blindness and doctrinal veils, darkening counsel and falsifying mysteries, to hinder those who have found the Lord from coming to a **clear knowledge of the truth.**

But how would Satan be interested in adding to the luster of the glory of our Lord Jesus Christ? Would it not rather be his work to detract from the glory of Christ? We answer, that it has always been Satan's policy to misrepresent the truth, to misrepresent the Bible, and to make its teachings appear unreasonable and self-contradictory, in order to hinder mankind from seeing the great beauty and reasonableness and harmony which inhere in the divine plan and Word. The more absurdities Satan can get interwoven into man's views respecting the Creator, the better he will succeed in separating from the service of God those who are of reasonable and logical mind; and proportionately the more unreasonable he succeeds in making the creeds of men, the more does he destroy real faith amongst those who advocate those creeds, and the more he does to favor mere credulity, instead of genuine faith.

Thus for centuries the great adversary has been working most successfully to rid the Church of all the most reasonably disposed, and to gather into it the more credulous and superstitious and unreasoning class. He has covered and hidden some of the most precious truths under the most specious and repulsive errors, and the progress of the Lord's people has been correspondingly slow. But, thank God, we are now living in the time when the veil of ignorance is being dissolved, and when the Lord's people are learning to look away from the creeds formed for their enslavement during the Dark Ages, and to look directly to the Word of God itself. But, alas, this comes too late for many, especially the worldly wise: they have already so associated the creeds with the Bible that in rejecting the former they are rejecting the latter also; and instead of seeking true light from the Word of God, they are more inclined to ignore or reject it and to lean to their own understandings—to human philosophies.

Hence it is that Higher Criticism, Evolution, Christian Science, Theosophy and other Bible-denying theories, are today making rapid progress; while the old creeds are falling to pieces or being abandoned. Only the comparatively few have learned that the mistake is not in the Bible, but in the creeds, and are seeking the "old paths," and the "faith once delivered unto the saints."—Jer. 6:16; Jude 3

But how could the doctrine of the Trinity ever become so widespread amongst Christians, if it were not the teaching of the primitive Church? Is it not one of the oldest doctrines in the Church, extending back to the third century? Yes, we answer: the doctrine of the Trinity had its **rise**, its small beginning, in the second and third centuries. It must be very evident to any one who will search the Scriptures with an unprejudiced mind that the doctrine of the Trinity was not received in any measure or degree during the first century, for this is clearly shown by the writings of the apostles in the New Testament. The doctrine of the Trinity arose in a very natural way—at first through combativeness.

The apostles, in their teachings during the first century, claim most emphatically for Christ, not that he was the Father, not that he was Jehovah, but that he was the Son of Jehovah, the Messiah, sent into the world to bless the world, and to establish God's Kingdom, and to finally bring order out of the present condition of sin and disorder. The claim that he was the Son of God was met by counterclaims: some claimed that Jesus was an **impostor**: some that he was merely a **good man**: some that he had a miraculous birth, but **never had a pre-existence;** and others held the truth, viz., that he had pre-existence as a Son of God on a spiritual plane, that he became the Son of God on a human plane, in order to redeem mankind and that now he is highly exalted, so that all are commanded to honor "the Son even as they honor the Father." But as is well known, the disposition to combat leads to exaggeration of claims; and hence it was that many of those who attempted to deny the various false views respecting our Lord went to the other extreme of claiming that he was the Father, Jehovah himself.

The Religious Dictionary, of which the Rev. Dr. Lyman Abbott, a professed Trinitarian, was one of the compilers and editors, on page 944 says:—

"It was not until the beginning of the fourth century that the Trinitarian view began to be **elaborated** and formulated into a doctrine, and **an endeavor made to reconcile it with the belief of the Church in one God**. . . . Out of the attempt **to solve** this problem sprang the doctrine of the Trinity. . . . Trinity is a very marked feature in Hindooism, and is discernible in Persian, Egyptian, Roman, Japanese, Indian and the most ancient Grecian mythologies."

The idea of more deities than one was very common in olden times, with all except the one nation, Israel. As everybody knows, Grecian mythology is full of deities, many of whom have practically the same power; and to these the Jewish idea of one God seemed ridiculous, and implied a scarcity of gods. Hence it would appear that the Trinitarian view would find ready acceptance amongst the Gentile converts: it was a compromise between the general view of the world, called Polytheism (the belief in more gods than one) and Monotheism (the doctrine of one God) held by Israel. The idea of claiming **three** Gods, and at the same time claiming that the three were only **one** God, was, no doubt, considered a masterstroke in theology, by which the views of many believers converted from amongst the Jews could be brought into closer accord with the general sentiments of the Gentiles, who, it was desired should be pleased and brought into the Church. Similarly Mariolatry—the worship of the Virgin Mary—was introduced to meet, to gratify and to attach itself upon, the superstition which had long prevailed amongst the heathen in respect to Isis, Diana, and the other goddesses, who had their millions of worshipers. It should be remembered that at the time of the introduction of these doctrines the leaders of the Church had abandoned their hope in the second coming of the Lord to establish his Kingdom, and had obtained a new hope namely, a hope of converting the world, and of thus **establishing** the earthly Church as a Hierarchy, or Kingdom of God, in which a representative or pope would reign instead of Christ, as his **vicegerent.***

The general acceptance of the doctrine of the Trinity, and the tenacity with which it is held, is based upon the superstitious fear inculcated by the Roman clergy, and later also by the Protestant clergy, under the implied threat that whoever denies the Trinity is taking the straight road to eternal torture. At the same time it is admitted that the doctrine is **incomprehensible,** and therefore that nobody really believes it, because nobody can in a true sense, believe an incomprehensible thing. And various doctrines and practices, not only of Protestantism, but also of Catholicism, deny the doctrine of the Trinity: note, for instance, that all Protestants pray to the Father, **"in the name** of Jesus," "for Jesus' sake," etc., thus recognizing the fact that they are two separate persons, and not one in person. Roman Catholics similarly recognize the distinction of person: for they pray to the lower saints to intercede for them with Mary, that she may intercede with Jesus, and have Jesus intercede for them with the Father.

So firmly entrenched is this false doctrine, received by Protestants from Papacy during the Dark Ages, and still held with tenacious grasp, that belief in this incomprehensible, unreasonable and unscriptural doctrine is made a test of orthodoxy. Whoever disbelieves this is declared to be a heretic, not only

---

*See SCRIPTURE STUDIES. Vol. II. Chap. 9; Vol. III, Chap. 4

The Author of the Atonement

by the Church of Rome, but by the greatest standard of authority amongst Protestants—The Evangelical Alliance. Truth is mighty and shall ultimately prevail: nevertheless, meantime, the conditions which God has permitted are such as to form tests of character and of loyalty to God and his Word amongst those who profess to be his people and to be taught of God. It therefore behooves every truthseeker to deal honestly with himself and with the Heavenly Father's Word, which alone is able to make us wise unto salvation. Let us remember that the truth alone sanctifies, and that error, on the contrary, always tends to evil.

GOD THE FATHER AND GOD THE SON

This may be the proper point at which to introduce and examine a few Scriptures supposed to favor the doctrine of the Trinity, although they do not state it.

It is claimed that our Lord Jesus is spoken of as God, and that there is but one God, and that hence God the Father and God the Son must be two names for the one person. Let us examine this question in the light of the divine Word, taking nothing for granted, but proving every step of our way. We labor under the disadvantage that almost all translators of the Old Testament have not been **exact** or **uniform** in their translations of the several appellatives to deity.*
For instance:—

APPELLATIONS OF DEITY IN THE OLD TESTAMENT

(1) The name **Jehovah** is properly rendered only four times, where it seemed impossible to do otherwise (Exod. 6:3; Psa. 83:18; Isa. 12:2; 26:4); it is rendered **God** 298 times, and **Lord** over 5,000 times.

---

*The appearance is that the Trinitarians who translated our Common Version Bible feared to render the name Jehovah as a proper name in every instance, lest the people should realize the fact which theology denies—that the title Jehovah belongs only to the great "I AM," the Father. Similarly Leeser's English translation made for the Jews

(2) The title **Adonai**, generally properly rendered **Lord**, is once rendered **God**.

(3) The title **Adon** is rendered **Sir, Master, Lord**.

(4) The word **elohim**, with its modifications **eloah, elah** and **el**, occurs over 2,500 times. These most frequently refer to Jehovah; but in many instances with evident propriety are applied to others: hence the connections must determine **who** is referred to. We will give Scripture illustrations which will make the matter perfectly clear, and prove beyond a doubt that **elohim** signifies **mighty**. It is properly applied to Jehovah, because he is **All-mighty**, all powerful. It is properly applied to any angel, for they are **mighty**, powerful, and in their visits to man recorded in the Old Testament they were specially **mighty** because representatives of Jehovah, the All-mighty. Great, influential men were also properly described as **elohim—mighty**. Like our English word "sheep," **elohim** is used either in the singular or plural as occasion may require.

These are facts, and our quotations from the Common Version Bible will substantiate them thoroughly; and thus will demonstrate the Scriptural propriety and consistency in referring to our Lord Jesus Christ as **God** (**elohim**) and as **Adon** (Master, Lord) and as **Adonai** (my Lord), and yet never as Jehovah.

---

covers the word; possibly because of fear that some of the Jews might stumble over some of the few uses of the word reviewed preceding.

The Jew prefers and uses the word Lord, possibly in the hope that fellow Jews will recognize the word Lord as applicable **only** to Jehovah and therefore feel a resentment toward those who speak of Jesus as "our Lord and Savior Jesus Christ"—thinking this blasphemy.

The Trinitarian translators probably preferred to use the word Lord instead of Jehovah, in order that Christians accustomed to use the word Lord as a title for our Savior, Jesus, might in reading the Old Testament think that he, and not the Father, Jehovah, is usually referred to.

ELOHIM [MIGHTY] TRANSLATED "ANGELS"

Psalm 8:5. "Thou [Jehovah, vs. 1] hast made him a little lower than the **angels** [**elohim**], and hast crowned him with glory and honor."

That this is a proper rendering of **elohim** is proven by the fact that the inspired apostle translated it thus into the Greek, **angelos**—when, referring to how our Lord humbled himself, he says—"Thou madest him a little lower than **angels**."—Heb. 2:7, 9

ELOHIM [MIGHTY] TRANSLATED "GODS"

In referring to false gods of the heathen, the word **elohim** [mighty] is used 196 times; and quite properly, too, for they were **mighty** or influential to their devotees.

JEHOVAH THE [ALL-MIGHTY] ELOHIM CONTRASTED WITH OTHER ELOHIM [MIGHTY ONES]

Psalm 86:6-8. "Give ear O **Jehovah** unto my prayer. . . . Among all the gods [**elohim**—mighty ones] there is none like unto thee."

Psalm 95:3. **Jehovah** is a great God [**el**—mighty one] and a great King above all **gods** [**elohim**—mighty ones]."

Psalm 50:1. "The mighty God [lit.—**God** of gods—**el elohim**—the mighty of the mighty], **Jehovah**, hath spoken."

Psalm 29:1. "Give unto **Jehovah** O ye **mighty** [**el**—gods], ascribe unto **Jehovah** glory and strength. Give unto **Jehovah** the honor of his name; and worship **Jehovah** in the beauty of holiness."

Genesis 17:1. "**Jehovah** appeared to Abraham and said unto him, I am the Almighty **God** [**el**]."

Exodus 15:11. "Who is like unto thee, O **Jehovah**, among the **gods** [**el**—mighty ones]."—See margin.

Genesis 14:22. "Abraham said, I have lifted up my hand unto **Jehovah**, the most high **God** [**el**], possessor of heaven and earth."

Psalm 96:4. **Jehovah** is great, and greatly to be praised: he is to be feared above all **gods** [elohim—mighty ones.]"

These instances suffice as samples: others may be found by those who desire and seek them.

ELOHIM APPLIED TO MEN

In the afore-mentioned 196 translations of **elohim** by the word **gods,** probably fully one-half refer to men—mighty ones—kings, princes, nobles, etc., but now we notice a few instances in which **elohim** is applied to the Lord's people.

Genesis 23:6. Abraham is styled **elohim**, the word being translated **mighty** in our Common Version Bible. "Thou art a **mighty** [elohim] prince among us."

Exodus 7:1. Moses is denominated the **god** [elohim] of Pharaoh. "I have made thee a **god** [elohim] to Pharaoh."

Exodus 21:6. The judges [rulers, **mighty** ones] of Israel were styled **elohim**. "His master shall bring him unto the **judges** [elohim]."

Exodus 22:8, 9. "If the thief be not found, then the master of the house shall be brought unto the **judges** [elohim] . . . Both parties shall come before the **judges** [elohim]; and whom the **judges** [elohim] shall condemn, he shall pay double unto his neighbor."

Exodus 22:28. "Thou shalt not revile **the gods** [elohim—margin, judges]." Note the apostle's sanction of this translation.—Acts 23:5

THE SAINTS CALLED ELOHIM

Psalm 82:6, 7. "I have said, Ye are **gods** [elohim—mighty ones], all of you sons of the highest, but ye shall all die like [other] men, falling like one of the princes [heads]." The saints must all die, but like Christ Jesus their "head," sacrificially, and not as Adam for his own sin.

This passage was quoted by our Lord Jesus, and applied to those who received the word of God at his lips—those having ears "to hear:" and it applies still

The Author of the Atonement

to the same class.* "Beloved, now are we the sons of God," reckonedly, hoping by divine grace to "become partakers of the divine nature."—John 10:34, 35; 1 John 3:2; 2 Pet. 1:4

ELOHIM RENDERED "GREAT," "STRONG," ETC.

This word is sometimes rendered **strong, power, great,** etc., in connection with inanimate things; as "Great [elohim—mighty] tremblings" (1 Sam. 14:15); "Great [elohim—mighty] wrestlings" (Gen. 30:8); "Great [el—mighty] mountains" (Psa. 36:6); "The **strong** [el] among the mighty" (Ezek. 32:21); "It is in the **power** [el] of my hand."—Gen. 31:29

"GOD" AND "LORD" IN THE NEW TESTAMENT

In the New Testament the matter is simplified by the use of fewer words; but it may be said that nothing whatever in the **words** used distinguishes the Father from the Son in the words rendered Lord and

---

*This entire Psalm (82) seems to refer to our Lord Jesus as the divinely appointed Deliverer and Judge of Christendom, now, in the time of his **parousia**. To him we apply the words, "God [elohim, Christ appointed by the Father to judge the world now] standeth in the assemblage of the mighty [amongst the financial, political and ecclesiastical princes]; he judgeth among [these] gods [elohim—mighty ones]." He is represented first as reproving these princes and calling for equity, but "They heed not, neither will they understand; they walk on in darkness [respecting what will be the result of their policy]: all the foundations of the earth [the social world] are out of the course"; is his decision: it is useless to attempt to patch present institutions; they must all be "dissolved," that the new heavens and new earth—the new social world—may come instead. Then verses 6 and 7 are addressed to his faithful "little flock." When they are gathered—when all the "elect" Church by dying shall have passed beyond the veil—then Christ will be called upon, "Arise O God [elohim], judge the earth: for thou hast inherited all nations." It will be to establish his Kingdom that he will let loose the judgments which in "a great time of trouble such as never was since there was a nation," shall abase the proud and exalt the humble and usher in the "times of restitution" long promised by all the holy prophets.—Acts 3:19-23

God. The matter is left entirely to the judgment of the reader, and indicated only by the construction of the sentence—except that where the word **Theos** is used twice in the same clause the Greek **Prepositive Article** is sometimes used, so as to give the effect of **the God** in contrast with **a God**. An illustration of this is found in John 1:1—"The Word was with **the** God [**ho theos**] and the Word was **a** God [**theos**]." But the careful student (freed from prejudice) will generally have no difficulty in determining the thought of the apostle. Indeed, the language is so explicit that the wonder is that we were heedless of it so long.

The word God in our New Testament, whether in referring to our Heavenly Father or to his Heavenly Son, our Lord Jesus, or to false gods, is almost invariably the translation of the Greek word **Theos**. Exceptions are that the word **kurios** is once translated **God** when it should have been rendered Lord or Master, namely in Acts 19:20; and Acts 17:18 **daimonion** is rendered gods, and should be **demons**.

The title "Lord," whether applied to Jehovah, or Christ, or man, or angels, is generally the translation of the Greek word **kurios** signifying Master, or Lord. It is frequently translated **Sir** and **Master**. Exceptions are that in five places Lord is the translation of **despotes**, where it would better have been translated **Sovereign** or **Autocrat**. The cases are:—

(1) Luke 2:29. "Lord [**despotes**] now lettest thou thy servant depart in peace."

(2) Acts 4:24 "Lord [**despotes**] thou art God which hast made heaven and earth. . . . The rulers were gathered together against the Lord [**kurios**] and against his Christ. For of a truth against thy holy Son Jesus, whom thou hast anointed, . . . were gathered."

(3) 2 Pet. 2:1. "Heresies, even denying the Lord [**despotes**] that bought them."

(4) Jude 4. "Denying the only Lord [**despotes**] God, and our Lord Jesus Christ."

(5) Rev. 6:10. "How long, O Lord [**despotes**], holy and true, dost thou not judge and avenge our blood?"

Rabboni [master] is once rendered **Lord.**—Mark 10:51

Kurieno [to be lords] is once rendered **lords.**— 1 Tim. 6:15

THE GODHEAD

The translators of our New Testament were extremely unfortunate in selecting and using the word "godhead" three times to translate three different words—none of which have any such significance as comes from this word to the mind of the ordinary English reader: namely—a God with several bodies and but one head. Its occurrences are:—

(1) **Ho Theios** is rendered **Godhead** in Acts 17:29 whereas it should be **"the Deity,"**—"We ought not to think that the **Godhead** [**ho Theios**—the Deity] is like unto gold or silver or stone." The same word is translated **divine** in the only two other instances of its occurrence in the New Testament; viz., 2 Pet. 1:3, 4.

(2) **Theiotes** is rendered **Godhead** in Romans 1:20; whereas it should be translated **Divinity** or **Deity**— "God hath showed it unto them, . . . even his eternal power and **godhead** [**Theiotes**—Deity]." This is the only occurrence of this word in the New Testament.

(3) **Theotes** is rendered **Godhead** in Colossians 2:9; whereas it should be translated **Deity**—"For in him dwelleth all the fullness of the Godhead [**Theotes** —Deity] bodily." This is the only occurrence of this word in the New Testament.

In the glorified Christ, who is the head of the Church, dwells all fullness—plenitude of wisdom, grace and power, not only to guide all the affairs of the Church, his body, but also as the Father's representative to do any and everything necessary to be done in carrying forward to successful completion the great divine plan committed to his care.

"THOU SHALT WORSHIP THE LORD THY GOD AND HIM ONLY SHALT THOU SERVE"
——Matt. 4:10——

It is claimed by some that the fact that our Lord Jesus received worship without rebuke signifies that he is **Jehovah**. Our Lord's words above quoted are supposed to imply that for any being but Jehovah to receive worship would be wrong. We answer, Not so! To so interpret these words is to think into them a meaning which they do not contain, and to make them contradictory to the teachings of other Scriptures. Jehovah's decree respecting Christ, "Thou art **my Son,** this day have I begotten thee," had already been recorded through the prophets; and also his decree, "Let all the angels of God **worship him.**" (Psa. 2:7; 97:7; Heb. 1:5, 6) Our Lord Jesus knew this. He also knew that the angelic messengers of Jehovah had in the past been **worshiped as representatives of Jehovah;** and that he himself was the chief messenger, the Only Begotten Son, the "Messenger of the Covenant," whom the Father had sanctified and sent into the world: he knew consequently that whoever honored him honored the Father also.

Indeed, his own words were, "He that honoreth not the Son honoreth not the Father which sent him." —John 5:23; Mal. 3:1

The Greek word translated **worship** in the New Testament is **proskuneo** which signifies **"to kiss the hand,"** as a dog licks the hand of his master. The significance is **reverence.**

The Hebrew word rendered **worship in the Old Testament** is **shaw-kaw** and signifies to **bow down.** The significance is reverence. The word occurs 170 times and only about one-half of this number refer to the worship of God. But this fact is hidden from the English reader by reason of its having been 74 times translated **bow down, bowed himself, did reverence, did obeisance,** etc., when referring to homage to great earthly beings. We will give examples:—

The Author of the Atonement

Abraham "**bowed himself [shaw-kaw]** toward the ground, and said, My Lords [**Adonai**] . . . let a little water be fetched and wash your feet, and rest yourselves under the tree." These words and acts were while he thought them merely "three men."—Gen. 18:2-4

Lot "**bowed down [shaw-kaw]**" to two of the same three.—Gen. 19:1

Abraham "**bowed down himself [shaw-kaw]**" to the people of Canaan.—Gen. 23:7, 12

Isaac blessed Jacob, saying, "Let nations **bow down [shaw-kaw]** unto thee; . . . and let thy mother's sons **bow down [shaw-kaw]** unto thee."—Gen. 27:29

"David stooped and **bowed himself [shaw-kaw]** to the earth" to king Saul.—1 Sam. 24:8

Abigail "**bowed herself [shaw-kaw]** to the ground" to David; and again to David's representatives.—1 Sam. 25:23, 41

The woman of Tekoah "fell on her face . . . and **did obeisance [shaw-kaw]**" to king David. And Joab and Absalom did likewise, translated "**bowed himself [shaw-kaw]**."—2 Sam. 14:4, 22, 23

"When Mephibosheth . . . was come unto David, he fell on his face **and did reverence [shaw-kaw]**."—2 Sam. 9:6

From these evidences it will be apparent to all that the prohibition of the First Commandment—"Thou shalt not **bow down thyself [shaw-kaw]** to them nor serve them," was not understood, nor meant to be understood, as a prohibition of **reverence, homage,** etc., to the honorable, or to those in honored positions among men. Nor did the Jews err in doing **reverence [shaw-kaw]** to angels who came with messages in Jehovah's name and acknowledging him. And such reverence was approved—never reproved. The Commandment warns against image worship or any worship of any **rival** gods. This Jehovah cannot tolerate. Hence there was no impropriety for any Jew who recognized Jesus as the "Sent of God" to do him **reverence, obeisance**; and much more proper is it for all those who recognize our Lord Jesus according to his **claims**—as the Son of God.

Indeed, we may be sure that those Pharisees who took up stones to kill our Lord because he declared himself the **Son** of God would have been wild beyond bounds, and not only have stoned our Lord Jesus, but also his **worshipers,** claiming idolatry, had they entertained as a people any such extreme thought of worship, obeisance (**proskuneo**), as is entertained by those whose extreme views respecting this word we are combating and have proved erroneous.

Exceptions to this liberty would be in cases where the **man** to whom **reverence, obeisance** or **worship** is rendered is the recognized **representative** of a false god—as a pseudo-Christ or false Christ—Antichrist. Homage to the popes would, we believe, come under this head of false or wrong worship; because in his office he claims falsely to be "Vicegerent Christ." It was on this ground that our Lord Jesus refused to acknowledge Satan and his great power in the world. It was an **actively evil** power, designedly opposed to the laws of Jehovah. Hence the proposition that by not opposing evil, by respecting or **reverencing** evil customs already established under Satan's regime, Satan would co-operate with our Lord in the establishment of his kingdom, was at once declined and the answer signified—I am in full accord with Jehovah God and therefore in full accord with the prophetic declaration: "Thou shalt **reverence** Jehovah thy God and him shalt thou serve"—and since you are his wilful opponent I can render no **reverence** to you or your methods, nor could I either serve your cause or co-operate with you. Our causes are distinctly separate. I will have nothing to do with you. Compare Matt. 4:10; Deut. 10:20, 21

Had our Lord Jesus set himself as **a rival** to Jehovah instead of as his Son and servant, any homage to him would have signified disrespect to the Father and would have been sinful—idolatrous. On the contrary, however, while accepting homage, **reverence**, as the Son of God he declared most positively and publicly—"The Father is greater than I," and taught his disciples to make their petitions to the Father saying, "Whatsoever ye shall ask of the Father in my name, he will give it you."—John 16:23

The Author of the Atonement

"I AND MY FATHER ARE ONE"
——John 10:30——

This text is considered a proof that our Lord Jesus is entitled to the name Jehovah—that he was both the Father and the Son—or that he had no Father and was not a Son.

Having vague, mysterious thoughts respecting "trinity," a remarkably large number of otherwise intelligent people seem to forget that there **is** any other kind of oneness than **personal** oneness. On the contrary, however, in **all other** uses of the word the thought is that of **harmony**—oneness of plan, purpose, will, mind. How blind a theory can make us is well illustrated by the fact that our Lord's own explanation and illustration of the manner in which he and the Father are **one** is very generally overlooked. He said in prayer to the Father—

"I pray not for the world but for them which thou hast given me, for they are thine . . . neither pray I for these alone, but for them also which shall believe on me through their word; **that they all may be one, as thou, Father, art in me and I in thee, that they also may be one in us** . . . that **they may be one, even as we are one**: I in them and thou in me, that they may be **made perfect in one**."—John 17:9, 20-23

Here the oneness of the Church, for which the Lord prayed, is specially stated to be exactly the **same as the oneness between the Father and the Son.** That the oneness of the Church is **oneness of mind** and **not a personal oneness** needs no discussion. Evidently the thought in the Redeemer's mind was oneness of heart, oneness of purpose, oneness of will, amongst his followers; and **that oneness identical with the oneness between the Father and himself.** And this oneness was to be **attained** on the part of the Church in the same manner exactly as the oneness between the Father and the Son was **attained.** The Son was at one with the Father because he fully accepted as his own **the Father's will,** saying, "Not my will but thine be done." So each member of the Church is to come into perfect harmony with the Father, and with the Son, by doing not their own wills, but by setting aside their own wills and accepting the **will of Christ**, which is the **will of the Father**. Thus, and thus only, will the Church ever come into the **oneness** for which our Lord here prayed, and which he refers to as of the same kind as the **oneness** between the Father and himself. How strange that any should attempt to misuse and pervert these our Lord's words, to make them support the unreasonable and unscriptural doctrine of a Trinity—three Gods in **one person**. On the contrary, how beautiful and reasonable is the Scriptural **oneness** of the spirit of the Father and Son and Church.

"HE THAT HATH SEEN ME HATH SEEN THE FATHER"

After our Lord had declared himself to be the Way, the Truth and the Life, and that no man could come to the Father but by him, and that whoever knew him would know the Father also, Philip said to our Lord Jesus, "Lord, show us the Father, and it sufficeth us." Jesus answered him, "Have I been so long time with you, and yet hast thou not known me, Philip? He that hath seen me hath seen the Father; and how sayest thou then, Show us the Father? Believest thou not that I am in the Father and the Father in me? The words that I speak unto you I speak not of myself: but the Father that dwelleth in me, he doeth the works."—John 14:7-10

We are asked to accept this statement by our Lord Jesus as proof that he is Jehovah (and not Jehovah's Son), and that as such the name Jehovah is properly applicable to him. But all should notice that the entire context shows a distinction between the Father and the Son, such as no reasonable person would use if he desired to give the impression which Trinitarians seek to draw from it. The whole question, therefore, is, What did our Lord wish us to understand by his words, "He that hath seen me hath seen the Father"? We answer, he meant us to understand that it is impossible for man (a fleshly, earthly being) to see God, a spirit being. Thus the Apostle John testified, "No one has seen God at any time: the Only Begotten of God—the One existing within the bosom of the Father—he interpreted [him]." (John 1:18— Rotherham's Translation) He meant them to understand what the Lord declared to Moses, "No man can see my face and live:" and hence that if the Father would show himself to humanity, it could only be either by miraculously opening man's eyes to discern the spiritual glory (thus exposing man to death), or else by **God's manifesting himself in a body of flesh**—in such a manner that men could discern something of his character by contact and intercourse.

And was not this exactly what God did do? God's mind, God's will, was **fully represented** in his Only Begotten Son, our Lord, when he was made flesh and dwelt amongst men. He therefore was the best, the closest, the most positive representation of God that it was or ever would be **possible to give mankind.** In seeing and knowing the Lord Jesus intimately, Philip and the other apostles knew the Father in the most absolute sense possible for humanity to know him. They knew him in the most absolute sense possible for the Father to **reveal** himself to mankind. There never was, there never would be, there never could be, a clearer, a more absolute, a more complete manifestation of God to man than in the person of the Lord Jesus Christ; for when "made flesh" he was "God manifested [Greek, **rendered apparent**] in the flesh." (1 Tim. 3:16) Similarly the apostle declares of the Church, the faithful members of Christ—We are delivered unto death, "that the life also of Jesus might be made manifest [Greek, **rendered apparent**] **in our mortal flesh.**"—2 Cor. 4:11

The **perfect man** is a **perfect image** of the invisible God, and hence the best conception or illustration that could be presented. Similarly during the Millennium the ancient worthies **perfected** will be the best representatives among men of the Heavenly Father, the Heavenly Son and the Heavenly Bride of

Christ. Whoever sees them will see God manifest in the flesh—God's **likeness** in flesh. And it will be to this sublime condition that the entire groaning creation will be privileged to attain, if they will, under the guidance of the Royal Priest and his "brethren" the under priests, ministering through the ancient worthies who, as the fleshly representatives of the kingdom, will be earth's "princes."—Psa. 45:16

THE BLESSED AND ONLY POTENTATE, THE KING OF KINGS AND LORD OF LORDS, WHO ONLY HATH IMMORTALITY
—1 Tim. 6:15, 16—

Many consider this passage to signify that at his appearing, at his second advent, our Lord Jesus will exhibit or make known to the world the Heavenly Father's greatness. But although that view has some reasonable aspects, we incline on the whole to apply the statement to the glory and honor of Christ—dating from the beginning of the Millennial age. True, he will cause all who accept his way to recognize Jehovah God also, but this will not be at his appearing but at the close of his reign, when he shall "deliver up the Kingdom to God, even the Father."—1 Cor. 15:24-28

To apply the passage to the Father would be to deny that our Lord possesses immortality, whereas the Scriptures explicitly teach that he and all who share in the First Resurrection obtain therein immortality and that thus the Father, who hath **life-inherent** (self-existence—immortality), **gave** to the Son that he should have **life-inherent** (self-existence—immortality).—1 Cor. 15:42-44, 53, 54; John 5:26

But to apply this Scripture to the Son seems to fit every condition perfectly, and by no means ignores the Father, Jehovah—nor proves that our Lord Jesus is the Father, Jehovah—for we are in all such cases to remember the invariable rule laid down by the inspired apostle—namely, that in comparisons, honors, etc., mentioned respecting the Son, the Father is **always excepted** as being inexpressibly above all comparisons. His words are, "It is manifest that he [the Father] is **excepted**," and not to be considered under or subject to our Lord Jesus and the various powers conferred by the Father upon him. For when the Son shall have subdued sin in the world, "then shall the Son also himself be subject unto him [the Father] that did put all things under him [the Son]." —1 Cor. 15:27

Another very similar statement of the glory of our Lord Jesus' kingdom given him by the Father is that "He is at the head of all principality and power." (Col. 2:10) The answer to this is the same. The Father's government and authority are never **contrasted** with that of the Son; for the latter is at **one** with the former and is his representative.

"THOUGHT IT NOT ROBBERY TO BE EQUAL WITH GOD"

In Phil. 2:6 our common English version represents the Apostle Paul as making the astounding statement that Christ, "being in the form of God, thought it not robbery to be equal with God." It should be noticed, first of all, that this passage surely does not teach the doctrine of the Trinity, nor that our Lord Jesus **is** the Father, Jehovah: for if so where would be the room for meditating a **robbery** or considering an **equality?** These words "robbery" and "equal" positively teach that the Father and the Son are not **one in person**, but two. But how strange it seems that the apostle's words are so different from those of our Lord on this subject. He declares, "The Father is greater than I"; "Of mine own self I can do nothing." We ask, Did our Lord Jesus lose his humility that he later concluded to be **equal** with God the Father?

But, secondly, we notice how much such a view conflicts with the lesson which the apostle was seeking to inculcate. Was the apostle seeking to have the

Church aspire to and grasp after the honor of the Father or the honor of each other? Surely not! On the contrary, he is urging against vainglory and in favor of lowliness of mind, and that each should esteem the other **better than himself.** He assures his readers that this humility of mind was our Lord Jesus' disposition, and says, "Let this mind be in you which was also in Christ Jesus." If the mind which was in Christ Jesus was to grasp the Father's glory and honor, and to think it not robbery to do so, then the same mind in the Lord's Church would mean that each one of us should be grasping after all the glory and honor possible to be attained, and should consider that the proper course, and that we thus would have the mind or disposition which Christ manifested.

But this is all wrong: It is the translation that is at fault. It is a wretched one, and gives the very opposite of the apostle's meaning. The Greek word, **harpagmos,** here rendered "robbery," only occurs this once in the New Testament, and has associated with it the thought of robbery, or unlawful acquisition, but the apostle's meaning is exactly reversed by the misarrangement of the sentence. His thought could be translated in almost the same words but with an opposite meaning, thus—"Who thought not by robbery to be equal with God." Our Lord Jesus' course is thus contrasted with that of Satan who did attempt to usurp God's position and honor. (Isa. 14: 12-14) This is clearly shown by the context preceding and following—that nothing be done for vainglory—that Christ was very **humble-minded,** and that we also should be **humble-minded** and thus walk in his footsteps. Note the following translations of this word **harpagmos,** preferred by eminent scholars of various denominations:

"Did not think it a matter to be earnestly desired." —Clarke

"Did not think of eagerly retaining."—Wakefield

"Did not regard . . . as an object of solicitous desire."—Stewart

The Author of the Atonement

"Who in God's form subsisting, **not a thing to be seized on** esteemed the being equal with God."—Rotherham

"Who being [margin, **originally**] in the form of God, counted it not a prize [**margin,** a thing to be grasped] to be on an equality with God."—Revised Version

"Who existing in the form of God, **counted not the** being on an equality with God **a thing to be grasped.**"—Amer. Rev. Committee

"Thought not . . . a thing to be seized."—Sharpe

"Did not eagerly grasp."—Neeland

"Did not violently strive."—Dickenson

"Did not meditate a usurpation."—Turnbull

The last definition seems to fit best with the context, and is the translation preferred and given in the Emphatic Diaglott, which renders the entire passage thus:—

"Who, though being in God's form, yet did not meditate a usurpation to be like God, but divested himself, taking a bondman's form."

This translation is consistent, not only with the facts of the case, but also with the apostle's argument, of which it forms a part. Its statement, amplified, is that when our Lord Jesus was a spirit being, when he had a God-like form and nature, he was not filled with an ambitious spirit, and a desire to usurp divine authority and power and glory and homage—he was not of the spirit of Satan, who strove to exalt himself, saying, "I will be as the Most High." On the contrary, although he occupied the highest position, next to the Heavenly Father, he was so humble minded that, in obedience to the Father's will, he divested himself of the glories and majesty of his spirit condition, exchanging that higher nature and glory for a lower condition, a human condition. "a little lower than the angels." The apostle then proceeds to show that not only was this humility manifested, but that subsequently a still greater humility was shown, in that our Lord Jesus, as the man Christ Jesus, became subject to death, even the ignominious death of the Cross. And all this humbling of himself, the apostle declares, was in obedience to the divine will, the Father's will. Then the apostle points out the result of this, saying, "Wherefore [**on this account**, because of his exhibition of loyalty, humility, and obedience even unto death] God [the Father] has highly exalted him, and given him a name that is above every name, that at the name of Jesus every knee should bow and every tongue confess . . . to the glory of God the Father."—Heb. 2:7, 9; 1 Tim. 2:5, 6; Phil. 2:11

Thus seen, this text, so far from being an aid or a comfort to the doctrine of the Trinity, most strongly opposes it, and places itself in full harmony with the entire Word of God, and with sanctified common sense and reason.

We leave this feature of our subject with an enhanced appreciation of the lengths and breadths and heights and depths of the Heavenly Father's greatness of person, character and plan, and with a greater esteem than ever for his great Son, whose wonderful love, loyalty and trust in the Father's wisdom, grace and power have been so royally rewarded; rejoicing, indeed to "honor the Son **even as** we honor the Father." And after full, explicit examination of the revelation given us in God's Word, we fully concur in the Apostle Paul's inspired testimony:—"To us there is but one [supreme] God, the Father, **out of** whom are all things and we **for** him, and one Lord Jesus Christ, **through** whom are all things and we **through** him."—1 Cor. 8:6

"Grace to you and peace from God our Father, and from the Lord Jesus Christ. Blessed be the God and Father of our Lord Jesus Christ, who hath blessed us with all spiritual blessings in the heavenlies, in Christ: according as he hath chosen us in him . . . having **predestinated** us unto the adoption of children **by** Jesus Christ **to** himself. . . . The God of our Lord Jesus Christ, the glorious Father, give unto you the spirit of wisdom and revelation in the knowledge of him."—Eph. 1:2-18

STUDY III

THE MEDIATOR OF THE ATONEMENT

THE ONLY BEGOTTEN ONE

"Who Is He?"—The Logos, a God—The Only Begotten of Jehovah—The Bible's Testimony—"He Who Was Rich"—"Before Abraham Was I Am"—"The First and the Last"—"Jehovah Possessed Me in the Beginning"—The Logos Made Flesh—Not Incarnated—He Humbled Himself—"He Who Was Rich for Our Sakes Became Poor"—No Hypocrisy in this Testimony—Our Lord's Conduct not Deceptive—The Holy, Harmless, Undefiled, Separate from Sinners.

"There is one God, and one Mediator between God and men, the man Christ Jesus, who gave himself a ransom."—1 Tim. 2:5, 6

IN PROPORTION as we value the work of the Atonement—our reconciliation to God, and the sacrifice for sin through which it is accomplished—in the same proportion will we esteem him whom the Heavenly Father set forth to be the propitiation for our sins, our Restorer and Life-giver. Hence, in approaching the question, Who is this great One whom Jehovah God has so highly honored, and who, by the grace of God, is our Redeemer and Savior? it is befitting that we realize, first of all, our own ignorance of the subject, and our incompetency to reach a conclusion except as the divine Word shall instruct us. Secondly, it is befitting, at the very outset of our investigation, that we remember the apostle's testimony respecting the greatness of this Mediator, and the honor due to him. He says, "Him hath God highly exalted, and given him a name that is above every name, that at the name of Jesus every knee should bow." It is written also, "That all men should honor the Son even as they honor the Father."—Phil. 2:9; John 5:23

Searching the Scriptures carefully to note just what they do say, and what they do not say, respecting our

Lord Jesus, we find their testimony very explicit, harmonious and satisfactory. We will first state, in synoptical form, what we find to be the Scriptural teaching, the proofs of which we will give further along.

(1) Our Redeemer existed as a spirit being before he was made flesh and dwelt amongst men.

(2) At that time, as well as subsequently, he was properly known as "a god"—a mighty one. As chief of the angels and next to the Father, he was known as the Archangel (highest angel or messenger), whose name, Michael, signifies, "Who as God," or God's representative.

(3) As he was the highest of all Jehovah's creation, so also he was the first, the direct creation of God, the "Only Begotten," and then he, as Jehovah's representative, and in the exercise of Jehovah's power, and in his name, created all things—angels, principalities and powers, as well as the earthly creation.

(4) When he was made flesh, to be our Redeemer, it was not of compulsion, but a voluntary matter, the result of his complete harmony with the Father, and his joyful acquiescence in carrying out every feature of the divine will—which he had learned to respect and love, as the very essence of Justice, Wisdom and Love.

(5) This humiliation to man's condition was not intended to be perpetual. It accomplished its purpose when our Lord had given himself, a human being, as our **ransom,** or "corresponding price." Hence, his resurrection was not in the flesh, but, as the apostle declares, "He was put to death in the flesh but quickened in spirit."—1 Pet. 3:18

(6) His resurrection not only restored to him a spirit nature, but in addition conferred upon him a still higher honor, and, as the Father's reward for his faithfulness, made him partaker of the **divine nature** —the very highest of the spirit natures,* possessed of immortality.

---

*Vol. I, Chap. x.

(7) It is this great One, who has been thus highly exalted and honored by Jehovah, whom we delight to honor and to worship and to serve, as one with the Heavenly Father, in word, in work, in purpose and in spirit.

SCRIPTURE TESTIMONY RESPECTING THE SON OF GOD

Let us now consider the Scriptural evidences substantiating these positions. We begin with the first chapter of John's Gospel. Here our Lord, in his pre-human existence, is referred to as "The Word" (Greek, **Logos**). "In the beginning was the **Logos**." Dr. Alexander Clarke says, concerning this word **Logos**: "This term should be left untranslated for the same reason that the names **Jesus** and **Christ** are left untranslated. As every appellative of the Savior of the world was descriptive of some excellencies in his person, nature, or work, so the epithet, **Logos**, which signifies a word, a word spoken, speech, eloquence, doctrine, reason, or the faculty of reason, is very properly applied to him." The Evangelist, in his epistle, uses the same title in respect to our Lord again, denominating him "the Word of life," or the "**Logos** of life."—1 John 1:1

The title, "Word of God"—"Logos of God"—is a very fitting one by which to describe the important work or office of our Master, prior to his coming into the world. The **Logos** was the Heavenly Father's direct **expression** of creation, while all subsequent expressions of divine wisdom, power and goodness were made through the **Logos**. It is said that in olden times certain kings made addresses to their subjects by proxy, the king sitting behind a screen, while his "word" or spokesman stood before the screen, and addressed the people aloud on subjects whispered to him by the king, who was not seen: and such a speaker was termed "The King's **Logos**." Whether or not the legend be true, it well illustrates the use of this word **"Logos"** in connection with the pre-human existence of our Lord and Master and his very grand office as the **Father's representative**, which the

Scriptures, in this connection and elsewhere, point out as having been his office.

Be it noted that the apostle, writing under inspiration, tells us that "The **Logos** was in the beginning with **the** God, and the **Logos** was **a** God." This is the literal translation of the Greek, as can be readily confirmed by anyone, whether a Greek scholar or not. The Greek article **ho** precedes the first word "God," in this verse, and does not precede the second word "God," thus intentionally indicating God the Father and God the Son in a case where without the article the reader would be left in confusion. Similarly the article precedes the word "God" in the second verse. The entire passage therefore reads:—

"In the beginning was the Word, and the Word was with [**ho theos**] the God, and the Word was [**theos**] a God. The same was in the beginning with [**ho theos**] the God."—John 1:1, 2

What "beginning" is here referred to? Surely not the beginning of the existence of Jehovah, the God, the Father; because he is "from everlasting to everlasting," and never had a beginning. (Psa. 41:13; 90:2; 106:48) But Jehovah's work had a beginning, and it is to this that reference is here made—the beginning of creation. The statement, thus understood, implies that our Lord Jesus, in his pre-human existence, as the **Logos**, was with the Father in the very beginning of creation. This confirms the inspired statement that the **Logos** himself was "the beginning of the creation of God:" this is the precise statement of the apostle, who assures us that our Lord is not only "the Head of the body, the Church," and "the first-born from the dead," but also the beginning of all creation—**"that in all things he might have the pre-eminence."** His words are: "He is the image of the invisible God—**first-born of all creation;** because by him were all things created, those in the heavens and those on the earth, visible and invisible—whether thrones, or lordships, or governments, or authorities: all things were created by him and for him, and he precedes all things, and in him all things have been permanently placed." (Col. 1:15-18) Hear also the word of prophecy concerning the Only Begotten, not only declaring his coming exaltation as King of earthly kings, but describing him as already being Jehovah's **first-born**, saying, "I will make him, my first-born, higher than the kings of the earth." (Psa. 89:27) Note also that our Lord (referring to his own origin), declares himself to be, "The faithful and true witness, **the beginning of the creation of God.**"—Rev. 3:14

In harmony with this thought of our Lord's preeminence from the very beginning, as the "first-born of every creature," and in harmony with the thought that he was the **Logos** or Expression of the Heavenly Father, in respect to every matter, is the next statement of the Evangelist's record, viz., "All things through him came into existence; and without him came into existence not even one thing which hath come into existence." (John 1:3, Rotherham's translation) What a grand thought this gives us respecting the majesty of the Only Begotten Son of God, the **Logos**! From this standpoint of his original greatness and pre-eminence, we have a clearer view than from any other of the import of the apostle's words, "He who **was rich**, for our sakes became poor, that we through his poverty might become rich." (2 Cor. 8:9) From this standpoint we can see how rich he was in the honor and glory of which he himself made mention in prayer, saying, "Father, glorify me with thine own self, **with the glory which I had with thee before the world was.**" (John 17:5) Although everything connected with the divine plan of redemption is wonderful, astounding in its manifestations of divine love, mercy, sympathy for fallen men, yet, from this standpoint of view, all is reasonable—consistent with the divine character and statement.

Those who hold that our Lord Jesus never had an existence until he was born a babe at Bethlehem have a very inferior view of the divine plan for man's succor; and they are left without a use for the many Scriptures above cited, and others, relative to our Lord's glory with the Father before the world was, relative to his great stoop, in which he humbled himself to take a nature a little lower than the angelic.

leaving therefor a nature that was above that of angels. And the Scriptural view relieves us of all the unreasonable and fallacious theories of men, by which, in attempting to honor the Son, they have gone beyond the Word of God, and have dishonored the Word of the Lord and the apostles, which declare him to have been the Son or offspring of God, and that the Father is greater than the Son. The false view has involved its millions of adherents in inextricable difficulty in every direction.

The truth alone is reasonable.

"———It's true:

It satisfies our longings as nothing else can do."

These statements respecting our Lord Jesus, that he was the beginning of the creation of God, and that he had, therefore, an existence long before he came into the world as a man, to be our Redeemer, are fully confirmed by various Scriptures, a sample of which is the statement, "God sent his only begotten Son into the world that we might have life through him." (1 John 4:9) Here the statement most positively is that he was God's Son before he came into the world, and that, as God's Son, he was given a mission in the world to perform. Nor should it be overlooked that here, as in many other instances, the **Logos** is designated "The Only Begotten Son" of God. The thought conveyed by this expression is that the **Logos** was himself the **only** direct creation or begetting of the Heavenly Father, while all others of God's sons (angels as well as men), were his indirect creation through the **Logos**. Hence the propriety, the truthfulness, of the statement, that he is the Only Begotten Son of God.

Take another illustration: "God sent not his Son into the world to condemn the world, but that the world through him might be saved." (John 3:17) Here again his pre-human existence is implied in the sending and mission. And these statements respecting the **Logos** are in full accord with the history of the matter, presented to us by the Evangelist, who declares, "He was in the world, and **the world was made by him,** and the world knew him not." And again. "The **Logos** was made flesh and dwelt amongst us.

full of grace and truth; and we beheld the glory of him, a glory as of an only begotten one from a father." (John 1:10, 14) Our Lord's own statements respecting his pre-existence are indisputable. He never acknowledged Joseph to be his father; nor did he ever acknowledge his earthly life to be the beginning of his existence.

On the contrary, notice that he continually referred to Jehovah as his Father. Remember his words, "Say ye of him whom the Father hath sanctified and **sent into the world,** Thou blasphemest, because I said, I am **the Son of God?**" (John 10:36) To Mary, his earthly mother, he said, "Wist ye not that I must be about **my Father's** business?" (Luke 2:49) To his disciples he declares, "I came down from heaven." "I am the bread of life which came down from heaven." (John 6:38, 51) Many in his day disbelieved this, and many disbelieve it still, but its truth remains. Some of those who heard said, "How can this be?" And some of his disciples said, when they heard it, "This is a hard saying: who can hear it?" "When Jesus knew in himself that his disciples murmured at it, he said unto them, Doth this offend you? What and if ye shall see the Son of man **ascend up where he was before?**" "But from that time many of the disciples went back and walked no more with him;" because of this claim of heavenly origin and pre-human existence.—John 6:60-66

Hear him again before the Pharisees, proclaiming the same truth, saying, "I know whence I came, and whither I go . . . I am from above, . . . I am not of this world; . . . I proceeded forth and came from God; neither came I of myself, but he sent me. . . . It is my Father that heareth me, and if I should say that I know him not, I shall be a liar." Then said the Jews unto him, "Art thou greater than our Father Abraham?" Jesus answered, "Your father Abraham rejoiced to see my day: and he saw it and was glad." (Abraham saw Christ's day with the eye of faith— believing the divine promise respecting Messiah. He may have seen his day of sacrifice, typified in the offering of Isaac, his only son, but at all events he saw Messiah's coming glory-day, the Millennium, and its blessings upon all the families of the earth, through this promised Seed. And no wonder the prospect made him glad. He with the eye of faith beheld the heavenly city, the New Jerusalem, the glorified Church, the Kingdom class, and he beheld similarly the heavenly country—the world blessed by that Kingdom.—Heb. 11:10, 16; 12:22; 13:14

"Then said the Jews unto him [Jesus], Thou art not yet fifty years old, and hast thou seen Abraham? [Abraham had been dead two thousand years.] Jesus said unto them, Verily, verily I say unto you, **before Abraham was, I am.**"—John 8:14, 23, 42-58

There can be no mistake about the meaning of these words. Our Lord avers that he **existed** before Abraham. Nor do the Scriptures in any place intimate that the existence of the Only Begotten ever ceased from the time it began, as "the beginning of the creation of God," until it ceased at Calvary for three days; after which he was raised from the dead to die no more, death having never more dominion over him. (Rom. 6:9) The incident of his birth as a human being, "a little lower than the angels," for the purpose of being man's sin-sacrifice, did not involve a death to the spirit nature preceding the birth as a human babe, but merely a transference of his life from a higher or spirit nature to a lower or human nature. Hence our Lord's words, "Before Abraham was I **am**," signify that there had been no cessation of his existence at any time in the interim, and positively identifies Jesus, the Son of God, in the flesh, with the **Logos**, the first-born of all creation. Of course our Lord's testimony was not received by many who heard it, nor has it been received by many since. There seems to be a perversity of disposition, which leads mankind to reject the simple, plain statements of the Lord's Word, and to prefer to regard our Lord either as a sinful member of the fallen race, or else as his own father. Only the meek are ready to "receive with meekness the engrafted word, which is able to make truly wise," and only for such is the Word of God's testimony intended. (Isa. 61:1; Jas. 1:21) As those who heard the Master, and rejected his testimony, took up stones against him, so some who hear the truth and reject it now are ready to stone, figuratively, all who accept and teach the Master's words, in their simplicity. And now, as then, the reason is because they know neither the Father, nor the Son, as they ought to know them—as they reveal themselves.

Our Lord's words are still applicable to the case, viz., "No man knoweth the Son but the Father, neither knoweth any man the Father save the Son, and he to whom the Son will reveal him." (Matt. 11:27) The world knew him not: knew not of his high origin, and his great humiliation on its behalf; and when we remember that a long period of time probably intervened between the beginning of the creation in the person of our Lord, and the time when he was made flesh, and when further we remember that during all that period he was with the Father, "daily his delight, rejoicing always before him," we cannot wonder that the Son knew the Father, as his disciples and the world knew him not—as we are learning to know him through his Word of revelation and the unfoldment of his wonderful plan of the ages. Hear him again declare, "O righteous Father, the world hath not known thee, but I have known thee."—John 17:25

The key to this wonderful knowledge of heavenly things is furnished in the statement, "He that is of the earth is earthy, and speaketh of the earth; he that cometh from heaven is above all, **and what he hath seen and heard, that he testifies.**" (John 3:31, 32) No wonder, then, that even his opponents asked, "Whence hath this man this wisdom?" (Matt. 13:54) And it was his knowledge of heavenly things, his intimate and long acquaintance with the Father, begetting absolute faith in the Father's promises, which enabled him, as a perfect man, to overcome the world, the flesh and the devil, and to present an acceptable sacrifice for our sins. Thus it was written beforehand through the Prophet: "By his **knowledge** shall my righteous servant justify many, while he will bear their iniquities."—Isa. 53:11

Now, only those who walk by faith, in the light of the divine Word, may know either the Father or the Son, or clearly and rightly appreciate the great work of atonement which they unitedly are accomplishing for humanity. But ere long, after the selection of the Church has been completed, after the Bride, the Lamb's wife, has been associated with her Lord in glory, and the Kingdom shall have come—then the knowledge of the Lord shall be caused to fill the whole earth, and the power of the Father, which, through the Logos, created all things, shall be exerted through him, as the Savior, in the restoration and perfecting of those who, when privileged to know him, shall yield to his righteous requirements, so that ultimately our Lord's power, as Jehovah's agent in creation, shall be fully equaled and exemplified in his power, as Jehovah's agent in restoring and blessing the world: and thus will be fulfilled the prediction of the Psalmist—"Thou hast the dew [freshness, vigor] of thy youth."—Psa. 110:3

Hearken to our Lord's words to Nicodemus, who sought to know something of heavenly things, but who was refused the knowledge, because he had not yet believed the earthly things. Our Lord, in explaining to him his knowledge of heavenly things, says, "No man hath ascended up to heaven but he that came down from heaven, even the Son of Man."* Our Lord then proceeds to show Nicodemus the provision which God has made for the world, that they should not perish, but have eternal life, declaring, "God so loved the world that he gave His **Only Begotten Son**, that whosoever believeth on him should not perish but have everlasting life."—John 3:13, 16

The **Logos**, the beginning of the creation of God, called also by Isaiah the Wonderful, Counselor, the

---

*The words "which is in heaven," are spurious—not found in old MSS.

The Only Begotten One

Mighty God, etc. (Isa. 9:6), we find described by Solomon, and represented under the name of Wisdom, yet with all the details which harmonize the statement with the account given by John the Evangelist (John 1:1, 18), as follows:—

"Jehovah possessed me in the beginning of his way, before his ways of old. I was set up from everlasting, from the beginning, or ever the earth was [formed]. When there were no depths [seas] I was brought forth: when there were no fountains abounding with water. Before the mountains were settled, before the hills was I brought forth; while as yet he had not made the earth, nor the fields, nor the highest part of the dust of the world. When he prepared the heavens I was there: when he set a compass upon the face of the depth: when he established the clouds above: when he strengthened the fountains of the deep: when he gave to the sea his decree, that the waters should not pass his command: when he appointed the foundations of the earth: then was I by him, as one brought up with him; and I was daily his delight, rejoicing always before him."—Prov. 8: 22-30

In addition to what we have here noted respecting the Logos—that he was not only the beginning of the creation of God, and the first-born, but additionally his Only Begotten Son, and that all other creations were by and through him—we find a beautiful corroborative statement in our Lord's own words, saying: "Fear not, I am the first and the last; I am he that liveth and was dead, and behold I am alive forevermore." And again, "These things saith the first and the last, which was dead, and is alive." (Rev. 1:17: 2:8) In no other sense or way than as the "Only" direct creation of God, through whom all else was created, could our Lord be the first and the last of God's creation. Any other view, therefore, would be an incorrect one, and in conflict with all the foregoing Scriptures.

"THE LOGOS WAS MADE FLESH AND DWELT AMONG US"—John 1:14

The common thought in respect to our Lord's manifestation in the flesh is usually expressed in the word **incarnation.** This usual thought we believe to be wholly incorrect, unscriptural. The **Incarnation** theory is that our Lord's human body, which was born of Mary, was merely a **clothing**, a **covering** for the spiritual body. The thought therefore attached to our Lord's earthly life, according to this theory, is that our Lord during his earthly life was still a spirit being, exactly as before, except that he used the flesh that was born of Mary, and that was known as the man Christ Jesus, as his veil or medium of communication with mankind, after the manner in which angels had appeared in human form in previous times—to Abraham, to Manoah, to Lot, and others. (Gen. 18:1, 2; 19:1; Judges 13:9-11, 16) Because of this incorrect premise, many confused and unscriptural ideas have been evolved respecting the various incidents of our Lord's life and death: for instance, this theory assumes that our Lord's weariness was not real, but feigned; because he, as a spirit being, could know no weariness. The logic of this theory would imply also that our Lord's prayers were feigned, because, says this theory, he was God himself, and to pray would have been to pray to himself; hence it is argued that his prayers were merely **pro forma**, to make an impression upon the disciples and those who were about. The same theory is bound to suppose that our Lord's death was merely an appearance of death, for they argue that Jesus was God the Father, who, being from everlasting to everlasting, cannot die; hence that the apparent agony and cry, "My God, my God, why hast thou forsaken me?" and the dying, were merely **pro forma**, to make the impression upon the minds of those who heard and saw. The logical arguments of this theory, therefore, is that there was no real death for man's sins, but merely an appearance of one, a spectacular effect, a dramatic show, a Cinematographic representation, **a deception** produced for a good purpose—to favorably influence the sympathies and sensibilities of mankind.

All of this is wrong, and violently in opposition to **the** truth on the subject, as presented in the Word of

God. The Scriptural declaration is not that our Lord **assumed** a body of flesh as a covering for a spiritual body as did the angels previously; but that he actually laid aside or, as the Greek renders it, "divested himself of" his pre-human conditions, and **actually took our nature,** or, as our text above declares, "**the Logos** was **made flesh.**" There was no fraud, no sham, about it: it was not that he merely appeared to humble himself while really retaining his glory and power: it was not that he seemed to become poor for our sakes, yet actually remained rich in the possession of the higher spiritual nature all the time: it was not that he merely put on the clothing, the livery, of a servant. No, but he actually became **a man** —"the man Christ Jesus, who gave himself a ransom for all."—1 Tim. 2:5

We shall see subsequently, when we come to consider particularly the ransom feature of his work, that it was absolutely necessary that he should be a man—neither more nor less than a perfect man— because it was a man that sinned, man who was to be redeemed, and the divine law required that a man's life should pay the redemption price for a man's life. "As by a **man** came death, by a **man** also came the resurrection of the dead." (1 Cor. 15: 21) But let no one misunderstand us by this to mean that our Redeemer became a man such as we are, full of inherited imperfections and blemishes. Quite to the contrary of this: the same Word of God declares that he was "holy, harmless, **separate from sinners.**"—Heb. 7:26, 28; Luke 1:35

His separateness from sinners is one of the difficult points with many. How could he be a man, and yet be free from the hereditary taint which affects the entire human family? We hope to see exactly how this could be, and how it was accomplished under the divine plan; but we require first to have thoroughly impressed upon our minds the fact that an imperfect man, a blemished man, one who through heredity had partaken of Adamic stock, and whose life was thus part with our life, **could not be our Redeemer.** There were plenty of sinful men in the world, without God sending his Son to be another.

There were plenty of these imperfect men who were willing to lay down their lives for the accomplishment of the Father's will. This is fully attested by the record of Hebrews 11, in which it is clearly shown that many "counted not their lives dear unto them," in their faithfulness to the Lord. But what was needed was not merely **a sacrifice** for sins, but **a sinless sacrifice**, which would thus pay the sinner's penalty. And since "all have sinned and come short of the glory of God," and since "there is none righteous, no, not one," **therefore,** as the Scriptures again declare, "None could give to God a ransom for his brother." (Rom. 3:10, 23; Psa. 49:7) It was because the Lord beheld and saw that there was no man competent to redeem the world that he laid help upon one who is mighty to save—able to save to the uttermost all who come unto the Father by him.—Psa. 89:19; Isa. 63:1; 59:16; Heb. 7:25

Next we want, if possible, to see clearly how our Lord Jesus laid hold upon our race, and became a member of it, through his mother Mary, without sharing in any degree its depravity, without inheriting its blight of sin, without its curse of death laying hold upon him: for if in any manner or degree he partook of the **life** of Adam, he would have been a partaker also of the death sentence upon Adam's life, and thus he would have come under the **sentence of death:** and if rendered thus imperfect, and under the sentence of death, he had no **life-rights** to give as man's ransom price, by which to purchase father Adam and his race from under the sentence of death imposed by divine Justice. We propose to examine this question in our next chapter. We hope to there prove that our Lord did not, in any manner or degree, become contaminated with sin or imperfection through his mother.

STUDY IV

THE MEDIATOR OF THE ATONEMENT

THE UNDEFILED ONE

Seemingly Conflicting Scriptures Reconciled—The Roman Catholic Doctrine of Mary's Immaculate Conception Not Sustained—The Birth of Jesus Separate from Sinners Essential to the Divine Arrangement—Otherwise no Ransom Possible—The Latest Deductions of Science in re the Union of Life and Protoplasm—The Logos Made Flesh—Born of a Woman yet Undefiled—How the Imperfect Mother Could and Did Bring Forth the Undefiled One—This Same Principle Operating in Other Features of the Divine Plan, as Testified by the Scriptures.

"Who can bring a clean thing out of an unclean? Not one."—Job 14:4

"He was manifested to take away sins and in him is no sin." "Such an High Priest was suitable for us—holy harmless, undefiled, **separate** from sinners."—1 John 3:5; Heb. 7:26

HERE are Scripture statements apparently in conflict: the first declaring, in harmony with our experience, that all of Adam's posterity is affected by virus of sin from the poisoned fountain: the latter declaring that our Lord Jesus was as a man different from other men—unblemished, undefiled, spotless. And since the entire theory of the Atonement, presented in the Scriptures, demands that of necessity our Redeemer must be an unblemished man—of our race and yet **separate** from it—this becomes a very important point before the minds of the Lord's thinking people. How did God accomplish in our Lord Jesus' case what is impossible to man, according to all human experience and according to Job's testimony? To give ample proof of how the divine arrangement did accomplish this desired yet seemingly impossible thing of producing a member of the race yet separate from its blemishes, to be its ransom—to give a corresponding price for the first **perfect man** whose sin and its curse blights the race—this is the pleasurable task of the present chapter.

Not that a knowledge of the **manner** is essential either to the faith or salvation of the true disciple taught of God; but that in the light of present-day destructive criticism (reasonable and unreasonable) it is expedient that this truth, so closely identified with the Atonement, the very center and foundation of true Christianity, should be solidly buttressed, to the intent that the faith of the Lord's people may be able to withstand the assaults of the Adversary against the doctrine of the ransom—from pulpit, press and pew. The Scriptural statement of the fact of our Lord's spotlessness was, thank God, quite sufficient for his saints for centuries; but now as "meat in due season" for the household comes the scientific and philosophic attestation to the possibility of all that is claimed in the divine Word on this subject— quite in harmony with "the laws of nature."

The Roman Catholic Church in its doctrine of "The Immaculate Conception" of Mary, attempts to establish faith in our Lord's mother, as immaculate, spotless, perfect; and thus to prove that Jesus could be born pure and separate from sinners: but this is not our claim. We admit that our Lord's mother was a member of Adam's race, in the same sense as all other members of it—that her life was derived from the Adamic stock, that she inherited human weaknesses and blemishes and unavoidably was, like all others, under the sentence of death. We claim that "the **man** Christ Jesus" was an exception—the only exception.

And it is well for us not to forget that God's providential care for the children of men is frequently manifested in the **exceptions** of nature. For instance, it is the rule of nature that heat causes expansion, while freezing causes contraction: but how fortunate it is for humanity that water is an exception to this principle—that water, contrary to the general rule, expands in freezing. Were it to follow the customary law of nature and contract with freezing, it would have the effect of making the ice heavier than the unfrozen water, and cause it to sink to the river bottoms, so that as a consequence our rivers would become solid ice, which even the summer heat would not dissolve. How fortunate, too, that antimony among the minerals is an exception to this law of nature also; otherwise it would be impossible for us to secure clear-cut edges on our printing types, secured by the mixing of this metal, which contracts, with other metals which expand under heat. So the one exception to sin-defilement in our race was its only hope—its ransom, its salvation under divine providence. With these thoughts we proceed to examine how the **Logos** was **"made flesh,"** "born of a woman," "of the seed of Abraham," and yet was uncontaminated, and could therefore be a suitable and acceptable ransom for Adam and his race.

The Scriptures hold out the thought that all **existence, living energy or being,** comes from the father and not from the mother. The mother receives the sperm or seed of life from the father, furnishes it a cell-nucleus out of which a form or body is produced, and nourishes the germ of being until it is able to maintain an independent existence; i. e., until it is able to appropriate to its maintenance the life-sustaining elements which the earth and air supply; —then it is born.

The word **father** has the significance of **life-giver.** Accordingly, God was the **"Father,"** or life-giver, while the earth was the mother, of Adam, and hence of the human race. (Luke 3:38) Adam's form or organism was of and from **earth** (which therefore served as his mother); but his spark of life which constituted him a man came from God (who thus was his Father or life-giver): and in the male of the human species has since resided the power to communicate that spark of life or living seed to progeny.

In harmony with this principle, children are spoken of as being **of** or from their fathers, and borne by their mothers. (Gen. 24:47) Thus the children of Jacob, counted through his sons, were seventy when he came down to Egypt. All of those seventy souls or beings are expressly said to have come out of the loins of Jacob. (Gen. 46:26, 27; Exod. 1:5) So of Solomon, it is said that he came out of the loins of David. (1 Kings 8:19; 2 Chron. 6:9) So also the Apostle Paul and Israelites in general claimed that they all came out of the loins of Abraham; and of Levi it is written that "he was yet in the loins of his father when Melchisedec met him."—Heb. 7:5, 10

Thus also the whole race was in and sprang from Adam their father, by mother Eve, but not from her. And thus it is written that "all in **Adam** die," but not all in Eve. Because the race came of Adam, it was tried in **his** trial, condemned in **his** failure and included under **his** sentence.

This, which the Scriptures teach, is the latest deduction of science on this subject of progeneration, as applied to humanity and to all mammalia. Scientists find abundant and conclusive proof in nature that **life** or being comes always from the male. The simplest form of illustration is a hen's egg: of itself it originally contains no life but is merely a cell-germ with its supply of nutriment ready to build up an **organism** as soon as vivified, fecundated or impregnated with the life-germ or life-seed from the male bird.

The egg contains not only the germ-cell but also the proper elements of nutrition and in proper proportion, adapted to the minute organism begotten in it by the sperm or life-seed; and under proper conditions that organism develops. The germ-cell, or "formative yolk," or protoplasm, receives the life-germ or sperm, and this becomes the embryo chick, which appropriates to its own development the "food-yolk" and the albumen, until it breaks the shell and is able to sustain itself by appropriating cruder elements of nutrition. The principles here involved are the same in human and other animals.

In view of these harmonious testimonies of the Bible and science, it is a reasonable deduction that if the father were perfect, the child would be perfect. Under even moderately favorable conditions a perfect sperm or life-seed in uniting with the female

The Undefiled One

germ-cell would produce a living embryo so vigorous and healthy as to be capable of appropriating the proper elements of nutrition, and voiding, throwing off or neutralizing the unfit. And the perfect being thus produced would likewise possess the power of neutralizing or repelling, by its perfect functions and without injury or inconvenience to itself, all elements not beneficial. On the contrary, in proportion as the sperm or life-seed be imperfect, the living embryo will be weak and unable to overcome the unfavorable conditions of its environment, and will appropriate whatever its mother furnishes—good or bad—and will be the prey of disease. Being imperfect, it is unable to reject wholly the poisonous elements and the consequence is weakness and disease.

The old proverb, "One man's meat is another man's poison," rests upon the principle here enunciated. A person possessed of good digestive powers can eat and extract nutriment and strength from food which would speedily sicken and eventually kill another of inferior powers. The more rugged extracts the good and avoids the injurious elements: the weaker is unable to do this and is really poisoned, frequently to the extent of sickness. Yet let us remember that no member of our race is nearly perfect —none are able to defend their imperfect systems against the myriads of foes that assail through food and drink and air. Consequently none are born perfect and none can avoid the encroachments of disease for long. It preys upon the weakest organs first and soon all collapse.

From this standpoint it follows that had mother Eve alone sinned the race would not have died; for had Adam remained perfect, his life unforfeited and unimpaired, his offspring would have been born without blemish. And even had the death sentence passed upon mother Eve, bringing imperfections to her, these would not have impaired her offspring: being **perfect**, they would have appropriated good elements, and have neutralized, voided or passed off naturally and without injury, any unwholesome elements of nutrition supplied them.

On the other hand, suppose that Adam had sinned

and Eve had remained sinless: Adam's condemnation and death would have affected the entire posterity just the same. However perfect the germ-cells and nourishment provided by mother Eve, only imperfect dying beings could be produced from diseased sperm or life-seed from Adam. Hence the appropriateness of the Scriptural statement that "All in Adam die," and "By one **man's** disobedience . . . death passed upon all."—1 Cor. 15:22; Rom. 5:12, 19

How wonderful the correspondence here between the first and second Adams and their brides. As the **death** of the race depended not upon Eve but wholly upon Adam, and yet she shared in the bringing of it, so the restored **life** of the redeemed race depends not at all on the bride of Christ, but upon Jesus, the Redeemer, though by divine favor it is arranged that his bride shall share in the restitution of "that which was lost."

The fountain, Adam, having become contaminated by sin and death, none of his posterity can be free from contamination; for, "Who can bring a clean thing out of an unclean? Not one." The reference here must be understood as applying to the man, and not to the woman: none coming from or out of the contaminated fountain can be clean. Hence, "There is none righteous, no, not one"; none can redeem his own life, much less give to God a ransom for his brother.—Rom. 3:10; Psa. 49:7

It is a well-recognized fact that the mind of a mother, during the period of gestation, has an important bearing upon the character and disposition of her children, for good or evil. There are many instances of mental as well as of physical "birthmarks." Whether at all or **how much** a perfect **embryo, begotten of a** perfect life-germ, might be injured by an evil **mind** in the mother, it would be impossible for humanity under present conditions to determine; for we have no opportunity for proofs along this line. Nor is it necessary to our argument to determine this proposition, for it was not under such conditions that the **"man Christ Jesus"** was born. The Scriptures explicitly point out: (1) That the Lord chose for the mother of Jesus a holy woman "blessed among women," who had "found favor with God" (Luke 1:28, 30, 42); (2) Mary was full of faith and the joy of the Lord, to be an instrument in his plan; and (3) not regarding fear of reproach from Joseph or the world, she lived rejoicing in God, saying—"My soul doth magnify Jehovah; my spirit rejoiceth in God my Savior." (Luke 1:45-47) Thus we perceive that the mind of Jesus' mother, instead of being antagonistic to his perfect development, co-operated to that result.

It follows, then, that the only obstacle to the generation of a perfect man of an imperfect, blemished, but well-willed mother is the lack of a perfect father to supply **perfect spermatozoa**. And hence the **consistency of the teaching of Scripture**, that in the case of Jesus a **perfect life** (not of or from the Adamic fountain) was **transferred** by divine power from a pre-existent condition to the embryo human condition, was born "holy" (pure and perfect), though of an imperfect mother. (Luke 1:35) That Jesus was thus uncontaminated with the imperfections, mental, moral or physical—which his mother in common with the entire human race shared, is entirely reasonable and, as we have just seen, in perfect accord not only with Scripture but also with the latest scientific findings and deductions.

Another fact which scientists are demonstrating to themselves, which seems to concur with the Scripture testimony, is, that though life or being comes from the father, **form** and **nature** come from the mother. The scientific proofs of this are more abstruse and less easily grasped by the ordinary mind; and this, because in wisdom God has not only separated the various **kinds** or **natures**, but in great measure has limited them, so that they cannot mix or blend beyond certains limits without losing the powers of fecundation. A common illustration of this is the mule, a hybrid which cannot propagate.

The old idea that form and nature came from the male is abandoned by modern students of nature, who now agree that the female furnishes **organism** as well as **sustenance**—in fact furnishes all except the life-seed or sperm, which comes from the father or life-giver. Take as a Scriptural illustration of the foregoing claims the improper union between "the daughters of men" and those angels which kept not their first estate or condition. (Gen. 6:2, 4; Jude 6; 2 Pet. 2:4) The angels, when they assumed human form, being perfect in vitality, begat children far superior to the then greatly fallen race of Adam in mental acumen as well as in physical powers, so that the record is—"the same were men of renown." These wonderful men, let us remember, were born of imperfect, dying mothers, but begotten by vigorous, unimpaired fathers.

The dying race of Adam would have had hard masters in those superior **Nephilim** (Hebrew, **fallen ones**) which were never recognized by God, either by a trial for life, or by a condemnation to death. It was a mercy indeed which, not having authorized their existence, blotted them from existence in the flood, and sparing as a new beginning for the race Noah and his family, with the comment—"Now Noah was perfect in his **generation,**" which implies that the majority of Adam's posterity had become greatly **contaminated** and more or less a new race by association with the angels in human form. We say a new race because of their new life and vigor coming from new fathers.

So great was the renown of these **"Nephilim,"** that the dread of them is to be found with more or less distinctness in heathen mythologies to this day; and hundreds of years after their destruction in the flood, the **false** report that some of these were yet alive caused a panic among the Israelites while flushed with the victory of recent battles. (See Num. 13:33; 14:36, 37) No doubt there were some large men in Canaan, as other Scriptures show, but never except in this **"evil report"** are they called **Nephilim.**

Another illustration of this principle that life (vitality) comes from the father, and organism (nature) from the mother, is found in the fact that Jehovah, himself of the divine nature has begotten **sons** of various natures. He is the father or **life-giver** to those

The Undefiled One

sons of angelic nature (Job 2:1; 38:7; Heb. 2:9), as well as to sons of human nature (Luke 3:38), as well to the **"new creatures"** who, in the first resurrection, shall be made partakers of his own **divine** nature. (2 Pet. 1:4) The spirit or **energy** of Jehovah operating upon spirit-substances produced and developed angels; the same energy or spirit operating upon earthly substances produced man and the lower animals. (Gen. 2:7; 1 Cor. 15:47) And when God would give us a clear conception of the generation of the new creatures to the divine nature, he represents them as **begotten** of his word of promise in the **womb of the Covenant** which he made with Abraham, which Covenant was symbolized by a woman, Sarah, telling us that as Isaac was the heir of Abraham and child of promise (by Sarah), **so** we, as or like Isaac, are children of God, being children of the promise, or Sarah Covenant.—See Gal. 4:23-31; 1 Pet. 1:3, 23; 2 Pet. 1:4

The same principle is illustrated in the fact that in the **typical** Jewish dispensation, prior to the Christian age, a child inherited blessings and privileges of its father, according to the favor and standing of its mother, thus again declaring that the mother's nature, rights, privileges and liberties attached to the child, though not of necessity the father's.—See Gen. 21:10; Ex. 21:4; Gal. 4:30

The foregoing arguments are clinched by the fact that our Lord Jesus was born of a woman. The "holy thing" born of a woman partook of the woman's nature, i. e., human nature—"of the earth, earthy." Though retaining all the purity and perfection of the pre-existent (spirit) state, the transferred germ of being (in harmony with this law we are examining) partook of the nature of the mother and was **"made flesh"** by being "born of a woman." Yet the "clean thing" came not out of the unclean race, but "proceeded forth and came from God" and was merely developed and nourished in Mary.—John 8:42; Gal. 4:4

It is yet further in harmony with this same principle that though our Lord Jesus has since been highly exalted to the **divine nature,** and is no longer human, yet it is declared of him that he shall be the **life-giver** or "father" of the whole human race, while it is also shown that his work for the race is to **restore** the perfection of **human nature,** which was lost for all through Adam's sin. Thus, while their "father" or life-giver will be on the divine plane, his children will be on the human plane, born out of a Covenant of restitution, illustrated by Keturah, Abraham's third wife.

Reviewing our subject then, we perceive that the "**miraculous**" birth of our Lord Jesus, perfect, **unblemished, of an imperfect mother, was** not contrary to the usual procedure of the Creator's arrangements, but in full harmony with them: we see that similarly father Adam was born into being perfect because he was born **of** God, though his mother (the earth) was still imperfect except the specially prepared Garden of Eden. The Scriptural assurance then that our Lord had a pre-human existence, the life-principle of which was transferred to Mary's womb and born of her "holy," is abundant assurance that he was as the same Scriptures declare "holy, harmless, **undefiled, separate from sinners.**" Just such an one "became us" or was suitable to the necessities of our case—such an one as could be accepted by Justice as our **ransom-price;** and then being made humanity's High Priest in things pertaining to God, would be able to compassionate the weak and burdened—having been touched with a feeling of human infirmities when he himself compassionately took our sicknesses.—Matt. 8:16, 17; Heb. 7:26

We pass on now to the consideration of how he could be thus without sin and yet be "made like unto his brethren."

STUDY V

THE MEDIATOR OF THE ATONEMENT

"MADE LIKE UNTO HIS BRETHREN"
AND
"TOUCHED WITH A FEELING OF OUR INFIRMITIES"

Who "His Brethren" are—In What the Likeness Consisted—How He was Tempted in all Points, Like as We are Tempted, Yet Without Sin—The Wilderness Temptations—Their Resemblance to ours—Some of which would "Deceive if it were Possible the Very Elect"—In What Sense our Lord was Made Perfect Through Sufferings—Though a Son, yet Learned He Obedience—How He was Made in the Likeness of Sinful Flesh—Yet Without Sin—"Himself took our Infirmities"—How He was "Touched."

"In all things it behooved him to be made like unto his brethren; that he might be a merciful and faithful High Priest in things pertaining unto God—to make reconciliation for the sins of the people."—Heb. 2:17

THE TWO popular but opposing lines of thought touch and conflict in respect to all the various Scriptural statements which declare our Lord's relationship to mankind; and the third or truth line alone is able to either reconcile the various Scriptures or to satisfy sanctified reason. Of the two false but popular theories one claims that our Lord Jesus was the Almighty God, Jehovah, who merely garbed himself in human flesh, without really having actual sensibility of humanity's trials, temptations and environments. The other theory claims that he was a sinful man, partaker of the blemishes of our race, just as others, but more successful than others in combating and resisting the motions of sin. We are endeavoring to show that both of these theories are erroneous, and that the truth lies between them, in the fact that the **Logos** "being in a form of God," a spirit being, when **"made flesh"** was really **a man**, "the **man** Christ Jesus," but **"separate** from sinners" a **perfect** man prepared to be the "corresponding price" for the first perfect man whose fall involved our race, and whose redemption also involves the race.

It is quite proper in this connection, therefore, in seeking to establish the Scripturally correct view of this subject, that we examine various Scriptures which have been distorted and misused to prove that our Lord was blemished, and subject to like passions with the fallen race. We hold that if he had been in this condition it would have been as impossible for him as it is impossible for us to keep absolutely and perfectly every feature of the Divine Law. The Divine Law is the full measure of the **perfect** man's ability and is beyond the measure and ability of any man who is not perfect. Hence, the very fact that in our Lord was no sin, the very fact that he was pleasing to the Father, and acceptable as a sin-offering, as a ransom-price for Adam (and the race lost in him), proves indirectly his perfection, as we hold that the Scriptures everywhere teach it.

But our Lord's "brethren" were not immaculate, were not separate from sinners. How, then, could he be "made like unto his brethren," and yet be separate from sinners? The answer to this question is found in the recognition of the fact that the world of mankind, sinners in general, are not the ones who are referred to as "his brethren." The man Adam, indeed, was a son of God at his creation, and up to the time of his transgression (Luke 3:38), but not subsequently. And all of his race are Scripturally designated "children of wrath." (Eph. 2:3) Only those who have "escaped the condemnation that is on the world," and who have gotten back into harmony with God, through Christ, are Scripturally authorized to consider themselves the sons of God. (John 1:12) Of the others, our Lord declares, "Ye are of your father, the devil, for his works ye do." (John 8:44) Our Lord Jesus never counted himself in as one of the children of the devil, nor as one of the "children of wrath," but declared that he "proceeded forth and came from God." Neither did he recognize as "his brethren" any of those who were still "children of wrath." The only ones recognized as the "Lord's brethren" are those who, having escaped the condemnation that is on the world, have been brought nigh to the Father through the blood of Christ, and have received "the spirit of adoption" into God's family, and the promise of full "adoption of sons" at the establishment of the Kingdom. (Rom. 8:15, 23; Gal. 4:5) It is because these are **justified,** reckonedly freed from Adamic condemnation and reckonedly constituted righteous, through the blood of Christ, that they are in any sense of the word like our Lord Jesus, "his brethren," on a similar footing of divine favor and separateness from the world. Of the consecrated of this class our Lord says, "They are not of the world, even as I am not of the world." I have chosen you out of the world." (John 15:19; 17:16). From this standpoint it can readily be seen that our Lord was "made like unto his brethren"—**exactly,** in every particular. Not that his "brethren" were in this condition at the time he humbled himself and was made flesh—he had no brethren at that time, except as this class was **foreknown** of God. (Eph. 1:5, 11; Rom. 8:9) But the divine arrangement was such that God foresaw that he could be just, and yet justify those of the sinner race who accepted divine grace through Christ, and whose sins were, on this account, covered, not imputed to them, but imputed to him who "bore ours sins in his own body on the tree." God forearranged, foreknew, his purpose to call out the Gospel Church to be "joint-heirs with Jesus Christ our Lord," to the inheritance, incorruptible, undefiled, and that fadeth not away, reserved in heaven. And it was in view of this prearranged plan that all who will constitute this class were spoken of in advance, through the prophets, as the "brethren" of Christ. Prophetically, our Lord is represented as saying to the Father, "I have declared thy name unto **my brethren;** in the midst of the Church have I sung thy praise." (Psa. 22:22; Heb. 2:12) Since this was the divine program—that our Lord should not only be the Redeemer of the world, but also a **pattern** for the "brethren" who would be his joint-heirs—therefore, in carrying out this divine program it was fitting that he should in all his trials and experiences be "made like unto his brethren."

"HE WAS TEMPTED IN ALL POINTS LIKE AS WE ARE, YET WITHOUT SIN"
——Heb. 4:15——

It will be noticed that this statement is not that our Lord was tempted in all points like as the world is tempted, but like as we, his followers, are tempted. He was not tempted along the lines of depraved appetites for sinful things, received by heredity, from an earthly parentage; but being holy, harmless, undefiled and separate from sinners, he was tempted along the same lines as his followers of this Gospel age—who walk not after the flesh but after the spirit; —and who are judged, not according to the infirmities of their flesh, but according to the spirit of their minds—according to their new wills, new hearts. —Rom. 8:4; 2 Cor. 5:16; John 8:15

This is seen very clearly in connection with our Lord's temptations in the wilderness, which immediately followed his consecration and baptism at Jordan.—Matt. 4:1-11

(1) The first was Satan's suggestion that he use the divine power which he had just received at Jordan, in ministering to his own wants, converting the stones into bread. This was not a temptation in any degree traceable to heredity or imperfection. Our Lord had been forty days without food, studying the divine plan, seeking to determine, under the enlightening influence of the Holy Spirit, just received, what would be his proper course in life, to fulfil the great mission upon which he had come into the world, viz., the world's redemption. The suggestion that he use the spiritual power conferred upon him, and which he realized was in his possession, to minister to the necessities of his flesh, would, at first thought, seem reasonable; but our Lord at once discerned that such a use of his spiritual gift would be wrong, would be a misuse of it, a use for which it was not intended, and hence he rejected the sugges-

tion, saying, "It is written, Man shall not live by bread alone, but by every word that proceedeth out of the mouth of God." The Lord's "brethren" sometimes have similar temptations of the adversary, suggestions to use spiritual gifts for the furtherance of temporal interests. Suggestions of this kind are insidious, and are the channels through which God's consecrated people not infrequently are led astray by the adversary to greater and greater misuse of divine blessings.

(2) The adversary suggested to our Lord fakir methods of introducing his mission to the people— that he leap from a pinnacle of the temple into the valley below in the sight of the multitude; so that their seeing him survive uninjured would be proof to them of his superhuman power, which would lead them at once to accept him as the Messiah, and to co-operate with him in the work before him. But our Lord saw at once that such methods were wholly out of harmony with the divine arrangement, and even the misapplication of a Scripture by the Adversary (**apparently** in favor of the wrong) did not swerve him from the principles of righteousness. He immediately replied to the effect that such a procedure on his part would be a tempting of divine providence, wholly unwarranted, and hence not to be considered for a moment. Where duty called or danger the Master did not hesitate, but realized the Father's ability to keep every interest; but true confidence in God does not involve a reckless exposure to danger, without divine command, and merely for a show, and in a spirit of braggadocio.

The Lord's brethren have temptations along this line also, and need to remember this lesson and example set before them by the Captain of our Salvation. We are not to rush unbidden into dangers, and esteem ourselves thus valiant soldiers of the cross. "Daredevil deeds" may not seem out of place to the children of the devil, but they are wholly improper in the children of God. The latter have a warfare which requires still greater courage. They are called upon to perform services which the world does not applaud, nor even appreciate, but often persecutes.

They are called upon to endure ignominy, and the scoffs of the world; yea, and to have the uncircumcised of heart "say all manner of evil" against them falsely for Christ's sake. In this respect the followers of the Captain of our Salvation pass along the same road, and walk in the footsteps of their Captain. And it requires greater courage to ignore the shame and ignominy of the world, in the disesteemed service of God, than to perform some great and wonderful feat, that would cause the natural man to wonder and admire.

One of the chief battles of those who walk this narrow way is against self-will; to bring their wills into fullest subjection to the Heavenly Father's will, and to keep them there; to rule their own hearts, crushing out the rising ambitions which are natural even to a perfect manhood; quenching these kindling fires, and presenting their bodies and all earthly interests living sacrifices in the service of the Lord and his cause. These were trials in which our Captain gained his victory and its laurels, and these also are the trials of his "brethren." "Greater is he that ruleth his own spirit [bringing it into full subordination to the will of God] than he that taketh a city:" greater also is such than he who, with a false conception of faith, would leap from the pinnacle of a temple, or do some other foolhardy thing. True faith in God consists not in blind credulity and extravagant assumptions respecting his providential care; it consists, on the contrary, of a quiet confidence in all the exceeding great and precious promises which God has made, a confidence which enables the faithful to resist the various efforts of the world, the flesh and the devil, to distract his attention, and which follows carefully the lines of faith and obedience marked out for us in the divine Word.

(3) The third temptation of our Lord was to offer earthly dominion and speedy success in the establishment of his kingdom, without suffering and death, —without the cross, upon condition of a compromise with the Adversary. The Adversary claimed, and his claim was not disputed, that he held control of the world, and that by his co-operation the Kingdom of

Righteousness, which our Lord had come to institute, could be quickly established. Satan's intimation was that he had become weary of leading the world into sin, blindness, superstition, ignorance, and that he therefore had a sympathy with our Lord's mission, which was to help the poor, fallen race. What he wanted to retain, however, was a leading or controlling influence in the world; and hence the price of his turning the world over to a righteous course, the price of his co-operation with the Lord Jesus in a restitutionary blessing of the world, was, that the latter should recognize him, Satan, as the ruler of the world, in its reconstructed condition—that thus our Lord should do homage to him.

We are to remember that Satan's rebellion against the divine rule was instigated by ambition to be himself a monarch—"as the Most High." (Isa. 14:14) We recall that this was the primary motive of his successful attack upon our first parents in Eden—that he might alienate or separate them from God, and thus enslave them to himself. We can readily suppose that he would prefer to be monarch of happier subjects than the "groaning creation:" he would prefer subjects possessed of everlasting life. It would appear that even yet he does not recognize the fact that everlasting life and true happiness are impossible except in harmony with Divine law. Satan was therefore willing to become a reformer in all particulars except one—his ambition must be gratified—he must be no less the ruler amongst men; and was he not already "the prince of this world"—and so acknowledged in Holy Writ? (John 14:30; 12:31; 16:11; 2 Cor. 4:4) Not that he had any divine commission to be "the prince of this world," but that by getting possession of mankind, through ignorance, and through misrepresentation of the false as the true, of darkness as the light, of wrong as the right, he had so confused, bewildered, blinded the world that he easily held the position of master or "god of this world, who now worketh in the hearts of the children of disobedience"—the vast majority.

The peculiar temptation of Satan's suggestion, therefore, was that it seemed to offer a new solution of the question of the recovery of man out of his condition of sin. And more than this, it seemed to imply at least a partial repentance on the part of Satan, and the possibility of his recovery to a course of righteousness, provided he could be guaranteed the continued success of his ambition to be a ruler over subjects more happy and more prosperous than it was possible for them to be while kept under his delusions and enslaved by sin, which was the only way in which he could retain man's loyalty: because in proportion as mankind rejects sin and appreciates holiness, in that proportion it becomes desirous to serve and to worship God.

Our Lord Jesus did not long hesitate. He had absolute confidence that the Father's wisdom had adopted the best and only adequate plan. Therefore he not only did not confer with flesh and blood, but neither would he bargain with the Adversary for **co-operation** in the work of the world's uplift.

Here also we see one of the special besetments of the Adversary against the Lord's "brethren." He succeeded in tempting the nominal Church, early in her career, to abandon the way of the cross, the narrow way of separateness from the world, and to enter into a league with the civil power, and thus gradually to become influential in the world's politics. By co-operation with "the princes of this world," fostered and aided by the Adversary secretly, she sought to establish the reign of Christ on earth, through a representative, a pope, for whom it was claimed that he was Christ's vicegerent. We have seen what baneful influences resulted: how this counterfeit Kingdom of Christ became really a kingdom of the devil, for his work it did. We have seen the result in the "Dark Ages," and that the Lord denominates the system "Antichrist."*

And although the Reformation started in boldly, we find that the Adversary again presented the same

---

*See Vol. II, Chap. ix.

temptation before the Reformers, and we see that they resisted it only in part, that they were willing to compromise the truth for the sake of the protection and aid of "the kingdoms of this world," and in the hope that the kingdoms of this world would in some manner become the Kingdom of our Lord. But we see that the combination of the Church and the world influence, as represented in Protestantism, while less baneful in its results than Papacy's combination, is nevertheless very injurious, and a great hindrance to all who come under its influence. We see that the constant conflict of the "brethren" is to overcome this temptation of the Adversary, and to stand fast in the liberty wherewith Christ has made us free—not of the world, but separate from it.

Moreover, we find that although the same temptation comes to all the "brethren," it comes in slightly modified form from time to time, and that the great Adversary very cunningly, in every instance, attempts to do with us as with the Lord, viz., to present himself as a leader along the lines of reform which he advocates—appearing to be in hearty sympathy with the work of blessing the world. His latest temptation along this line comes in the form of the suggested "social uplift," which he is successfully bringing before the minds of many of the "brethren." He suggests now, that however necessary it once was to walk the "narrow way," the way of the cross, it is no longer necessary so to do; but that now we have reached the place where the whole matter may be easily and quickly accomplished, and the world in general lifted up to a high plane of social, intellectual, moral and religious standing. But the plans which he suggests always involve combination with him: in the present instance it is the suggestion that all who would be co-workers in the social uplift shall join in **social** and **political** movements, which shall bring about the desired end. And he has become so bold and so confident of the support of the majority that he no longer pretends to favor reform along the line of individual conversion from sin and salvation from condemnation, and reconciliation with the Father, through a personal faith in and consecration to the Lord Jesus Christ: his proposition is a social uplift, which shall ignore individual responsibilities and sins, and merely regard social conditions and make society outwardly "clean." He would have us disregard the Lord's teaching, to the effect that only those who come unto the Father through him are "sons of God," and his "brethren:" instead, he would have us believe that all men are brethren, and that God is the Father of all humanity, that none are "children of wrath," and that it is criminally unchristian and uncharitable to believe our Lord's words that some are of their "father, the devil." He would thus, without always so saying in specific terms, have us ignore and deny man's **fall into sin,** and ignore and deny the **ransom from sin,** and all the work of atonement—under the specious, deceptive watchword, "the Fatherhood of God and the Brotherhood of man," and the Golden Rule.

This temptation of the Adversary before the "brethren" today is deceiving many, and probably will yet deceive all except "the very elect." (Matt. 24:24) These very elect "brethren," are those who follow closely in the Master's footsteps, and who, instead of hearkening to the Adversary's suggestions, hearken to the Word of the Lord. These very elect "brethren," instead of leaning to their own understandings, and to Satan's sophistries, have faith in the superior wisdom of Jehovah and his divine plan of the ages. Hence these are all "taught of God," and know thereby that the work of the present age is the selection of the "brethren" of Christ, and their testing, and finally their glorification with the Lord in the Kingdom, as the seed of Abraham, to bless the world; and that in the next age will come God's "due time" for the world's uplift, mental, moral and physical. Hence the very elect cannot be deceived by any of the specious arguments or sophistries of their wily foe. Moreover, the "brethren" are not ignorant of his devices, for they were forewarned along this line, and they are looking unto Jesus, who not only is the Author of their faith, through the sacrifice of himself, but also is to be the finisher of it, when he shall grant them a part in the first resurrection, and make them partakers of his excellent glory and divine nature.

Such are the points of temptation to the "brethren," and such were the points of temptation to their Captain. He was **"tempted in all points like as we are"** tempted; and he knows how to succor those who are tempted, and who are willing to receive the succor which he gives, in the way in which he gives it—through the teachings of his Word and its exceeding great and precious promises. The weaknesses which come to us through heredity were no part of our Lord's temptation. He did not have a drunkard's appetite; he did not have a murderer's passion, nor a thief's avarice; he was holy, harmless, separate from sinners. Nor do his "brethren" have these besetments, as their temptations. Those who have become his "brethren" through faith, and consecration, and begetting of the Holy Spirit of adoption, have lost the disposition which seeks to do injury to others, and have received instead the new mind, the mind of Christ, the spirit of Christ, the spirit of a sound mind, the Holy Spirit—the spirit of love; which seeks first of all the Father's will, and secondly, seeks to do good unto all men, as it has opportunity, especially to the household of faith.—Gal. 6:10

And though there remains in the flesh of these "new creatures," possessed of the new mind or new will, a weakness of heredity, a tendency toward passion or strife, so that they may need continually to keep on guard against these, and may occasionally be overtaken in a fault, contrary to their wills, nevertheless these unintentional weaknesses are not counted unto them as sins, nor as the acts of the "new creature," but merely as defects which belong to the old nature, which, so long as the new nature opposes them, are reckoned as covered by the merit of the ransom—the great sin-offering made by the Captain of our Salvation. It is the "new creature" alone that is being tried, tested, fitted, polished and prepared for joint-heirship with Christ in his Kingdom, and not the body of flesh which, of such, is reckoned dead.

"MADE PERFECT THROUGH SUFFERING"

"It became him [the Father] for whom are all things, and by whom are all things, in bringing many sons to glory, to make the Captain of their Salvation perfect through sufferings."—Heb. 2:10

Having in mind the foregoing, it will be easy to see that our Lord was **not made perfect as a man**, through the things which he suffered as a man; nor did he suffer anything before he became a man. The thought of this Scripture is that our Lord, when in the world, when he was already perfect as a man, the very image of the Father in the flesh, holy, harmless, undefiled, separate from sinners, attained, by his experiences and sufferings, another perfection—a perfection on another plane of being, gained since then. It was one thing that the Logos was perfect when with the Father before the world was—perfect in his being, and in his heart or will—perfectly loyal to the Father; it was another thing that when voluntarily he humbled himself to be made flesh, and to take our nature, a lower nature, he was perfect as a man—separate from sinners: it is still a third thing that he is **now perfect** in his present highly exalted condition, a sharer of the divine nature. It is to this latter that our text relates. So high an exaltation to the "glory, honor and immortality" of "the divine nature," made it proper in the divine wisdom that certain **tests** should be applied, the meeting of which should **make perfect** the title of God's Only Begotten Son to share all the riches of divine grace, and "that all men should honor the Son even as they honor the Father."

We are to remember that it was in connection with these **tests** of his obedience to the Father that there was set before him a certain joy or prospect, as it is written—"For the **joy** that was set before him he endured the cross, despising the shame." (Heb. 12:2) This joy before him, we may reasonably suppose, was:—

(1) A joy to render a service which would be acceptable to the Father.

(2) A joy to redeem mankind, and make possible their rescue from sin and death.

(3) A joy in the thought that by the accomplishment of this redemption he would be accounted **worthy of the Father to be the mighty** ruler and blesser, King and Priest of the world; to reveal to the world a knowledge of the divine plan, and to lift up from sin to divine grace whosoever would accept of the terms of the New Covenant.

(4) A joy that the Father had promised him; not only a return to the glory of spirit-being which he had with the Father before the world was, but a more excellent glory—to be exalted far above angels, principalities and powers, and every name that is named, and to be made an associate in the Kingdom of the Universe, next to the Father—on the right hand of the majesty on high; and partaker of the divine nature, with its inherent or immortal life.

But all this joy set before our Lord was made contingent or dependent upon his full obedience to the Father's will. True, he had always been obedient to the Father, and delighted in the Father's way, but never before had he been put to such a test as now. Hitherto it had been pleasurable and honorable to do the Father's will; now the test was to be whether or not he would do that will under conditions that would be distressing, painful, humiliating—conditions which would bring him finally not only to death, but even the ignominious death of the cross. He did stand this testing, and never faltered, never wavered, but manifested in every particular, and to the utmost, faith in the Father's Justice, Love, Wisdom, and Power, and unhesitatingly endured all the oppositions and contradictions of sinners against himself, with all other besetments of the Adversary; and by this means; through suffering, he **"made perfect"** his title to all the joys set before him, and in consequence was perfected as a being of the very highest order, viz., "of the divine nature." Thus it was true of the Only Begotten of the Father that—

"THOUGH HE WERE A SON YET LEARNED HE OBEDIENCE BY THE THINGS WHICH HE SUFFERED AND BEING MADE PERFECT HE BECAME THE AUTHOR OF EVERLASTING SALVATION UNTO ALL THEM THAT OBEY HIM"
——Heb. 5:8-10——

The inspired apostle thus explains that our Lord, already undefiled, perfect, already a "Son," already fully obedient to the Father under favorable conditions, learned what it meant to be obedient under most adverse conditions, and being thus tested and proved worthy of perfection on the highest plane of being, the divine nature, he was perfected in it when the Father raised him from the dead to the excellent glory set before him—to be, first, the Deliverer of the Church which is his body, and afterward, "in due time," of all who, being brought to a knowledge of the Truth, will obey him.

Note the harmony between this and the Apostle Peter's testimony—"The God of our fathers raised up Jesus. . . . Him hath God exalted with his right hand, to be a Prince and a Savior."—Acts 5:31

Thus our Lord Jesus demonstrated before the Father, before angels, and before us, his "brethren," his fidelity to the Father and to the principles of the Father's government. Thus he magnified the Father's law and made it honorable: demonstrating that it was not too exacting, that it was not beyond the ability of a perfect being, even under the most adverse conditions. We, his followers, may well rejoice with all of God's obedient and intelligent creation, saying, "Worthy the Lamb that was slain, to receive power and riches and wisdom and strength and honor and glory and blessing."—Rev. 5:12

And as our Lord glorified is the Captain of our Salvation, it implies that all who would be soldiers of the cross, followers of this Captain and joint-heirs with him in the Kingdom, must likewise be made perfect as "new creatures" through trial and suffering. And as the sufferings through which the Captain was made perfect as a new creature were the things which he endured through the opposition of the world, the flesh and devil, and through the submission of his own will to the Father's will, so with us: our sufferings are not the ordinary sufferings of pain, such as the "groaning creation" shares, and which we share to some extent, as members of the world. The sufferings which count in the development of the "new creature" are those **voluntary** and **willing** endurances on account of the Lord and the Lord's Word and the Lord's people—the hardness which we endure, as good soldiers of the Lord Jesus Christ, while seeking to do not our own wills, but to have perfected in us the will of our Captain, the will of our Heavenly Father. Thus we are to walk in his footsteps, realizing his watchcare, and availing ourselves at the throne of the heavenly grace of his helps by the way; and trusting his promise that all things shall work together for good to us, and that he will not suffer us to be tempted above that we are able, but will with every temptation provide a way of escape; and that in every trial he will grant grace sufficient—for every time of need. Thus are his "brethren" also now on trial and now being **made perfect** as new creatures in Christ—"made meet for the inheritance of the saints in light."—Col. 1:12

"IN THE LIKENESS OF SINFUL FLESH"

What the Law could not do, in that it was powerless because of the flesh [because all flesh was depraved through the fall, and incapable of rendering absolute obedience to the Law], God accomplished by sending his own Son in the likeness of the flesh of mankind [that had come under the dominion of Sin], even by an offering for sin, which, though it condemned sin in the flesh, opened up a new way of life under which the righteousness of the Law might be fulfilled by us [who are not walking according to the flesh but according to the Spirit]. To such, therefore, there is now no condemnation, for the Law of the spirit of life in Christ Jesus [under the precious blood] hath made us free from the Law Covenant which convicted all imperfect ones as sinners and condemned them to death.—Rom. 8:1-4, paraphrase.

Those more or less disposed to consider our Lord a sinner, a member of the fallen race, have seized upon this Scripture, and attempted to turn it out of harmony with reason, and out of harmony with the other Scriptures, to support their theory: to prove that Christ was made exactly like "sinful flesh," and not like flesh that had not sinned—namely, Adam before his transgression. But from the above paraphrase of his text, we believe that the apostle's thought is clearly brought before the mind of the English reader. Our Lord left the glory of the spirit nature, and was "made flesh," made of the same kind of nature as the race which he came to redeem—the race whose nature, or flesh, had come under the bondage of sin, which was sold under sin, through the disobedience of its first parent, Adam. Nothing here intimates, except in the gloss given through the translation, that our Lord himself was a sinner. Indeed, it is one of the simplest propositions imaginable, that if he were a sinner, or in any manner a partaker of the curse which rested upon the human family, he could not have been our sin-offering, for one sinner could not be an offering for another sinner. Under the divine law, "the wages of sin is death." Our Lord, if he had been in any sense or degree a sinner, would thereby have forfeited his own life, and would have been valueless as a **ransom-price** for Adam or for any other sinner.

"HIMSELF TOOK OUR INFIRMITIES"
——Matt. 8:17——

"Surely he hath borne our griefs and carried our sorrows; yet we did esteem him stricken, smitten of God and afflicted. But he was wounded for our transgressions; he was bruised for our iniquities; the chastisement of our peace was upon him; and with his stripes we are healed." —Isa. 53:4, 5

Perfection is the opposite of infirmity, and the fact that our Lord had infirmities might logically be argued as proof that he was not perfect—that he had inherited some of the blemishes of the fallen race. It will be remembered that on the night of his agony in the Garden of Gethsemane our Lord sweated "as it were great drops of blood," and this is set down by some medical authorities as a disease, which, altho very rare, has been known to affect others of the human family. It gave evidence of a great nervous strain and weakness. Again, tradition says that when on the way to Golgotha our Lord was compelled to carry the cross, and that he fainted under it, and that it was on this account that Simon, the Cyrenian, was compelled to bear the cross for the remainder of the journey. (Matt. 27:32) It is further claimed that our Lord's death on the cross, so much sooner than was usual, was occasioned by a literal breaking of his heart, the rupture of its muscles, and that this is indicated by the flow of both blood and water from the spear-wound in his side after death. At all events, our Lord did not manifest that fullness of vigor which was manifested in Adam, the first perfect man, whose vitality was such that he lived for nine hundred and thirty years. The question arises, Did not these evidences of infirmity on the part of our Lord indicate imperfection: that either through heredity or in some other manner he lacked the powers of a perfect man, and was therefore a blemished man?

On the surface the matter has this appearance, and only under the guidance of the divine Word are we enabled to explain satisfactorily to our own minds, or to others, the consistency between these facts and the Scriptural assurance that our Redeemer was "holy, harmless, undefiled, **separate** from sinners." The key to the matter is given in the Scripture under consideration. The prophet declares what would naturally appear to ourselves or to others, viz., that our Lord, like all the remainder of the race, was stricken, was under sentence of death, was smitten of God and afflicted—as much under the sentence of death as the remainder of the race: but then he shows that what thus seems or appears is not the fact, explaining that it was for our sins, and not for his own sins, that he suffered; his infirmities were the result of bearing our griefs and carrying the load of our sorrow; his death was in consequence of his taking our place before the divine law, and suffering, "the just for the unjust, that he might bring us to God." Speaking for fleshly Israel at the first advent, the Prophet says—We did esteem him to be **stricken, smitten and afflicted of God:** and explaining that such a view was incorrect, he declares— But it was for our transgressions that he was wounded; it was for our iniquities that he was bruised: our peace with God was secured by the chastisement for sin which he bore; our healing was secured by the punishment which he endured for us.

Matthew calls attention to the fulfilment of this very prophecy, declaring—"They brought unto him many that were possessed with devils; and he cast out the spirits with his word, and healed all that were sick: that it might be fulfilled which was spoken by Isaiah the prophet, saying, Himself took our infirmities, and bare our sicknesses."—Matt. 8:16, 17

The connection between the healing of disease, on our Lord's part, and his taking of infirmity upon himself, is not very apparent to the majority of those who read the record. It is generally supposed that our Lord merely exercised a power of healing that cost himself nothing—that he had an inexhaustible power from a spiritual source, unseen, which permitted all manner of miracles, without the slightest impairment of his own strength, his own vitality.

We do not question that "the power of the Highest," bestowed upon our Redeemer without measure, would have enabled him to do many things entirely supernatural, and hence entirely without self-exhaustion: nor do we question that our Lord used this superhuman power—for instance in the turning of the water into wine, and in the miraculous feeding of the multitudes. But, from the record of the Scriptures, we understand that the healing of the sick, as performed by our Lord, was not by the superhuman power at his command, but that on the contrary, in healing the sick he expended upon them **a part of his own vitality:** and consequently, the greater the number healed, the greater was our Lord's loss of vitality, strength. In proof that this was so, call to mind the record of the poor woman

Like Unto His Brethren

who "for twelve years had an issue of blood, and had suffered many things of many physicians, and had spent all that she had, and was nothing bettered, but rather worse," etc. Remembering how with faith she pressed close to the Lord, and touched the hem of his garment, saying within herself, "If I may touch but his clothes I shall be whole." The record is that "straightway the fountain of her blood was dried up, and she felt in her body that she was healed of that plague. And Jesus, immediately knowing within himself that virtue [**vitality**] had gone out of him, turned him about in the press, and said, Who touched my clothes? And the disciples said unto him, Thou seest the multitude thronging thee and sayest thou, Who touched me? And he looked round about to see her that had done this thing, and he said unto her, Daughter thy faith hath made thee whole; go in peace, and be whole of thy plague."—Mark 5:25-34

Notice also Luke's account (6:19) which declares. "And the whole multitude sought to touch him: for there went virtue [**vitality**] out of him, and healed them all." This, then, was the sense in which our dear Redeemer took the infirmities of humanity, bearing our sicknesses. And the result of thus day by day giving his own vitality for the healing of others, could be no other than debilitating in its effect upon his own strength, his own vitality. And we are to remember that this work of healing, lavishly expending his vitality was in connection with his preaching and travels, our Lord's almost continuous work during the three and a half years of his ministry.

Nor does this seem so strange to us when we consider our own experiences: who is there of deeply sympathetic nature who has not at times, to a limited degree, witnessed the fact that it is possible for a friend to share the troubles of a friend, and sympathetically to relieve in a measure the depressed one, and to some extent to impart increased vitality and lightness of spirit? But such a helpful influence, and such feeling of the infirmities of others, depends very largely upon the degree of **sympathy** inspiring the one who visits the sick and the afflicted. Not only so, but we know that certain animals have varying degrees of sympathy; the dove, for instance, being one of the most gentle and sympathetic, was one of the typical representatives of our Redeemer under the Mosaic dispensation. Because it has been found helpful in many instances, doves are sometimes brought into the chamber of the sick, and are found beneficial to the sufferers. The dove, perhaps because of its sympathetic nature, takes on a certain proportion of the disease, and imparts a certain proportion of its own vitality. This manifests itself in the fact that the birds grow sick (have their limbs drawn up, as with rheumatism, etc.), while the patient is proportionately relieved.

When we remember that our loves and sympathies are only such as have survived the fall of six thousand years, and when we remember that our dear Redeemer was perfect and that therefore in him this quality of sympathetic love abounded in greatest measure, we can realize faintly, how "he was touched with the feeling of our infirmities." His sympathy was touched, because his nature was fine, perfect, touchable—not hard, not calloused with selfishness and sin, either through heredity or personal acquirement. Again, we read of him that he was "moved with compassion," and again, "He had compassion on the multitude," and again, when he saw the Jews weeping, and Martha and Mary weeping, he was moved with sympathy, and "Jesus wept." So far from these sympathies indicating weakness of character, they indicate the very reverse; for the true character of man, in its image and likeness to the Creator, is not hard and heartless and calloused, but tender, gentle, loving, sympathetic. Hence all these things go to show to us that he who spake "as never man spake" also sympathized, as none of the fallen race could sympathize, with the fallen conditions, troubles and afflictions of humanity.

Not only so, but we are to remember the very object for which our Lord came into the world. That object was not to simply manifest power without cost to himself, but, as he himself explained it, **the Son of Man came to minister to others, and to give his life** a ransom for many. True, the wages of sin was not suffering, but death; and hence suffering on our Lord's part would not alone pay the wages of sin for us; it was absolutely necessary that he should **"taste death** for every man." Hence we read, "Christ **died for our** sins, according to the Scriptures." (1 Cor. 15:3) Nevertheless, it was appropriate that in **taking the sinner's place** our Lord should experience all that was implied in the curse—the penalty of death: and inasmuch as the human family has died, by a process of gradual loss of life, through weakness, sickness and infirmity, it was correspondingly appropriate that our dear Redeemer should pass through this experience also. And since he himself was not the sinner, all **the** penalties of sin which could rest upon him must be as the result of his **taking** the sinner's place, and **bearing for us the** stroke of Justice.

Our Lord did this, so far as sickness and pain and weakness were concerned, in the best and most helpful manner, viz., by voluntarily pouring out his life, day by day, during the three and a half years of his ministry, giving away his vitality to those who appreciated not his motive—his grace, his love. Thus, as it is written, "He poured out his soul [being, existence] unto death:" "He made his soul [being] an offering for sin." (Isa. 53:10, 12) And we can readily see that from the time of his consecration, when he was thirty years old, and was baptized of John in Jordan, down to Calvary, he was constantly **pouring out** his soul: vitality was continually going out of him for the help and healing of those to whom he ministered. And while all this would **not have been sufficient,** as the price of our sins, yet it was all a part of the dying process through which our dear Redeemer passed, which culminated at Calvary, when he cried, "It is finished," and the last spark of life went out.

It would seem to have been just as necessary that our Lord should thus sacrifice, spend his life-forces, and be touched with the experiences of our dying process, as that later, when on the cross, he should be obliged to experience, if only for a moment, the sinner's position of **complete separation** from the Heavenly Father, and with the withdrawal of all superhuman help, at the time when he cried, "My God! My God! Why hast thou forsaken me?" As the sinner's **substitute**, he must bear the sinner's penalty in all its particulars, and not until all this was accomplished was his sacrificial mission finished—not until this had been faithfully endured had he passed all the tests deemed of the Father requisite to his being made "the Captain of our Salvation," and exalted far above all angels, and principalities, and powers, to be the Father's associate in the throne of the Universe.

All of these **experiences** through which the Heavenly Father caused his Beloved Son to pass before exalting him to his own right hand of majesty and committing to his charge the great work of blessing all the families of the earth, were not merely **tests** of the fidelity of the Only Begotten, the **Logos**: the Scriptures assure us that they were necessary also to fit our Lord to sympathize with those whom he thus redeemed, that he might be able to sympathize with and "succor" such as would return to full fellowship with God through him—the Church during this age, the world during the Millennial age: "That he might be a merciful and faithful High Priest in things pertaining to God"; "in all points tempted like as we are"; one who can have compassion on the ignorant and them that are out of the way; for that he himself also was compassed with infirmities." "Wherefore he is able also to save them to the uttermost that come unto God by him." Verily, "Such an High Priest was suitable for us—one holy, harmless, undefiled, separate from sinners, and exalted higher than the heavens."—Heb. 2:17, 18; 4:15, 16; 5:2; 7:25, 26

STUDY VI

THE MEDIATOR OF THE ATONEMENT

DAVID'S SON AND DAVID'S LORD

How David's Son—Joseph's Genealogy Through Solomon—Mary's Genealogy Through Nathan—Abase the High, Exalt the Low—Whence Christ's Title to be David's Lord—How He was Both Root and Branch of David—Meaning of His Title, "The Everlasting Father"—How Secured and How to be Applicable—Who are Children of Christ—The Church His "Brethren"—Children of the God and Father of our Lord Jesus Christ.

"Jesus asked them, saying, What think ye of Christ? Whose son is he? They say unto him, The Son of David. He saith unto them, How then doth David in spirit [by inspiration] call him Lord, saying, The Lord [Jehovah] said unto my Lord [**adon**, master, ruler], Sit thou on my right hand, till I make thine enemies thy footstool? If David then call him Lord [**adon**, master] how is he his Son?"—Matt. 22:42-45

IT SHOULD be noticed, first of all, that the discussion of this question does not relate to our Lord's pre-existence, but merely to his relationship to the human family. He became related to the human family, as we have seen, by taking our nature through his mother Mary. Mary's genealogy, as traced by Luke, leads back to David, through his son Nathan (Luke 3:31*), while Joseph's genealogy, as given by Matthew, traces also back to David, through his son, Solomon. (Matt. 1:6, 16) Joseph having accepted Mary as his wife, and adopted Jesus, her son, as though he were his own son, this adoption would entitle Jesus to reckon Joseph's genealogy; but such a tracing back to the family of David was not nec-

---

*Joseph is here styled "the son of Heli," i. e., the son of Eli, Mary's father, by marriage, or legally; or as we would say, son-in-law of Eli. By birth, Joseph was the son of Jacob, as stated in Matt. 1:16.

essary, because, as we have seen, his mother came also of David, by another line.

But, be it noticed that our Lord's claim to the throne of Israel does not rest upon his mother's relationship to Joseph, as some have inferred. On the contrary, had he been the son of Joseph, he would have been debarred from any ancestral right to David's throne, because, although David's successors in the kingdom came through the line of his son Solomon, and not through the line of his son Nathan, nevertheless certain Scriptures distinctly point out that the great heir of David's throne should not come through the royal family line of Solomon. If we shall demonstrate this, it will be an effectual estoppel of the claims made by some, that our Lord must have been the son of Joseph, as well as of Mary. Let us therefore carefully examine this matter.

The divine proposition, clearly stated, was, first, that unequivocally and unquestionably the great heir of the throne of the world, the great King of Israel, should come of David's line. Secondly, it was also declared that he should come of the line of Solomon, of the reigning family, only upon certain conditions. If those conditions were complied with, he would come of that line; if those conditions were not complied with, he would come of some other line, but in any event must come through David's line and be both David's son and David's Lord.

Note the Scriptural statement:—

"The Lord hath sworn in truth unto David; he will not turn him from him: Of the fruit of thy body will I set upon thy throne. **If thy children** will keep my covenant, and my testimony that I shall teach them, **their children** shall also sit upon thy throne forevermore."—Psa. 132:11, 12

"And of all my sons (for God hath given me many sons) he hath chosen Solomon my son to sit upon the throne of the Kingdom of the Lord over Israel. And he said unto me, Solomon thy son shall build my house. . . . Moreover, I will establish his king-

David's Son and Lord

dom forever, **if he will be constant** to do my statutes and my judgments as at this day."—1 Chron. 28:5-7

"If thy children take heed to their way, to walk before me in truth, with all their heart and with all their soul, there shall not fail thee [be cut off from thee from the throne—**margin**] a man from the throne of Israel."—1 Kings 2:4

The promise of the Messianic Kingdom in Solomon's line, and in the line of his posterity according to the flesh, is thus made clearly and specifically **conditional,** contingent upon a certain faithfulness to the Lord; and by all rules of interpretation of language, the implication of this is that unfaithfulness to the Lord would assuredly bar the posterity of Solomon and his line from the throne of Israel, as related to the Messianic Kingdom, according to the flesh. The question therefore arises, Did Solomon and his successors upon the throne of Israel "take heed to their way to walk before me [God] in truth, with all their heart and with all their soul"? If they did not, they are barred from being of the ancestral line of the Messiah, according to the flesh.

We must go to the Scriptures to ascertain the answer to this question. There we find most unmistakably that Solomon and his royal line failed to walk after the divine precepts. Hence we know of a surety that that line was cut off and abandoned from being the Messianic line, and that it must come through another ancestral line, from David. Hear the word of the Lord:—

"And thou, Solomon, my son, know thou the God of thy father and serve him with a perfect heart. . . . If thou seek him he will be found of thee, but if thou forsake him he will cast thee off forever." —1 Chron. 28:9

"And the Lord was angry with Solomon, because his heart was turned from the Lord God of Israel. . . . Wherefore the Lord said unto Solomon, Forasmuch as this is done of thee and thou hast not kept my covenant and my statutes which I have commanded thee, I will surely rend the kingdom from thee. . . . Nevertheless in thy days I will not do it

—for David thy father's sake; but I will rend it out of the hand of thy son. Howbeit, I will not rend away all the kingdom, but will give one tribe to thy son, for David my servant's sake and for Jerusalem's sake which I have chosen."—1 Kings 11:9-13

In harmony with this, the record is that the ten tribes were rent away from the Solomonic line directly after Solomon's death—ten of the tribes never acknowledging allegiance to Rehoboam, Solomon's son and successor. But let us hearken to the word of the Lord respecting the tribe of Judah, and its consort Benjamin, which remained for a time loyal to the line of Solomon, and thus apparently associated with the promised antitypical Kingdom, and Messiah, the great King. The last three kings of Solomon's line who sat upon his throne were Jehoiakim, his son Jehoiachin (called also Jekoniah and Coniah), and Zedekiah, Jehoiakim's brother. Let us mark the testimony of the Lord's Word against these men, and his assurance that none of their posterity should ever again sit upon the throne of the Kingdom of the Lord—actual or typical. We read:—

"As I live, saith the Lord, though Coniah the son of Jehoiakim, king of Judah, were the signet upon my right hand, yet would I pluck thee hence. . . . Is this man Coniah a despised broken idol? Is he a vessel wherein is no pleasure? Wherefore are they cast out (he and his seed), and are cast into a land which they know not? O earth, earth, earth, hear the word of the Lord: thus saith the Lord, Write ye this man childless, a man that shall not prosper in his days: for no man of his seed shall prosper, sitting upon the throne of David, and ruling any more in Judah.—Jer. 22:24-30

"Thus saith the Lord of Jehoiakim, king of Judah, he shall have none to sit upon the throne of David."—Jer. 36:30

Concerning Zedekiah we read:—

"Thou profane and wicked prince of Israel, whose day is coming, when iniquity shall have an end: Thus saith the Lord God, Remove the diadem, and take off the crown: this shall not be the same: exalt him that is low, and abase him that is high. I will overturn, overturn, overturn it: and it shall be no more until he come whose right it is; and I will give it to him."—Ezek. 21:25-27

Here the complete overturning of the Solomonic line is declared: it was the line that was exalted, and which should thenceforth be debased, while the debased or obscure line of Nathan, which had never made any pretensions to the throne, was to be exalted in due time in its representative, the Messiah, born of Mary, according to the flesh.

Who could ask more positive testimony than this, that the Messiah could not be expected through the line of Solomon—all the rights and claims of that line, under divine promises and conditions, having been forfeited by wickedness and rebellion against God? Thus the claim that our Lord must have been the son of Joseph, and thus have inherited his rights and claims through Joseph, are proven utterly false, for no man of that line shall ever sit upon the throne of the Lord.

This changing of the kingdom from the branch of Solomon to another branch of the house of David is clearly foretold in other Scriptures, as we read, "Behold the day is coming, saith the Lord, that I will **raise unto David a Righteous Branch**, and a king shall reign and prosper. . . . In his days Judah shall be saved and Israel shall dwell safely; and this is his name that Jehovah proclaimeth him, Our Righteousness."—Jer. 23:6—See Young's Translation.

Mary, the mother of Jesus, seems to have caught this proper thought, or else was moved to speak by the Holy Spirit prophetically, when she gave utterance to the remarkable song of thanksgiving quoted by Luke (1:46-55): "He [God] hath scattered the proud in the imagination of their heart; he hath **put down the mighty** from their seats, and exalted them of **low degree**. He hath filled the hungry with good things, and the rich he hath sent empty away." Here the favored family of Solomon's line is contrasted with the humbler family of Nathan's line. The diadem and crown were removed from Zedekiah, and from the line of Solomon, to be given to him whose right it is—the Righteous Branch from the Davidic root.

We have seen how our Lord is the branch, or offspring or son of David, and the line through which his genealogy is properly to be traced, and the full accordance of the Scriptures thereto: let us now see in what respect he was David's Lord. How could Jesus be both the Son and the Lord of David?

We answer that he is not David's Lord by reason of anything that he was as a spirit being before he was "made flesh," and dwelt amongst us—no more than he was David's Branch or Son in his pre-human existence. Our Lord Jesus **became** David's Lord or superior, as well as "Lord of all" (Acts 10:36), by reason of the great work which he accomplished as the Mediator of the Atonement. "**To this end** Christ both died and rose and revived, **that he might be Lord** both of the dead and living."—Rom. 14:9

True, the **Logos** might properly have been styled a Lord, a high one in authority, as he is styled a God. a mighty or influential one.* Likewise the man Christ Jesus, before his death, might properly be styled a Lord, and was so addressed by his disciples, as we read, "Ye call me Lord and Master, and ye do well, for so I am." (John 13:13) As the special messenger of the Covenant, whom the Father had sanctified and sent into the world to redeem the world, and whom the Father honored in every manner, testifying, "This is my beloved son, in whom I am well pleased"—it was eminently proper that all who beheld his glory, as the glory of an Only Begotten of the Father, full of grace and truth, should reverence him, hear him, obey him, and worship him—do him homage—as the representative of the Father. But, as indicated by the apostle in the text

---

*It will be remembered that we are not now discussing the word "Jehovah," so frequently translated "Lord" in the Old Testament. We are discussing other words rendered "Lord" as in the text above quoted. "The Lord [Jehovah] said unto **my Lord** [**Adon**—my master]. Sit thou on my right hand." etc.

David's Son and Lord

above cited, there was a **particular** and different sense in which our Lord Jesus **became** a Lord or Master by virtue of his death and resurrection.

This particular sense in which the risen Christ was "Lord of all"—"Lord both of the dead and the living" —is vitally connected with his great work as Mediator of the Atonement. It was for this very purpose that he became a man. Humanity in its depraved condition, "sold under sin" through the disobedience of Father Adam, was helpless—under the dominion of Sin and the sentence of death: and its deliverance from these evils, in harmony with the divine law, required that the penalty of Adam entailed upon his family should be fully met. The race required to be **bought back** from sin, and Christ became its purchaser, its owner—"Lord of all." For this very purpose he left the glory of his pre-human condition, and became **the man** Christ Jesus. And the Scriptural declaration is that he "gave himself a ransom" —**a purchase price**—for the race condemned in Adam. Thus the whole world was "**bought** with a price, even the precious blood [life] of Christ."

But though by virtue of his having **bought the race**, he has, in the eye of Justice, become its **owner**, its **master**, "Lord of all," he did not purchase the race for the purpose of enslaving it, but for the very reverse object of setting at liberty from sin and death all who will accept the gracious gift of God through him. And the very object of the establishment of the Messianic Kingdom is that through it may be bestowed upon the human family the rights and privileges of the sons of God—lost in Eden, redeemed, bought with a price, at Calvary. It was to obtain this **right to release** man that our Redeemer became the purchaser, owner, Lord of all. Thus by his death Messiah became David's Lord, because David was a member of the race purchased with his precious blood.

"THE ROOT AND OFFSPRING OF DAVID"
——Rev. 22:16——

Much of the same thought is presented in these

our Lord's words to the Church. According to the flesh, our Lord Jesus was, through his mother, the son, the branch, the offshoot or offspring of David. It was by virtue of his sacrifice of his undefiled life that he became the "root" of David as well as his Lord: for the thought suggested by the word "root" differs somewhat from that furnished in the word "Lord." The "root" of David signifies the **origin**, source of life, and development of David.

The Scriptures declare that David was "a **stem** out of Jesse:" his father therefore was his root, according to natural generation. When and how did Christ become David's root or father? We answer, Not before he "was made flesh"—it was when made flesh that, as the man Jesus, he became related to Adam's race through his mother. (Heb. 2:14-18) And in that relationship to the race and to David he was "branch," not "root." How and when did he become the "root"? We answer, By the same means and at the same time that he became David's Lord: the **means** was his death, by which he purchased **life**-rights of Adam and all his race, including David's; the **time** was when he was raised from the dead, Adam's Redeemer, the race's Redeemer and hence David's Redeemer.

It was therefore not the pre-human **Logos** nor yet the man Jesus that was David's Lord and David's Root; but the resurrected Messiah. When David in spirit (i. e., speaking under the prophetic spirit or influence) called Jesus Lord, saying, "Jehovah said unto my Lord [Jesus], Sit thou on my right hand." etc., the reference was not to the sacrificing one, "the man Christ Jesus," who had not yet finished his sacrifice, but to the victor Jesus, the Lord of life and glory, "the first born from the dead, the prince of the kings of earth." (Rev. 1:5) It was of this one that Peter said, "Him God raised up the third day. . . . He is Lord of all." (Acts 10:36, 40) Of this one also Paul declared that at his second coming he will display himself as "King of kings and Lord of lords."*
—1 Tim. 6:15

---

*See page 78.

"THE SECOND ADAM"

The first "root" or father of the human race, Adam, failed, because of disobedience to God, to bring forth his family in his own likeness, the image of God; he not only failed to give to his posterity everlasting life, but forfeited his own right to the same, and entailed upon his offspring a legacy, a heredity of sin, weakness, depravity, death. The **Logos** was made flesh, became the man Christ Jesus, in order that he might be the Second Adam, and take the place of the first Adam, that he might undo the work of the first Adam, and give to him and to his race (or so many of them as will accept it upon the divine terms), **life more abundant,** everlasting life, under its favorable conditions, lost through disobedience.

It is a great mistake of some, however, to suppose that **"the man** Christ Jesus" was the Second Adam. Oh no! As the apostle declares (1 Cor. 15:47), "The second Adam is the Lord from Heaven"—the Lord who will come from heaven, and at his second advent assume the office and duties of a father to the race of Adam, which he redeemed with his own precious blood at Calvary. The purchase of the race of Adam from under the sentence of Justice was necessary before it would be possible for our Lord Jesus to be the Life-giver or Father of the race: and this great work alone was accomplished by our Lord at his first advent. He comes, at his second advent, to lift up mankind by processes of restitution, and to give eternal life, and all the privileges and blessings lost through the first Adam. The interim is devoted, according to the Father's program, to the selection from amongst the redeemed world of a class whose qualifications were predestined—that they should all be "copies of God's dear Son." (Rom. 8:29) This class is variously called the under-priests of the Royal priesthood, the body or Church of Christ, and the Bride of Christ, the Lamb's wife, and joint-heir with him in all the honors and blessings and service of his Kingdom.

Accordingly, the work of the future, the work of the Millennial age, the grand object for which Messiah will reign, is expressed by the word **regeneration**. The world was generated once through Father Adam, but failed to get life; it was generated only to sin and its sentence, death. But the new Father of the race, the second Adam, proposes a general regeneration. The time of this regeneration, as it shall become available to the world, is distinctly indicated by our Lord's words to his disciples to be the Millennial age. He said, "Ye that have followed me, in the regeneration shall sit upon twelve thrones judging the twelve tribes of Israel," etc. The fact that the Church, selected during this Gospel age, experiences a regeneration, is generally recognized by Bible students, but many have overlooked the fact that another and separate regeneration is proposed, and has been provided for the world of mankind, as a whole: not that all shall experience the full regeneration, but that all shall have an opportunity, which, if rightly used, would lead to full, complete regeneration.

It is well, in this connection, to notice more particularly the wide distinction between the regeneration of the Church and the regeneration of the world: in the case of the Church many are called to the regeneration offered during this Gospel age, and few are chosen—few experience the full regeneration to which they are invited—namely, to become new creatures in Christ Jesus, partakers of the divine nature. The regeneration provided for the world, as we have already seen, is not to a new nature, but to a restoration or restitution of the human nature in its perfection.

And so it is written, "The first Adam was made a living soul [an animal being], the last Adam a quickening spirit. However, the spiritual was not first, but the animal—afterwards the spiritual." (1 Cor. 15:45-47—See Diaglott) Verily our Lord Jesus in the days of his flesh did take hold on or become identified with the **first Adam and his race**, through the seed of Abraham (Heb. 2:16), and was made "lower than the angels, for the suffering of **death** . . . that he by the grace of God might taste death **for every man.**" But having accomplished that object he was raised from the dead a partaker of the divine nature, the purchaser of the human family, but no longer of it—no longer "of the earth earthy," but the heavenly Lord—the Second Adam, a **life-giving spirit.**

The first Adam was the original "root" out of which the entire human family has been produced, and hence our Lord Jesus in the flesh, son of Mary, son of David, son of Abraham, was in the same sense a shoot or branch out of Adam (but supplied, as we have seen, with an unimpaired life from above, which still kept him separate from sinners). It was his **sacrifice** of himself as the **man** (in obedience to the Father's plan) that not only secured his own exaltation to the divine nature, but purchased to him all the race of Adam and Adam's right as father or "root" of the race. Thus by purchasing Adam's place and rights, our Lord is the Second Adam. As he **gave his own human life for that of Adam,** so **he sacrificed also the possibilities of a race** which he might have produced in a natural way, for Adam's children—that he may in due time accept "whosoever will" of Adam's family as his own children, **regenerating** them, giving them everlasting life under reasonable terms. No longer a "branch," out of the root of Jesse and David, our Lord is a new root, prepared to give **new** life and sustenance to mankind—Adam, Abraham, David and every other member or branch of the sin-blighted human family who will accept it on the terms of the "Oath-bound Covenant."

Like the **first** work of the Lord for his Church of this age will be his work for all of mankind who will accept it during the Millennial age. His **first** work for his Church now is **justification** to life (human life) in harmony with God, in fellowship with God: the same enjoyed by the perfect man Jesus, prior to his consecration to death at baptism; and the same enjoyed by the perfect man Adam before he transgressed—except that theirs was **actual** while ours is merely a **reckoned** perfection of life. (Hence the statement that we are **"justified—by faith."**)

Our Lord represents himself and his Church as a grapevine; and it furnishes us a good illustration of the **branch** and **root** proposition. Adam and his race were the original vine and branches, attacked by the virus of sin, producing bad fruit and death. Our Lord Jesus became a new branch, and was grafted into the Adamic vine, and bore a different kind of fruit. It is a peculiarity of the grapevine that its **branches** may be buried and become **roots**. So our Lord, the branch ingrafted upon Adamic stock, was buried, ceased to be a **branch** and became a **root**. His Church during this age are "branches" in him, and likewise have their "fruit unto holiness" (Rom. 6:22) the new life being drawn from him. But all the branches of this age are required not only to "bear much fruit" as branches, as he did, but also like him eventually to be buried and with him become parts of the **root** that during the Millennial age shall invigorate and sustain the **regenerated** human race.

The fallen root, Adam (with the first Eve, his helpmate,) generated the human family in bondage to sin and death; the Second Adam, Christ, (with his Bride and helpmate), having bought the rights of the first as well as him and his race, will be prepared to **re**generate all the willing and obedient. This is termed "restitution" (Acts 3:19-23)—giving back to the worthy the earthly privileges and blessings lost in the first Adam, that, as the Lord's vine, humanity restored may bear much fruit to God's praise. But be it noted, this privilege of becoming the "root" is confined to the Christ, Head and body, "elect according to the foreknowledge of God through sanctification of the spirit and the belief of the truth" during this Gospel age. (1 Pet. 1:2) David and other worthies of the past (who died before the "branch" was buried and became the "root") can never become parts of the root; nor will the faithful of the Millennial age. All, however, will be **satisfied** when they attain his likeness, whether it be the earthly or the heavenly. Mankind will be privileged to attain his likeness as the perfect **man** Christ Jesus, the holy "branch," while the Church, his "bride," his "body," his faithful under-priests, who now fill up that which is behind of the sufferings of Christ and are "planted with him in the likeness of his death," shall bear his heavenly image.—1 Cor. 15:48, 49; Heb. 11:39, 40

"THE EVERLASTING FATHER"

"His name shall be called Wonderful, Counselor, The Mighty God, The Everlasting Father, The Prince of Peace.'—Isa. 9:6

We have already noted the propriety of the title "The Mighty God" as applied to our Lord Jesus; and few will dispute that he is indeed the Wonderful One of all the Heavenly Father's family; none will dispute that he is a great Counselor or Teacher; or that, although his Kingdom is to be introduced by a time of trouble and disturbance incident to the death of present evil institutions, our Lord is nevertheless the Prince of Peace—who will establish a sure and lasting peace upon the only proper basis—righteousness—conformity to the divine character and plan. Now we come to the examination of the title, "The Everlasting Father," and find it as appropriate and meaningful as the others.

It does not, as some have surmised, contradict the multitudinous Scriptures which declare Jehovah to be the Father everlasting—"the God and Father of our Lord Jesus Christ," as Peter expresses it. (1 Pet. 1:3) On the contrary the Scriptures clearly show a particular sense in which this title will apply to our Lord at his second advent—that he will be the Father of the human race regenerated during the Millennium. Indeed, this title is merely the equivalent of those we have just considered—the new "Lord" of David and of mankind, the new "Root," the Second Adam merely signifies the Everlasting Father, who gives everlasting life.

Since our Lord purchased the world of mankind at the cost of his own life, and since it is by virtue of that purchase that he became its Lord, its Restorer, its Life-giver, and since the very central thought of the word **father** is **life-giver**, our Lord could take no more appropriate name or title than "Everlasting Father" to represent his relationship to the world about to be regenerated—born again from the dead by restitution, resurrection processes. The world's life will come directly from the Lord Jesus, who, as we shall shortly see, by divine arrangement **bought** it and paid Justice the full price for it. Nevertheless, the restored world will, after the restitution process is finished, recognize Jehovah as the great original fountain of life and blessing, the author of the great plan of salvation executed by our Lord Jesus—the Grand Father and Over-Lord of All.—1 Cor. 15:24-28; 3:23; Matt. 19:28

In full accord with what we have just seen is the prophetic statement which for centuries has perplexed the wise and the unwise, the scholar and commentator as well as the student; namely—

INSTEAD OF THY FATHERS SHALL BE THY CHILDREN WHOM THOU MAYEST MAKE PRINCES IN ALL THE EARTH
——Psalm 45:16——

The patriarchs and prophets, and especially such as were in the genealogical line upon which our Lord took hold, through his mother Mary, were long honored with the title of "fathers," progenitors of Messiah: just as the texts before cited declare David to be the root out of which the Messiah, the righteous Branch, should spring; and that the Messiah should be David's son. But all this is to be changed, when the Church, the body of Christ, shall be completed, and joined to Jesus the Head in glory, and as the Everlasting Father of mankind begin the world's regeneration. Those previously the fathers will then be the children. Abraham, Isaac, Jacob, David—none of these had **life**, in the proper sense of that word: they were all members of the death-condemned race. And when Jesus took hold upon our humanity, and became identified with the seed of Abraham and of David, and accomplished the work of redemption, it applied not only to the world in general, but as well to these, his progenitors according to the flesh. He bought all, and none can obtain life (complete, perfect, everlasting) except through him. "He that hath the Son hath life, he that hath not the Son shall not see life." (John 3:36) Hence, Abraham, Isaac and Jacob and David and all the prophets, and all the remainder of the world, must receive future and everlasting life from Christ, or not at all; and outside of him is only condemnation. Therefore it is true, that when in God's due time they shall be awakened from death, it will be by the great Life-giver, Jesus, who will thus be their Father or Life-giver.

In this connection it is well to notice also that the Scriptures clearly point out the Heavenly Father as the begetter in the regeneration of the Church, the Bride of Christ. In proof of this, note the Scriptural statements on this subject. The Apostle Peter declares, "The God and Father of our Lord Jesus Christ . . . **hath begotten us.**" (1 Pet. 1:3) The Apostle John also declares that **we are "begotten of God."** (1 John 5:18) The Apostle Paul also declares, "To us there is one **God, the Father.**" (1 Cor. 8:6) He hath sent forth his spirit into our hearts, whereby we are enabled to **cry unto him,** "Abba, Father." (Rom. 8:15) Our Lord Jesus testified to the same thing, saying, after his resurrection, "I ascend to my Father and to your Father, to my God and to your God." (John 20:17) John's Gospel testifies to the same, saying, "To as many as received him, to them gave he liberty to become the sons of God," and declares of such that they are "begotten, not of blood, nor of the will of the flesh, nor of the will of man, but of God." (John 1:12, 13) The Apostle James declares of the Father of lights that "Of his own will **begat he us** with the Word of truth, that we should be a kind of first-fruits of his creatures."—Jas. 1:18

Indeed, everything respecting the Church indicates that the faithful of this Gospel age are not the children of Christ, but children of his Father, begotten of the Father's spirit and to the Father's nature, and intended to be "heirs of God, **joint-heirs with** Jesus

Christ our Lord, if so be that we suffer with him, that we may be also glorified together."—Rom. 8:17

Our relationship to our Lord Jesus, on the contrary, is specifically and repeatedly indicated to be that of brethren, and not sons. Speaking of the Church the apostle says, "He is not ashamed to call them brethren," as had been prophetically stated; "I will declare thy name unto my brethren; in the midst of thy church will I sing praises unto thee"; and again, "Behold I and the children [of God] which God hath given me." These are the "many sons" whom the Father is bringing to glory, under the lead of the Captain of their Salvation, Christ Jesus, and as respects this Church, it is again stated that our Lord Jesus, in his resurrection, was "firstborn among many brethren."—Rom. 8:29; Heb. 2:10-13

This great work of lifegiving to the world in general is deferred until the Body of the Life-giver has been completed, until the "brethren," with their Lord and Redeemer, shall be received as sons of glory, and enter upon the work of restitution. Even in the case of those of the world (the ancient worthies), whose faith and loyalty to the divine will has already been tested and approved, there can be no lifegiving until the body of the great antitypical Moses (the Church) has been fully completed (Acts 3:22, 23), as it is written, "They without us [the overcomers of the Gospel age, the Body of the Anointed] shall not be made perfect"—not inherit the earthly good things promised to them.—Heb. 11:39, 40

From this standpoint of the redemption which is in Christ Jesus, and in view of the authority or lordship of earth lost by Adam and thus redeemed by Christ, purchased by his precious blood, we see Christ's title to the office of Life-giver and Father to all of the race of Adam who will accept the blessings of restitution under the terms of the New Covenant, and from this standpoint only can we see how our Lord Jesus could be both the Root and the Offspring of David, both David's Son and David's Father, David's Lord.

In this connection it may be proper to inquire, How comes it that the Church of this Gospel age, a part of the world, "children of wrath even as others" (Eph. 2:3), and needing to experience as much as the others the forgiveness of sins through the merit of the great atonement, is, in any **just** sense, separate and distinct from the world, so that they should be designated "sons of God," while the world should be designated sons of the Life-giver, the Christ.

This distinction lies in the fact that the world not only had its human life-rights purchased by the Lord Jesus, but the obedient of mankind will have that **purchased life restored to them** by him, through the gradual processes of the Millennial age. The Church, on the contrary, does not receive the **restitution** of human life which her Lord purchased for her. The restitution life is merely **reckoned** to believers of this Gospel age, in that they are justified (or made perfect, restored as human beings) **by faith**—not actually. And this faith-reckoned human perfection is for a specific purpose: namely, that such may **sacrifice** the reckoned or imputed human life and its rights and privileges in the divine service, and receive in **exchange therefor** the hope of sharing the **divine nature.**

Earthly life and earthly blessings were lost by Adam, and the same and no others were redeemed for men by our Lord, and these and none others he will eventually bestow during the times of restitution. But the Church, the body, the Bride of Christ, is called out from mankind first, a specially "elect" class, called to a **"heavenly** calling," a "high calling," —to be joint-heir with Jesus Christ, her Lord and Redeemer. As Jesus offered his perfect sacrifice, "the man Christ Jesus," and was rewarded with the divine nature, so the believers of this Gospel age are permitted to offer their imperfect selves (justified or reckoned perfect through the merit of the precious **blood of Jesus) on God's altar; and so doing are begotten of the spirit to be** "new creatures," "sons of the Highest," accepted as Christ's brethren—members of the "royal priesthood" of which he is the Chief Priest.

These are drawn of the Father, not drawn of the Son, as will be the case with the world during the Millennium. (Compare John 6:44 and 12:32) Those whom the Father draws to Christ he, as an elder brother, receives as "brethren," and assists in walking in his footsteps in the narrow way of self-sacrifice, even unto death. Thus they may become dead with him, and be reckoned as joint-sacrificers with him, and thus be reckoned also as worthy to be joint-heirs with him in the Kingdom and work which is to bless the world and give eternal life to as many as will receive it. These, we are distinctly told, are to "fill up that which is behind of the afflictions of Christ"—to "suffer with him, that they may also reign with him" (Col. 1:24; 2 Tim. 2:12) Thus the position of the Church is particularly different from that of the world in general, even as their calling is a high calling, a heavenly calling, and even as its reward is to be the divine nature.—2 Pet. 1:4

This is the great "mystery" or secret which, as the apostle declares, is the key, without which it is impossible to understand the promises and prophecies of the divine Word. (Col. 1:26) The heavenly Father purposed in himself the creation of a human race, a little lower than the angels, of the earth earthy, and adapted to the earth in its Paradisaic condition: but he foreknew also the result of the fall, and its opportunity for manifesting divine justice, divine love, divine wisdom and divine power. As he forearranged that his Only Begotten Son, the Logos, should be given the opportunity of proving his fidelity to the Father and to the principles of righteousness, by becoming man's Redeemer and thus heir of all the riches of divine grace, and chief over all, next to the Father, that in all things he might have the preeminence, so he also designed that before the world of mankind in general should be uplifted by their Redeemer, he would make a selection, according to character and according to faithfulness, of a "little flock," to be joint-heirs with the Only Begotten One,

David's Son and Lord

and his associates in the Kingdom, far above angels, principalities and powers, and every name that is named:

Accordingly, the apostle declares, we are "elect according to the foreknowledge of God the Father, through sanctification of the spirit." (1 Pet. 1:2) The Apostle Paul corroborates the thought, saying, "Whom he did foreknow he also did **predestinate to be conformed to the image of his Son,** that he might be the first-born among many brethren." Further he desired that the eyes of our understanding might be enlightened, so that we "may know what is the hope of his calling, and what the riches of his inheritance in the saints, and what the exceeding greatness of his power to us-ward who believe." He declares that this mercy toward us came without our having done aught to merit it. God, "When we were dead in sins, hath **quickened us together with Christ,** and hath raised us up together, and hath made us sit together in heavenly places in Christ Jesus: that in the ages to come he might show the exceeding riches of his grace in his kindness toward us, through Christ Jesus. . . . For we are his workmanship, created in Christ Jesus unto good works."—Eph. 1:17-19; 2:4-10

GIVE STRENGTH, BLEST SAVIOR

"We seek not, Lord, for tongues of flame,
    Or healing virtue's mystic aid;
But power thy Gospel to proclaim—
    The balm for wounds that sin has made.

"Breathe on us, Lord; thy radiance pour
    On all the wonders of the page
Where hidden lies the heavenly lore
    That blessed our youth and guides our age.

"Grant skill each sacred theme to trace,
    With loving voice and glowing tongue,
As when upon thy words of grace
    The wondering crowds enraptured hung.

"Grant faith that treads the stormy deep
    If but thy voice shall bid it come;
And zeal, that climbs the mountain steep,
    To seek and bring the wanderer home.

"Give strength, blest Savior, in thy might;
    Illuminate our hearts, and we,
Transformed into thine image bright,
    Shall teach, and love, and live, like thee."

STUDY VII

THE MEDIATOR OF THE ATONEMENT

"THE SON OF MAN"

What this Title Does not Mean—What It Does Mean—Its Honors Indisputable, Can be Claimed by None Other—The Son of Man as Seen by the World—Pilate's View, Rousseau's View, Napoleon's View—Significance of Statements, "No Beauty in Him that we Should Desire Him"; and "His Visage Was So Marred"—"The Chiefest Among Ten Thousand"—"Yea, He is Altogether Lovely."

AMONG the many titles applied to our Lord, and one of the most frequently used by himself, is "The Son of Man." Some have been inclined to consider this a concession on our Lord's part that he was a son of Joseph; but this is wholly wrong: he never acknowledged Joseph as his father. On the contrary, it will be noticed that this title which he applies to himself is used, not merely respecting his earthly life, but also as respects his present condition and glory. And from this fact some have swung to the other extreme, and claim that it indicates that our Lord is now **a man** in heaven—that he still retains human nature. This, as we shall endeavor to show, is a thought wholly without warrant, a misapprehension of the title, "The Son of Man." But meantime let us notice that such a thought is wholly at variance with the entire drift of the Scripture teaching. The Scripture statement is most emphatic, that our Lord's humiliation to the human nature was not perpetual, but merely for the purpose of effecting man's redemption, paying man's penalty, and thereby incidentally proving his own fidelity to the Father, on account of which he was immediately afterward highly exalted, not only to the glory which he had with the Father before the world was, but to a more excellent glory, far above angels, principalities, and powers—to the divine nature, and the right hand, place of favor with the Majesty on high.

Notice carefully a few of the uses of this title by our Lord, as follows:—

"The Son of Man shall send forth his angels," in the harvest of this Gospel age.—**Matt. 13:41**

"So shall it be in the presence of the Son of Man," in the harvest, the end of this age.—**Matt. 24:27, 37**

"When the Son of Man shall come in his glory, and all the holy angels with him."—**Matt. 25:31**

"Of him shall the Son of Man be ashamed, when he cometh in the glory of the Father."—Mark 8:38

"What and if ye shall see the Son of Man ascend up where he was before?"—John 6:62

"He that came down from heaven, even the Son of Man."—John 3:13*

These Scriptures identify "The Son of Man" with the Lord of glory, and with the man Christ Jesus, who gave himself, and with the pre-human **Logos**, which came down from heaven and was made flesh. And evidently the Jews did not have the thought that the title "The Son of Man" signified the son of Joseph, or, in the ordinary sense, the son of a man, to receive life from a human father: this is shown by the fact that they inquired, saying, "We have heard out of the law that Christ abideth forever: and how sayest thou, The Son of Man must be lifted up? Who is this Son of Man?" (John 12:34) The Jews evidently identified the expression, "The Son of Man," with their hoped-for Messiah, no doubt basing their hopes in large measure upon the statement of Daniel (7:13) "I saw in the night visions, and behold one like unto the Son of Man came with the clouds of heaven, and came to the Ancient of Days, and they brought him near before him, and there was given him dominion and glory, and a kingdom, that all people, nations and languages should serve him: his dominion is an everlasting dominion, which shall not pass away, and his kingdom shall not be destroyed." Our Lord identified himself with this description in his Revelation (14:14) where he

---

*"Which is in heaven" omitted by oldest MSS.

represents himself as one "like unto the Son of Man, and having on his head a golden crown, and in his hand a sharp sickle"—the Reaper of the harvest of the Gospel age.

Nevertheless, even though assured that this title in no sense refers to Joseph's son, and though the evidence is conclusive that the human nature, taken for the purpose, was **sacrificed forever,** and that now he is a quickening spirit being of the highest order (Heb. 2:9, 16; 1 Pet. 3:18; John 6:51; Phil. 2:9), the question still arises, Why did our Lord choose such a name, such a title? Have we not reason to suspect that there must be some particular reason for it, else this particular title would not be used, since each of our Lord's titles has a peculiar significance, when understood?

There is a most important reason for the use of this title. It is a title of high honor, because a perpetual reminder of his great Victory—of his faithful, humble obedience to all the Heavenly Father's arrangements, even unto death, even the death of the cross, by which he secured the title to all his present and prospective honor and glory, dignity and power, and the divine nature. By this title, "The Son of Man," both angels and men are referred directly to the great exhibition of humility on the part of the Only Begotten of the Father, and to the underlying principle of the divine government—he that exalteth himself shall be abased, and he that humbleth himself shall be exalted. Thus every time this name is used it speaks a volume of valuable instruction to all who shall be taught of God, and who are desirous of honoring him, and doing those things which are well pleasing in his sight.

In the same sense that our Lord was made "of the seed of David," and "of the seed of Abraham, Isaac and Jacob," he was also of the seed of Adam, through mother Eve—yet, as we have seen, "undefiled, **separate** from sinners." "The seed of the woman" is referred to as being the antagonist of the seed of the serpent, yet there is no intimation that Eve would have any seed apart from her husband, Adam. And in the same sense that it is proper to think of and speak of our Lord as the seed of David, it is equally proper to think of him as the seed of Adam, through Eve. And this, we believe, is the thought lying back of this title—"The Son of Man."

Adam, as the head of the race, and its appointed life-giver, failed to give his posterity lasting life, because of his disobedience; nevertheless, the divine promise looked forward to the time when Messiah, identified with Adam's race, should redeem Adam and his entire posterity. Adam was **the man** preeminently, in that he was the head of the race of men, and in him resided the title to the earth and its dominion. Note the prophetic reference to Adam, "What is man that thou are mindful of him, or the son of man that thou visitest him? Thou hast made him a little lower than the angels, and hast crowned him with glory and honor. Thou madest him to have dominion over the works of thy hands; thou hast put all things under his feet: all sheep and oxen, yea, and the beasts of the field, the fowl of the air, the fish of the sea, and whatsoever passeth through the paths of the sea."—Psa. 8:4-8

This earthly right, kingship, dominion, fell into disorder, was lost, through the fall, but was part and parcel of that which was redeemed by the great sin-offering. As it is written of our Lord, prophetically, "Unto thee shall it come, O thou Tower of the flock, **even the first dominion.**" (Micah 4:8) Thus we see that the hope of the world, under the divine arrangement, rested in the coming of a great son and heir of Adam, a great son of Abraham, a great son of David, a great son of Mary. Nor does this imply that the life of this son would come either through Adam or Abraham or David or Mary. As we have already seen, a son-in-law, under the divine arrangement, is counted as a member of the family, able to redeem and to take up a forfeited possession. In the case of our Lord, we have clearly seen that his life came not through earthly parentage, but merely his physical organism—that the life proceedeth forth and came from God, and that originally he was known as the **Logos.**

And the more we investigate this subject the more evident all the foregoing appears, for the student of the Greek may readily inform himself of the fact that in all the instances in which our Lord made use of this term, "The Son of Man," he used it in an emphatic form, which is not distinguishable in English translation, and which, to be appreciated in English, would need to be expressed with emphasis upon the two words "the"—"the Son of the Man." And our Lord's right to this title is indisputable. As Adam alone was perfect, and all others of his race degenerate, except this one Son who attached himself to Adam's race, to be the **Redeemer** of all his lost possessions, so when he was in the act of redeeming the race, and since he has redeemed it from the curse or sentence of death, the title to be **the** son of **the** man came legally and indisputably into his possession.

And not only was that title properly his during the period of his giving the great "ransom for all," but it is properly his during this Gospel age while the selection of his co-workers in the grand restitution program is in progress. And much more will this title properly belong to our Lord during the term of his Millennial Kingdom, when he will as **the** (now highly exalted and changed) Son of **the** man (Adam) prosecute the work of restitution, "the redemption [**deliverance**] of the purchased possession."—Eph. 1: 14; Ruth 4:1-10

"THE MAN CHRIST JESUS,"
AS VIEWED BY UNBELIEVERS

Not merely the devoted followers of the Lord Jesus Christ have recognized his wisdom and grace, and noted that he was "filled with all the fullness of God," but even his opponents recognized him as far beyond the ordinary of our race, as we read, "And all bare him witness, and wondered at the gracious words which proceeded out of his mouth." (Luke 4. 22). Others said, "Never man spake like this man." (John 7:46) And Pilate, loth to destroy this life of the noblest Jew he had ever seen, endeavored, as a last resort, to placate the malevolence of the multitude, perceiving that it was instigated by the scribes and Pharisees, who were envious and jealous of our Lord's popularity. Pilate finally caused Jesus to be brought forth to face his accusers, evidently with the thought that a look upon his noble features would turn back their hatred and their malice. So presenting him, Pilate exclaimed—"Behold the Man!" with an emphasis on the words which is not apparent in our English translation, unless the word "the" be read with emphasis—"Behold **the** Man!" As though he would have said, The man whom you are asking me to crucify is not only **the** Jew above all other Jews, but **the** Man above all other men. And it was concerning our Lord's manhood that John declares, "The **Logos** was made flesh. . . . and we beheld his glory, the glory as of the only begotten of the Father—full of grace and truth."—John 1:14; 19:5

And in this connection let us remember the oftquoted and well-known eulogy of "The Son of **the** Man," and his teachings, by Rousseau, the celebrated Frenchman, as follows:—

"How petty are the books of the philosophers with all their pomp, compared with the Gospels! Can it be that writings at once so sublime and so simple are the work of men? Can he whose life they tell be himself no more than a man? Is there anything in his character of the enthusiast or the ambitious sectary? What sweetness, what purity in his ways, what touching grace in his teachings! What a loftiness in his maxims! What profound wisdom in his words! What presence of mind, what delicacy and aptness in his replies! What an empire over his passions! Where is the man, where is the sage, who knows how to act, to suffer, and to die, without weakness, without display? My friends, men do not invent like this; and the facts respecting Socrates, which no one doubts,

The Son of Man

are not so well attested as about Jesus. Those Jews could never have struck this tone or thought of this morality. And the Gospel has characteristics of truthfulness, so grand, so striking, so perfectly inimitable, that their inventors would be even more wonderful than he whom they portray."

The following eulogy on the Son of the Man is credited to the renowned Napoleon Bonaparte:—

"From first to last Jesus is the same; always the same—majestic and simple, infinitely severe and infinitely gentle. Throughout a life passed under the public eye, he never gives occasion to find fault. The prudence of his conduct compels our admiration by its union of force and gentleness. Alike in speech and action, he is enlightened, consistent and calm. Sublimity is said to be an attribute of divinity: what name, then, shall we give him in whose character was united every element of the sublime?

"I know men, and I tell you Jesus was not a man. Everything in him amazes me. Comparison is impossible between him and any other being in the world. He is truly a being by himself. His ideas and his sentiments, the truth that he announces, his manner of conference, are all beyond human and the natural order of things. His birth, and the story of his life; the profoundness of his doctrine, which overturns all difficulties, and is their most complete solution; his Gospel; the singularity of that mysterious being, and his appearance; his empire, his progress through all centuries and kingdoms; all this is to me a prodigy, an unfathomable mystery. I see nothing here of man. Near as I may approach, closely as I may examine, all remains above comparison—great with greatness that crushes me. It is in vain that I reflect—all remains unaccountable! I defy you to cite another life like that of Christ!"

Aye, truth is stranger than fiction, and the perfect man Christ Jesus, anointed with the spirit of the Highest, was so different from the imperfect race of which he took hold, for its redemption, that the world is certainly excusable for questioning whether he was not more than a man. Assuredly he was more, much more than a **mere** man—much more than a sinful man: he was separate from sinners, and, as a perfect man, was the very image and likeness of the invisible God.

"NO BEAUTY IN HIM THAT WE SHOULD DESIRE HIM"

"Yea, he grew up like a small shoot before him, and as a root out of dry ground: he hath no form nor honor, and when we observe him there is not the appearance that we should desire in him. He is despised and rejected of men; a man of sorrows and acquainted with grief: and we hid our faces from him, as it were."—Isa. 53:2, 3—Compare Young's and Leeser's translations.

Some have suggested that these Scriptures indicate that our Lord's personal appearance was inferior to that of other men, and hence have regarded this as a **proof that he was not separate** from sinners, but a partaker of sin and of its penalty of degeneration. We dissent from this, however, as being contrary to the entire trend of the Scriptural testimony, and incline on the contrary to bend this statement into harmony with the general testimony of Scripture on the subject, if it can be done without violence to the proper principles of interpretation, and we think this can be done and shown.

There are various types of honorableness, beauty, comeliness—strikingly different are the ideals of various peoples, and of the same people under various circumstances. The ideal of beauty satisfactory to barbarians is repulsive to the more civilized. The Indian warrior, painted in red and yellow, and bedecked with shells and dyed feathers, and with a girdle of gory scalps, would be the desirable ideal before the mind of certain savages. The pugilist in the prize ring, stripped for battle, is the ideal of manly form in what is known as "the manly art"—to some. To others, the richly dressed matador, or bullfighter, is the grand ideal of manly development, which captures the admiration and applause of the multitude. And so ideals vary according to times, circumstances and conditions. Since this Scripture deals with our Lord Jesus at his first advent, it should be understood as signifying that he did not come up to the Jewish ideal. This is very evident, since the very one of whom Pilate exclaimed, "Behold the Man!" was the very one of whom the Jews cried out the more lustily, "Crucify him! Crucify him! We have no king but Caesar!"

We are to remember that at the time of the first advent the Jewish nation was in subjection, under the Roman yoke: and that it had been "trodden down of the Gentiles" for over six hundred years. We should remember also the hopes of Israel, begotten of the divine promises to Abraham, Isaac and Jacob, and reiterated through all the prophets, to the effect that in God's due time he would send them his Anointed One, a greater law-giver than Moses, a greater general than Joshua, and a greater king than David or Solomon. We should remember that at this very time Israel was looking for Messiah according to their ideals: as it is recorded, all men were in expectation of the Messiah. But when Jesus was announced to be the Messiah, his presentation was so different from all they had expected that their proud hearts were ashamed of him; and as it were they hid their faces from him—turned their backs upon him—especially the leaders and prominent ones of that nation, whose guidance the common people followed.—Luke 3:15

They were expecting a great general, great king, and great law-giver combined, full of dignity, full of hauteur, full of ambition, full of pride, full of self-will—haughty and domineering in word and in act. This was their **ideal** of what would constitute the necessary qualifications of the King who would conquer the world, and make Israel the leading nation. They saw the pride, insolence, arrogance, of Herod, appointed by the Roman Emperor to be their king; they saw something of the Roman generals and governors, centurions, etc.; they imagined the Roman

Emperor, to be still more strongly marked in **all these** various characteristics, leading him up to predominance in the empire: and taking their cue from these, they expected the Messiah to possess many of these qualities still more markedly, as representing the still greater dignity, honor and glory of the Heavenly Court and its authority transferred to earth.

No wonder, then, that with such expectations they were unprepared to accept the meek and lowly Nazarene, who welcomed to his company publicans and sinners and whose only weapon for conquering the world was "the sword of his mouth." No wonder that when he was announced to be the hope of Israel, the King of the Jews, the Messiah, they turned their backs upon him. No wonder that, with their false expectations long cherished, they were sorely disappointed. No wonder they were ashamed to acknowledge "Jesus, the King of the Jews," and said, His is not the kind of beauty, honor and dignity which we desired: he is not our ideal of the soldier, statesman and king befitting our nation's needs or likely to fulfil its long-cherished hopes. Ah yes! like a similar class today looking for the Messiah's second advent, they took for granted that their expectations built upon "traditions of the elders" were correct, and correspondingly neglected to honestly and earnestly search the Scriptures, which would have made them "wise unto salvation."

That it was to **such undesirableness** of appearance, and to such lack of the "honor" (beauty) they looked for, that the prophet referred, seems evident. It would be inconsistent to translate and interpret the **prophecy** out of harmony with the **historic facts** admitted to be their fulfilment: and also out of logical harmony with the repeated declarations of his purity, as the Lamb of God which taketh away the sin of the world—holy, harmless, undefiled, separate from sinners.

"HIS VISAGE WAS SO MARRED"
——Isa. 52:14, 15——

Here again a faulty translation has given rise to

erroneous thoughts respecting our Lord's appearance: and yet even the most careless readers who have seen faces of human creatures seriously marred by debauchery, by disease, or misshapen by accident, have found it impossible to realize that our Lord's visage or countenance "was more marred than that of any man, and his form more than the sons of men." **Evidently** something is amiss in such a statement, for not such an one would Pilate present before the people, saying, "Behold **the** man!" Not such an one would the common people hail as the Son of David, and think to take by force to make him a king. Besides, have we not the assurance that not a bone of him was broken? But how changed is this prophetic statement for the better—how much more consistent with the facts of Scripture history and the logical deductions of his holiness and purity—when rendered thus:—

"As astonished at thee have been many (so marred by man was his appearance, and his form by the sons of men) so shall he astonish many peoples." As the people of his day were surprised that he would submit to the abuses of those who crowned him with thorns and smote him and spat upon him and crucified him and pierced him, so others of all nations, now and in the future, hearing of the endurance of "such contradiction of sinners against himself" (Heb. 12:3) have wondered and will wonder at such patience and such meekness.

"Before him shall kings shut their mouths; for what was not recorded [of others] they will see [exemplified in Him]; what they had never before heard of they shall understand." The great ones of earth never heard of any king voluntarily submitting to such indignities at the hands of his subjects, and in order that he might do them good. Verily, "His is love beyond a brother's." No wonder if all are astonished "in due time."

Undoubtedly also our dear Redeemer's face bore marks of sorrow, for as we have seen, his deeply sympathetic heart was **"touched"** with a feeling of our infirmities: and no doubt those marks increased, until the close of his ministry at Calvary. We must remember that the finer the organism and the more delicate its sensibilities, the more it is susceptible to pain. We can readily discern that scenes of trouble, sickness, pain and depravity, to which we become more or less inured through our own share in the fall, and through continual contact with human woe, would be many-fold more serious matters to the perfect one—holy, harmless, undefiled and separate from sinners.

We find the same thing illustrated to some extent in our own experiences. Those of comparatively fine sensibilities who have been accustomed to luxury, refinement, beauty, and favorable surroundings, if they visit the slums of a great city, and note the degradation, the unfavorable conditions, the bad odors, the incongruous sounds, the wretched sights of squalor, are sure to become sick at heart: involuntarily the countenance becomes drawn, and the thought arises, How terrible life would be under such circumstances; what a boon death would be. Yet, perhaps, while thus soliloquizing, the eye catches sight of children playing merrily, and perhaps the washerwoman, from her task, catches up a snatch of a song, or a man is seen contentedly reading a newspaper, or a boy is heard attempting music with an old instrument. These things indicate that those who have become accustomed to such sights and sounds and smells and general conditions are far less influenced by them than are those who have been accustomed from infancy to refinement.

And this lesson illustrates in a very small measure the disparity between our Lord's view of the earth's sinful and woeful condition and ours. As a perfect being, who had left the courts of heavenly glory, and had humbled himself to become a partaker of man's woe, his sympathizer and his Redeemer, he surely felt much more than we the miseries of "the groaning creation." What wonder, then, if the weight of our sorrows cast a shade over the glorious beauties of his perfect face! What wonder if contact with earth's troubles, and his voluntary sharing of the human weakness and diseases (at the cost of his own life, his own vitality, as we have seen), marked deeply the face and form of the Son of the Man! And yet we cannot for a moment question that his communion with the Father, his fellowship of the Holy Spirit and the approval of his own conscience, that he did always those things which were pleasing in the Father's sight, must have given to our Redeemer's face a peaceful expression, which would make it a combination of joy and of sorrow, of trouble and of peace. And his knowledge of the Heavenly Father's plan must have enabled him to rejoice in the things which he suffered, realizing how they would shortly work out, not only a blessing to himself, but also "salvation unto the ends of the earth." If, therefore, the sorrows of men shadowed his countenance, we may be sure that his faith and hope were also marked in facial expression, and that the peace of God which passeth all understanding kept his heart, and enabled him to be always rejoicing, in the midst of the greatest contradictions of sinners against himself.

"THE CHIEFEST AMONG TEN THOUSAND"

To the sinful, envious, hateful heart of the fallen nature, everything akin to beauty, goodness, truth and love is distasteful, there is no beauty in it, nothing desired—it is a reproof. Our Lord expressed this matter forcefully when he said, "The darkness hateth the light, and they that are of the darkness come not to the light, because the light makes manifest their darkness." (John 3:19, 20) We see a further illustration of this fact, that an evil heart may at times hate and despise a glorious countenance, a lovelit countenance, not only in the fact that our dear Redeemer was thus despised by those who cried, "Crucify him," but also in the cases of the others. Note the various records of martyrdom for the Truth's sake, and note how little was the melting influence of the countenances of those who could look up from their personal sufferings, and pray for blessings upon their persecutors. The testimony respecting the first Christian martyr—Stephen—is to the effect that his face was radiant and beautiful, so as to be even comparable to the face of an angel. "All that sat in the council looking steadfastly on him, saw his face as it had been the face of an angel." (Acts 6:15) And yet, because of the hardness of their hearts, so far from loving his angelic face, which must have been much less angelic than that of the Master, and instead of heeding his wonderful words, which were much less wonderful than those of the Great Teacher, "they ran upon him with one accord . . . and they stoned Stephen," even as they cried out to Pilate to have the Lord of glory crucified.

"Yea, he is altogether lovely."

* * *

"The heav'ns declare thy glory, Lord;
   Through all the realms of boundless space
The soaring mind may roam abroad,
   And there thy power and wisdom trace.

"Author of nature's wondrous laws,
   Preserver of its glorious grace,
We hail thee as the great First Cause,
   And here delight thy ways to trace.

"By faith we see thy glory now,
   We read thy wisdom, love and grace;
In praise and adoration bow,
   And long to see thy glorious face.

"In Christ, when all things are complete—
   The things in earth and things in heav'n—
The heav'ns and earth shall be replete
   With thy high praises, ever given."

STUDY VIII

THE CHANNEL OF THE ATONEMENT

THE HOLY SPIRIT OF GOD

The Operation of the Holy Spirit—Now and in the Millennium—Various Descriptive Names of the Holy Spirit, "Spirit of Love," "Spirit of Truth," etc.—In Contrast, the Unholy Spirit, "Spirit of Error," "Spirit of Fear," etc.—Personal Pronouns Applied—The Significance of the Word Spirit—"God is a Spirit"—"The Holy Spirit Was not yet Given"—Gifts of the Spirit—The Transforming Power of the Holy Spirit—The Spirit by Measure and Without Measure—"The Spirit of the World," Antichrist—The Battle Between this and the Holy Spirit—Spirit Fightings Without and Within the Saints—The Spirit that Lusteth to Envy—Taught of the Spirit—the Parakletos, the Comforter—He Shall Guide You into all Truth and into Full Atonement—The Spirit's Supervision None the Less Since the Miraculous Gifts Were Discontinued.

"For as many as are led by the Spirit of God, they are the sons of God . . . Ye have received the spirit of adoption, whereby we cry, Abba, Father. The Spirit itself beareth witness with our spirit that we are the children of God."—Rom. 8:14-16

"And it shall come to pass, afterward, that I will pour out my Spirit upon all flesh."—Joel 2:28

THE GREAT work of the Atonement could not be properly considered, nor clearly understood, if the work of the Holy Spirit, in connection therewith, were overlooked or ignored. The Holy Spirit has much to do with the presentation of the Atonement—**making manifest to the believer the divine forgiveness, as well as guiding him into full reconciliation of heart to God.** It was under the begetting influence of the Holy Spirit, received by our Lord Jesus at his baptism, at the beginning of his ministry, that his consecrated heart was enabled to see clearly and distinctly the Father's will, the proper course, the narrow way of sacrifice, and to appreciate the exceeding great and precious promises, whose fulfilment lay beyond his humiliation, ignominy and death at Calvary. By the Holy Spirit, therefore, our Redeemer was enabled to perform his great work, being guided thereby to do that which was pleasing and acceptable before the Father, and which provided the ransom for all humanity. Similarly the Holy Spirit is identified with the Church: all who have accepted the merits of the great sin-offering, and who have come unto the Father through the merit of the Son's sacrifice, and who have presented themselves living sacrifices, in harmony with the high calling to the divine nature held out to such during the Gospel age, have needed and had the Holy Spirit's aid. Only in proportion as any receive the Holy Spirit of God are they able to come into proper lines of fellowship with the Father, and with the Son, so as to be able to "prove what is that good and acceptable and perfect will of God," and to do it. Only by the Holy Spirit are we guided beyond the mere letter of the divine testimony, into a true appreciation of "the deep things of God," and all those things which God hath in reservation for them that love him, which the human eye hath not seen, the human ear hath not heard, neither have entered into the human heart to understand and appreciate.—1 Cor. 2:9, 10

The Holy Spirit's office will be equally important during the Millennial age, in bringing the world of mankind back into harmony with God under the terms of the New Covenant, through the merits of the dear Redeemer's sacrifice. Accordingly, through the prophet Joel (2:28, 29), the Lord has drawn attention to this fact, pointing out that while he will pour his Spirit only upon his servants and handmaidens during this Gospel age, yet **"afterward"** his Holy Spirit shall be generally poured upon the world of mankind, "all flesh."* During the Millennial age,

---

*The order of this blessing is reversed in the prophetic statement; quite probably, in order to obscure the matter until the proper time, and thus to hide some of the length and breadth and height and depth of the divine plan, until the due time for it to be known and appreciated.

then, the world's progress will be in full harmony with the Holy Spirit; and only in proportion as men shall come into full harmony with that Holy Spirit will any of them become eligible to the eternal conditions of life and joy and blessing which lie beyond the Millennial age. The fact that the Holy Spirit will co-operate with the glorified Church in the blessing of all the families of the earth is also testified by our Lord. After picturing to us the glories of the Millennium and its abundant supply of truth as a mighty river of the water of life, clear as crystal, he says, "And the Spirit and the Bride say, Come! And whosoever will may come, and take of the water of life freely."—Rev. 22:17

But this subject of the Holy Spirit, its office and operation, has been grievously misunderstood by many of the Lord's people for centuries: and only in the light of the rising Sun of righteousness—in the light of the **parousia** of the Son of Man—is this subject becoming thoroughly clear and reasonable, as it evidently was to the early Church, and in harmony with all the various Scriptural testimonies pertaining to it. The doctrine of the Trinity, which, as we have seen, began to rise in the second century, and reached a large development in the fourth century, is responsible, in considerable measure, for much of the darkness which blends with the truth on this subject in many Christian minds, much to their disadvantage—confusing and mystifying all religious convictions.

There is consistency in the Scripture teaching that the Father and Son are in full harmony and **oneness** of purpose and operation, as we have just seen. And equally consistent is the Scripture teaching respecting the Holy Spirit—that it is not another God, but the spirit, influence or power exercised by the one God our Father, and by his Only Begotten Son— in absolute oneness, therefore, with both of these, who also are **at one** or in full accord. But how different is this **unity** of the Father, the Son and the Holy Spirit from that held and taught under the name of Trinitarian doctrine, which in the language of the Catechism (Question 5 and 6) declares—There are three persons in the One God—the Father, the Son, and the Holy Ghost: "these **three** are **one** God, the **same in substance**, equal in power and glory." This view suited well "the dark ages" which it helped to produce. The period in which **mysteries** were worshiped instead of unraveled found a most choice one in this theory, which is as unscriptural as it is unreasonable. How could the **three be one in person**, in substance? And if only **"one** in substance," how could they be **"equal?"** Does not every intelligent person know that if God is **one** in person he cannot be **three?** and that if **three** in person there can be only one sense in which the three could be **one**, and that not in person but in purpose, in mind, in will, in co-operation? Verily, if it were not for the fact that this trinitarian nonsense was drilled into us from earliest infancy, and the fact that it is soberly taught in Theological Seminaries by gray-haired professors, in many other ways apparently wise, nobody would give it a moment's serious consideration. How the great Adversary ever succeeded in foisting it upon the Lord's people to bewilder and mystify them, and render much of the Word of God of none effect, is the real mystery which will probably not be solved until we "know even as we are known," in glory.

The careful student of the preceding chapters has found abundant testimony from the Scriptures, to the effect that there is but one All-mighty God—Jehovah; and that he has highly exalted his First Begotten Son, his Only Begotten Son, to his own nature and to his own throne of the universe; and that next to these in order of rank will be the glorified Church, the Bride, the Lamb's wife and joint-heir—otherwise styled his "brethren." These shall be made associates of his glory, as in the present age they are required to be associates in his sufferings. The students have noticed also, that all Scriptures harmonize and agree in the above testimony; and further, that there are no Scriptures whatever which,

The Holy Spirit

either directly or indirectly, actually or apparently, conflict with these findings. The question then arises, Who, Where, What, is the Holy Spirit?

Let us follow in respect to this question the same course of investigation followed in the others. Let us go to the law and to the testimony of God for all our information. Let us not go to man. Let us not accept the doubts and speculations of good people who are dead, or of good people who are living, nor yet our own. Let us remember the apostle's declaration that the Word of the Lord is given with the intention—"that the man of God may be perfect, thoroughly furnished unto every good work." (2 Tim. 3:17) Let us place our reliance wholly upon the Lord, and seek to know the meaning of what he declares respecting the Holy Spirit, bringing every Scripture testimony into harmony; assured that the truth, and it only, will stand such a searching examination. So doing, prayerfully and carefully, our efforts shall be rewarded. To him that knocketh, the door of knowledge shall be opened; to him that seeketh, the knowledge of the Holy Spirit shall be revealed.—Isa. 8:20; Matt. 7:7, 8

The Holy Spirit is variously defined in the Scriptures, and to rightly understand the subject these various definitions must be considered together, and be permitted to throw light upon each other. Notice that the Holy Spirit is variously styled—"The Spirit of God," "The Spirit of Christ," "The Spirit of Holiness," "The Spirit of Truth," "The Spirit of a Sound Mind," "The Spirit of Liberty," "The Spirit of the Father," "The Holy Spirit of Promise," "The Spirit of Meekness," "The Spirit of Understanding," "The Spirit of Wisdom," "The Spirit of Glory," "The Spirit of Counsel," "The Spirit of Grace," "The Spirit of Adoption," "The Spirit of Prophecy."

These various titles, repeated many times, and used interchangeably, give us the full, proper assurance that they all relate to the same Holy Spirit—indeed, frequently the word "holy" is added in, combined, as for instance, "The Holy Spirit of God," "The Holy Spirit of Promise," etc. We must seek an understanding of the subject which will reject none of these appellations, but harmonize them all. It is impossible to harmonize these various statements with the **ordinary idea of a third God**; but it is entirely consistent with every one of them to understand these various expressions as descriptive of the spirit, disposition and power of one God, our Father; and also the spirit, disposition and power of our Lord Jesus Christ, because he is **at one** with the Father—and also to a certain extent it is the spirit or disposition of all who are truly the Lord's, angels or men, in proportion as they have come into oneness, or harmony, with him.

It may be helpful to some to notice that there is another spirit mentioned frequently throughout the Scriptures, and in opposite terms, namely, "The Spirit of Fear," "The Spirit of Bondage," "The Spirit of the World," "The Spirit of Error," "The Spirit of Divination," "The Spirit of Antichrist," "The Spirit of Slumber." No one thinks that these various definitions, if unitedly considered, would justify the thought that there are **two** or more Satans. All naturally and properly enough recognize the meaning of these terms, as signifying in general the **wrong spirit**—the spirit, disposition or power which has its chief exemplification in Satan; the spirit manifesting itself in all who are in harmony with sin and Satan. Very properly also, none think of these as personal spirits. No more should any one consider the various applications of the word "spirit" in a good sense, as signifying different spirit beings, nor as signifying unitedly **another** God. These terms, considered unitedly, represent various features of the character, the disposition, the Spirit of our God, Jehovah, and proportionately the spirit or disposition of all who have received his Spirit, become partakers of his disposition and come into harmony with the divine mind.

Certain unscriptural ideas, and therefore false

The Holy Spirit

ideas, respecting the spirit of man, which will be examined in a succeeding chapter, lie close to the foundation of the unscriptural and false view of the Holy Spirit, now so generally prevalent. And the wrong thoughts respecting the Spirit of God and the spirit of man have been intensified and deepened by the fact that the translators of our Common Version English Bible have ninety-two times used the phrase "Holy Ghost" without the slightest authority—the original Greek word being **pneuma**—spirit. And the word "ghost," to the uneducated, has a very vague meaning, which, nevertheless, is very positively identified with the thought of personality. It is worthy of note that in the Revised Version of the New Testament twenty-one of these occurrences of the word "Ghost" were changed so as to read "Spirit," and that the American Revision Committee recorded its **protest** in respect to the use of the word "Ghost" in the remaining seventy-one occurrences. And yet both the English and American Committees were composed of strict Trinitarians.

There is absolutely no ground whatever for thinking of or speaking of the Holy Spirit of God as another God, distinct in personality from the Father and the Son. Quite to the contrary of this, notice the fact that it was the Father's Spirit that was communicated to our Lord Jesus, as it is written, "The **Spirit of** the Lord God is upon me, because he hath anointed me to preach the Gospel." (Luke 4:18) Turning to the prophecy from which this quotation is made, we read there, in the Hebrew, "The **Spirit of** the Lord Jehovah is on me, because Jehovah hath anointed me to proclaim good tidings to the humble." (Isa. 61:1) And to the same purport we read again, "And the **Spirit of** Jehovah shall rest upon him, the **spirit of** wisdom and understanding, the **spirit of** counsel and might, the **spirit of** knowledge and of reverence of Jehovah." (Isa. 11:2, 3) Similarly the same Spirit in Christ is referred to as "The Spirit of Christ," the mind of Christ—"Let this mind be in you which was also in Christ Jesus our Lord."—Phil. 2:5

It is urged by some that our Lord's reference to the Holy Spirit, recorded in John 14:26, proves that the Spirit is a person, because our Common Version renders this passage thus: "But the Comforter, which is the Holy Ghost, **whom** the Father will send in my name, **he** shall teach you all things, and bring all things to your remembrance, whatsoever I have said unto you." But a glance at the Greek text of this passage shows that the translators were influenced by their prejudices on the subject, for there is no ground for the use of the words "whom" and "he." The Diaglott renders this verse thus: "But the helper, the Holy Spirit **which** the Father will send in my name, shall teach you all things and remind you of those things which I said to you."

The same criticism is applicable to the seventeenth verse of the same chapter, which, in our Common Version, reads: "The Spirit of truth, **whom** the world cannot receive, because it seeth **him** not, neither knoweth **him**, but ye know **him**, for **he** dwelleth with you, and shall be in you." Here the expression, "Spirit of truth," is evidently used in contrast with the "spirit of error." The passage has no reference whatever to a person, but to the influence of the truth, and the effect of the same upon the Lord's people. The Diaglott translation of this verse reads: "The Spirit of truth, **which** the world cannot receive, because it beholds **it** not, nor knows **it**; but ye know **it**; because **it** operates with you and will be in you."

Take another illustration—"When **he** the Spirit of truth is come, **he** will guide you into all truth; for **he** shall not speak of **himself**; but whatsoever **he** shall hear that shall **he** speak; and **he** shall show you things to come. **He** will glorify me for **he** shall receive of mine and shall show it unto you." (John 16:13, 14) In this passage the Greek word, **heautou,** is translated "himself," yet the same word is frequently properly translated "itself." In our Common Version this word **heautou** is rendered in the masculine, feminine, common, and neuter genders. For instance, in the above text it is rendered in the

The Holy Spirit

masculine;* in 1 Cor. 11:5 it is in the feminine gender—"dishonoreth her head"; similarly in Rev. 2:20—"which calleth herself a prophetess"; and again in 1 Cor. 13:5—"Love seeketh not her own." In 1 Cor. 11:31 it is rendered in the common gender—"would judge ourselves"; likewise in 1 Cor. 16:15—"have addicted themselves"; again, Luke 22:17—"divide it among yourselves"; again, John 6:53—"ye have no life in you." As illustrations of the translation of the word **heautou** in the neuter form, in our Common Version, note the following:—

"Let the morrow take thought for the things of itself."—Matt. 6:34

"If a kingdom be divided against itself."—Mark 3:24

"If a house be divided against itself."—Mark 3:25

"As the branch cannot bear fruit of itself."—John 15:4

"There is nothing unclean of itself."—Rom. 14:14

"The whole body . . . maketh increase of the body unto the edifying of itself in love."—Eph. 4:16

"Faith, if it hath not works, is dead, being by itself."—James 2:17

Similarly, the word **ekinos**, rendered, "he" in the passage under consideration might with equal propriety, be rendered "that," "this," "those," "the same," "she," "it," and in our Common Version English Bible it is rendered in all these different forms and **more frequently** than as the masculine pronouns, "he," "his," "him." Anyone skeptical on this subject can readily convince himself by consulting a Greek-English Concordance of the New Testament, which shows the various translations of these words. We will give one example of each of these translations of the word **ekinos**:—

"It shall be more tolerable in that day for Sodom than for **that** city."—Luke 10:12

---

*The pronoun follows its noun here, Comforter (Gr. masculine, but arbitrarily so, regardless of sex—as in the German, which makes stove and table, masculine; fork, feminine; woman, neuter gender).

"**She**, supposing him to be the gardener, saith."—John 20:15

"But know **this**, that if the goodman of the house."—Matt. 24:43

"I do not say that ye shall pray for **it**."—1 John 5:16

"On one of **those** days as he taught."—Luke 20:1

"**The same** day was the Sabbath."—John 5:9

"The child was cured from **that** very hour."—Matt. 17:18

It is not infrequent, however, to attach to a virtue or quality the gender of the person or thing to which it belongs; thus, for instance, because the heavenly Father is designated as masculine, therefore it would be but proper that his power, his spirit, his every influence and characteristic should be similarly designated in the masculine form. Nor is it rare for things which are neuter of themselves to be designated as masculine or feminine, according as they are strong and active, or passive and delicate. Thus, for instance, the sun is universally referred to as "he," and the moon as "she." Hence, if it were not for the general misconception on the subject, and the prevalent thought that the Holy Spirit is a person (and not merely the divine spirit, influence or power—the **spirit** of the Father), there could be no criticism made of the use of the masculine pronouns in respect to the Holy Spirit; because God is recognized as masculine, as the Author and source of life and blessing. So, then, let us not overlook the fact that the use of the personal pronouns does not prove the Holy Spirit of God to be another person from the Father and the Son—another God. The Holy Spirit or influence is the Father's spirit or influence, and the Son's also, for these are one in purpose and influence.

THE MEANING OF THE WORD "SPIRIT"

The question, then, properly arises, what senses or meanings attach to the words "Holy Spirit" as used

The Holy Spirit

in the Scriptures? What qualities or qualifications of the divine character or power are represented by the word "spirit"? The answer will best be found by first of all examining the strict meaning of the word "spirit," and then examining all the different methods of its use throughout the Scriptures.

(1) The word "spirit," in the Old Testament, is the translation of the Hebrew word **ruach**, the primary significance or root-meaning of which is **wind**. The word "spirit" in the New Testament comes from the Greek word **pneuma**, whose primary significance or root-meaning likewise is **wind**. But let no one hastily conclude that we are about to attempt to prove that the Holy Spirit is a holy wind, for nothing could be farther from our thought. But we desire to present this obscure subject in such a manner as will be helpful both to the learned and the unlearned: hence we begin with the acknowledged root-meaning of these words, that we may ascertain **how** and **why** it was used in this connection.

Because the wind is both **invisible** and **powerful**, these words, **ruach** and **pneuma**, gradually took on much wider meanings, and came to represent any **invisible** power or influence, good or bad. And since divine power is exercised through channels and by agencies beyond human sight, therefore this word "spirit" came more and more to be applied to all of the Lord's dealings. Naturally also it came into common use in connection with such human influences as are invisible; for instance, to represent the **breath** of life, the **power** by which the man lives, which is invisible, designated the "spirit," or "breath of life"; also for the **power** of the mind, which is **invisible**, called "the spirit of the mind." Life itself is a power and is invisible, and hence it also was called spirit by the ancients. A few illustrations of these various uses of the Hebrew word **ruach** and the Greek word **pneuma** may be helpful.

Ruach in the Old Testament is translated "blast" 4 times, "breath" 28 times, "mind" 6 times, "smell" 8 times, "wind" and "windy" 91 times. In every instance the thought behind the word is an **invisible power or influence**. Samples of these translations of ruach are as follows:—

"With the **blast** of thy nostrils the waters were gathered together."—Exod. 15:8

"All flesh wherein is the **breath** of life."—Gen. 6:17; 7:15

"In whose hand is the . . . **breath** of all mankind."—Job 12:10

"They have all one **breath**: so that a man hath no pre-eminence."—Eccl. 3:19

"Which was a grief of **mind** unto Isaac."—Gen. 26:35

"Jehovah **smelleth** a sweet savor."—Gen. 8:21

"Noses have they but they **smell** not."—Psa. 115:6

"God made a **wind** to pass over the earth."—Gen. 8:1

"Thou didst blow with thy **wind**."—Exod. 15:10

"Stormy **wind** fulfilling his word."—Psa. 148:8

"The trees of the wood are moved with the **wind**."—Isa. 7:2

Pneuma in the New Testament is translated (besides "ghost" and "spirit") "life," "spiritual," and "wind," as follows:—

"To give **life** to the image of the beast."—Rev. 13:15

"Forasmuch as ye are zealous of **spiritual** gifts."—1 Cor. 14:12

"The **wind bloweth** where it listeth and ye hear the sound thereof."—John 3:8

And let us not forget that all of these various translations were made by Trinitarians. We do not object to these translations—they are quite proper: but we call attention to them as proofs that the words **ruach** and **pneuma**, rendered "spirit," **do not signify personality**, but do signify **invisible power or influence**.

"GOD IS A SPIRIT"

(2) "God is a Spirit"; that is to say, he is a powerful but invisible being; likewise the angels are called

spirits, because they also, in their natural condition, are invisible to men, except as revealed by miraculous power. Our Lord Jesus, while he was a man, was not designated a spirit being, but since his exaltation it is written of him, "Now the Lord is that Spirit"—he is now a powerful and invisible being. The Church of this Gospel age is promised change of nature, to the likeness of her Lord, as it is written, "We shall be like him, for we shall see him as he is." The Church is spoken of as being spiritual, inasmuch as she is in harmony with the Lord and is declared to be begotten again by the Spirit to a new nature, a **spirit nature**, with the assurance that that which is begotten of the Spirit will, in the resurrection, be born of the Spirit. This use of the word spirit, it will be perceived, is related to personality—spirit beings.—2 Cor. 3:17; 1 John 3:2; John 3:6

(3) Another use of the word spirit is in the sense of generative power or fecundity, as in Gen. 1:2, "And the Spirit of God **moved** upon the face of the waters"—that is to say, the power of God, his vehicle of energy, fecundated waters, or rendered them fruitful, prolific. Similarly, "Holy men of old spoke and wrote as they were **moved** by the Holy Spirit," the holy influence or power of God, fecundated their minds, causing them to bring forth thoughts such as God wished to have expressed. (2 Pet. 1:21) Similarly, the skilled workmen whom Moses selected to prepare the paraphernalia of the Tabernacle were brought under the influence of the divine power, to the energizing or quickening of their natural faculties, without affecting them in any moral sense, even as the waters of the great deep were not affected in a moral sense. Thus it is written:—

"The Lord hath called by name Bezaleel . . . and hath filled him with the **Spirit** of God, in wisdom, in understanding, in knowledge, in all manner of workmanship, and to devise curious works; to work in gold, and in silver, and in brass; and in covering of stones, to set them; and in carving of wood, to make any manner of cunning work. And he hath put in his heart that he may teach, both he and Aholiab, . . .

them hath he filled with wisdom of heart to work all manner of work, of the engraver and of the cunning workman, and of the embroiderer."—Exod. 35:30-35; 28:3; 31:3, 4

Likewise, we are informed that Jehovah God put upon Moses and the elders of Israel **his Spirit**, with special power for judging in Israel's affairs, preserving order, etc. (Num. 11:17-26) After the same manner God's Spirit was with the kings of Israel, so long as they were loyal to him. Notice, for instance, the case of Saul (1 Sam. 11:6); and that this Spirit of wisdom or judgment pertaining to the government of Israel departed from Saul, and was conferred upon David, whose discreetness thereafter is specially noted. (1 Sam. 16:13, 14) Thereafter, instead of the Spirit of wisdom and courage and confidence, as a servant of the Lord, Saul had an evil spirit, more literally a spirit of sadness, of dejection, loss of confidence, in the realization that he was no longer recognized as the Lord's representative on the throne. And this spirit of dejection, which brooded on calamities, is said to have been from the Lord—probably in the sense that it resulted from the Lord's dealings, in removing from Saul his recognition and sustaining power and direction in the affairs of Israel.

"THE HOLY SPIRIT WAS NOT YET GIVEN"

But no manifestation of the Spirit of God, prior to the first advent of our Lord Jesus, was exactly the same as the manifestation and operation of the Lord's Spirit upon our Lord Jesus, from the time of his baptism until his crucifixion, and upon the Church of Christ from the day of Pentecost until now—until the very end of this Gospel age, and the completion of the Church's course in the first resurrection. In harmony with this we read, "The Holy Spirit was not yet given [except to our Lord Jesus], because Jesus was not yet glorified."—John 7:39

The **operation** of God's Spirit during this Gospel age is widely different from its operation in previous times; and this difference is expressed in the words "Spirit of adoption," "Spirit of sonship," "Spirit of holiness," "Spirit of truth," and kindred expressions. As we have already seen, after Adam's fall none of his posterity were accepted as **sons** of God prior to the first advent: the very highest title given to the father of the faithful, Abraham, was that of friend: "Abraham was called the friend of God." But, as the Apostle John explains, when the **Logos** was made flesh, he presented himself to his own people, Israel, and to as many as received him (then and since) **gave he power** (privilege, opportunity) **to become the sons of God;** and these, he declares, were **begotten** of God—begotten of the Spirit, as "that which is born of the Spirit is spirit."—John 1:12, 13; 3:3-8

The Holy Spirit, in this sense of the word, is guaranteed only to the house of sons; and the house of sons was unknown until the Beloved Son was manifested in the flesh and **redeemed** the world, and granted to those who accept him the opportunity to receive the adoption of sons. (Gal. 4:5; Eph. 1:5) This adoption, as the apostle informs us, primarily was the inheritance of Israel, but since there was not a sufficient number in Israel ready to complete the predestinated number to be adopted, therefore, after accepting Israel's remnant, "God did visit the Gentiles, to take out of them a people for his name," to be the sons of God, joint-heirs with Christ, and this was foreknown and foretold through the prophets.—Rom. 9:4, 29-33; Acts 15:14

But in what respects does this manifestation of the divine power, influence or Spirit, during this Gospel age, differ from the manifestation of it in previous times? The Apostle Peter answers this question, assuring us that the ancient worthies, although highly honored of God, and moved upon by his Holy Spirit, spoke and wrote things which they did not understand. God used them as his servants to write out things not due to be understood by them, but which in due time would be revealed to us, the house of sons, by the operation of the same Holy Spirit or holy power of God upon those begotten of his Spirit. In the past the Spirit's operation was chiefly **mechanical**: to us its operation is chiefly **explanatory** and sympathetic, expounding the divine plan through apostles and teachers specially "set in the Church" from time to time, the object being to enable the sons "to comprehend with all saints the length and breadth, the height and the depth" of the divine wisdom and goodness, as exemplified in the divine plan and its revelation. Indeed, from the apostle's language, it is evident that even the angels (who were sometimes used of the Lord as his channels in communicating with the prophets, the mediums of his Holy Spirit) were not permitted to understand the meaning of their communications, any more than were the prophets who wrote out the revelations for our benefit. Note the apostle's words:—

"Of which salvation the prophets have inquired and searched diligently, who prophesied of the grace that would come **unto you:** searching what [time] or what manner of time [literal or symbolic] the Spirit of Christ which was in them did signify, when it testified beforehand the sufferings of Christ, and the glory that should follow. Unto whom it was revealed, that **not unto themselves**, but unto us they did minister the things which are now reported unto you by them that have preached the gospel unto you with the Holy Spirit sent down from heaven: which things also the angels desire to look into."—1 Pet. 1:10-12; 2 Pet. 1:21

GIFTS OF THE SAME SPIRIT, THE SAME LORD, THE SAME GOD

"There are diversities of gifts, but **the same Spirit,** as there are differences of administration, but the **same Lord;** there are divers operations, but it is **the same God** which worketh all in all. But a manifestation of the Spirit is given to every man [in the Church] to profit withal. For to one is given, by the

The Holy Spirit

Spirit, the word of wisdom; to another the word of knowledge, by the same Spirit; to another faith, by the same Spirit; to another, the gifts of healing, by the same Spirit; to another, the working of miracles; to another, prophecy; to another, discernment of spirits; to another, divers kinds of tongues; to another, the interpretation of tongues; but all these worketh that one and selfsame Spirit, dividing to every man severally as he will."—1 Cor. 12:4-11

Here are enumerated some of the **gifts** given by the Holy Spirit to the Church, but we are to distinguish sharply between the Holy Spirit itself and these gifts or manifestations granted in the early Church. As they were not to understand that different spirits were operating in the different members of the Church, because of the differences of their gifts, so they were not to understand that it was a different Lord or Master that gave these gifts, but all were to be identified as of the one holy influence shed forth by the one Lord, the representative of the one God over all, Jehovah; and to be explained as **"differences of administration,"** or of operation. Not only so, but the Spirit of God, the Holy Spirit, has varied its administration in the Church: so that, whereas **"gifts"** of the kind here mentioned were general in the early Church, the day came, as the apostle explained it would come, when prophecy would fail, tongues would cease, and special inspirations of knowledge would vanish away. (1 Cor. 13:8) All of these **"gifts"** were evidently necessary at the inauguration of the Church, at the start of the new age, but became unnecessary after the Church had been established and the canon of the inspired writings had been completed. These, the apostle declares, are sufficient, "that the man of God may be thoroughly furnished unto all good works."—2 Tim. 3:17

True, not all of these gifts have vanished away or ceased; nor does the cessation of those which have been discontinued prove that the Lord has less power today than he had eighteen centuries ago; nor do they prove that the Lord's people are less worthy or less favored of the Lord. On the contrary, they indicate a "diversity of manifestation," and imply that God's people no longer have need of those cruder methods of instruction and proofs of their acceptance with the Lord. Now, instead of having such gifts miraculously bestowed, the operation of God's Spirit or power seems to be upon each of his consecrated people—partly in proportion to their natural qualifications, and partly in proportion to their zeal for his service. And hence we find that the apostle, in this connection, and in later epistles, incites the Church to seek to **develop** spiritual gifts, powers, abilities, in and for the service of the Lord and his people and his Truth.

These **personally** developed gifts are to be esteemed more highly than those **miraculously bestowed;** and hence the apostle says, "I show unto you a more excellent way"; "follow after love and desire [cultivate] spiritual gifts, especially that ye may prophesy [publicly expound]." (1 Cor. 12:31; 14:1) The apostle points out that the speaking with tongues was merely for "a sign," that the attention of the unbelievers might be drawn to the Church and her methods. (1 Cor. 14:22) And this gift, therefore, which was highly esteemed by some of the Corinthians, he points out as being one of the least spiritual—adapted less to the development of the spiritual Church, and chiefly useful in connection with the unregenerate world. This gift, and others of a somewhat similar class, quickly disappeared from the Church after she had obtained a footing and a recognition in the world.

On the contrary, the **"fruits** of the Spirit" are to be encouraged, to be cultivated more and more, that they may yield the full, perfect fruitage of love toward God, to each other, and the love of sympathy toward the world. These fruits of the Spirit are designated by the apostle to be "love, joy, peace, longsuffering, gentleness, goodness, faith, meekness, temperance." (Gal. 5:22, 23) The word "fruit," it will be noticed, conveys a double thought, that it is a

The Holy Spirit

gift, but of gradual development and maturity, and the result of labor. So with the gifts of the Spirit: "Every good gift and perfect gift cometh down from our Father," but such-like fruits are not miraculous gifts but gradual and indirect gifts, inspired by our Father's promises, and by our Lord's instructions through the apostles and prophets. They are wrought out in us in proportion as we come into harmony and obedience of thought and word and deed with the Spirit of our Father, by which we are begotten, and by which, if obedient, we are having developed more and more of the fruits of holiness, or fruits of the Holy Spirit or disposition in likeness of God's dear Son, our Lord and Redeemer. Thus, under the ministration of the Holy Spirit of the Truth, the faithful are being fitted to be "born of the Spirit" in the first resurrection, spirit beings; as they were begotten of the Spirit at the moment of consecration. Thus perfected as spirit beings, the Church will be heirs of God, joint-heirs with Jesus Christ, our Lord, in fullness of unity and fellowship with the Father and with the Son, complete in him, who is the head of all principalities and powers, and the Father's associate in the Kingdom, and full of the Spirit of the Father and of the Son—the Holy Spirit.

It will be seen from the foregoing general views of the subject that the same Spirit or power of the heavenly Father, Jehovah, which operated in the creation of the world, and which operated differently upon his servants of the past, is, during this Gospel age, operating still differently, for the development of the Church, in the bringing of the Church into harmony with God, and in fitting and preparing it as the "Body of Christ" for a joint share in the Kingdom. And it will be the same Holy Spirit or influence of God that will operate still differently during the Millennial age, through Christ and the Church glorified, to bring the world into harmony and unity with the principles of righteousness, and with the King of kings and Lord of lords. Nothing connected with this work in any sense or degree makes necessary another God. Quite the contrary. The fact that it is the one God who is operating under various circumstances and conditions, and by various means, for the accomplishment of his one purpose, gives us all the more assurance that all his good purposes shall be accomplished, and that, as he declares, "The word that goeth forth out of my mouth, it shall not return unto me void, but shall prosper in the thing whereto I sent it."—Isa. 55:11

DIVINE WILL, INFLUENCE, POWER, SPIRIT

From the foregoing we perceive that a broad definition of the words "Spirit of God," or "Holy Spirit," would be—the divine **will, influence,** or **power,** exercised any and everywhere, and for any purpose in harmony with the divine will, which, being a holy will, implies that the steps and operations of the Holy Spirit will be in harmony with holiness. God exercises his Spirit or energy in many ways, using various agencies in accomplishing various results. Whatever is accomplished by the Lord through either mechanical or intelligent agencies, is as truly his work as though he were the direct actor, since all those agencies are of his creation. Just as, amongst men, the contracting builder may not be actually working on every part of the construction, but every workman is his representative and under his control: the work, as a whole, is the contractor's work, though he may never have lifted a tool upon it. He does it with his materials and through his representatives and agents.

Thus, for instance, when we read, "Jehovah God created the heavens and the earth" (Gen. 2:4), we are not to suppose that he personally handled the elements. He used various agencies—"He spake and it was done [he gave orders and they were promptly executed]; he commanded, and it stood fast." (Psa. 33:6, 9) Creation did not spring instantly into order; for we read that time was used—six days or epochs. And while we are distinctly informed that "All things are of the Father"—by his energy, his will, his Spirit, yet that energy, as we have previously seen, was exercised through his Son, the **Logos**.

The transforming power of God's Holy Spirit, as it operates during this Gospel dispensation, to bring his people into full **at-one-ment** with himself, is a more abstruse, a less easily understood operation, than the exercise of his power mentioned in Genesis 1:2. It deals with a higher subject—with mind and free will instead of senseless matter.

In the light of the Scriptures we may understand the Holy Spirit to mean:—

(a) God's power exercised in any manner, but always according to lines of justice and love, and hence always a holy power.

(b) This power may be an energy of life, a physically creative power, or a power of thought, creating and inspiring thoughts and words, or a quickening or life-giving power, as it was manifested in the resurrection of our Lord, and will again be manifested in the resurrection of the Church, his body.

(c) The begetting or transforming power or influence of the knowledge of the Truth. In this aspect it is designated "The Spirit of Truth." God rules his own course according to truth and righteousness; hence, God's Word, the revelation of his course, is called Truth—"Thy word is Truth." Similarly, all who come under the influence of God's plan of Truth and righteousness are properly said to be under the influence of the Spirit or disposition of the Truth: they are properly described as begotten of the Truth to newness of life.

The Father draws sinners to Christ through a general enlightenment of the mind, a conviction of sin and of their need of a Redeemer. Those who accept Christ as their Savior and Advocate, and come to the point of full consecration to God, through Christ, are said to be **begotten** of God, "begotten by the word of truth," begotten by the Spirit of God to a newness of life. That is to say, having come into harmony with divine conditions and regulations.

God accepts this consecrated attitude as the proper one, and passing by or covering the weakness of the flesh with the robe of Christ's righteousness—justification by faith, he accepts such as "new creatures in Christ Jesus," whose desire is to be guided by his Spirit into all truth, and to be led by that holy disposition or Spirit into full obedience to the extent of self-sacrifice, even unto death. Such are said to have received "the Spirit of adoption," because from thenceforth God, through Christ, enters into a special covenant with these as sons. And the Father, through the Captain of their Salvation, guarantees to such that if they abide in **the Spirit of the Truth** he will cause that all the affairs and incidents of life shall work together for good to them—to the development in them of more and more of the spirit of righteousness, truth, peace, joy; they shall have more and more of the Holy Spirit, as they progress in obedience to the Spirit of Truth. Hence the exhortation to such is, "Be ye filled with the Spirit," "walk in the Spirit," "let the Spirit of Christ dwell in you richly and abound, and it shall make you to be neither barren nor unfruitful." This Holy Spirit operating in the believer from the time of his full **consecration to the Lord, is the same** Holy Spirit or **disposition of the Father** which operated in our Lord Jesus Christ, and hence it is also styled "the Spirit of Christ," and we are assured, "if any man have not the Spirit of Christ he is none of his."—Rom. 8:9

THE SPIRIT BY "MEASURE" AND "WITHOUT MEASURE"

Our Lord Jesus was begotten of the Holy Spirit at his baptism, his consecration; and so likewise the members of his body, his Church, we have seen, are "begotten" at their "baptism into his death," at the moment of their full consecration: but there is a distinction to be always remembered; viz., that our Lord Jesus, the Head of the Church, received the Holy Spirit **without measure,** unlimitedly (John 3:34), while his followers receive it by measure, or limitedly—a measure of the Spirit is given to every man (in the Church). (1 Cor. 12:7; Rom. 12:3) The reason for this difference is that our Lord was a perfect man, while we, his followers, although accepted as reckonedly perfect (justified by faith), are actually very imperfect. The perfect man as the very image of God could be in the fullest harmony with God and with his Spirit of holiness, in every and all particulars; but in proportion to the degradation through the fall, our harmony with God and with his Spirit of holiness has been impaired, though it is the duty and privilege of each to thoroughly seek to know and to do the Lord's will and to have no will in opposition to his; yet no member of the fallen race is capable of receiving the Lord's Spirit to the full—to be in absolute harmony with God in every particular. And hence, amongst those who believe, and who consecrate themselves, and who receive the Holy Spirit of adoption, we find it possessed in different measures, these measures depending upon the degree of our fall from the divine image, and the degree of grace and faith attained since coming into the body of Christ. And the rapidity with which we may acquire more and more of the Holy Spirit, coming into fuller and fuller knowledge and accord with every feature of the divine plan, is dependent largely upon our realization of our own imperfections, and the degree of our consecration to the Lord—to the study of his will, in his Word, and to the practice of the same in the affairs of life.

To the extent that the consecrated believers resign themselves to the Lord, and, ignoring their own wills and preferences, seek to walk in his way, they are "led of the Spirit," "taught of the Spirit," and can "serve the Lord in **newness of Spirit.**" To continue under this leading and instruction they must have a "Spirit of meekness" (Gal. 5:22, 23; 6:1), so that the "God of our Lord Jesus Christ, the Father of glory," can give unto them the **"Spirit of wisdom and revelation,** in the knowledge of him; the eyes of their understanding being enlightened, that they may know what is the hope of his calling, and what the riches of the glory of his inheritance in the saints."—Eph. 1:17, 18

In these various presentations of the work of the Holy Spirit, and in many others which will come to the attention of Bible students, nothing can be found to necessitate **another** God. Quite the contrary: a proper conception of the one God shows that his **omnipotent power and resources are abundantly sufficient, and** that he who said to Israel, "Hear, O Israel, Jehovah thy God is one," is not in need of assistance. Indeed, to be consistent, those who claim that another God is necessary to attend to matters referred to as the operation of the Holy Spirit of God, might with equal consistency claim many spirit Gods —a spirit of adoption, spirit of meekness, spirit of Christ, spirit of the Father, spirit of love, spirit of justice, spirit of mercy, spirit of holiness, spirit of truth, spirit of patience, spirit of glory, spirit of knowledge, spirit of grace—a separate God for each department. But, as the apostle explains, all these variations of operation belong to the one Spirit of the one omnipotent Jehovah.

THE SPIRIT OF THE WORLD
—THE SPIRIT OF ANTICHRIST

The spirit of the world is the opposite to the Spirit of God. Since the whole world is in a fallen condition, and is under the blinding and seducing influences of the Adversary, its spirit or disposition necessarily is in constant conflict with the holy, the true, the just, the loving Spirit or disposition of God: in conflict therefore with the Holy Spirit received by his people through his Word, and all his holy influences variously exercised upon them. As Satan's spirit of selfishness, hatred, envy and strife works in and largely controls the children of this world, so the Holy Spirit of God, the Spirit of love, gentleness, meekness, patience, goodness, brotherly kindness.

works in and largely controls the children of God. And these two spirits or dispositions, the one of love and goodness, the other of selfishness and evil, are in conflict continually, and wholly irreconcilable.

The Scriptures speak of this spirit which is working in the world in opposition to the Holy Spirit, as "the spirit of Antichrist"—the spirit or disposition which is opposed to Christ. First, it desires to ignore him entirely, to dispute that he ever came into the world; then if unsuccessful in this, it will claim that our Lord Jesus was a mere man, a sinful man; if this position be disproved, it will still claim that anyway he accomplished nothing, or that he was merely an example, and not a Redeemer. Hence we are enjoined by the Scriptures to test, to try, to prove the spirits (the doctrines that present themselves to us, claiming to be of the spirit of truth). We are to test them, not merely by their outward appearance and claims, but by the Word of God. "Beloved, believe not every spirit, but try the spirits, whether they are of God . . . and know the Spirit of truth and the spirit of error."—1 John 4:1, 6

HOLY AND UNHOLY INFLUENCES AT WARFARE

God's perfections of character are the standards for holiness, righteousness and truth for all his creatures. Every thing and every creature opposed to or not in full accord with the standards is unholy, untrue, unrighteous. These adverse influences are sometimes credited to Satan because he is the arch-enemy of God and was the first conspirator against righteousness—the originator of error, "the father of lies" and deceptions. But we are to distinguish between evil spirit beings and evil spirit influences just as we do between holy spirit beings and holy spirit influences. The trend of evolutionary thought among educated people who neglect the Bible (including so-called Higher Critics), is to ignore the personality of Satan and his associated wicked spirits in exalted positions (Eph. 6:12), and to claim that there is no evil influence **per se,** and that man merely contends with his own ignorance and misdirection of his own good qualities. Similarly, others, still farther advanced (in error), still more highly educated (in untruth), and still further panoplied with philosophies (falsely so called), are reaching the conclusion that there is no **personal God** but merely good influences which they claim inhere in man and are gradually being evolved to perfection.

But we are giving heed to the oracle of God, his Word, which the apostle assures us is able to make wise unto salvation, and which we have found to contain a fountain of life and light and Holy Spirit of truth with which human theories and lights cannot compare. It shows us that God is a Holy Spirit (**being**), and that his Holy Spirit (**influence**) is always exercised in harmony with righteousness, and that all who are in harmony with God and in **at-one-ment** with him must have his Spirit of holiness—The Only Begotten Son in whom dwells the fullness of the divine Spirit—the holy angels who have no other will than the Father's holy will or Spirit—the Church from among men who have some measure of the mind or Spirit of their Head (else they are none of his), and who are seeking to be more and more filled with this Spirit of holiness and divested of all unholy disposition and influences. Likewise the Word teaches that Satan is a spirit (being) and has an unholy spirit, mind, disposition; and exercises an unholy spirit or influence through various channels and agents.* The fallen angels, also spirit beings, fell by losing their spirit of holiness and devotion to God and his righteous standards, and are now of unholy spirit or disposition, and exercise an evil influence or spirit as they have opportunity.† And the world of mankind, falling through Adam, have become servants of sin: some sin voluntarily for the

---

*ZION'S WATCH TOWER, Aug. 1, 1894.

†See chapter, "Spirits and Spiritism," in the booklet, "Hope Beyond the Grave." Price 10 Cents.

The Holy Spirit

pleasures of sin; some involuntarily, though "feeling after God," and blinded and deceived by the Adversary, and controlled by the spirit of error.

Mankind—the minds or "hearts" of men—is the battle ground on which the Holy Spirit of light, love, justice, truth, holiness, the Spirit of Jehovah and of his Son, man's Redeemer, contends with the evil spirit of Satan, sin, darkness, untruth, hatred, envy, malice, etc. Sold under sin, by our first parent, Adam, his family became "slaves of sin" "through frailty," through the weakness of heredity. (Rom. 5: 12, 21; 6:16-23; 7:14; 8:20, 21) In this captive condition they have been blinded by the god (ruler) of the present evil world (condition) who puts evil before their minds as good, and darkness for light (2 Cor. 4:4; Eph. 6:12; Isa. 5:20), and having thus perverted the vast majority, and made it easy to do evil and difficult to do good, and having ranged all the advantages of the present time on the side of evil and made it impossible to attain these except by conforming to his unholy spirit, which is "the spirit of the world," he has general control, first of the masses through ignorance, and secondly, of the more intelligent through pride, selfishness, etc.

The **battle** did not begin until our Lord's first advent; for the Spirit of Truth came first upon our Lord Jesus and at Pentecost upon his Church.* The world was dark when our Lord Jesus appeared in it filled with the Spirit of God, the light of divine truth, which constituted him "The Light of the world"; and at once the **battle** began; the true light, the holy Spirit, since Pentecost, being represented, not by the nominal churches, but by the true members of Christ's body, possessors of the Holy Spirit of their

---

*The **battle** of the Law of Righteousness was confined to the one little nation, Israel, and as God foresaw "The Law made nothing **perfect**"—none of the fallen race could or were expected to win in that fight. It was really to manifest Christ Jesus, the only Law-keeper, as the channel of divine mercy; and incidentally to discipline a people and make "a remnant" of them ready for the Spirit Dispensation and its conflicts by pointing to Christ.

Head. The battle could not commence sooner because none of mankind (all being sinners) could be the channels of God's Holy Spirit, his representatives, —ambassadors for righteousness and truth, soldiers of the cross. **Atonement for man's sin** must first be made before there would be any mission for the Holy Spirit to perform—before there would be anything to **battle for.** Mankind was sentenced to death—to everlasting destruction, as enemies of righteousness: why battle for the doomed? why try to influence them to righteousness, when no hope of reward for their efforts could be held out? Properly therefore the **ransom** came first; and it was as a result of the acceptance of that ransom by the Father that the Holy Spirit was granted to those adopted into his family as sons through Christ.

But some one may observe that the **battle,** ever since it began, seems to be against the Holy Spirit and in favor of the spirit of evil—since the servants of sin today by natural increase of population are many times more numerous than they were when the battle began, and are still increasing much more rapidly than even nominal Christianity, though the battle has been in progress for nearly nineteen centuries.

Furthermore the spirit of evil and malice and error triumphed against the Holy Spirit in our Lord to the extent of crucifying him: and similarly it has triumphed against all the faithful members of the body of Christ—misrepresenting, slandering and evilly entreating them, variously, according to time, place and circumstances. The object of these attacks of the spirit of evil and its servants upon the Spirit of holiness and its faithful is ever the same—to undermine the influence of the Spirit of the truth; to make the holy appear unholy; to cause that the pure and unselfish shall appear selfish and impure; to put darkness for light. Nor do the servants of unholiness always realize what they do: becoming imbued with the spirit of evil, the spirit of hatred, malice, envy, strife, it blinds them so that they "know not what they do," and often, evidently, "verily think that they do God service." Why this defeat of the Spirit of holiness? Will it always be thus?

We answer that this defeat of the Spirit of holiness is merely a seeming defeat and not an actual one. Actually the Spirit of holiness has been triumphing ever since the battle began. Its two-fold mission during this Gospel age has been well accomplished.

(1) It was to be **in God's people** according to the degree of their consecration and zeal toward God and his righteousness, and by reason of the prevalence and power of the spirit of evil in the world about them was to prove a test of their characters, present conditions demanding that whosoever would **live godly** in this present time must suffer persecution—must be willing to have "all manner of evil" falsely spoken against them and yet take it patiently, as did their Master, continuing, nevertheless, faithful to the Lord and his cause at any cost—counting not their earthly lives dear unto them.—2 Tim. 3:12; Matt. 5:11; 1 Pet. 2:23; Acts 20:24

(2) The light of the Spirit of holiness in God's people was to so shine forth **upon** the world that it would attract all not thoroughly blinded by the perverse spirit of the Adversary. It was to shine into the darkness of sin **reprovingly**—witnessing against all unrighteousness; thus awakening the conscience of even the blinded to a realization of responsibility to God and a future day of reckoning. Thus our Lord instructed his followers that after receiving the Holy Spirit they were to **witness** to the Truth amongst all nations—whether the people hear or whether they forbear.

The Holy Spirit has triumphed in both the objects for which it was sent. It has selected a faithful "little flock" of "overcomers," followers of the way of righteousness—Jesus the Captain and his faithful band of soldiers of the cross, all of whom consecrated "even unto death"; and to whom the Kingdom reward will soon be given—when the last members have been fully tested and made perfect through sufferings for righteousness' sake. It has also triumphed in respect to **witnessing** to the world. Our Lord foretold that the effect of the witnessing would be to convince the world of sin, of righteousness and of a coming day of righteous judgment, in which evil deeds of the present life will have a just retribution, according to the degree of light enjoyed by the transgressor.

This witness has gone far and near, and today the world as a whole recognizes these three items which the Spirit of holiness in the Church has set before it—sin, righteousness and judgment. True, the world has not clear and correct ideas of righteousness, nor of sin, nor does it understand the character and object of the coming judgment—nor that it will be a thousand-year day: nor does the world understand clearly the Church's call during this age, to escape judgment with the world and to become its judges in that judgment day by now **voluntarily sacrificing** earthly interests for righteousness' sake—following in the footsteps of the Redeemer. It is not necessary for the world to know these particulars—they do not concern it. These are among "the deep things of God," which none can appreciate except as they become heartily obedient to the Lord's call to righteousness, and consecrating themselves receive of the Spirit of the Father, and as sons are thus made acquainted with the minutiae of the divine plan.—1 Cor. 2:10, 11

In reply to the query, Will it always be thus? we answer, No. As soon as this age has developed the "little flock," called to be joint-heirs with Christ, it will cease. The next operation of Jehovah's Holy Spirit or power will be the establishment of that Kingdom: and with its establishment the Holy Spirit's operation will be along the Kingdom lines—establishing judgment and justice in the earth. It will lay judgment to the line and justice to the plummet, and falsehood and deception of every kind will give place to clear knowledge of the Truth. Instead of longer witnessing to the world a **"judgment to come,"** it will witness to it that judgment has commenced and that every transgression will promptly receive a just recompense of punishment. Instead of witnessing to the Church, "Judge nothing **before the time**," it will witness to the contrary that they as God's instruments have been specially qualified to judge the world with a righteous judgment. Instead of those in harmony with God and possessed of his Spirit of righteousness and truth being required to suffer for righteousness' sake they will be crowned kings and priests of righteousness and commissioned to reign over the earth for its blessing and restitution to perfection, to righteousness, and the "cutting off from life," in "everlasting destruction" of all who wilfully reject the opportunities of the blessed day of judgment secured by the love of God through the ransom given by our Lord Jesus. Thus shall the great Jehovah and his Spirit of holiness and all who ally themselves thereto finally triumph, and sin and Satan and the spirit of evil shall be forever extinguished and there shall be no more curse.—Isa. 28: 17; 1 Cor. 4:5; 6:2; Acts 3:23; 2 Thess. 1:9; Rev. 22:3

SPIRIT FIGHTINGS WITHOUT AND WITHIN THE SAINTS

We have considered the battle as a whole: let us glance at some of its present phases. While it may be considered as the Church's conflict it is nevertheless an **individual** conflict with sin. While the Church will come off conqueror, it will be composed only of the individual victors. And as the victory in the Church is a victory of God's Holy Spirit, power or influence against the spirit of evil, of unrighteousness, it is the same in the individual saint.

The majority of Christian people (nominal Christians, even including so-called "spirit wrestlers," "sanctificationists," etc.) know little about the real spirit battles and victories, because the majority have never made the proper consecration, and have never received the Holy Spirit of the Truth. Some have consecrated themselves to a sect, and have received a sectarian spirit of love for the sect, devotion to the sect, service and sacrifice for the sect, etc. Others have recognized one or more moral principles and have consecrated themselves never to violate those moralities: these receive the spirit of moralities, a self-satisfied spirit, a self-righteous spirit. Others have singled out some virtue which they worship and whose spirit they receive—for instance, patience—and they are fully satisfied when they have attained a good degree of patience and its spirit. Others consecrate themselves to "work" for Jesus and seem satisfied only when they are in a bustle of exciting activity; it matters little to them what kind the work is, so that it is not openly serving Satan and so that there is plenty of it and they have a prominent place: it is not so much results they seek as work, and hence they are quite content to "beat the air," hoping that in the end they will find that they have not done much harm. For these to take time to study God's Word and to ascertain the kind of workmen he seeks, and the kind of work he desires to have done, would be to them a violation of their covenant of consecration—for they consecrated themselves to work and are satisfied of heart only when they are in a fever of excitement. Others more wise, but not truly wise either, consecrate themselves to a particular kind of service, for God and man—the service which **they** think needs them most. If they **consecrate** to "temperance work," they receive the spirit of that work and have whatever blessing comes with it. Or if they **consecrate** to social reform work they get the spirit of social reform and its blessings.

All of these consecrations, and the spirits or dispositions resulting, have both good and evil influences. Any of them is far better than a consecration to evil and its spirit of evil. Any of them is far better even than consecration to self and the spirit of selfishness accompanying it. Any of them is far better even than an aimless life consecrated to nothing. But none of these can compare in any sense to the consecration taught in the Scriptures and exemplified in our Lord Jesus Christ, the Redeemer of the world, the exemplar of his body, the Church. This, the true consecration, alone brings to the heart the Holy Spirit, the Spirit of the Truth, which the world cannot receive.

This true, proper consecration differs from all others. It has but the one shrine at which it bows: it bows to Jehovah's will, surrendering self and self-will a living sacrifice on the Lord's altar, a reasonable service. It makes no stipulations or reservations. The language of the Chief Priest is that of each member of the "royal priesthood:" "I came not to do mine own will, but the will of him that sent me." "Lo I come (as in the volume of the book it is written of me) to do thy will, O God." Such are made partakers of the Holy Spirit.

Those who have consecrated their wills, and accepted unreservedly the Word and will of God, through Christ, are said to be heavenly or **spiritually minded.** These are so transformed, so entirely different from what they were in their former earthly condition, that they are called New Creatures, and this name would not be inappropriate to them if it signified nothing more than the radical change of heart or will which they have experienced. But it does mean more; it means that these who are now being selected from the world by the Holy Spirit of Truth, and who are approaching God through the new and living way which was opened up by the great sacrifice for sins, are really embryo new creatures, whose perfection in the divine nature only waits for the resurrection change, in the end of this age, conditioned wholly upon their faithfulness as new creatures to the leadings of the Holy Spirit.

However, this new mental creation, or transformed mind, the embryo of the new creature, which shall come fully into being in the resurrection, is still identified with a human body, and thus the apostle says of this class, "We have this treasure [the new mind, the new nature] in earthen vessels." (2 Cor. 4:7) Speaking of the same thing, the apostle assures us that when the earthly house is dissolved, sacrificed, dead with Christ, we shall, nevertheless, have a building of God, a new house, a glorious body, in harmony with and in every way fitted for the indwelling of the new mind and its Spirit of holiness (2 Cor. 5:1), if we are of the faithful over-comers who continue to the end of the pilgrimage of the narrow way, walking in the footsteps of our Captain.

The word **holy** is derived from the word **whole** and signifies completeness; hence the Holy Spirit is a whole or a complete spirit. And thus we see without surprise that those who have received the Holy Spirit or complete spirit in any good measure are thereby rounded out on all sides of their characters —better balanced than ever before in their judgments—they have "the Spirit of a sound mind," however the enmitous blinded spirit of the world may declare of them, "Thou hast a devil and art mad"; because they live for, labor for and enjoy the things unseen as yet, everlasting in the heavens.— 2 Tim. 1:7; John 10:20; 6:27

Individually considered, one of the most serious foes of those who have been begotten to holiness of spirit through the divine counsels and promises, is the evil spirit of fear. It would persuade us that probably there is some mistake: either that God did not inspire the exceeding great and precious promises, or that they are not for us, or that for some reason we can never attain them. All of God's people are liable to attack from this wrong spirit of doubt and fear—some more and some less persistently; and all have need to fight down this evil spirit courageously and to destroy it, lest it kill the fruits of the Holy Spirit and finally quench it—drive it out of us entirely.

Yet "the spirit of fear" is neither a spirit god nor a spirit devil that has gotten into our hearts: it is simply a mental influence natural to every fallen human being of humble mind. It is begotten of the realization of personal imperfection and unworthiness of divine favors. The antidote for this spirit of fear is the Holy Spirit of Truth, and its instructions accepted and held in full assurance of faith.

The Holy Spirit

The Spirit of Truth tells us that there were good reasons for our entertainment of the spirit of fear; but that those reasons no longer exist since we have come into Christ as new creatures. It points us away from our unintentional weakness to the great Atonement accomplished by our Lord Jesus, and cites to us the words of the inspired apostle:—

"If God be for us, who can be against us? He that spared not his own Son, but delivered him up [to death] for us all, how shall he not with him also freely give us all things [needful]? Who shall lay anything to the charge of those whom God chooses? It is God that justifieth. Who could condemn these? It is Christ that died [paying their penalty—making good all their deficiencies], yea, rather that [glorified and highly exalted Christ who] is risen again, who is even at the right hand of God, who also maketh intercession for us."—Rom. 8:31-34

If the "Spirit of faith," one of the phases or operations of the "Spirit of holiness," the "Spirit of the Truth," thus comes forward and is accepted and supported by the new creature, the victory over the spirit of fear is speedily won, and peace and joy in the Holy Spirit of faith and love and confidence in God results. Nevertheless, these battles must be fought time and again in every Christian's experience. And, indeed, the "spirit of fear" may be made a valuable **servant** of the new creature, while it cannot be tolerated as a master, nor as a friend and a resident of the heart. Make it the watchdog, and kennel it just outside the door of the heart, and it may serve a very useful purpose in calling attention to thieves and robbers who approach stealthily to rob us of our treasures of holiness, joy, peace, love and fellowship with our Father and with the brethren. As the apostle urges, "let us fear" attacks from without after we have gotten all right with God by casting out all opposing influences and receiving his Spirit into our hearts. Let us fear lest as those who are ready to go forth with the Bridegroom in the early morning any of us should be overcome with a spirit of slothfulness, a spirit of carelessness, a spirit of slumber, and so, like the "foolish virgins" be unprepared for the great event—"the marriage" —for which all our preparations have been made.

Let us remember, then, that however useful as a servant, the spirit of fear is not of God, and must never be admitted within the castle of the Christian heart, which must be fully given over to the occupancy of the various members of the Holy Spirit family—love, joy, peace, etc., for perfect love casteth out fear as well as all the members of the unholy spirit family—anger, malice, hatred, jealousy, fear, discontent, pride, worldly ambitions etc. The apostle declares—"God hath not given us the spirit of fear; but the Spirit of superhuman strength and of love, and of a sound mind."—2 Tim. 1:7

Sometimes the attack comes from the rear and not from the front—fear for friends, fear for the world, etc., an unwillingness to trust God for others though willing to trust him for one's self. This is a serious matter, too; for it largely drives out the spirit of peace and joy and misdirects the energies. The **"spirit of fear"** says, It is a great mistake to think that Christ died for all; and it is a great presumption to believe that all must eventually obtain some blessing of opportunity for life, as a result of the ransom. Or, if fear fail to win us, its evil companion, the **"spirit of error,"** may attempt to lead in the opposite direction, to get us to believe in universal salvation to eternal life—suggesting pride on God's part, that would hinder him from destroying the wilfully wicked.

The "spirit of error" assumes to be wiser than the Word of God, and suggests to human reason that it should judge God according to its own standards, rather than correct its own standards by the Word of divine revelation. Thus, in various ways, the spirit of error, the spirit of fear, and the spirit of bondage, which are all elements of the spirit of the Adversary, the unholy Spirit, give the lie to the statements of the Spirit of Truth, which declare that "Christ Jesus by the grace of God tasted death for every man," and that the blessed opportunity of coming into harmony with God, under the conditions of the New Covenant, shall ultimately be extended to every creature; and that when each one is brought to a knowledge of the Truth he is judged thereby, and either approved unto everlasting life, or condemned to everlasting destruction, the second death. "Hereby discern we the Spirit of Truth from the spirit of error."—1 John 4:5, 6; Acts 3:23

The Spirit of God, the Spirit of holiness, is a spirit of joy and peace in all who receive it, in proportion as they receive it—in proportion as they come into accord with the heavenly Father and with the Redeemer who has the same mind or disposition. The Spirit of the Lord leads to faith in God's promises; the spirit of error leads in the contrary direction, to unbelief in the promises of God, and to human speculations and credulity and superstition—to the believing of things which God has not spoken, and which are unreasonable to those who have the "Holy Spirit," "the Spirit of a sound mind." The Spirit of Truth leads to activity and energy in the divine cause, appreciating the privilege of being a co-worker together with God to any extent; the spirit of error, on the contrary, is a "spirit of slumber" and of carelessness in heavenly things, and of carefulness for earthly things—of carelessness for the true Church and its bond of love, and of carefulness for human organizations and their creed-bonds.—Rom. 11:8

THE SPIRIT THAT LUSTETH TO ENVY

As already noted, God's consecrated children—**spirit-begotten** "new creatures" are at present **dual** beings; the new not fully developed, not yet "born," and having no body suitable, lives in the old body of flesh reckoned dead—captured by the renewed will for its use and service during the period of its development. (This however does not imply that Christians are of two **natures,** for such a thought is contrary to the science of the Bible.) The new spirit, the mind of Christ, the holy disposition or will, alone is recognized by God, and should alone be recognized by the "holy brethren, partakers of the heavenly calling"; nevertheless there is a continual warfare between this new disposition begotten by the Word of God and the old will, spirit or disposition of our fallen flesh. Sometimes in Scripture the contrary will or disposition of our flesh is spoken of as our spirit, as when we read, "Do ye think that the Scripture saith in vain, The spirit that dwelleth in us ['In our flesh dwelleth no perfect thing.'] lusteth to envy?"—James 4:5

The new spirit, the new creature, that begotten of the Holy Spirit of love, does not envy; as it is written, "Love envieth not, is not puffed up, etc." (1 Cor. 13:4) Whenever, therefore, we find the spirit of envy, hatred, strife or vainglory in any degree controlling our actions or words or thoughts, it is a sure sign that our former evil spirit is gaining a victory over us as new creatures. And proportionately as we can and do put away all these and are filled with the elements of the Holy Spirit—gentleness, goodness, meekness, brotherly kindness, love—we are growing in the image of Christ, who is the image of the Father—in that proportion we are being filled with the Holy Spirit. Not filled with a **spirit person,** but filled with the spirit, influence or will of a person, even of our Father Jehovah—the same spirit which was and still is in the Only Begotten Son.

The Apostle Paul also writes respecting this same battle between the spirit, disposition or mind of our flesh and the new spirit, disposition or mind to which we have been regenerated. But he treats the subject from the **reckoned** standpoint—as though our flesh were no longer we but our enemies, and we recognized only as new creatures and the Holy Spirit our only spirit or disposition. He says:—"This I say then, Walk in the Spirit and ye shall not fulfil the lust [desire] of the flesh. For the flesh lusteth [desires] against the Spirit, and the Spirit against the flesh: and these are contrary the one to the other: so that ye cannot do the things that ye [new creatures] would"—the continual opposition and deceitfulness of the flesh being a hindrance to perfect **deeds**, though by God's grace this does not hinder our acceptance with God as "new creatures," whose hearts, spirits, intentions, are holy and acceptable to the Father in the Beloved One.—Gal. 5:16, 17

TAUGHT OF GOD THROUGH THE SPIRIT

From what we have learned respecting the Spirit of the Lord, and its operation upon his people, through its enlightening influence upon their minds, its removal of errors, and its illumination of the Word giving the living truth, we are prepared to understand and appreciate the apostle's words: "Eye hath not seen, nor ear heard, neither have entered into the heart of man [the natural man], the things which God hath in reservation for them that love him. But God hath revealed them unto us by his Spirit; for the Spirit searcheth all things, yea, the deep things of God." (1 Cor. 2:9, 10) That is to say, having submitted our wills to the Lord, that we might be taught of him, and walk in his way, we have come into harmony with his will, mind, Spirit; and we are prepared, from this new standpoint—the standpoint of a new mind, rightly directed—to see things in a new light—all things become new to us. The new mind, the new will, prompts us to search into the deep things of God, to study the Word of God, that we may know and do his will, as obedient sons. Having the mind or Spirit of our Father, we will take heed to his instructions, in every detail, and seek to walk in harmony with him. "For what man knoweth the things [mind, will, plan] of a man, save the spirit [mind] of man which is in him? Even so the things of God knoweth no man, but the Spirit of God." (1 Cor. 2:11) That is to say, as no man can know another man's mind and plan, except as they are revealed to him, so no one can understand the divine mind and plan, except he come into harmony with the divine mind—receive the Holy Spirit.

"Now we have received the Spirit [mind, disposition or will] of God, that we might know the things that are freely given unto us of God . . . but the natural man receiveth not the things of God, for they are foolishness unto him, neither can he know them, because they are spiritually discerned." They are understood only by those who have the Spirit or mind of God, the Spirit of his plan, the Spirit of the Truth. All such must have dispositions in harmony with righteousness and truth, so far as they understand these principles, and must daily seek to know more of the mind of God, the will of God, and to have more of his Spirit, disposition. Such obedient sons are more and more "filled with the Spirit" of Truth, and the spirit of obedience to it. But they do not gain this condition by comparing spiritual things with natural things, as the natural man is disposed to do, but by following the divine counsel, and "comparing spiritual things with spiritual." (1 Cor. 2:13) "He that is spiritual [who has received the Holy mind or Spirit] judgeth all things [he is able to understand and to properly estimate both human and spiritual things in the light of the divine plan], yet he himself is judged of no man." No natural man can understand or rightly judge the motives which prompt the spiritually minded "new creature" to willingly sacrifice things valuable to the natural man, for hopes and prospects which, to the latter, seem unreal and unreasonable. Hence, the followers of the Lord are "counted as fools" by the worldly-minded, by those who have the spirit of the world.—1 Cor. 2:12-16; 4:10

THE PARAKLETOS, THE COMFORTER

Parakletos is rendered Comforter in John 14:16, 26; but the thought usually conveyed by the word comfort (namely to soothe, to pacify) is not here the correct one. The correct thought is that of help, encouragement, assistance, strengthening. Thus our Lord's promise implied that the Holy Spirit which the Father would send in Jesus' name and as Jesus' representative would be near his followers, a present help in every time of need—the holy power by which he would guide and direct his people and enable them to "walk by faith and not by sight." Indeed, our Lord gives us to understand that all the ministrations of the Spirit are his own ministrations, saying, "I will not leave you orphans, I will come to you" (vs. 18): he thus identifies the Holy Spirit with himself. "If any man have not the Spirit of Christ he is none of his"—and has not the **parakletos,** the divine aid.

This power of God is with the whole Church, yet each receives his share of the holy influence personally—by individual connection with channels of the Spirit. The Truth itself is the main channel of the Spirit of the Truth; but all who are closely connected with the Truth and have its Spirit are to that extent also channels through which the Spirit aids and influences others.

The power or Spirit of God is invisible to men; but its effects are tangible and visible. This may be illustrated by the electric current in the copper wire; it is invisible, but the moment the car, properly supplied with a motor, touches the wire with its arm or "trolley" the power is manifest in the movement of the car. The same current by another arrangement lights the car, and by still another device furnishes it with heat, and by yet a different device communicates by telegraph or telephone. All these are its blessings under favorable arrangements, yet it may so be arranged as to be a death-dealing influence, as in the electrocution chair. So the Holy Spirit is the spiritual energy or power of God—it moves, enlightens, warms and instructs all who, having the proper conditions in themselves, are brought into connection with it through its proper channels; and it may bring death—Second Death, to all wilful sinners. How needful, then, that each of the Lord's people have the proper **equipment** and the proper connections in order to be filled with the Spirit and made active unto all good works!

Nothing connected with this reference to the Holy Spirit as another comforter or helper or strengthener implies that another God is meant or another **person** of a trinity of Gods. The connections show on the contrary that the comforting or strengthening Holy Spirit is the Spirit of the Father and the Spirit of the Son. In verses 18 and 23 the Father and the Son are referred to as the ones who strengthen and guide and comfort the Church—through the Spirit. Thus again our Lord declared, "Lo, I am with you always, even unto the end of the age"—by the Holy Spirit, not in flesh.

It should be remembered that the words **he, him, himself,** used in referring to the **parakletos,** might with equal propriety be translated **she, her, herself, or it, itself. Heautou,** rendered **himself** in this connection, is rendered **itself** nine times in our Common Version Bibles. **Ekinos,** rendered **he** in this connection, is much oftener rendered **that** and **those.** **Ekinos** is rendered **it** in 1 John 5:16—"I do not say that ye shall pray for **it** [the sin unto death]."

HE SHALL GUIDE YOU INTO ALL TRUTH

Our Lord indicated the channel through which this power of God, "the Spirit of the Truth," would come to his people, saying, "The words that I speak unto you, they are spirit and they are life." That is to say, My words express the mind, the will, the Spirit of God. Hence we have continually set before us, as necessary to our victory, the study of the Word of Truth. We hear our Lord's injunction, "Search the Scriptures." We hear the Apostle Paul commending the Bereans' noble conduct, in that "they searched the Scriptures daily." We hear him again saying that "we ought to take the more earnest heed to the words which we have heard"; and we have his exhortation to Timothy, which assures us

The Holy Spirit

that "the Word of God is profitable, that the man of God may be thoroughly furnished unto every good work." We hear the Apostle Peter also urging that "we have a more sure word of prophecy [of divine revelation], to which we do well that we take heed." —John 5:39; Acts 17:11; Heb. 2:1; 2 Tim. 3:17; 2 Pet. 1:19

The promise of being "filled with the Spirit" or mind of God is not to those who merely possess the Word of God, nor to those who merely read the Word of God, but is to those who search it earnestly, seeking to understand it; and who understanding it are willing, nay, anxious to obey it. If we would be **filled** with the Spirit of God, we must drink deeply of the fountain of Truth—his Word. And since our earthen vessels are imperfect, leaky, it is easy to let spiritual things slip (Heb. 2:1); in which case the spirit of the world, which surrounds us constantly, quickly rushes in to fill the vacuum. Indeed, there is a constant **pressure** of the spirit of the world upon the Lord's people, tending to displace the new spirit, the new mind, the Spirit or disposition of holiness. Therefore it behooves all of the Lord's faithful new creatures to live very close to the fountain of Truth, the Lord, and very close to his Word, lest the Spirit of God be quenched, and we be filled instead with the spirit of the world.

It seems expedient to caution some that although a knowledge of the Truth, a knowledge of the Scriptures, is important, essential to the possession of the Spirit of the Truth, nevertheless, one might have much knowledge of the Word of God without having any of its Spirit. To receive the **Spirit** of the Truth is to come into heart harmony with the Truth, to come into mental accord and co-operation with the Divine will expressed in the Word. This condition can be attained in one way only: by first accepting the Lord Jesus as our Redeemer and Justifier, and secondly, consecrating ourselves unreservedly to seek to know and to do his will.

But this "Spirit of the Truth" this "Holy Spirit" or mind in harmony with God and his righteousness, should not be confounded with the **"gifts of the Spir-**

it," nor yet with the **"fruits** of the Spirit," though its possession always yields the latter, "the peaceable fruits of righteousness,"—meekness, patience, gentleness, brotherly kindness, love. The Spirit of the Truth must be ours **before** it can produce such fruits in our daily lives: and in some the period of developing mature fruits, of good size and flavor, is longer than with others; but each should remember our Lord's words, "Herein is my Father glorified, that ye bear much fruit—so shall ye be my disciples." We should remember also his parable of the Vine, in which the branches represent severally his consecrated disciples. Of these he declares, "Every branch in me that beareth **fruit** the Father purgeth [pruneth] it, that it may bring forth more fruit, and every branch that beareth not fruit he taketh away."—John 15:2

The Christian is a branch from the moment of his consecration, and is a partaker of the sap from the root, a partaker of the Holy Spirit, and yet it is not to be expected that he will instantly bear all the fruits of the Spirit, nor any of them in their perfection. The first evidences of the relationship to the Church-Vine will be an association with the other branches, a connection with the root, and evidences of life. Next there will be the feelers or tendrils, by which progress will be sought and attained. Next will come the leaves, or professions; and next to be looked for should be the flower, and later the fruit. But the fruit is extremely small at first, and sour; it requires time to develop grapes of size and flavor acceptable to the great Husbandman. Such are "the fruits of the Spirit" of Christ expected in every "branch" of the Vine—in every member of the body of Christ, the Church. Unless in due time these fruits of the Spirit—meekness, gentleness, patience, brotherly kindness, faith, hope, love—appear, the branch will cease to be considered a branch, and as a "sucker" will be cut off from further affiliation and privilege.

We have already seen that **"the gifts** of the Spirit" granted at the beginning of the Gospel age, for the

The Holy Spirit

establishment of the Church, differed from **"the fruits of the Spirit."** The "gifts" were conferred by the laying on of the hands of the apostles: they came spontaneously only in exceptional cases (Acts 2:4; 10:45): Simon Magus, though baptized and granted a gift for his own use, was unable to confer the gifts to others and was reproved by Peter for offering money to obtain this purely **apostolic** power. (Acts 8:13-21) And the same account makes clear that even Philip the Evangelist, though able to perform "signs and great miracles," could not confer the **gifts** of the Spirit but was obliged to send for the apostles to do this for his converts. All this agrees fully with the statement of the Apostle Paul that many of the gifts would "fail," "vanish away": it was necessarily so when, all the apostles having died, all those upon whom they had conferred those "gifts" died also. The **gifts** of faith, hope and love which the apostle declared would abide were not miraculous gifts but **growths**—"fruits" as he elsewhere describes them.—1 Cor. 13:8; John 15:16

Amongst the gifts of the Spirit the apostle specifies—(1) apostles, (2) prophets, (3) teachers. We still have with us the gift of apostles, in that we have their teachings in the New Testament, so full and complete as to require no addition; and hence the twelve apostles have no successors, and need none, since there are but "twelve apostles of the Lamb"; they are "the twelve stars," the crown of the Church; they are the "twelve foundations" of the Church glorified, the New Jerusalem. (John 6:70; Rev. 12:1; 21:14) We have also still, in the Church, the gifts of prophets or expounders and teachers, servants of God and his Church speaking various languages; but no longer does the Spirit supply these instantly and miraculously without education and talents by the laying on of the apostolic hands. Such miracles are no longer necessary and no longer employed—assuredly not to the same extent as formerly. Instead, the Lord generally makes choice of some who by natural qualifications and education are fitted to his service: nevertheless we are to remember that the condition of the heart is far more important in the Lord's sight than all other qualifications combined; and that he is fully able to use those whom he chooses (because full of his Spirit) to be his special servants and ambassadors: he can providentially supply them with assistance in any manner he may please; as, for instance, to Moses —his special servant who was slow of speech—he gave Aaron to be a mouthpiece.

The Lord's people are not to forget that, although the administration or method has changed, the same Lord by the agency of the same Holy Spirit is still guiding the affairs of his Church—less manifestly, less outwardly discernible, but no less really, no less carefully, and in every detail of its affairs. And all of the Lord's flock led of his Spirit, and taught of his Word, are to judge discriminatingly respecting those who seem to be teachers and evangelists, presenting themselves as such. The Lord's people are not to receive as such all who profess to be teachers and evangelists, but only those whom they discern to be marked of the Lord as having these gifts; and one of the tests is in respect to their fidelity to the Word of God—that they preach not themselves, but Jesus Christ, and him crucified—the power of God and the wisdom of God to every one that believeth. If any man come unto us with any other gospel, we are instructed particularly that we are not to receive him as a teacher of the Truth, but to consider him as a servant of error, whether knowingly or ignorantly so.

Thus does the Spirit or influence of God, the Holy Spirit or influence of the Truth, instruct his people, guiding them (directly or indirectly) in a knowledge of God. Thus it is the channel of at-one-ment now to the Church, and somewhat similarly it will be the channel of at-one-ment to the world in the coming age, when "the Spirit and the Bride [the glorified Church] shall say, Come, take of the water of life freely."—Rev. 22:17

STUDY IX

THE BAPTISM, WITNESS AND SEAL
OF THE
SPIRIT OF AT-ONE-MENT

Spirit Baptism, One Only—In Three Parts—The Significance of this Baptism—"The Keys of the Kingdom of Heaven"—Another Baptism of the Spirit Promised "Upon all Flesh"—Its Significance—Prayer for the Spirit—The Witness of the Spirit—Its Importance—No Peace With God Without It—Few Know Whether They Have It or Not—" 'Tis a Point I Long to Know"—How to Recognize the Spirit's Witness—Differences of Administration—The Spirit's Testimony—"Sanctified by the Spirit"—"Filled With the Spirit" —The Seal of the Spirit—"The Promise" which it Seals— Unto the Day of Deliverance—The Highest Attainment to be Sought—and Retained.

"When the day of Pentecost was fully come, they were all with one accord in one place. And suddenly there came a sound from heaven as of a rushing mighty wind, and it filled all the house where they were sitting. And there appeared unto them cloven tongues like as of fire, and they sat upon each of them. And they were all filled with the Holy Ghost, and began to speak with other tongues, as the Spirit gave them utterance."—Acts 2:1-4

THE DAY of Pentecost was a most notable one in the history of the Gospel Church. It indicated that our Redeemer had appeared in the presence of God for us, as our great High Priest; that he had offered before the Father the merits of his sacrifice, finished at Calvary fifty days previously; that the Father had accepted the sacrifice fully; and consequently that the apostles and believers who had accepted Jesus, and who were desirous of approaching to the Father, and becoming **sons** of God (John 1:12), were now recognized as such—the Holy Spirit thus testifying their acceptance: hence it is termed the "Spirit of adoption" into the family of God. It was appropriate that so important a matter should be clearly demonstrated: it was not only important that the apostles and believers should receive the Holy Spirit, the Spirit of divine favor, in their hearts, but that they should have an outward manifestation which would be a satisfactory proof, not only to themselves but to all subsequent believers, that God had fully accepted the Church as sons and joint-heirs with Christ.

But nothing in connection with this narrative in any sense of the word necessitates the thought of a personal Holy Spirit, separate from the Father and the Son. Quite the contrary: the fact that the Holy Spirit was received in them all of itself implies that the Holy Spirit is not a person, but an influence, a power exerted by a person—the power or influence of God exerted in and upon his newly adopted children. This is further evidenced by the fact that the various powers and talents of the apostles were energized, quickened and enlarged by this influence.

The apostle explains that it was here that our Lord Jesus "gave gifts unto men"—spiritual gifts. (Psa. 68:18; Eph. 4:8) The great gift of his own life had already been given, and constituted the **redemption price** for the whole world—and a portion of the ransomed myriads, a little flock, having been especially given to Christ to be his joint-heirs and associates in the Kingdom, and the selection of this little flock having already begun, as represented in those who waited for the Pentecostal blessing, the time had come for their recognition. It was the Father who there recognized the Church of Christ, in the sense that the impartation of his Holy Spirit, as an influence and power, implied the reconciliation of believers; so that they were no longer treated as sinners and aliens, nor even as servants; now as sons they were made "partakers of the heavenly gift." We are informed that this Holy Spirit, holy influence, holy power, which emanates from its fountain or source, the Father, was poured out, nevertheless, appropriately

Its Baptism, Witness and Seal

by God's honored representative, through whom every blessing of God has come and will come, namely, Christ Jesus our Lord and Head.

The Apostle Peter, speaking under the inspiring influence of the Holy Spirit, explained the matter, that it was **of** the Father and **by** the Son, saying, "Jesus—being by the right hand of God exalted, and having received of the Father the promise of the Holy Spirit, he hath shed forth this which ye now see and hear." (Acts 2:33) Accordingly, there cannot be too much stress laid upon this baptism of the Holy Spirit, seeing that it marks the acceptance of the Church, and that without it we would have no proof of the acceptance of our Lord's sacrifice and of our justification.

However, we must most emphatically object to the common but erroneous and thoroughly unscriptural idea which prevails amongst many very earnest Christians, to the effect that frequent baptisms of the Holy Spirit are to be expected and sought. Such an expectation not only is unwarranted by any promises given us in the Word of God, but is thoroughly at variance with the divine arrangement therein laid down. It should be noticed that the Scriptures mention only three baptisms of the Holy Spirit; and the necessity for each of these, and for no more, is manifest—the three being parts or divisions of the one baptism. (1) The baptism of our Lord Jesus. (2) The baptism at Pentecost. (3) The baptism of Cornelius, the first Gentile convert accepted as a "son." Let us examine these baptisms of the Spirit in this order.

(1) Not only was our Lord's baptism of the Holy Spirit necessary to himself, that he might be a partaker of the divine power; as the divine agent, and as the earnest of his inheritance, his begetting to the divine nature; but it was proper also that there should be such an outward manifestation or recognition of him as would permit others to know him as God's Anointed. The manifestation was that of a dove descending and lighting upon him. Nor are we given to understand that the people in general wit-

nessed this manifestation of divine favor; the understanding rather is that John the Baptist, who was at the time doing a reformatory work in Israel, and who was recognized as a prophet, a servant of the Lord, alone witnessed the descent of the Spirit upon our Lord, and he bore testimony to the fact. The statement is, "And John **bare record**, saying, I saw the Spirit descending from heaven, like a dove, and it abode upon him; and I knew him not [knew not that he was the Messiah]: but he that sent me to baptize with water the same said unto me, Upon whom thou shalt see the Spirit descending and remaining upon him, the same is he which baptizeth with the Holy Spirit. And I saw, and bare record, that this is the Son of God."—John 1:33

(2) The baptism of the Church at Pentecost, as John here explains, was to be done by Christ, "he which baptizeth with the Holy Spirit." Peter confirms this, as we have seen, declaring that Christ did shed forth his Holy Spirit. He alone can so baptize, because he has redeemed the world, bought all with his precious blood; and because no man cometh unto the Father but by him, and because the **Father judgeth no man, but hath committed all judgment unto the Son**; and because the Son, highly exalted, acts as the Father's representative, to introduce into full fellowship with the Father those who come unto the Father by him. We have already seen that this baptism of the Church with the Holy Spirit was necessary, as a testimony, as a witness, in the same manner that it was necessary that the baptism of the Spirit upon our Lord Jesus should be witnessed and testified.

The rushing wind filling the place, and the "cloven tongues of flame" which "sat on each of them" (probably the eleven apostles only—designating them as the Lord's special representatives and the Holy Spirit's mouthpieces—see verse 14), were not the Holy Spirit, but merely **manifestations** to their senses representing the invisible. Similarly the dove which John saw was not the Spirit but a manifestation to his senses. The dove, the emblem of peace and purity, fitly represented the fullness of Jehovah's

Its Baptism, Witness and Seal

spirit of love in Jesus; as the cloven tongues fitly represented the mission of the apostles to be, under the Holy Spirit, to testify as "witnesses."—Acts 2:32; 3:15; 5:32; 10:39, 41; 13:31

(3) A special manifestation of the divine power in connection with the acceptance of Cornelius, the first Gentile convert, was necessary; because hitherto Gentiles had been outcasts, unacceptable to God even as servants; consequently it would not occur to the Jewish believers that the Gentiles would be accepted into the high position of **sons** of God, unless some pointed manifestation of divine favor to that effect were granted.

As already seen, it was not the divine program that any Gentiles should be accepted until the end of the "seventy weeks" of Jewish special favor, three and a half years after Pentecost;* hence the fact that converts from among the Gentiles were to be fellow-heirs (on an equality) with converts from among the Jews, could not be indicated in the baptism of the Spirit at Pentecost. And in view of the deep-rooted prejudices of the apostles as well as other Jews, it was most appropriate that the acceptance of Cornelius should be **manifested** to the senses of the apostle by the **same** evidences given at Pentecost. Nor is it necessary to suppose that the "cloven tongues of flame" sat on Cornelius: in common with the converts from Judaism, he probably received some of the "gifts" which came upon **all** at Pentecost.

How else could we have ever known that the Gentiles were accepted of the Lord? If the baptism of the Spirit and the Pentecostal blessings had come only upon the believers who were of the natural seed of Abraham, it might have left us in doubt all the way down through the Gospel age, as respects the standing of the Lord's people who by natural progeniture were Gentiles. But by the baptism of the Holy Spirit coming upon Cornelius, the Lord made fully manifest the fact that there was no longer any difference between Jew and Gentile, bond and free,

---

*See SCRIPTURE STUDIES, Vol. II, Chap. 7.

male and female, so far as acceptance with him in Christ was concerned. None are acceptable of themselves, in their own unrighteousness—hence only those who come unto the Father through the Beloved One are accepted in him.—1 Cor. 12:13

Aside from these three baptisms of the Holy Spirit there is no other reference to the subject in the Scriptures: consequently the thought of many of the Lord's people, that they must expect, labor for and pray for another or repeated baptisms of the Holy Spirit is quite unwarranted. Such baptisms are wholly unnecessary, because the one baptism at Pentecost, supplemented by that upon Cornelius, fills every requirement. Those baptisms came not merely upon the individuals who enjoyed the blessing, but representatively were for and upon the Church, the Body of Christ, as a whole. The fact that this representative work for the Church was made in two parts —upon the first Jewish believers at Pentecost, and upon the first Gentile believers in the house of Cornelius, is only in harmony with our Lord's statement on the subject to Peter, before his crucifixion, saying, "I will give unto thee the keys of the Kingdom of Heaven." (Matt. 16:19) A key signifies power to unlock, to open; and keys, in the plural implies that more than one door was to be opened. As a matter of fact, there were just two doors, and just two keys; and the Apostle Peter used both keys—doing the opening work to both Jews and Gentiles, as the Lord had predicted. He used the first key at Pentecost, where he was the first, chief, principal speaker, who introduced the new dispensation of the Spirit to the three thousand who at once believed and entered the door. (Acts 2:37-41) Again, when the due time had come for the Gospel to be preached to the Gentiles, the Lord, in accordance with his choice, sent Peter to do this work, telling Cornelius to send for Peter, and telling Peter to go to Cornelius, and to speak the words of the Gospel to him and his household. On this occasion Peter used the second key, opening the Gospel door before the Gentiles, God witnessing to the fact by the miraculous manifesta-

Its Baptism, Witness and Seal 215

tions of his Holy Spirit upon Cornelius and the other consecrated believers from among the Gentiles with him.

The proper thought respecting the baptism of the Holy Spirit is that of an outpouring, a shedding forth, an anointing, which, however, is so complete (**covering** every member of the body) as to be properly designated an **immersion**, or "baptism." And this same anointing or baptism continues upon the Church down through the age—covering, permeating, sanctifying, blessing, anointing, from then until now, each one who **comes into** the anointed, "body." And this will continue until the last member has been received and fully anointed. The Apostle John speaking also of this baptism styling it an anointing, says, "The anointing which ye have received of him abideth in you." (1 John 2:27; Psa. 133:2) He does not say, the numerous anointings which you have received, but **the** anointing, the one anointing, more being quite superfluous and out of harmony with the divine arrangement.

From the divine standpoint the entire Church is recognized as one—as a whole, for, "As the body is one, yet hath many members, so also is Christ . . . Ye are members in particular of the body of Christ." (1 Cor. 12:12, 27) In harmony with this thought the scriptural presentation of the matter is that although the Lord considers us individually, and in many respects deals with us individually, yet our standing before the Father is not so much as units, but as members or parts of a unit, which unit is Christ, head and body. Hence we are informed that after we have believed our next step is to get into the body of Christ—to be baptized into his body.

We will not here discuss the subject of baptism in general, leaving that for future consideration, but we note the fact that believers are invited to be baptized into Christ, in order that they may come into or under his baptism of the Holy Spirit. The Holy Spirit not being a person, but a Holy Spirit or power possessed by the Church, all who would have this blessing must come into relationship with **this Church,** Christ's body. It is not to be obtained otherwise. Nor do we mean by this a membership in an earthly Church—a Methodist body, a Presbyterian body, a Lutheran body, a Roman Catholic body, or any other body of human organization. We mean a membership in the **ecclesia,** whose members can be assuredly recognized only by their possession of the Holy Spirit of love—attested by its various fruits and witnessed to as we have seen foregoing.

Whoever becomes truly united with Christ, and thus truly united with all the members of the body of Christ, needs not to pray for present or future Pentecostal blessings, but may look back with joy and confidence to the original Pentecostal blessing and the blessing upon Cornelius, as the evidences which the Father gave, through Christ, of his acceptance of the Church as a whole: and with the divine arrangement all should be fully content. We do not say that our Lord is wroth with those who, with mistaken thoughts, ask, contrary to his will, for numerous Pentecosts, rather, we will suppose that he will have compassion upon their ignorance and misdirected prayers and without altering his own plans and arrangements will pour them out a blessing—as much of a blessing as their erroneous expectations and neglect of his Word will permit—accepting the groanings of their spirits for heavenly communion.

It is strange that these dear friends who continually pray for baptisms of the Spirit have never noticed that the apostles did not pray for future Pentecosts, neither did they instruct the Church so to pray. Do such friends think themselves wiser than the inspired apostles, or holier than they, or more anxious to be filled with the Spirit? We will trust that they have no such egotistical and presumptuous imaginations, and that their feelings are merely those of ignorant children, who thoughtlessly and sometimes peevishly tease indulgent parents for unnecessary and unpromised blessings and mercies, which cannot be granted them.

THE GENERAL BAPTISM OF THE SPIRIT

"Afterward I will pour out my spirit upon all flesh."—Joel 2:28

The Holy Spirit is to be the channel of reconciliation between the Almighty and the race of sinners redeemed with the precious life of Christ. As the object of the sacrifice of Christ was to open up the way by which God could be just, and yet be the justifier of all who believe in him, and who seek to come unto the Father by him, so his work, as the glorified Mediator, is to bring back into full fellowship with God so many of the redeemed race as are willing to return when granted full knowledge and opportunity. We have seen that this work of bringing back the members of the fallen race into harmony with God is divided into two parts: (1) the Church of this Gospel age, and (2) so many as will of the remainder of mankind, during the coming Millennial age.

We have seen that the basis of harmony is not that God condones sin, and excuses it, and permits us to return to his favor as sinners, but that the sinners are to put away their sins, accept heartily the divine standard of righteousness, and to come back into full harmony with God; so that they will seek and attain, through appointed channels, and under the supervision of Christ, the heavenly Father's Holy Spirit, mind, will, disposition—receiving it as their own mind, will or disposition, and thus be transformed by the renewing of their minds. This, which we have seen is God's program for the Church, is also declared to be God's program, through Christ, for the reconciliation of the world unto himself during the next age. Not one iota of the divine law will be modified; sin and imperfection will not be excused and counted as perfection and righteousness.

The world of mankind will be in the hands of the Christ for reformation and restoration to the image of God, lost through father Adam through transgression; and as a part of the means for bringing the world back into harmony with God, the influence of Satan, which now is upon the world, binding and blinding mankind, will be removed (2 Cor. 4:4; Rev. 20:2), and thereafter, instead of the world being under the influence or spirit of deception and error and ignorance and superstition, it shall be under the influence or Spirit of truth and righteousness and love. Instead of outside influences being a pressure upon the hearts of men, to fill them with anger and malice, hatred, strife and selfishness, this influence or spirit will be restrained and ultimately destroyed, and the contrary influence or Spirit of righteousness, goodness, mercy, sympathy, love, will be developed. Thus through Christ, the Holy Spirit of God will be poured out upon the world of mankind—first, in giving them enlightenment; secondly, in giving them help, assistance, strength, to overcome their own inherited tendencies; and third, in instructing them and leading them back to the image and likeness of God, lost through father Adam's disobedience.

While these prospective privileges and blessings for the world are glorious, and rejoice our hearts far beyond anything that the Lord's people have seen in times past, they nevertheless offer no comfort to enemies of the Lord, or to those who, when they have the opportunity, refuse to receive of his Holy Spirit, and to be filled by it. It will be poured out for all flesh, but it will be necessary for those who would enjoy it and be profited thereby to avail themselves of its privileges: just as it is necessary for believers of this Gospel age, who would come under and be blessed by the Holy Spirit, to make use of the means; —to consecrate themselves and to eat the truth, that they may have "the Spirit of the truth." When the great Prophet and Life-giver, the great Priest after the order of Melchizedek (Christ, head and body, complete), stands forward to bless the world, it will mean a blessing for all who will receive the words of that prophet, and obey them. and obtain the blessing of eternal life, by obedience; and it will mean the destruction by the Second Death for all those who refuse to hear him, as it is written, "Every soul which will not hear [obey] that Prophet shall be destroyed from among the people."—Acts 3:23

Joel's prophecy, it will be noticed, is stated in the reverse order to that of its fulfilment; the blessing of all flesh is stated first, and the blessing upon the Church last.

No doubt this order of statement was of the Lord's design, so as to cover or hide some of the glorious features of this great promise, until the due time for it to be understood. (Dan. 12:9, 10) Although it has been read over for centuries, it could not open up and disclose all of its wonderful treasure until God's "due time" had come. Throughout this Gospel age the Lord has poured out his Spirit upon his servants and handmaidens only; and blessed has been the experience of all those who received it—all who were immersed into the body of Christ, and made partakers of his anointing as sons; and it was to this feature that the Apostle Peter referred in his discourse at Pentecost. He quoted both parts of the prophecy, but, under the guidance of the Holy Spirit, he did not expound or illuminate the first part; because the time for it to be understood had not yet come. Hence, instead of explaining the **difference** between the Holy Spirit upon the servants and the handmaidens during this Gospel age ("**in** those days"), and the Holy Spirit upon all flesh "**afterward**," in the next age, he merely says, referring to the Holy Spirit upon himself and the other believers. "**This** is that which was spoken by the Prophet Joel" —a part of that, the beginning of that which was spoken. It will not all be complete until the pouring out of the Spirit upon all flesh, which is not yet. Moreover, the prophet mentions other things, which are not yet fulfilled. He refers to the darkening of the sun and the moon, and the coming of the great and notable day of the Lord, which are events now nigh at hand, the great day of wrath, which intervenes and separates between the outpouring of the Holy Spirit upon the Church, "the servants and handmaidens," in these days and "all flesh," afterward

As we have seen, there will be no difference between the Spirit of God, as it will come upon the world in the next age, and the Spirit of God as it comes upon the Church in this age, because it is the **same** Spirit of truth, Spirit of righteousness, Spirit of holiness, Spirit of sanctification, Spirit of harmony with God—the Spirit or influence which God will exert in favor of righteousness and goodness and truth. Nevertheless, it will not mean the same thing in every particular then that it means now. To receive the Holy Spirit of God now, and to live in harmony therewith, means necessarily a conflict with the spirit of the world, which abounds on every hand. For this reason it is that those who receive the Holy Spirit now, and who walk in harmony with it, are instructed to expect persecution and opposition from all who do not have the Spirit—the vast majority.

To receive the Holy Spirit in the future will not mean persecution, because the order, arrangement, government, of the next age will be very different from the present one: whereas the prince of this world is Satan, the prince of the world or age to come will be Christ; and whereas the majority of mankind are now under the influence of Satan, willingly or unwillingly, knowingly or unknowingly, in the next age the whole world will be under the influence of Christ and his righteous government. And the Truth will then be made free and common to all, from the least unto the greatest. Since the law of the next age will be the law of righteousness, truth, goodness, and will be **ruling**, as the Kingdom of God, those who come into harmony with that government and its law, and who have the Spirit of Truth, will not suffer persecution as a result thereof, but, on the contrary, will experience favor and blessings and make progress in proportion as they receive of that Spirit of holiness.

The possession of the Holy Spirit, during the Millennial age, will not as during this age signify a **begetting** of the Spirit to a spirit-nature, nor will it signify an acceptance to joint-heirship with Christ

Its Baptism, Witness and Seal

in the Kingdom. That promise belongs only to this Gospel age, to the servant and handmaiden class, who receive the Holy Spirit and are actuated by it during this age, when, in consequence of the present prevalence of evil, they are obliged to **suffer for righteousness' sake;** and upon whom, therefore, "the Spirit of **glory** and of God resteth."—1 Pet. 4:14

The possession of the Holy Spirit during the Millennial age will simply signify that the recipient has come into harmony with Christ, the Mediator, and is to that extent in harmony with God and in line with the blessings which God has provided for mankind in general, which blessings are not a **change of** nature, to the divine, but a **restitution** to all that was lost through the failure of the first Adam. (Acts 3:19-21) The possession of the Holy Spirit by such will be an evidence that the work of regeneration by the second Adam to perfection of human nature "bought" for them by the great sin-offering has commenced in them; and that if continued it will ultimately bring perfection of restitution to the human likeness of the divine Father.

We are to remember that the blessings which Christ will give to the world during the Millennial age, as the regenerator of the world, are the blessings which he bought for them by the sacrifice of himself. As he gave himself, as "the man Christ Jesus," a corresponding price for the man Adam, upon whom the condemnation came, so it was the manhood, rights, privileges and life and kingdom of Adam that were purchased by the great sacrifice for sins; and these purchased things are the things which are to be **restored** to the regenerated world, through their regenerator or father, Christ Jesus our Lord, the second Adam.—Eph. 1:14; Acts 3:19-23

The fact that our Lord Jesus was not the second Adam while in the flesh, but is the second Adam as a spirit being (since his resurrection), would not imply that he, as the second father of the race, would give to mankind spirit life or spirit being in their regeneration. On the contrary, we are to remember that the thought conveyed by the word "father" is merely "life-giver," without respect to the nature. Thus in father Adam's creation he is called a son of God, because created in the moral likeness and image of God, and not as implying that he was created in the divine nature; for we know that he was of the earth, earthy, while God is a spirit. The principle underlying this power by which God, as the life-giver, has become the Father of all creation, through his active agent, our Lord, is more particularly shown in a preceding chapter, under the caption, "The Undefiled One": we merely call attention to the matter here, to guard against misapprehension. God's purpose in connection with the creation of the world, and man as its inhabitant and lord, and the lower animals as his subjects, has not been changed by reason of the permitted disobedience and fall: the original plan remains as at first. After the evil attempted by the Adversary shall be ultimately expunged, the divine plan, as originally designed, will be fully accomplished through Christ. The Church of this Gospel age, which shall, as we have seen, be highly exalted and glorified as the Bride and joint-heir of Christ, is an exception to the restitution of mankind: it is called out or selected for a special purpose, and is particularly tried and tested, fitted and prepared for high exaltation, joint-heirship with Christ—a change from the human nature to a nature above the angelic nature—"far above angels, principalities and powers," partakers of the divine nature.

But while we ought not to pray for unpromised new baptisms of the Holy Spirit, we are taught most positively to seek and pray for the Spirit as a satisfying portion.

PRAYING FOR THE HOLY SPIRIT

"If ye then, being evil, know how to give good gifts unto your children, how much more shall your heavenly Father give the Holy Spirit to them that ask him."—Luke 11:13

Although "all things are by the Son," yet here as everywhere he gives the glory and honor, as the fountain of blessing, to the Father. The entire work of redemption and reconciliation is the Father's work—through the Son. And our Lord declares that it is the Father's good pleasure that we should have more and more of his Spirit of holiness. He bids us seek for and ask for this, as the great supreme blessing. As for earthly blessings, our Redeemer tells us that our Heavenly Father knoweth what things we have need of—he knoweth better than we know what earthly blessings will be helpful, and which would be injurious to us. We need not, therefore, as do the unregenerate and the heathen, think of and pray for earthly blessings; but rather, as those who have come into the relationship of sons, and who have full confidence in the Father's provision, we may expect that he will give what is best, and we may rest ourselves content in that promise and faith.

The Heavenly Father is pleased to have us desire and ask for more and more of the Holy Spirit—a disposition more and more fully in harmony with his Spirit: and all who thus desire and ask and seek it shall obtain their good desires; the Father will be pleased to so order the affairs of such that hindrances to the Spirit, whether in them or in their environment, shall be overcome, that his loving Spirit may abound in them—that they may be filled with the Spirit. But in this there is no suggestion of necessity for fresh baptisms of the Holy Spirit: the baptism came at the beginning, and now all there remains to do is to open the sluices in every direction, so as to let the Holy Spirit of love and truth penetrate into and permeate every action, word and thought of our beings. We need divine aid, the operation of the Lord's wisdom and providence, to show us what clogs the sluices and to help us to remove the obstructions.

The Spirit of holiness in abundance can only be received by those who earnestly desire it and seek it by prayer and effort. The mind or spirit of the world must be driven out of our hearts, in proportion as we would have them filled with the Holy Spirit, mind, influence. Self-will must also give place.

And because it is in proportion as we are emptied of all things else that we are ready to receive of his fullness, therefore the Lord would have us come into this condition of earnest desire for filling with his Spirit of holiness, that we may be willing and anxious to displace and eradicate every other contrary influence and will.

This evidently is the thought of the apostle, in his prayer for the Church at Ephesus, that "Christ [the Spirit of Christ] may dwell in your hearts by faith [that figuratively he may sit as king, ruler, director of every thought, word and deed]; that ye being rooted and grounded in love [the Holy Spirit or disposition] may be able to comprehend with all saints what is the breadth, and length, and depth and height, and to appreciate the love of Christ, which passeth knowledge, that ye may be filled with **all the fullness of God."** (Eph. 3:19) He who is filled with the Spirit of Christ, and with a full appreciation of the love which he manifested, will have the Father's Spirit in full measure.

Nothing in the Scripture under examination can in any manner be construed to imply that the Heavenly Father would be pleased to have his children ask him for another God—a third person of a trinity of co-equal Gods. Such a thought is repugnant to the passage and its connections: and those who entertain such an erroneous view must necessarily be blinded to that extent to the true beauty and force of this promise. It would be strange indeed if one member of a co-equal trinity of Gods referred to another as able and willing to give the third as earthly parents give bread, fish and eggs to their children. (See preceding verses.) The entire passage is consistent only when the Holy Spirit is properly understood to be the divine mind or influence bestowed variously for **the comfort and spiritual upbuilding of God's children.**

Our text institutes a comparison between kind earthly parents giving natural food to their children, and our kind heavenly Parent giving his Holy Spirit to them that ask him. But as the earthly parent sets the food within the reach of his family, but does not force it upon them, so our heavenly Parent has set within the reach of his spiritual family the good provisions of his grace, but he does not force them upon us. We must hunger and thirst for them, we must seek for them, not doubtfully, but with faith respecting his willingness to give us good gifts. When, therefore, we pray for the Holy Spirit, and to be filled with the Lord's Spirit, we are to look about us and find the provision which he has made for the answer to these prayers, which he has thus inspired and directed.

We find this provision in the Word of truth; but it is not enough to find **where** it is: if we desire to be filled we must eat; assuredly we must partake of the feast or we will not experience the satisfaction which the eating was designed to give. He who will not eat of a full table will be empty and starved, as truly as though there were no food. As the asking of a blessing upon the food will not fill us, but thereafter we must partake of it, so the possession of the Word of God, and the offering of our petition to be filled with the Spirit, will not suffice us; we must eat the Word of God, if we would derive his Spirit from it.

Our Master declared, "The **words** that I speak unto you, they are Spirit and they are life" (John 6:63); and of all who are filled with the Spirit it is true, as spoken by the prophet, "Thy words were found and **I did eat them.**" (Jer. 15:16; Rev. 10:9) It is absolutely useless for us to pray Lord, Lord, give us the Spirit, if we neglect the Word of truth which that Spirit has supplied for our filling. If we merely pray for the Spirit and do not use the proper means to obtain the Spirit of truth, we will continue to be at most only "babes in Christ," seeking outward signs, in proof of relationship to the Lord, instead of the inward witness, through the Word of truth, which he has provided.

THE WITNESS OF THE HOLY SPIRIT

"The Spirit itself beareth witness with our spirit that we are the children of God."—Rom. 8:16

Few doctrines are of more importance to God's people than this one; because on it depends to a considerable extent their possession of "the peace of God which passeth all understanding." (Phil. 4:7) How can they have "full assurance of faith" (Heb. 10:22) **if they lack the witness of the Spirit testifying to their sonship**—to their adoption into the family of God? Yet how few have the slightest conception of what is meant by this expression "witness of the Spirit," or what kind of experiences should be expected and looked for as constituting the Spirit's witness to our sonship.

The question is therefore a very important one— How does the Holy Spirit witness to us respecting our at-one-ment with the Father—that we have become sons of God, and that under divine providence we are being prepared for the glorious things which God hath in reservation for them that love him, and who are to be joint-heirs with Jesus Christ our Lord, in the Millennial Kingdom? On few subjects have Christians in general felt more disturbed than on this—the witness of the Spirit. Not knowing what the witness of the Spirit is, many of the best of the Lord's people must confess that they know not whether they have it or have it not. Others, more full of assurance than of knowledge, claim that they have the witness of the Holy Spirit, and refer to their happy feelings as the evidence. But soon or later such, if candid, must confess that the "witness" they rely on is a most unsatisfactory one: it fails them in the times of greatest need. When all men speak well of them, when health is favorable, when they are financially prosperous, when friends are numerous, they feel happy; but in proportion as some or all of these conditions are reversed they feel unhappy: they lose what they suppose was the "wit-

Its Baptism, Witness and Seal

ness of the Spirit," and cry in anguish of soul:—

> "Where is the blessedness I knew,
> When first I found the Lord?"

Such are deceived and misled by their feelings: they feel themselves happier and think themselves drawing nearer to God at times when really they are, under the Adversary's leading, going straight into temptations. This accounts for some of the frequent and sudden "falls from grace" which some experience and which astonish themselves as well as their friends. Deceived by an unreliable "witness" they felt secure, were off guard and fell an easy prey to temptation at the very time they felt "so happy in the Lord"(?). Again, the trials and disappointments of life designed to draw us near to our Father, and to make us most appreciative of our Savior's loving sympathy and care, are partially lost upon this class; because losing the witness of their feelings, which they falsely consider the witness of the Spirit, they feel so bereft, and so hungry and thirsty for a return of the good feelings, that they lose many precious lessons obtainable only when leaning confidently on the Lord's bosom and communing with him, whilst passing through life's Gethsemanes.

Another class of Christians learning the unreliability of the "witness" of feelings seem to conclude that God has denied (to them at least) any reliable evidence of his favor—any sure "witness" on the subject of their acceptance as "sons" into his family. Their doubts are expressed in the well-known hymn:

> "'Tis a point I long to know—
> Oft it causes anxious thought:
> Do I love the Lord or no?
> Am I his or am I not?"

This uncertainty arises in part also from a misapprehension of the doctrine of election: and yet these friends are quite correct in concluding that their changeable feelings could not be a proper criterion by which to judge of their sonship. Others, because the Scriptures declare, "Thou wilt keep him in perfect peace whose mind is stayed on thee," judge of their sonship by their peace of mind: but when they look at the heathen and at the worldly, and see that many of them apparently have peace of mind too, their view of the Spirit's witness proves insufficient to sustain their hopes, or to give them assurance. Then the dark hour comes, and they say, How easy a matter to be deceived, and are in torment lest they have grieved the Spirit—for "fear hath torment."

Persons of large credulity (misnamed **faith**) will imagine they hear the Spirit's "whisper" to an inner ear and they congratulate themselves accordingly— even though they should subsequently ascertain that the information "whispered" was absolutely untrue. Other Christians of more logical mind, who cannot thus delude themselves, are perplexed that their friends should so confidently assert the witness of the Spirit, while they themselves have no such assurance.

The difficulty lies largely in the erroneous view that the Spirit is a person, and which seeks to apply personality to its witnessings. When the fact is recognized that the Spirit of God is any power or influence which God may be pleased to exercise, the subject is clarified and the "witness of the Spirit" becomes a matter easy of distinguishment. It will be a blessing to those who have this witness to know it of a surety: and it will be a blessing to those who have not this witness to ascertain their lack; so that they may fulfil the conditions and obtain the witness, without which none are authorized to consider themselves sons of God, in acceptable standing with the Father.

But what a joy and peace divine comes to those who have the true witness—to those who have the correct experiences and who have learned how to read them! It is to them indeed joy in sorrow, light in darkness, comfort in affliction, strength in weakness. And the full and explicit directions on this subject, as on all subjects, are found in that wonderful book, our Father's Word—the Bible. In it and through its testimonies God's Spirit witnesseth with our spirits.

> "How firm a foundation, ye saints of the Lord,
> Is laid for your faith in his excellent Word.
> What more can he say than to you he hath said:
> You who unto Jesus for refuge have fled!"

HOW TO KNOW THE SPIRIT'S WITNESS

A man's mind or spirit may be known by his words and conduct; and so we may know God's mind or Spirit by his words and dealings. The testimony of his Word is that whosoever cometh unto him (by faith, and reformation from bad works and dead works, through Jesus) is accepted. (Heb. 7:25) Hence the questions to be asked of themselves by those who are seeking a witness of the Spirit respecting their sonship are:—

Was I ever drawn to Christ?—to recognize him as my Redeemer, through whose righteousness alone I could have access to the heavenly Father, and be acceptable with him?

If this can be answered in the affirmative, the next question would be:—

Did I ever fully consecrate myself—my life, my time, my talents, my influence, my all—to God?

If this question also can be answered in the affirmative, the inquirer may rest fully assured that he has been accepted with the Father, in the Beloved One, and recognized of him as a son. And if scrutinizing his own heart's desires and sentiments he finds it still trusting in the merit of Jesus, and still consecrated to do the Lord's will, he may allow the sweet confidence and peace which this thought of harmony and relationship to divinity brings, to fully possess his heart. This conviction of the Lord's grace toward us in Christ constructed from facts of our own experience, built upon the unalterable character and Word of God, is not mutative, not changeable, as it would be if built upon the shifting sands of feelings. If doubts or fears intrude in some dark hour, we have only to take the "Lamp" (God's Word) and examine afresh the facts and the foundation, and if our hearts are still loyal to the Lord, faith, joy and peace will instantly return to us; if we find our faith in "the precious blood" crumbling, or our consecration slipping away, we know the true condition of affairs, and can at once make the proper repairs and thus re-establish our "full assurance of faith." (Heb. 10:22) But be it noticed that each one who would have this assurance must "set to his seal that God is true" (John 3:33): that our Lord changeth not, but is "the same yesterday, today and forever." The Lord's people may therefore rest assured that having once come into the conditions of divine favor, they may continue under those conditions so long as their hearts are loyal to God and their desires in harmony with his will: so long as they are at heart obedient to the divine commands—briefly comprehended in the word Love—to God and men. —Heb. 11:6; 13:8

Whoever has taken the specified steps has the assurance, the "witness" of the Word of God, that he is a child of God; and this, during the Gospel age, signifies that he is a branch of the true vine, a probationary member of the true Church. (John 15:1) To such the Word of God witnesses that they have joined the true Church, which is Christ's body. This witness is given to their spirit, their mind, by God's Spirit, which testifies through his Word. And the same Spirit of Truth assures such that if their hearts continue faithful to the Lord to the close of their probation—if they willingly and gladly take up the cross daily, seeking as best they are able to follow in the Master's footsteps, their probationary membership in the Church of Christ will shortly be changed to actual membership—after they have finished their course, and been made sharers in his resurrection, the first resurrection.—Phil. 3:10

However, the Spirit of God, through his Word, witnesses with equal clearness that it is possible for those who have already become branches of the true Vine to be cut off, if unfaithful—if they fail to bring forth the proper fruits of the Spirit of love. "Every branch in me that beareth not fruit he [the Father] taketh away, and every branch that bringeth forth fruit he purgeth [pruneth] it, that it may bring forth more fruit." The Spirit of God, through his Word, thus testifies or witnesses to us the rule of our heavenly Father's dealing with his sons—chastisements, pruning, taking away of the dross, and a development of the fruit-bearing qualities. Hence, to have these experiences, after having become identified with the 'Vine," is to have the witness of the Spirit that we are still in the "Vine," and still recognized as "branches" of it—still under our Lord's care and discipline. On the contrary, if any one lack these disciplines, prunings, etc., after having become identified with the Vine, he lacks this "witness of the Spirit," and correspondingly has reason to doubt his acceptance with the Lord.—Heb. 12:7

If we were all perfect, absolutely perfect, and had been proven so by tests, the case would be different; God would then love us for our perfection and harmony with himself; then chastisement and bitter experiences would be signs of his disfavor. But as it is, we all know that all are imperfect, that we all come far short of the divine standard; and that our new hearts, our new wills, our transformed minds or spirits, alone are acceptable with God—and that through the merit of Christ, and in a probationary sense, with a view to our testing, development and final perfecting. Only in proportion as we learn to appreciate the divine perfections, and our own deficiencies, can we appreciate the many and important lessons to be learned, and the necessity for the trying experiences we are required to undergo in order to develop in us the divine likeness.

The Scriptures inform us that the Heavenly Father is preparing a glorious spiritual Temple, in and through which the world of mankind is to have the privilege of coming to at-one-ment, reconciliation with himself. We see in the Scriptures the great Architect's ideal in respect to this temple—that the ideal of the whole was represented in the person of our Lord Jesus Christ, its chief corner stone, and "top-stone," "laid in Heaven." We can see the better what is required of all those who will be acceptable to God as the "living stones" of that Temple—to be built together with Christ the Head, "for an habitation of God through his Spirit." And we discern our own roughness by nature, our inharmony with the graceful lines of the Temple, delineated in its "top-stone." We can readily discern that much chiseling and much polishing are absolutely necessary to us, if we would be fitted and prepared for the place in this Temple to which, through the grace of God, we aspire. And hence those who find that they are not receiving the blows from the Lord's hammer and chisel, lack this "witness" which the Spirit of God through his Word testifies must come to all the living stones of his Temple: and which even the grand Top-stone did not escape. If divine providence does not mark out for us a "narrow way" with a certain amount of difficulty and adversity—if we are simply permitted to rest without afflictions, trials, etc., then we may know of a surety that God is not dealing with us as with the living stones which shall form part of the Temple—the sons—because we lack this "witness" of our acceptance and preparation. A realization that such is our condition ought to send us promptly to the Lord to inquire why we have no tribulations and adversities, and to "examine ourselves" whether or not we be still in the faith (2 Cor. 13:5); and whether or not we are still endeavoring to walk faithfully in the footsteps of our Master, in fullness of consecration to the Father's will. But if we have this "witness" of chiselings, polishings, prunings, disciplines, chastisements, let us take them patiently, joyfully, appreciatively, as evidences of our Father's love essential to our attainment to our high-calling—in full accord with the Spirit's testimony or witness—that we are sons of God, "heirs of God, joint-heirs with Jesus Christ our Lord, [only] **if so be that we suffer with him**, that we may be also glorified together."—Rom. 8:17

THE SPIRIT'S "DIFFERENCES OF ADMINISTRATION"

"Whom the Lord loveth he chasteneth, and scourgeth every son whom he receiveth. If ye be without chastisement, then, are ye bastards and not sons." (Heb. 12:8) Afflictions and troubles come upon the world, as well as upon the Lord's saints, but these are **not marks of sonship**, except to those fully consecrated to the Father's will and work. The Spirit and Word of God "witness" only to his sons. Nor are the prunings and chastenings in the Lord's family always the same. As earthly children require different kinds and degrees of discipline, so with God's children: to some, a look of disapproval is sufficient; to others a word of rebuke is necessary, while still others must be scourged, and some repeatedly. An earthly parent rejoices most in the obedient and promptly submissive child, for whom the word or look of reproof is sufficient to prune away the evil; and so also our Father in Heaven declares his approval of those who "tremble at his word."—Isa. 66:5

Such co-operate with God in the development of their own character, noting their own defects and seeking to correct them—hearkening for the Father's voice of direction, instruction or loving reproof, and ever seeking his approving smile: their sentiments are well described by the words of the poet:—

> "Sun of my soul, my Father dear,
>   I know no night when thou art near.
> O let no earthborn cloud arise.
>   To hide thee from thy servant's eyes."

This is the class of whom the apostle writes, who judge themselves, and who, therefore, need less chastening of the Lord. (1 Cor. 11:31) To be of this class requires fullness of consecration; and these are and will be the overcomers, who shall be deemed worthy of joint-heirship with Christ Jesus their Lord in his Kingdom. To this class, obedient and watchful, the Lord says, "I will guide thee with mine eye,"—"Thou shalt guide me with thy counsel and afterward receive me to glory." Those who can be guided only by continual scourging are not of the overcoming class, and will not be accounted worthy to be of the Lord's Bride, and have such a "witness" from the Lord through the Spirit of the Truth.—Psa. 32:8; 73:24; contrast Rev. 7:9, 14

Nor are chastenings always proofs of faults, or a "witness" of the Lord's disapproval. On the contrary, as with our Lord, so also with his faithful followers, divine providence leads the faithful and obedient into the path of suffering and self-denial, not as chastisement of a contrary will, but as tests, by self-sacrifice, of the measure of love and devotion to the Father's will, and to the cause of righteousness. As our Lord was chastened for our transgressions, not his own, when he bore the sins of many, so his followers in many respects suffer, not for their own wrong-doings, but by reason of the wrong-doings of others, for they are called as the apostle declares, to "fill up that which is behind of the afflictions of Christ, for his body's sake, which is the Church."—Col. 1:24

WHAT THE HOLY SPIRIT WITNESSES

In the light of the foregoing, let each of the Lord's professed sons examine himself whether or not he have "the witness of the Spirit," that he is one of the children of God: and let us repeat the examination frequently, and thus "watch" and keep ourselves in the love of God, rejoicing in the witness of his Spirit.

Are we being pruned continually? Are we passing through such experiences, great or small, as are removing from us more or less rapidly the fleshly tendencies, which war against the soul—anger, malice, hatred, envy, strife, selfishness, rudeness, and all things contrary to the law of the Spirit of life in Christ Jesus—the Spirit of love? If so, to the extent that we can realize this pruning work in progress, we will no doubt be able to recognize growth in the proper direction—in meekness, patience, gentleness, brotherly kindness, love. Whoever, after a careful examination along these lines, marked out in the Lord's Word, can realize such experiences in progress may know of his continued acceptance with God, because he has **this witness of the Spirit.**

Again, the Spirit witnesses that "Whosoever is born [begotten] of God, sinneth not." (1 John 5:18) The child of God may be overpowered by his old nature (reckoned **dead,** but not fully, actually so); he may be overtaken in a fault, may err in judgment or in word, but he will never **willingly** transgress the divine law. So then, if our hearts can respond that we delight to do God's will, and would not willingly violate or in any manner oppose it—that we would rather have God's will done, and his plan fulfilled, even though it should dash our fondest hopes and break every tender tie—then we have this witness that our spirit or mind agrees with the witness of the Spirit of the Truth here recorded: and this is a witness, not only that we were once accepted into God's family, but that we are there still.

The Spirit witnesses, through the Word of God, that those who are the Lord's people are separate from the world—that their hopes and aims and general spirit, disposition, are different. "If ye were of the world, the world would love his own; but because ye are not of the world, therefore the world hateth you." "Yea, and all that will live godly in Christ Jesus shall suffer persecution."—John 15:19; 2 Tim. 3:12

Can our hearts testify that these words properly represent our experience in life? If so, the Spirit (mind) of God is thus again witnessing with our spirit (mind) that we are his. Nor should we forget that the world spoken of by our Lord includes all the worldly-minded ones, in whom the spirit of the world has a footing. In our Lord's day this was true of the nominal Jewish Church: in fact, all of his persecutions came from professors of religion. Hence, we must not marvel if all who are walking in our Lord's footsteps should have a similarly disappointing experience, and find that the spirit of the world, in its most antagonistic form will be manifested in a quarter where we might naturally expect it least—amongst those who profess to be the children of God. It was the chief religionists of our Lord's day who called him Beelzebub, a prince of devils. And the Holy Spirit witnesseth through our Lord's Word, saying, "If they have called the Master of the house Beelzebub, how much more shall they call them of his household." (Matt. 10:25) If, therefore, we have been evilly spoken of, because of our identification with the Truth, and our service of it, we have in this an additional evidence or witness of the Spirit that we are in the right pathway.

Had our Lord Jesus joined hands with the popular leaders in the Jewish Church, and abstained from speaking the truth in love, abstained from pointing out the false doctrines of his day, he would not have been "hated," nor "persecuted"; on the contrary, he probably would have been "highly esteemed amongst men." But, as he himself declared, much that is "highly esteemed amongst men is an abomination in the sight of God."—Luke 16:15

Had our Lord simply kept quiet and refrained from exposing the hypocrisies, shams, long prayers and false teachings of the Scribes and Pharisees, they no doubt would have let him alone, would not have persecuted him; and he would not have suffered for the Truth's sake. So also it is with his followers: from a similar class, the Truth and those who have the Spirit of the Truth, and who follow the Lord's instruction, letting their lights shine, will now incur hatred and persecution. And if some, for these reasons, and while doing their best to speak the truth in love, suffer therefor, happy are they, for as the

Its Baptism, Witness and Seal

apostle said, "The Spirit of glory and of God resteth on you." They have this witness of the Spirit to their faithfulness in the narrow way.—1 Pet. 4:14

Again, the Holy Spirit witnesses, through our Lord's testimony, that whosoever is ashamed of the Redeemer and of his Truth which he taught, of him will the Lord be ashamed when he comes to make up his jewels. (Mark 8:38) Whoever, therefore, finds his heart so in love with the Lord and his Word that he takes pleasure, on every suitable occasion, in acknowledging Jesus as his Redeemer and Master, and to faithfully present the Word of his testimony, so long does such an one have this as another witness of the Holy Spirit that he is a child of God, and an heir of the Kingdom. Such have reason to rejoice in the Master's promise that they are just the kind whom he will be glad to confess before his Father and before the holy angels. But if any have not this witness—if, on the contrary, their hearts witness that they are ashamed of the Lord, ashamed to confess themselves his followers, ashamed to own his "brethren," the members of his body, and ashamed to confess the doctrines which he taught— any who have these experiences have the witness of the Spirit that if this condition of things be not altered the Lord will be ashamed of them at his second coming, and will not confess them before the Father and his holy messengers.

Further, the Holy Spirit witnesses that, "Whosoever is born [begotten] of God **overcometh** the world: and this is the victory that overcometh the world, even your **faith**." (1 John 5:4) Let us examine our hearts, our spirits, our minds, in the light of this testimony of the Holy Spirit. Are we overcomers, according to this standard? The standard is that to be the Lord's we must be out of harmony with the world, in conflict with it—its aims, its hopes, its ambitions. The thought of conflict is contained in the expression, "overcometh the world." And we can readily see that no one can be an overcomer of the world who is in sympathy and affiliation with it, and its general spirit of selfishness, pride, ambition, etc.

Before we decide positively whether we are overcoming the world or not, let us notice that we are not to overcome the world by flattery nor by joining with it in its follies and attempting to give these a religious twist; nor are we to overcome the world by engaging in some moral or religious work, such as teaching a Sunday-school class, or helping the poor, or joining a sectarian church. In none of these ways does the Lord indicate or "witness" that we can overcome the world. His statement is positive, that the victory which overcometh the world is our **faith**. The Spirit thus witnesses that to be overcomers we must "walk by **faith**, and not by sight." We must look not at the things that are seen—popularity, worldly show, denominational greatness, etc.—but must look at the things which are not seen— the spiritual and eternal things. (2 Cor. 4:18) We are to have the faith expressed by the poet's words:—

> "I would rather walk in the dark with God,
> Than go with the throng in the light."

Furthermore, the Holy Spirit witnesses to us, through the Word, that if we are the children of God we will not be ignorant of things present nor of "things **to come**," because we will be enlightened and taught of God, through the Word of his grace— the Word of his Spirit. As we mature, "grow in grace," we will desire and seek and obtain, in addition to the milk of the Word, the "strong meat" which the apostle declares is for those of fuller development. (1 Pet. 2:2; Heb. 5:13, 14) The development in the graces of the Spirit, faith, fortitude, knowledge, self-control, patience, piety, brotherly kindness, love, will bring us into closer fellowship with the Father and with the Lord Jesus, so that the Lord will be able and willing to communicate to us more and more clearly a knowledge of his gracious plans, as well as of his own gracious character.

Referring to this growth, the Apostle Peter says: "If these things be in you and abound, they make you that ye shall be neither barren nor unfruitful in the **knowledge** of the Lord Jesus Christ; but he that lacketh these things is blind, **and cannot see afar off.** . . . For if ye do these things ye shall never fall; for so an entrance shall be ministered unto you abundantly into the everlasting kingdom of our Lord and Savior Jesus Christ."—2 Pet. 1:5-11. Compare John 16:12, 15

Each should ask himself whether or not he has this witness of the Spirit, this testimony to his growth as a new creature in Christ Jesus, and whether or not he is developing and maturing the kind of fruit here specified. Let us remember also that our growth in love and in all the fruits of the Spirit is dependent largely upon our growth in knowledge; and our growth in knowledge of divine things is dependent also upon our growth in the fruits of the Spirit. Each step of knowledge brings a corresponding step of duty and obedience, and each step of duty and obedience taken will be followed by a further step in knowledge, for so, **the Spirit witnesseth,** shall be the experience of all those who shall be taught of God in the school of Christ. If we have this witness of the Spirit of growth, both in grace and in knowledge, let us rejoice therein, and let us follow on in the same pathway until it shall bring us, under divine guidance, to that which is perfect, both in knowledge and in grace.

THE HOLY SPIRIT'S FUTURE TESTIMONY

The Holy Spirit will witness to the reconciled world of mankind in the next age, very similarly as to manner, but very dissimilarly as to facts. Those possessing the Spirit will no longer be the few special servants and handmaids, but as the Prophet Joel declares "all flesh." (Joel 2:28) The Spirit's "witness" will no longer be "whosoever will live godly shall suffer persecution"; for no persecution will then be permitted. It will no longer "witness" to a "narrow way" of sacrifice, for the day of sacrifice will be past: "A highway shall be there" and it shall be without stumbling stones. (Isa. 35:8; 62:10) It will "witness" that "Evil-doers shall be cut off: but those who wait upon the Lord, they shall inherit the earth." (Acts 3:23; Psa. 37:7-11) It will "witness" blessings to the well-doer and punishments and destruction to wilful evil-doers. It is the same Spirit of God but under differences of administration.

Having learned **how** the Holy Spirit "witnesses" and **what** are some of its testimonies through God's holy Word, we do indeed find these very much more satisfactory than all the doubts and fears inspired by mental and physical conditions—feelings, falsely called by some the witness of the Holy Spirit. Nevertheless, we should call attention to the fact that all Christians cannot have the same witnessings from the Spirit of God with their spirits or minds. All Christians of large experience and development should have testimony or witness on **all** these points, and on other points set forth in the Scriptures: but there are young Christians who have not yet progressed far enough to have all of these witnessings; —some, perhaps, may be truly begotten of the Lord, and as yet have but few of them. The great Husbandman does not expect fruitage, neither green nor yet the developed and ripe fruit, from the fresh and tender sprout of a branch.

The first witness that the newly begotten may have is, that they are accepted with the Lord; that they are young branches in the true Vine; and that the Spirit of the Vine is in them—the desire to grow and to be like the Vine, and to bring forth fruitage. Nor should it be long after the branch first shoots forth, before the sign of leaves and the buds of promise for fruit will be discernible. The new-born babe in the spiritual family manifests its relationship to the older and more developed members of the family, not by its eating of the strong meat, which might strangle it, but by desires for the strengthening milk, to grow thereby.—1 Pet. 2:2

Those who find themselves possessed of any of the foregoing witnessings of the Spirit should rejoice correspondingly; and every particular they are lacking they should endeavor to cultivate and develop, so that they may ultimately have the witness of the Spirit in their favor on every point of the scriptural testimony respecting the pathway and experiences of the Lord's faithful people. Such will no longer need to sing—"'Tis a point I long to know." On the contrary, they will know, will have full assurance of faith, and will be rooted and grounded and built up and established in the faith. This is the divinely arranged way: we wholly escape from fear—from "Doubting Castle"—for our trust rests securely in the divine promises, which never fail. This is as true in the time of trial and adversity and darkness as when we are more particularly enjoying the light of our heavenly Father's smile. The poet expresses the correct thought, saying:—

> "When darkness seems to veil his face
> I rest in his unchanging grace.
> His oath, his covenant, his blood,
> Support me in the whelming flood.
> When all around my soul gives way,
> He then is all my hope and stay."

SANCTIFIED BY THE SPIRIT

"But ye are washed, but ye are sanctified, but ye are holy, in the name of the Lord Jesus, and by the Spirit of our God."—1 Cor. 6:11

Sanctification signifies a **setting apart** or separating. All who are sanctified, set apart, fully consecrated to God, must first be washed or **justified**—either actually cleansed from sin, or reckonedly cleansed—"justified by faith." Actual justification will be the route of approach toward God on the part of the world during the Millennium, under the guidance and help of the great Mediator, and as part of the process of the Atonement. A justification no less vital, although merely by faith—is the arrangement which operates during this Gospel age, by which we who are sinners by nature, and in whose flesh dwells no perfection, are reckoned clean, holy, justified, acceptable to God through our acceptance of Christ as our Redeemer. We believe the Scriptural testimony that "Christ died for our sins, according to the Scriptures"; and believing this, and desirous of escaping from sin, we are accepted of God as though perfect, sinless, as justified through the merit of the precious blood. Being thus justified by faith, we have peace with God, and can approach him, and will be received by him, and can begin to **do works acceptable** to the Father, through the merit of our Lord Jesus Christ. The evidence which we have of our justification and sanctification comes to us through the Word, and is called the "seal" and "witness" of the Spirit in us.

The **power** which enables us to live up to our consecration vows is the Holy Spirit or holy mind of God, which we receive as a result of our faith in Christ, and our consecration to be "dead with him." The Spirit of the Truth, which we obtain through the study of our Father's Word, in our spirit of obedience thereto, furnishes us the needed strength for overcoming the world and our own perverted appetites. Accordingly, **the text under consideration declares that all the cleansing** which we have experienced, all of our justification, and all of our setting apart to righteousness, and our separation from sin—all the victories and blessings in these directions have come to us through the merit of our Lord Jesus, and by or through the channel of the Spirit of holiness, the Spirit of God, which we have received.

Other Scriptures are in full harmony with these findings. The same Apostle Paul prayed for the Church, "The very God of peace sanctify you wholly." (1 Thess. 5:23) He is not here contradicting the statement foregoing, that it is the Holy Spirit of God, which sanctifies. It is God who sanctifies, and the medium, method or channel is his Holy Spirit and not another person.

Its Baptism, Witness and Seal

The Apostle Peter declares the Church to be "elect [chosen] through sanctification [setting apart] of the Spirit unto obedience." (1 Pet. 1:2) The thought here is that those whom God now recognizes as his chosen ones, and who are exhorted to make their calling and election sure, are chosen, not arbitrarily, but according to fixed principles, viz., that if the Holy Spirit of God (influence of the Truth) operating upon them shall bring them to the condition of full obedience (sanctification) to the Father's will and plan and providence, then they shall constitute the elect.

The Apostle Paul, in another of his epistles (Eph. 5:26), attributes this sanctification and cleansing power in the Church to the Word of God, saying, "Christ loved the Church, and gave himself for it, that he might **sanctify** and **cleanse** it with the washing of water by the Word." We are not to suppose that the apostle is here contradicting his previous statement, to the effect that **God** sanctifies the Church, nor contradicting his other statement, that it is the **Spirit** of God that sanctifies the Church. Clearly and unmistakably, his thought in every instance is, that it is the Holy Spirit of God, operating through the Word of his truth, that he has designed shall produce in us cleansing, justification, sanctification.

Thus also our Lord Jesus prayed, "Sanctify them through thy Truth: thy Word is truth." (John 17:17) Thus we see that the various Scriptures upon the subject taken together, teach that the sanctification of the Church is accomplished by the Spirit of the Truth, imparted to the consecrated ones through the Word of God which he provided for this very purpose.

All who are thus sanctified are thenceforth **"new creatures in Christ Jesus,"** and are addressed as "them that are sanctified in Christ." (1 Cor. 1:2) Yet this sanctification in Christ is not aside from the Spirit of God, nor aside from the Word of God; for it is by reason of our acceptance of the divine plan and provision, by reason of our coming to the point of sanctification of the Spirit, that we are one with Christ our Lord. And this is further shown by the Scripture which says, "Both he that sanctifieth and they who are sanctified are all of one [of one spirit, of one mind, begotten of the Spirit of Truth]: for which cause he is not ashamed to call them brethren." (Heb. 2:11) Thus it is that we are "washed, sanctified, justified, in the name of our Lord Jesus and by the Spirit of our God"—the Spirit of Truth.

BE YE FILLED WITH THE SPIRIT

"Be ye filled with the Spirit; speaking to yourselves in psalms and hymns and spiritual songs, singing and making melody in your heart to the Lord; giving thanks always."
—Eph. 5:18-20

The intimation of this Scripture is that the Lord's people may have a greater or less degree of fullness of his Spirit. To be his they must have some of his Spirit for "if any man have not the Spirit of Christ he is none of his." (Rom. 8:9) It rests with ourselves largely with our use of the means which God had provided, how fully we may be filled with his Spirit and disposition, his influence—the Spirit or influence of his Truth, which he has revealed for the very purpose of sanctifying our hearts and lives, and separating us from those who have the spirit of the world.

Nothing in this and similar texts involves the thought of a personal Holy Spirit: quite the contrary. If a person were meant, it would be inconsistent to urge the recipient to a greater or less filling. The person who could enter could alone have to do with the filling; if he is great, he will fill the more, if small, he will fill the less. The Holy Spirit conceived of as a person, one of a trinity of Gods, equal with the Highest, could not be supposed to get into the small compass of an imperfect man, and then not even fill that little heart. But when the correct thought of the divine power and influence is understood the apostle's exhortation is thoroughly reasonable. **We should continue seeking to be filled with the holy**

Its Baptism, Witness and Seal 245

mind or disposition of our God, so beautifully exemplified in the person and obedience of our dear Redeemer, his Only Begotten Son.

And this thought of being filled with the Holy Spirit is in harmony with the apostle's suggestion in another place, that our mortal bodies are like leaky vessels, cracked, marred, which God permits to be filled with his Holy Spirit. The apostle's suggestion is that in view of what we know of our own imperfections, and our liability to let slip from us the holy influence, inspired of God through the Gospel, we should give the more earnest heed lest we should let these things slip from us, because "we have this treasure [the Holy Spirit, the renewed mind in harmony with God] in earthen vessels." (Heb. 2:1; 2 Cor. 4:7) It behooves all who would walk in the footsteps of our Master, who would share in the sufferings of Christ, and in the glory that shall follow, to seek in the Lord's way to be filled with his Spirit. To this end we need to keep close to the Lord, and to the fellow-members of his body—close in sympathy, in love, in co-operation; and we need also to keep close to the Word, which is the fountain of the sanctifying influence to the entire Church. "Sanctify them through thy Truth: thy Word is truth."

It is in vain that we seek to be filled with the Holy Spirit if we do not give attention to the divine arrangement provided for this very purpose. If we neglect the Word of God we are neglecting this sanctifying power; if we neglect prayer we are neglecting another privilege, and the helpfulness which it brings. If we neglect to assemble ourselves with those who are the Lord's people, and in whom we see the "seal" of this Spirit, we will fail to get the benefits and helps which "every joint supplieth"—including the helps which God has promised to the Church as a whole, through various members which he sets in the body for the exposition of his Word, and the obtaining therefrom of its sanctifying power or Spirit.—1 Cor. 12:25-28; Eph. 4:16

The exhortation, therefore, "Be ye filled with the Spirit," implies much: it implies that we should make use of the various arrangements and provisions which the Lord has made for our spiritual development. Though we cannot have personal contact with the Lord, we may have intercourse through prayer and through the members of his body, and through the Scriptures. Though we cannot have actual contact with the apostles, we may have contact with their words. If we cannot have actual contact and personal fellowship with the members of the Church, we may have intercourse with them through the mails, and through the medium of the printed page. If we desire to be filled with the Lord's Spirit, we must obey these, his instructions.

THE SEAL OF THE SPIRIT

"In whom [Christ] ye also trusted, after that ye heard the word of Truth, the gospel of your salvation; in whom also, after that ye believed, ye were sealed with the holy Spirit of the promise, which is the earnest of our inheritance."—Eph. 1:13, 14

Seals in olden times were used for various purposes. (1) As a signet or signature, a mark of attestation or acknowledgment. (2) To make secret, to render secure against intrusion—as in Matt. 27:66; Rev. 10:4; 20:3.

It is in the first of these senses that the Lord's people are said to be "sealed with the Holy Spirit of the promise." The apostle does not say, as some seem to suppose, that we were sealed by the Holy Spirit as a person, the so-called third person of a trinity of co-equal Gods: he declares that we were sealed "with the Holy Spirit of the promise"; quite a different thought, as all will perceive. The Holy Spirit is from the Father: he does the sealing through Christ with the Holy Spirit, which itself is the seal. This is attested by the apostle (Acts 2:33), and is in full accord with the record respecting our Lord Jesus, who was the first of the house of sons to be thus sealed. We read, "Him hath God the Father sealed" —with the Holy Spirit.—John 6:27

Its Baptism, Witness and Seal

The expression "Spirit of the promise," like other terms used in reference to the holy influence of God, as the "Spirit of holiness," "the Spirit of Truth," is descriptive: it shows that there is a connection between this sealing and the **promise** which God has given us. It is an advanced evidence or attestation of God's covenant with the "sealed" one, that "the exceeding great and precious promises" of the "things which God hath in reservation for them that love him [supremely]" are true; and that he shall inherit those promised blessings after he has endured faithfully the **tests** of his love and devotion which God will apply.

The apostle refers to this same sealing later on in the same epistle, and there identifies the "promise" with the "day of deliverance." (Eph. 4:30) In other words then, the seal of the Spirit of promise unto the day of deliverance is but another form of expressing the thought—we (the Church) "have the **first-fruits** of the Spirit"—the hand-payment as it were, binding the contract or covenant between the Lord and us, and assuring us that if we faint not we shall inherit the promise to the full.

This seal of covenant relationship, of sonship and heirship, is not an outward sign upon our foreheads; nor is it a mark or manifestation of God's favor in earthly affairs, in worldly prosperity; nor is it now, nor was it ever, the "gifts" of healing, or of speaking with tongues, etc., for many who possessed those miraculous "gifts" lacked the seal and witness of the Spirit.—Acts 8:13-23; 1 Cor. 13:1-3

The seal or pledge of the Holy Spirit is in the heart of the sealed, and hence it is that no man knoweth it save he that receiveth it (Rev. 2:17), except as others may see the fruits of it in his daily life. "He who establisheth us with you in Christ, and hath anointed us, is God; who hath also sealed us and given the earnest of the Spirit in our hearts."—2 Cor. 1:21, 22

This earnest or seal of sonship is the Spirit of love which is at-one with the Father and all his holy arrangements, crying out, Abba, Father; I delight to do thy will, O my God. He who has this seal or mark of sonship is he who not only seeks to do the will of the Father, but doing it finds it "not grievous," but delightsome.—1 John 5:3

The Spirit of adoption or sealing as sons, the possession of the first-fruits or earnest of the coming inheritance, is, then, one of the most advanced "witnesses" of the Spirit—the very cream of Christian experiences in the present life. Before attaining this stage of experience we must receive our share of the **anointing** by coming into the anointed body of Christ, the Church, by being **begotten** of the Spirit of Truth unto sanctification of our spirits to know and do the Lord's will. This experience comes after we have been quickened of the Spirit to the service of righteousness: it is an evidence, so to speak, that we have passed from the embryo condition to one in which God can consider us sons and seal us as such.

As all believers should seek to come under the anointing and begetting influence of the Holy Spirit of God, the Spirit of the Truth—so all who have been thus begotten of the Spirit to sonship should seek to attain that position of fullness of harmony with the Father that he can acknowledge and seal. And having attained this position, let all be careful not to mar or blur the seal—not to quench or extinguish this precious treasure—not to turn this spirit of love and joy in the Holy Spirit of fellowship and communion into a spirit of heaviness, darkness, grief. Not to spoil this seal, but to keep it ever bright and fresh, should be the constant effort of all who receive it.

STUDY X

THE SPIRIT OF A SOUND MIND

THE Spirit of God in His People Casts Out the Spirit of Fear—Mankind in General Unsound Mentally and Physically—The Sense in Which the Holy Spirit is the Spirit of a Sound Mind—The Operations Producing this Result—The Evidences of the Spirit of a Sound Mind.

"God hath not given us the spirit of fear, but of power and of love and of a sound mind."—2 Tim. 1:7

BY EVERY law of language, the spirit of fear is here put in contrast with another spirit. If the Spirit of love, power, a sound mind, be a person, or three persons, then in all reason the Spirit of fear should be considered another person. The fallacy of such an argument is so apparent as to need nothing more than a mere statement for its disproof.

In proportion as the Lord's people are filled with his Holy Spirit or influence and are expanded more and more by it, and enlarged, they have the less of the spirit of fear. The spirit of fear in a Christian is the spirit of doubt, and marks a lack of faith, a lack of the Holy Spirit. The spirit of fear is a fruitful source of evil in spiritual matters, in every feature of the Christian growth, individually and as a Church; and it is also closely identified with physical weakness and disabilities. The child of God who is filled with the Holy Spirit is a giant in comparison with his own natural self; because his fears are quelled, his heart is established, his faith is rooted and grounded, and his soul is anchored sure and steadfast, within the veil. Thus he is held from being driven onto the rocks of disaster, when the stormy winds of trouble prevail. The Holy Spirit is thus a power to those who possess it, which has often caused amazement to their enemies.

It is not our claim that the Gospel of Christ takes hold upon the strong minded and strong bodied, and that therefore those who are his are strong; quite to the contrary of this, we hold, as a matter of fact, as well as a matter of scriptural testimony, that the Gospel of Christ usually takes hold upon the weaker ones, who feel their weakness, and who realize more than do the stronger their need of help. Yet such is the transforming influence of the Holy Spirit upon those who receive it, that in their weakness they are made strong. The weak things of this world are made mighty through God (through the Spirit, the power of God) to the pulling down of strongholds of error and sin, and to the endurance of a good fight as good soldiers of the Lord Jesus Christ, much to the surprise of those naturally their superiors.— 1 Cor. 1:27; 2 Cor. 10:4; 2 Tim. 2:3, 4

This was true in times past, when the weak ones of the world espoused the cause of Christ, and were firm to the very end of life, as martyrs, enduring unwaveringly trials and difficulties before which the strongest of the world quailed. And the same thing is still true of the same class, for although the particular features of persecution have greatly changed, nevertheless it is still necessary to "endure hardness as good soldiers," and to "lay down our lives for the brethren": and the weak things of the world, yea those that are naught, whom God hath chosen, are still confounding the wisdom and might of this world.—1 Cor. 1:27, 28

This Spirit of God in us is not only a Spirit of power, but a Spirit of love, says the apostle. The love here mentioned is not the natural love possessed to some extent by all mankind, and even by the brute creation—in large measure a spirit of selfishness. In those who receive the Holy Spirit of love this natural love should become intensified, broadened, deepened, and should more and more lose its selfish characteristics, and become a generous love, a self-sacrificing love, based not upon selfishness, but upon principles of righteousness, truth, goodness, and the possession in general of the Spirit, disposi-

The Spirit of a Sound Mind

tion of God. And this Spirit of love should continue, increasing and abounding more and more until that which is perfect is come and that which is in part will be done away.—1 Cor. 13:10

There is no more wonderful manifestation of the Holy Spirit in the Lord's people than that which the apostle in our text denominates "the Spirit of a sound mind." The Lord's people, by nature, are not more sound of mind than are the world's people, Quite the contrary. As we have already seen, the tendency of the Gospel is to attract the more imperfect, who realize their own impotency and their need of grace and strength from on high, rather than to influence those who are of stronger and sounder minds—who, comparing themselves with others, have a self-satisfied, self-righteous spirit or mind.

But whenever the Truth is received into good and honest hearts and brings forth its legitimate fruitage, and the Lord's people become partakers of his Holy Spirit, whether naturally strong or weak, they thereby obtain the "Spirit of a sound mind"—their **judgments are clearer, truer, more trustworthy, than before;** because they have before their minds, first of all, the explicit directions of the Lord's Word in respect to what they should do, and what they should not do—directions which cover almost every feature and aim of life. Those who have accepted the Lord as their instructor and teacher, and who have his Spirit of obedience to the Father's will, have the "Spirit of a **sound** mind," because they do not trust merely to their own judgment, not merely to their own understanding, but by obedience to the Lord's directions they are preserved in the vicissitudes of life from the snares and difficulties which befall those who have not the guidance and direction of superhuman wisdom.

As a result of the fall of our race into sin and its condemnation, death, the whole world is unsound, mentally as well as physically—but in varying degrees, according to circumstances and heredity. As some are physically less sound than others, so some are mentally less sound than others, yet all are unsound, as the Scriptures declare, "There is none righteous [perfect, sound, either in mind or body], no not one." (Rom. 3:10) Figuratively, all are covered with wounds and bruises and putrefying sores—mental and physical. (Isa. 1:5, 6) The curse of sin has laid its heavy hand on the entire man—mind and body.

It is a well-recognized fact that suffering in one member of the body causes ailment to the entire body, including the mind. The mind could not be perfectly sound, while supported and nourished by an unsound body. The deranged stomach of a dyspeptic has a direct effect upon his mind, as well as upon his entire physical system. The person whose lungs are diseased cannot avoid a degree of mental impairment corresponding; likewise, when other organs, the heart, the liver, the kidneys, are diseased and perform their functions imperfectly, the effect unquestionably is disordered blood, and a disordered nervous system, the center of which is the brain. Likewise the brain that is harassed by pain or imperfectly nourished through malnutrition, or fevered through failure of the action of the secretive organs, is sure to be impaired in all its various functions: it cannot think and reason as correctly, as logically, as if in perfect condition. Derangements of the mind are so common, that the word derangement is not applied except in quite extreme cases of more than average unsoundness, unbalance. But no one of judgment and experience will question these conclusions.

The question arises, How or wherein does the impartation of the Holy Spirit to the Christian serve to repair his judgment, and become to him the Spirit of a sound mind? We answer that the divine mind is perfect, "sound," and consequently to whatever extent Christians are able to set aside their own minds or judgments, on any or all matters, and to accept instead the divine mind, will, judgment, for the control of their lives, to that extent they will have the spirit or disposition of a sound mind—God's mind.

The Spirit of a Sound Mind

We do not mean by this that the brains of Christians undergo a change or a reversal of the order of nature in their operation, but that under the guidance of the Holy Spirit, the Spirit of the Truth, such learn gradually to **rectify the errors** of their own judgments in respect to all the various questions which come before them, to harmonize with the teaching of the Holy Spirit through the Word of God. To illustrate: **suppose we had a clock, a poor timekeeper,** and without means for regulation; suppose also that we had access frequently to a chronometer of absolute correctness, which showed us that our clock lost thirty minutes every twenty-four hours, we would learn how to correct it, by resetting every twenty-four hours. Moreover, we would learn also how to estimate its error at any point in the day. So with our judgments, and the various matters and affairs of life: when we measure them with the perfect standard, we find that we are either too fast or too slow, too weak or too strong, in our mental and physical emotions. And while we are quite unable to alter our methods of thought and action so as to have them perfect and in full accord with those of our Lord Jesus, our standard, nevertheless we are enabled to regulate our thoughts, our judgments, according to the standard which is before our minds, in a way and to a degree which those who have not this perfect standard, or who are not seeking to be regulated by it, will neither appreciate nor be able to copy.

Who has not noticed in his friends and his neighbors (as well as in himself) abundant evidence of such unsoundness of mind that they are unable to manage their affairs creditably, and who nevertheless cause great annoyance by their attempts to manage the affairs of others? Through self-conceit they are judging others, gossiping busybodies in other men's matters, though evidencing thorough incapacity for the management of their own affairs. Is not this one evidence of an unsound mind—a measure of insanity? Do we not find that the same principle, carried to a still greater extreme, is noticeable in the cases of all whose judgments are so unsound that they are obliged to be confined in an asylum? Undoubtedly self-conceit, approbativeness and fear are the bases of the mental troubles in the majority of those who are confined in insane asylums—many of the remainder being demoniacal obsession. If we enter an insane asylum we find some of the inmates laboring under the delusion that they are very wealthy, or that they are kings, or queens, or nobles, or princes, and correspondingly full of pride and touchiness, and easily offended. Others have endured fancied wrongs, and imagine that they are not sufficiently appreciated, and their friends are endeavoring to get them out of the way, for fear of their influence, or to hide their ability, or to prevent them from securing a fortune. Others, through fear, imagine that every one is seeking their life, that the whole world is mad, and that they alone are sane; or that God is against them, and that their fate is eternal torment, because they have committed unpardonable sins, etc.

All these are but **extremes** of mental conditions and characteristics which the observing may see about them every day in all the walks of life. The tendency of the world and the spirit of the world, with its ambitions and pride, its superstitions and errors and fears, is to intensify these natural conditions; and as a result we find that insanity in the extreme form is making rapid increase throughout the civilized world.

What these need—what we and all mankind need —are sound minds: but the time for the general healing of a world's mental and physical ailments at the hands of the Great Physician is the Millennial age, when fully introduced; but that age cannot be introduced, and its relief and blessings cannot come, until the due time. Meantime, however, the called-out Gospel Church obtains, through her Lord and his Word, **his** Holy Spirit—the Spirit of **his** sound mind, which is the same as the Father's mind or Spirit. And in proportion as each member utilizes his privileges in this connection he will be helped over the natural mental and physical troubles which beset us in common with the whole world of mankind. The Word of the Lord through the apostle directs us thus—"I say . . . to every man that is among you not to think of himself more highly than he ought to think; but to think soberly [not according to the flesh, but according to his new nature] according as God hath dealt to every man the measure of faith." (Rom. 12:3) It is a life work with many, to conquer their too high appreciation of themselves, and to obtain the Spirit of a sound mind as respects their own talents, but they are assisted in this work of rectifying their pride, by the words of the Master, which say, "Blessed are the meek, for they shall inherit the earth." They are assisted also by the words of the apostle, which declare that "God resisteth the proud, but giveth grace [favor] to the humble." "Humble yourselves therefore under the mighty hand of God, that he may exalt you in due time."—Matt. 5:5; Jas. 4:6; 1 Pet. 5:5, 6

But, as a matter of fact, not many great, not many wise, according to the course of this world and according to their own estimation of their own wisdom, hath God chosen; but rather the poor of this world, rich in faith—who trust not to their own wisdom, nor to their own righteousness, but accept Christ as their wisdom, their justification, their all.

Likewise, also, those who have the "spirit of fear" are helped to counteract it by the "Spirit of truth," the "Spirit of love," if they receive it—for, "Perfect love casteth out fear." (1 John 4:18) As they learn to know God through his Word and the gracious plan of the ages therein set forth, it removes from their minds the great incubus of fear and dread which torments so many. It gives them instead of fear, hope—a hope that maketh not ashamed, because the love of God is shed abroad in their hearts through the Holy Spirit—the Spirit of a sound mind.

Thus also those who are too humble (too lacking in self-confidence) ever to accomplish anything in life, are encouraged and uplifted and made useful to themselves and to others, by the same Spirit of truth which reproves and corrects those who are over-confident, self-assertive, self-conscious, self-conceited. The former are encouraged by assurances of God's aid; the latter are restrained, moderated, brought into subjection and taught what is pleasing to God and helpful to themselves: as the apostle says, "If any man [confidently] think that he knoweth anything [of his own wisdom], he knoweth nothing yet as he ought to know." (1 Cor. 8:2) But transformations of character, let us remember, come not from saying, Lord, Lord, nor from having a Bible in one's possession; nor from joining a human organization called a church; but from joining Christ, and receiving from him the Spirit of his Word, the Spirit of truth, the Spirit of holiness, the Spirit of a sound mind—his Holy Spirit and the Father's.

The man who has, by the grace of God, and his own acceptance of that grace, come into possession of the Spirit of a sound mind, has much advantage every way over the remainder of mankind; for the Spirit of a sound mind is a Spirit of wisdom. Such an one values more correctly than others the things of this life—wealth, fame, social position, etc. From his new standpoint he sees things connected with all these which others do not notice. His mind, instructed from the Lord's Word, discerns that if he should amass all the wealth of the world, he could take none of it with him when he dies. He sees that fame is a very hollow and very transitory thing, and that in the busy rush of life the dead are soon forgotten. He sees that society is shallow, and its profession of esteem, etc., often insincere, and that its effervescence terminates with death—if not sooner in financial disaster. They see, in the language of the world, that—"The game [of chance for earthly fame and wealth and pleasure] is not worth the candle." And indeed, from the standpoint of the average man and woman of the world, life is but a game of cards—unsatisfactory in its results, because even to

The Spirit of a Sound Mind

the most successful it means comparatively nothing in the end.

On the other hand, the children of God, now begotten of the Holy Spirit to the "high calling" of this Gospel age, have something offered to them which attracts their minds away from trifles and delusions which captivate and often frenzy the minds of mankind in general. Theirs are higher joys, higher ambitions—for a higher social standing, for greater riches and for a Kingdom—for heavenly riches and a heavenly and eternal Kingdom. The ambitions inspired by these heavenly promises are **holy** ambitions, full of mercy and good fruits, and operate along the lines of love, while the operations of the earthly ambitions are along the lines of selfishness.

The man or woman whose aim is lifted from these earthly toys and vanities and ambitions, and placed upon the heavenly, certainly has much better opportunities for exercising a sound judgment in respect to all the affairs of this present life—because he looks upon them from a comparatively disinterested standpoint. He is in the world, and obliged to live, and to this end to provide things needful and decent and honest in the sight of all men; but being relieved of inordinate ambitions toward worldly things, he is proportionately relieved from the pressure of avarice, covetousness, pride, etc., and the better enabled to think and to act justly, and to exercise kindly sympathy toward all. This Spirit of a sound mind, or better judgment of the experienced Christian, is not reckoned as a correction or repair of his earthly or fleshly mind, but as a new mind or disposition, begotten in him from above by the exceeding great and precious promises of the Word of the Lord. (2 Pet. 1:4) He is thus helped by reason of his new disposition, the Spirit or disposition of a sound mind, the Holy Spirit of the Lord. And his mind will be sound in proportion as he receives and is filled with the

Holy Spirit. And this will be rapid or slow in proportion as his love for the Lord and his righteousness is fervent or cool.

It was the Master who inquired, "For what will a man exchange his soul [his being—his existence]?" (Matt. 16:26) A man with a sound mind would not exchange the most valuable thing which he possesses (his being), for anything—wealth, fame or office. And in proportion as any receive the Spirit of a sound mind, this will be their estimate. On the contrary, we see the world today doing the reverse, and thus proving their mental unsoundness. What are known as the wisest men of the world are spending their labor for that which satisfieth not—in the accumulation of wealth; in strife for honor, social standing and preferment; in vainglorious display and pleasures of sin. Even were there no future life, all who have the Spirit of a sound mind can see that such courses are unwise; for the majority spend the present life in getting ready for enjoyment, and then lie down in death, realizing that they have not obtained what they sought—and that the wealth or fame which they leave behind them will soon be scattered, or if not scattered, that it will remain a monument of their folly, avarice and unsoundness of mind.

The world's life, devoid of reasonable aims and ambitions, is what the apostle calls "your **vain** [fruitless] conversation [life] received by custom from your fathers." (1 Pet. 1:18) The custom of laboring for unworthy objects is hereditary; men do not stop to reason the matter out, but drop into the grooves in which their parents moved. But the apostle points out that our change of course is because we have learned that we were **redeemed** by the precious blood of Christ. We have discovered through the Word of grace that the course of the world is vain and that all follow the vain course because of depravity—unsoundness of mind through the fall—and

The Spirit of a Sound Mind

having learned of the great purchase we gladly consecrate to him who redeemed us and receive of his Spirit—the Spirit of a sound mind.

When the present life is viewed from the standpoint of the Holy Spirit, presented in the Holy Word, it is seen to be but a schooling season, a preparation for a future life, for all who see that prize and hear the "call." However, only those whose eyes are opened and who see from the inside can realize how unwise is the course of the majority, who, so far from curbing their own selfish propensities, and cultivating the nobler and truer elements of their fallen nature, are in many instances undermining character, and leaving the world at death weaker in character than when they were born into it, with oftentimes a legacy of weakness also entailed upon their offspring.

On the other hand, while the Word of God and the Holy Spirit of that Word restrain our ambitions for earthly riches, and assure us that the "love of money is the root of all evil" (1 Tim. 6:10), they protect us from the opposite extreme of slothfulness, indolence—instructing that each should provide things honest in the sight of all men, and especially for the necessities of his own household. They exhort us to be "Not slothful in business, but fervent in spirit, serving the Lord." (Rom. 12:11) Thus, those who have the Lord's Spirit are guarded against the folly of those who spend life with Bunyan's "muck-rake," gathering to themselves treasures of no real worth; they are also guarded against the unsoundness of indolence, and exhorted to be energetic in all good services, which will be helpful to humanity and which will meet with the divine approval, and be accepted as a service "done unto the Lord," which will have his abundant reward in the life everlasting.

The Spirit of a sound mind sees in the present life opportunities for the attainment of riches of character, riches of grace, and for the laying up of treasures which neither moth nor rust will consume.

but which will be enduring—eternal joys. Not that the Spirit of a sound mind leads us to live in the future, to the neglect of the present: rather it lives wisely in the present, by keeping in memory the future.

The Spirit of a sound mind broadens and deepens character along all its good lines; it not only helps its possessor to take correct views of himself, but also to take correct views of his fellows in degradation, and it enlarges his sympathies. He realizes the impairment of his own mind and body through the fall, and his own need of mercy and helpful correction, as well as the similar derangement of the whole world of mankind, and the general need for sympathy and aid for correction. As he learns to rectify the deficiencies and inequalities of his own mind, he sympathizes the more with others who are without this regulating principle, this Spirit of a sound mind, and who are hindered from accepting it by reason of the opposition of the Adversary, "the god of this world," who blinds the minds of them that believe not, lest the glorious light of divine goodness, in the face of Jesus Christ, should shine into their hearts, and should bring to them the Spirit of a sound mind. —2 Cor. 4:4

In proportion as he develops in this Holy Spirit of his adoption, a "new creature in Christ Jesus," he becomes, through its operation, gradually more patient, more sympathetic, more generous more loving—more Godlike. And these benevolences of character will affect not only the outward acts of his life, but also his words and his thoughts. In proportion as his Holy Spirit discountenances a dishonorable or dishonest action, in the same proportion it discountenances a dishonorable or a dishonest word, in respect to friend or neighbor or enemy; and similarly it discountenances the slightest injustice or unkindness of thought to any of these.

The Spirit of a sound mind will therefore gradually but surely make the husband a better husband, the father a better father, the son a better son, the wife a better wife, the mother a better mother, the

The Spirit of a Sound Mind

daughter a better daughter. It will do this, because the basis of thought and word and conduct has changed from selfishness to love. The one possessed of this Spirit of a sound mind, the Holy Spirit, the Spirit of love, will in proportion as he comes into possession of it, be less touchy in respect to his own rights, privileges, preferments, and more considerate for the rights and feelings and preferences of others. The will of the Lord must, of course, stand first, but next to pleasing the Lord he will take pleasure in pleasing others with whom he may come in contact, especially those of his own family: and in harmony with this desire to serve and to please the Lord first, and then the Lord's family, and all men as he may have opportunity, his thoughts will operate, his words be guided and regulated, and his conduct shape itself.

It does not follow that the man or woman who has received the Spirit of a sound mind will therefore be the best husband, the best wife, the best brother, the best sister, the best father, the best mother, in every particular; because, as we have already suggested, the mission of the gospel of Christ, in its effect upon the civilized world, is to take hold of the mean things of this world, and the things that are not [of value], and to uplift these in proportion as they come into consecration to the Lord, and receive the Spirit of a sound mind. On the contrary, some much better born, on a higher plane, are more inclined to self-righteousness, and to decline the assistance which the Lord offers. These may be noble husbands, noble wives, noble children, noble parents, by reason of being of more noble birth, by reason of inheriting through Christian parents minds of better poise and greater wisdom. But unless such accept the Savior, and the offer of the new mind, they are very sure to degenerate, and their kindness, gentleness, etc., to become more of a matter of outward form, covering an inward selfishness, which soon or later will crop out in their posterity, bringing them in turn to a lower plane.

The thought we wish to impress is that on whatever plane of mental decrepitude, immorality or unwisdom the truth and grace of God shall reach a man or woman, it will lift him up and make him or her the nobler, the purer, the kinder, the gentler, the more considerate of others—in proportion as he or she receives this new mind, the Spirit of a sound mind.

The unsoundness of the human mind in general is illustrated in the matter of the reckless propagation of the human race. It progresses almost without regard to the laws of health, and almost without provision for the proper sustenance of the offspring, and in utter violation of the laws of nature, recognized in breeding of lower animals, cattle, sheep, horses, dogs. No wonder the apostle enjoins upon the believers the exercise of a sound mind in the use of man's highest natural power, procreation, saying, "Husbands, deal with your wives according to knowledge." (1 Pet. 3:7) If this advice were followed, if the Spirit of a sound mind prevailed, how much more consideration would be shown for delicate and overburdened wives, by husbands who truly love them—dealing with them according to knowledge.

But only the servants and handmaids of the Lord have yet received this Holy Spirit of God—this Spirit of a sound mind. Thank God the time is near when through the ministries of these servants and handmaids, glorified and empowered with the King of glory, all the world shall be blessed and the Lord shall pour out his Holy Spirit, the Spirit of a sound mind "upon all flesh."

STUDY XI

THE HOLY SPIRIT OF AT-ONE-MENT

SUPPOSED OBJECTIONS CONSIDERED

Apparently Contradictory Scriptures Examined—Quench not the Spirit—Grieve not the Holy Spirit—The Spirit of Truth—The Comforter—Filled with the Holy Spirit—Lying to the Holy Spirit—Tempting the Spirit of the Lord—Sin Against the Holy Spirit—"The Spirit Said"—"It Seemed Good to the Holy Spirit"—"Forbidden of the Holy Ghost"—"The Holy Ghost Witnesseth"—"The Holy Ghost hath Made You Overseers"—The Holy Spirit a Teacher—"An Unction from the Holy One"—The Spirit Maketh Intercessions with Groanings—How the Spirit Reproves the World—"Hereby Know Ye the Spirit of God" from "the Spirit of Antichrist."

IN CONSEQUENCE of the translating of the Scriptures having been done by Trinitarians (both the Common Version and the Revised), many passages have been given a bias or twist which causes an apparent disagreement between some of these and what we have seen foregoing to be the scriptural as well as the reasonable view of the subject under discussion—that the Holy Spirit of the Father and by the Son is in the Lord's people the Spirit of at-one-ment. We will, therefore, now take up a variety of Scriptures—all that we can think of as likely to be confusing to the minds of many. Let us examine these together, with our hearts fully loyal to the Word of God, and desirous of being led by the Spirit of Truth: then we will proceed to other phases of the subject, which cannot so well be understood until these supposed objections are removed.

"QUENCH NOT THE SPIRIT"
1 Thess. 5:19

To quench signifies to extinguish, as when we quench a fire, or extinguish a light. The Greek word here rendered "quench" occurs eight times in the New Testament, and in every other instance it refers to quenching fire or light. Carrying this thought with us, let us remember that by reason of our possession of the Holy Spirit or mind of God, enlightening us, we are called "the light of the world" (Matt. 5:14): thus we see that the apostle meant that if we should be seduced into worldliness by the spirit of the world, the effect would be to extinguish or quench the light of the holy mind or Spirit of God in us, and shining from us upon others. In harmony with this is our Lord's expression, "If the light that is in thee become darkness [be extinguished], how great is that darkness."—Matt. 6:23

"GRIEVE NOT THE HOLY SPIRIT OF GOD, WHEREBY YE ARE SEALED UNTO THE DAY OF REDEMPTION"
Eph. 4:30

To seal signifies to mark or designate. The children of this world may be distinguished by certain marks, and the children of God, the new creatures in Christ, by other marks or characteristics. The mark of the one class is the spirit (mind, disposition, will) of the world; in the other class the seal or mark is of the Spirit (mind, disposition, will) of God. From the moment of true consecration to God, the evidence, marks or sealing may be noted in the words, thoughts and conduct. These marks grow more and more distinct as the new mind grows in grace, knowledge and love. In other words, the Spirit (mind) of God becomes **our** mind or spirit, in proportion as we give up our human will or spirit, and submit in all things to the will or Spirit of God. Thus we are exhorted to permit or let the same mind be in us which was also in Christ Jesus our Lord—a mind or disposition to do only the Father's will. Hence, our new mind or Spirit is holy or God-directed. In the text under consideration the apostle urges that we do nothing which would be a violation of our covenant—that we do nothing to cause grief to our new minds or smiting of conscience from dereliction of duty—nothing that would wound our conscience, as new creatures in Christ. Grieve not the Holy Spirit, mind of God, in you, which is your seal of divine sonship.

"THE SPIRIT OF THE TRUTH"

"The Spirit of Truth. . . . shall not speak of himself, but whatsoever he shall hear he shall speak, and he will show you things to come."—John 16:13

This Scripture has already had consideration on page 170, but some additional features require consideration here. The disciples, as Jews and natural men, had been looking at matters from an earthly standpoint, expecting a human deliverance, and an earthly kingdom in the hands of fallen men. Our Lord had talked to them concerning the Kingdom of God, but not until now had he explained that he must die, must leave them, and go into a far country, to receive the Kingdom authority, and to return to establish his Kingdom and glorify his faithful ones with himself as joint-heirs in that Kingdom. (Luke 19:12) Consoling them, in view of the disappointment awakened by his declaration, he assures them that they shall not be left wholly alone, but that as the Father had sent him to do a work, so, during his absence, the Father would send another Comforter, in his name, or as his representative for the time. They must not get the idea that the coming Comforter is to be another Messiah or a different teacher; hence he says, "He shall not speak of himself"; he shall not teach independently and out of harmony with my teaching, which you already have received; "but whatsoever he shall hear that shall he speak."

That is to say, this Comforter will be merely a channel of communication between the Father and myself, on the one hand, and you, my faithful followers, on the other: the Spirit of Truth, as my representative, will elaborate and bring to your attention more particularly various truths which I have already stated to you, but which you are not yet prepared to clearly comprehend—which, indeed, it is not proper for you to understand until first I shall have paid your ransom, and have ascended into the Father's presence, and presented it before him on your behalf. Then in harmony with the Father's plan, I shall be enabled, through this Comforter, to communicate to you the spiritual things, for which you are now unprepared, and to which now, being not yet atoned for, you have no right. And as future things become due to be understood by you, this Spirit of the Father, my Spirit, sent in my name, and as a result of my redemptive work, shall guide you step by step into the full understanding of everything necessary and proper for you to understand— "He [the Father's Holy Spirit, influence or power] shall glorify me, for he shall receive of mine, and shall show it unto you. All things that the Father hath are mine [his plans and mine are in perfect union]; therefore said I that he shall take of mine and show it unto you."

You are not, therefore, to expect a new teaching, subversive of my teaching, but rather a further development and instruction along the lines of my teaching: for all the teachings of the coming Comforter will be in harmony with mine, and designed to show you more fully that I am the Messiah. Neither need you doubt the truth of this Comforter's teachings, for it is the very Spirit of Truth, and proceeds from the Father. This Spirit of Truth will be my messenger to communicate to you my doctrines, and will show you things to come.—John 16:13

And thus it has been: the Spirit of Truth has been showing to the Church throughout this Gospel age more and more respecting the sufferings of Christ and the necessity for every member of his "body" to share them, and the pathway that we should take in following our Redeemer and Lord: showing us also the height of the glory of his reward, and our privilege of becoming "heirs of God, joint-heirs with Jesus Christ our Lord, if so be that we suffer with him, that we may be also glorified together." Jehovah, the Father of all, is the Author of all this truth, and hence all that we have received throughout this age has proceeded from him, from whom cometh every good and every perfect gift. He has sent it through channels long since prepared—through the prophetic and typical teachings of the past opened up to us through the inspired words of our Lord Jesus and his inspired apostles: and by receiving of the Holy Spirit in our hearts, and by conduct in harmony with the Father's Word and plan, we are enabled to appreciate the things which God hath in reservation for them that love him, and to walk by faith and not by sight.

"BUT THE COMFORTER, WHICH IS THE HOLY GHOST, WHOM THE FATHER WILL SEND IN MY NAME"
——John 14:26——

We have already examined this misleading word "ghost" (page 169), but we now notice the statement that the Holy Spirit is to be sent by the Father, which indicates that it is an influence or power wholly under the Father's control; and not another being equal in power and glory, as the creeds of men falsely assert. All of God's powers are fully under his own control, as our powers are under our control, and hence the declaration that the Father would send his Spirit, or, as the prophet has expressed it, "I will put my Spirit within thee." Moreover, the Holy Spirit is declared to have been sent in Jesus' name—just as a servant is sent in the name of his master and not in his own name. Here we have another contradiction of the unscriptural theory of three Gods of equal power and glory. Here the Father's superiority is clearly stated: the Holy Spirit is the Father's Spirit, power, influence, sent at the instance and in the name of our Redeemer,

Jesus. Why in the name of Jesus? Because the entire work of redemption and restitution of sinners, the entire work of Atonement, has been committed unto the Son, and the Holy Spirit of the Father is the channel by which the Son operates in conferring the blessings purchased by his precious blood.

When the Holy Spirit of the Father came upon our Lord Jesus at his baptism and consecration, it was a comfort indeed, a great blessing, but it nevertheless meant to him the sacrifice of every earthly aim and hope in the execution of the divine plan. Had our Lord been otherwise minded, self-willed and self-seeking, the guidance of the Holy Spirit, instead of being comforting to him, would have been disquieting; his heart would have been full of dissatisfaction, discontent, rebellion. And so it is with the Lord's people: the more of the mind of the Lord the natural man can discern, the more unhappy and uncomfortable he becomes, because it conflicts with his spirit, mind or will, and reproves him. But the "new creature in Christ," whose own will is dead, and who seeks to know the Father's will, and to do it—to him the clear apprehension of the Father's will and plan and the leading of divine providence in connection with the instruction of the divine Word, are comforting indeed—bringing peace, joy and contentment, even in the midst of tribulations and persecutions. In harmony with this thought is the apostle's declaration respecting the Word of truth, whose Spirit must be received and appreciated in order to give comfort. He says, "Whatsoever things were written aforetime were written for our admonition, that we through patience and comfort of the Scriptures might have hope."—Rom. 15:4

"FILLED WITH THE HOLY SPIRIT"

"They were all filled with the Holy Spirit, and began to speak with tongues, as the Spirit gave them utterance."—Acts 2:4

This text describes a twofold operation of the Holy Spirit: (1) It was the mind, disposition, Spirit of God, operating in the disciples, as the Spirit of adoption, bringing their hearts into closeness of sympathy and touch with the Father and with the glorified Redeemer. (2) God's Holy Spirit or power or influence acted also **upon** them, conferring special miraculous gifts for a testimony to the world, and for the establishment of the Church. While it would be unreasonable in the extreme to think of a God getting personally into one man, and still more unreasonable to think of God getting personally into a hundred, a thousand, or a million men, there is not the slightest unreasonableness in the thought that the power of the Highest, the power, the influence of Jehovah could be in and upon hundreds, thousands or millions without in anywise interfering with the personal presence of Jehovah upon the throne of the universe.

LYING TO THE HOLY SPIRIT

"Peter said, Ananias, why hath Satan filled thy heart, to lie to the Holy Spirit, and to keep back part of the price of the land?"—Acts 5:3

Satan filled Ananias' heart in the same manner as God fills the hearts of his people—by his Spirit, his influence. Satan's Spirit is one of covetousness and selfishness, which does not hesitate at deceit to accomplish its ends. Peter, who had been made the recipient of a special "gift of discerning of spirits," was able to read the heart, to read the mind, and thus could see that Ananias and Sapphira were acting dishonestly, pretending to do what they were not really doing. It will be noticed, in this connection, that the apostle uses the words "God" and "Holy Spirit" interchangeably, saying, in verse 3, that they had lied unto the Holy Spirit, and, in verse 4, that they had lied unto God. The thought is the same. God's Holy Spirit, acting through the apostles, was God's representative, most emphatically; and consequently, in lying to the apostles who represented God and his Holy Spirit, Ananias and Sapphira were lying to God, lying to the Holy Spirit of God, whose agent and representative Peter was.

TEMPTING THE HOLY SPIRIT

"Then Peter said unto her [Sapphira], How is it that ye have agreed together to tempt the Spirit of the Lord?"—Acts 5:9

This is to be understood in the same way as the foregoing, but the same Spirit is here referred to as being "the Spirit of the Lord," by which the apostle probably meant the Lord Jesus. We can readily see the reasonableness of this also. The Spirit of the Father, the Holy Spirit, was especially in the Church, the representative of the Church's Lord or Head—operating through the mind of his "body"—in this instance his Spirit-inspired and actuated apostle.

SIN AGAINST THE HOLY SPIRIT

"Whosoever speaketh against the Holy Spirit, it shall not be forgiven him, neither in this world, neither in the world to come."—Matt. 12:32

The thought generally deduced from this statement by those who consider the Holy Spirit to be a personal God, separate and distinct from the Father and the Son, is that the Holy Spirit is a much more important personage than either the Father or the Son. But as we have already seen, the Scriptures nowhere acknowledge more than one God, the Father, of whom are all things, and he superior to all; and one Lord, Jesus Christ, by whom are all things, and he next to the Father exalted to that position by the Father's power. The Holy Spirit was of the Father and by the Son, and hence could not be superior to them, if a person; but we have seen that there is no personality connected with the Holy Spirit; rather it is the Spirit of a person or being, the Spirit of the Lord, his influence, his power, and in this sense of the word, himself, representative of all his wisdom, majesty, power and love. Let us see then, what the passage does signify.

From the context, we notice that our Lord Jesus had just been using this divine power, or Holy Spirit, conferred upon him by the Father, to cast out a

Supposed Objections Considered

devil. The Pharisees who saw the miracle, and could not deny it, sought to turn aside its force by claiming that it was performed by Satanic power. In reply to them our Lord distinctly disclaimed the power he used as being his own, and asserts that it was divine power or influence, saying, "I cast out devils by the Spirit of God." He then upbraided the Pharisees for being so **malicious** as to attribute to an evil source that which they could not deny was a good work, and accompanied by no evidence whatever of sin, selfishness, or even ambition. He denominates them a generation of vipers, so set upon the traditions of their church that their minds were blinded to most simple and manifest truths. It was plainly evident that the power or influence which had possessed the afflicted one was devilish, malignant; and that any power which would dispossess it must be out of harmony with that evil disposition, so that these teachers were inexcusable, when they claimed, without any cause, that the miracle was performed by the power of Satan.

Our Lord pointed out further, that although they had not intentionally blasphemed Jehovah, nor had they particularly blasphemed himself, they had blasphemed against the holy **power** or Spirit which was operating in him. For them to have misunderstood and misrepresented the invisible God would have been a much lighter offense; and to have spoken evil of our Lord Jesus and to have misinterpreted his motives, claiming that he was merely trying to usurp a throne and to exalt himself in power, would also have been a comparatively light offence—measuring his motives by their own selfish ambition and pride. But their conduct was worse: after they had witnessed the manifestation of divine power in performing a good deed for the relief of one of their fellow-creatures from the power of the devil—to blaspheme this holy power, meant a degree of wickedness and animosity of heart of much deeper dye than either of the other offenses would have implied.

Our Lord pointed out to them that in their ignorance and blindness they might have misinterpreted him, his words, his efforts; and in similar blindness they might have misinterpreted many of God's dealings, and spoken evil thereof; but when once the power of God had been witnessed by them, in direct contrast with the power of the devil, the fact that they spoke evil of it implied most unmistakably that their hearts were in a most unholy condition. Sins of ignorance may be forgiven men—will be forgiven men—because the ignorance came through the fall, and a ransom has been paid for all who shared in the fall and its curse. But sins against clear manifestations of divine grace cannot be attributed to weakness of the flesh and heredity, but must be properly charged up as wilful viciousness of the heart, which is unforgivable.

Wilful, intentional evil will never have forgiveness—neither in this age, nor in the coming age. God's proposition is not to force men into harmony with himself; but after redeeming them he will furnish to all an opportunity of coming to a knowledge of the truth and witnessing the goodness of God through the operation of his Holy Spirit: whoever then continues out of harmony with the divine arrangement proves himself a wilful sinner, an intelligent opponent of the holy power of God—for such the Lord has no further provisions of grace.

Whether or not the scribes and Pharisees came to a sufficiently clear appreciation of God's holy power to constitute them amenable to the Second Death, for reproaching it as an evil power, we are not able to judge, because we are unable to read their hearts, and because our Lord did not fully state the matter in this connection. If assured they sinned against clear light, sinned to the full against the power of God, we could have no further hope for them, but should merely expect them to perish in the Second Death, as wilful rejectors of God's grace. But if they did not receive a sufficiency of light and knowledge, sufficient contact with the holy power of God, to constitute for them a full trial, they must ultimately come to such a full trial, before they could suffer the full penalty—Second Death.

But **every** sin against the Holy Spirit, against **clear light and knowledge of divine power, is unforgivable,** because wilful. If it be a wilful sin against a measure of light, then "stripes," punishment, will result, unavoidably; if it be wilful **sin against a larger measure** of light and a greater favor in connection with the holy power of God, then a greater measure of stripes; but if the transgression involves a full, clear conception of right and wrong, and full, knowing opposition to the holy power of God, it would mean everlasting destruction, the Second Death, the full wages of sin. The **forgiveness** of sins secured by the ransom covers sins of ignorance or weakness resulting from the fall, and not personal, wilful, deliberate sins against light. We are not to forget, however, that many sins which contain a measure of wilfulness blend with it a measure of weakness or of ignorance of right principles or of both. To the proportion of its ignorance and weakness any sin is **forgivable** through the grace of God in Christ—through faith in and acceptance of his atonement; and to the proportion that any sin was wilful, intentional sin it is unforgivable—must be **expiated** by punishment— "stripes," so long as some forgivable quality inheres in the sin; death, destruction, when no forgivable quality can be found in the sin.

Thus seen, all wilful sin is sin against light, sin against the Holy Spirit of truth—and such sin hath never **forgiveness.**

"THE SPIRIT SAID UNTO PHILIP, GO NEAR, AND JOIN THYSELF TO THIS CHARIOT"
——Acts 8:29——

Nothing associated with these words, nor with the context, seems to imply the necessity for another God. On the contrary, every requirement is met, and harmony with the remainder of the Scriptures maintained, when we understand that the Lord, by his Spirit, influence, power, directed and instructed Philip to approach the chariot of the eunuch. In what manner Philip was directed of the Holy Spirit we are not informed and it would be unwise to speculate. Our God has at his disposal unlimited means for communicating his wishes to his people.—Compare verse 39

"THE SPIRIT SAID UNTO HIM, BEHOLD, THREE MEN SEEK THEE"—Acts 10:19

The same answer is applicable to this as to the preceding objection. It is quite immaterial to us how the power, influence, Spirit of God addressed Peter, giving him this information. It is sufficient that we know that the Lord did direct the apostle, and in such a manner that the apostle clearly discerned it, and that correctly, as is shown by the sequel of the narrative.

"THE HOLY GHOST SAID, SEPARATE ME BARNABAS AND SAUL FOR THE WORK WHEREUNTO I HAVE CALLED THEM"—Acts 13:2

Here, as in other instances, the Holy Spirit uses the personal and masculine form of expression, according to our text. No objection certainly can be found to this, since God everywhere uses the personal and masculine form of expression respecting himself. It is not less appropriate here, in speaking of Jehovah's power, and the information which he gave. In what manner the Holy Spirit communicated, "said," or indicated the setting apart of Paul and Barnabas we are not informed. We do know, however, that all the Lord's consecrated people are called by his Spirit to be ministers or servants of the truth, and according to their abilities and opportunities they should be faithful and active servants. The Spirit says to all such through the general call, "Why stand ye here idle? . . . Go ye also into the vineyard." And special ability and favorable opportunity should be recognized as a special call of the Lord to more public work in the service of the truth. But while the talents possessed by Paul and Barnabas should be considered as emphasizing the general call of the Holy Spirit to them, to render services for

Supposed Objections Considered

which they had special talents, it is quite probable that the Holy Spirit at this time made use of one of the "gifts" which were then operative in the Church —the gift of prophecy—to indicate the Lord's will respecting Paul and Barnabas, for we read: "Now there were in the Church that was at Antioch certain prophets."—Acts 13:1

We are to remember, however, the apostle's words to the Galatians (1:1) respecting his call to the ministry. He declares that his authority came from the Father and the Son, but entirely ignores the Holy Spirit as another and coequal God, saying: "Paul, an apostle, not of men, neither by man, but by Jesus Christ, and God the Father who raised him from the dead." If the Holy Spirit were a person, if it were the God, whose special providence it is to appoint the ministers of the truth (and this is the general claim), such an omission to mention the Holy Spirit would be thoroughly inconsistent, unreasonable; but when we have the proper view of the Holy Spirit, viz., that it is the Spirit, influence, power, or authority of the Father and of the Son, or of both conjointly, because their purposes are one, then all is harmonious and reasonable.

"IT SEEMED GOOD TO THE HOLY SPIRIT AND TO US"—Acts 15:28

The apostles met as a Conference, to answer the questions of the Church at Antioch, respecting the obligations to the Jewish or Law Covenant of those who were not Jews by birth. The decision reached was, we are assured, not merely the judgment of the apostles themselves; but additionally, their judgment was corroborated in some manner by the Lord, and they had the evidence that their decision was the mind of the Lord, the Spirit of the Lord, the will of the Lord.

The Apostle James, the chief speaker of the council, gives a clue as to how God's will or mind was then ascertained; and we find it the same method commended to the entire Church, and used by the faithful today; namely, through searching the Scriptures in the light of divine Providence. He reasons out the mind of the Lord on the subject, by reviewing the special providential leading of Peter—sending him to Cornelius, the first Gentile convert—he followed this by an appeal to an unfulfilled prophecy, which he quotes. The conclusion drawn from these, he and all the Church accepted as the Holy Spirit's teaching. Examine Acts 15:13-18.

"FORBIDDEN OF THE HOLY GHOST TO PREACH THE WORD IN ASIA"—Acts 16:6

The form of expression here would seem to imply the common thought, that the Holy Spirit is a person, and spoke and forbade, etc. Yet an examination of this text in the light of its context shows it to be in full accord with all that we have seen on the subject: corroborating the thought that the Holy Spirit is the holy influence or power of Jehovah God, and of our Lord Jesus Christ, by which the will of the Father and the Son are brought to the attention of the consecrated—whatever the process. We are not informed specifically how the apostle and his companions were forbidden to prosecute the preaching work in Asia, but apparently they were hindered or not permitted to go into Asia—unfavorable circumstances preventing. But no matter how they were hindered; the lesson is that God himself was guiding his own work, and that the direction and course of the apostles was a matter of divine supervision; —they were directed by the Lord's Spirit; he used invisible power to direct them as his servants.

In any event, we may be sure that the Lord's guidance was more than a mere mental impression to the apostle. An illustration of one of the Spirit's ways of leading in such matters is furnished by the context—A vision appeared to Paul in the night. There stood a man of Macedonia, and prayed him, saying, Come over to Macedonia, and help us; and after he had seen the vision, immediately they endeavored to go into Macedonia, assuredly gathering

that the Lord had called them to preach the Gospel
unto them. (Verse 9) These various dealings show
us that the methods by which God taught and led
in those days were not so very different from those
he now employs in the guidance of his servants. And
all such indirect, non-personal instructions are properly described as from or by the Lord's Holy Spirit
or influence or power. Had an angel delivered the
message, as to Peter in prison (Acts 5:19; 12:7), or
had our Lord addressed Paul personally, as he did
when he was on the way to Damascus (Acts 9:4; 1
Cor. 15:8), it would not be credited to the Holy Spirit
or power of the Lord but to the Lord himself or to
the angel.

"THE HOLY GHOST WITNESSETH IN EVERY CITY, SAYING THAT BONDS AND AFFLICTIONS ABIDE ME"
——Acts 20:23——

Nothing here necessitates the thought of the personality of the Holy Spirit. On the contrary, as an
illustration of the agencies by which God's holy will
or Spirit informed Paul of the bonds awaiting him
at Jerusalem, note the account of one of these oc-
casions of witnessing at Caesarea. In the Church at
that place was one named Agabus, who had the gift
of prophecy common at this time. The record is,
"When he was come unto us, he took Paul's girdle,
and bound his own hands and feet, and said, Thus
saith the Holy Ghost, so shall the Jews at Jerusalem
bind the man that owns this girdle, and shall deliver
him into the hands of the Gentiles." (Acts 21:11)
The friends of the cause attempted at first to dis-
suade the apostle from going to Jerusalem, but he
determined that he would in no manner interfere
with the Lord's program in respect to himself; declaring, on the contrary, that he was not only ready
to be bound, but also to die at Jerusalem, for the
name of the Lord Jesus. (It should be noticed that
the apostle did not refer to the Holy Spirit— that he
would be willing to die for the Holy Spirit's name.)

When the friends at Caesarea perceived the apostle's steadfastness, they said, "The will of the Lord be done." Thus, in every instance, the testimony of the Holy Spirit was accepted by the early Church as merely being the will of our Lord Jesus, whose will was also the Father's will.—Acts 21:10-14

THE HOLY SPIRIT MADE SOME OVERSEERS

"Take heed therefore unto yourselves, and to all the flock, over which the Holy Ghost hath made you overseers, to feed the Church of God."—Acts 20:28

These words were addressed to the Elders of the Church at Ephesus. The apostle here calls attention to the fact that their position in the Church as servants of the truth was not merely a self-appointment, nor merely an appointment or recognition by the Church; but that the Lord had operated by his Holy Spirit in the matter of their selection. He would have them realize that all the virtue of their office was in view of the fact that it had the divine recognition, and that they were servants of the Church, by the Lord's appointment, through his Holy Spirit or influence which had guided, directed and overruled in the matter of their selection. So, in another place, the apostle says, addressing the Church, not the world, "The manifestation of the Spirit is given to every man [in Christ] to profit withal . . . **God hath set** some in the Church, first apostles, secondarily prophets, thirdly teachers. . . . And there are diversities of operations, but it is the same God that worketh all [things] in [among] all."—1 Cor. 12:6, 7, 28

In this statement the apostle shows that the appointment of all the servants of the Church is of God, by or through the manifestation of his Holy Spirit—and not a work of the Holy Spirit separate and apart from the Father and the Son. God in Christ supervises the affairs of his own people, the Church, by **his Spirit**—his holy power operative omnipotently and omnisciently—throughout his universe. This contradicts the thought that the Holy Spirit is another person, and shows that the work was accomplished by the Lord through his Holy Spirit. Those elders of the Church had consecrated themselves to the Lord's service, and were chosen to be ministers, teachers, elders, of the Church, because of special fitness and talent under the direction of the Holy Spirit—in accord with the will, or Spirit, or mind, or purpose of God. And although called to office through human instrumentality, they had accepted the service as of God's direction and appointment, and were to consider the responsibilities of their position accordingly.

THE HOLY SPIRIT A TEACHER

"God hath revealed them unto us by his Spirit; for the Spirit searcheth all things, yea, the deep things of God . . . which things also we speak, not in the words which man's wisdom teacheth, but which the Holy Ghost teacheth."—1 Cor. 2:10, 13 and context.

This scripture, as we have already suggested, proves that the Holy Spirit or mind of God, when received by his children, fits or prepares or enables their minds to comprehend his plan. Only by coming into full harmony with God, through his Word of truth, and through the spirit or real meaning of that Word, are we enabled to comprehend the deep things of God. Here the apostle, it will be noticed, contrasts "the Spirit which is of [from] God," which operates in us, with "the spirit of the world," which dwells in and influences the natural man. How clear it is that the spirit of the world is not a person, but a worldly mind or disposition or influence! Likewise the Spirit of God in his people is not a person, but the holy mind or influence or disposition of God in them.

"THE THINGS OF THE SPIRIT OF GOD"

"But the natural man receiveth not the things of the Spirit of God, for they are foolishness unto him. Neither can he know them, because they are spiritually discerned."
—1 Cor. 2:14

This is a very forceful statement, and fully in harmony with all that we have seen. The man who is filled with the worldly spirit is proportionately unprepared to see and appreciate the deep, hidden, glorious things of God—"the things which God hath in reservation for them that love him." These deep things, or as our Lord designates them, "pearls," are not for the swinish, the selfish, full of the spirit of this world; but for those who are cleansed by the washing of water through the Word, who are brought nigh to the Lord through faith in the precious blood, and sanctified, fully consecrated to the Lord. To these God is pleased to reveal his deep things, yea, all the riches of his grace, step by step—as the various items of truth become "meat in due season."

This is a very crucial test, as all may discern. It distinguishes sharply between the fallen man and the new creature, the spiritual. Whoever is blind to the deeper spiritual truths certainly lacks the **witness** or evidence here mentioned as proof of his sonship, his relationship to the heavenly Father, and his fidelity under such a relationship. Those who are indifferent to the matters which the apostle here mentions, "The things which God hath in reservation for them that love him," have, in this statement, a suggestion that the reason for their indifference is that they lack the Lord's Spirit. And yet we have known professed teachers in the church who not only admitted their own ignorance of these things, but who boasted of that ignorance. Thereby they proclaim that they have not the mind of God, do not know of his plans, and hence cannot have much of his Spirit, the Spirit of the truth—and proportionately they cannot have much of the truth. The test is here given of our possession of the Spirit, and our ability to discern and appreciate the things of God, which are hidden from the worldly—"**God hath revealed them unto us by his Spirit.**"

AN UNCTION FROM THE HOLY ONE

"Ye have an **unction** from the Holy One and ye know all things."

"The **anointing** which ye have received of him abideth in you, and ye need not that any man teach you: but as the same **anointing** teacheth you of all things and is truth and is no lie, and even as it hath taught you, ye shall abide in him."—1 John 2:20, 27

These words **unction** and **anointing** awaken in intelligent Bible students recollections of the holy anointing oil poured upon the heads of each successor to the offices of High Priest and King in Israel. As the people of Israel were typical of "the true Israel of God," so their priests and kings were typical of Christ, the great antitypical High Priest and King. And as their priests and kings were anointed with the "holy anointing oil" as an induction into office, so our Lord Jesus was anointed with the Holy Spirit at the time of his consecration. He thus became the Christ—the anointed of Jehovah.

The elect church is to be a "royal priesthood" (king-priests) under their Lord and Head—"members of the body of the Anointed [the Christ]." The Holy Spirit of anointing which came to our Lord Jesus at his baptism at Jordan, and with "all power in heaven and in earth," when he was raised from the dead by the Holy Spirit or power of the Father (Matt. 28:18; Eph. 1:19, 20), he with the Father's approval "shed forth" or poured out as the antitypical anointing oil upon the representatives of his Church at Pentecost. There (keeping in thought the type) the anointing oil passed from the "Head" to his "body," the Church, and thenceforth the faithful, abiding in the body, were recognized in the divine Word as "the very elect" of God, anointed of him (in Christ) to rule and bless the world after being first "taught of God" under the guidance of the anointing Spirit.

The signification of **unction** (and of its Greek original **chrisma**) is smoothness, oiliness, lubrication. From custom the word carried with it also the thought of fragrance, perfume. How beautifully and forcefully this word represents the effect of God's **influence** toward goodness, upon those who come under this antitypical anointing—holiness, gentleness, patience, brotherly kindness—love! What a sweet, pure perfume does this anointing of the Holy Spirit of love bring with it to all who receive it!

However ungainly or coarse or rude or ignorant the outer man, "the earthen vessel," how speedily it partakes of the sweetening and purifying influence of the treasure of the "new heart," the new will within—anointed with the Holy Spirit and brought into harmony with "whatsoever things are true, whatsoever things are honest, whatsoever things are just, whatsoever things are pure, whatsoever things are lovely!"—Phil. 4:8

These words "unction" and "anointing" are in full accord with the correct view of the Holy Spirit— that it is an **influence** from God, an invisible power of God exercised through his precepts, his promises, or otherwise as may seem good to the all-wise omnipotent One. These words certainly do not convey the thought of a **person.** How could we be anointed with a person?

But some one perhaps will suggest that in the expression, "an unction from the Holy One," not the **unction** but the **Holy One** represents the Holy Spirit. We answer, No; the Holy One is the Father. Peter, describing the Pentecostal blessing, declares that it was "shed forth" or **poured out**—as anointing oil, but not as a person would be said to be sent. He says, speaking of Jesus, "Having received of the Father the Holy Spirit promised [in Joel] he hath **shed forth** this which ye see and hear"—this miraculous power or influence which manifests itself variously, in quickening thoughts, in tongues of flame and divers languages uttered by unlearned men. Again Joel's prophecy was "I will **pour out** my Spirit." Can any one claim that this would be appropriate language to use respecting any **person?** That he was **given** by the Father to the Son, and that he was poured or shed forth and seen and heard as **"this"?** Surely not. And surely such language would be disrespectful, if applied to a third person of a trinity of Gods "equal in power and glory."

The item however which strikes everyone as most astounding is that those who have this unction **"know all things."** How many of the Lord's people have felt absolutely certain that they did not "know all things," and therefore doubted if they had received the anointing of the Holy Spirit! How the matter is simplified when translated, "Ye have an unction from the Holy One and ye all know it!"* Yes, indeed; all the true children of God know very well the difference between the natural mind or heart or will and the new heart, new mind, new disposition, controlled by love and righteousness.

And how many of God's best and humblest children have read with amazement the words, "The anointing which ye have received of him abideth in you and **ye need not that any man teach you!**" Alas! they said, we have received no such anointing, for we have very much need that some man teach us, and know very little that has not come to us either directly or indirectly through human instrumentality. And these humble souls would feel greatly cast down and discouraged by reason of their honesty of thought, did they not see that the very best of the saints of their acquaintance similarly need and appreciate human teachers. On the other hand, some of the less honest, less candid, less saintly, endeavor to deceive themselves and others by claiming that they have learned nothing of men but have been taught all they know by direct inspiration of the Holy Spirit. They see not that they are thus claiming infallibility for their thoughts and words, in the most absolute sense. They fail, too, to see that their **errors** of thought, word and deed, claimed to be under plenary inspiration of the Holy Spirit, reflect against God's Holy Spirit, as the author of their errors and follies.

Taking this passage just as it stands, it contradicts the general testimony of Scripture. Does not the Apostle Paul mention among the Spirit's **gifts** to the Church—apostles, prophets [orators], pastors, teachers, evangelists? And why give these if the Church had no need that any man teach them? What does the apostle say of the **reason** for setting these special gifts in the Church? Hear him: "For the perfecting of the saints for the work of the ministry, for the edifying of the body of Christ: till we all

---
*The words "all things" are omitted by oldest Greek MSS

come to the unity of the faith and the knowledge of the Son of God."—Eph. 4:11-13. Compare 1 Cor. 12:28-31.

It is not supposable that the Apostle John was contradicting the Apostle Paul and the other apostles—all of whom were teachers and who instructed the Church to seek out the Spirit's choice of pastors, teachers and overseers, and to honor those who thus had the "rule over" the Church and who were to watch for the interests of souls as those who must give an account to the Lord. (Heb. 13:17) It was undoubtedly in full accord with the Apostle Paul's advice that the Church had need to select as its servants men "apt at teaching," able by sound doctrine both to exhort and to convince the gainsayers," and when necessary to "rebuke sharply that they may be sound in faith." They were to recognize undershepherds, who would not "lord it over God's heritage," but would **feed** the flock" with meat in due season—avoiding teachers having ears which itched for popularity and flattery.—1 Pet. 5:2-4; 1 Tim. 3:2; 2 Tim. 2:25; Titus 1:9, 13

Furthermore, John himself was a teacher, and in this very epistle was teaching what he and we appreciate as sound doctrine—necessary to be taught. Surely no one reading John's writings could draw the inference that he meant them merely as social letters, devoid of doctrine or teaching. Does he not open the epistle by saying, "That which we have seen and heard declare [**teach**] we unto you, that ye also may have fellowship with us?" (1:3) Again he says, "These things write I unto you [to teach you] that ye sin not." (2:1) Again, "A new commandment [**teaching**] I write unto you." (2:8) Again "Little children, let no man deceive you [but heed my **teaching**]: he that doeth righteousness is righteous." (3:7) Again, "We are of God: he that knoweth God heareth us [obeys our instructions, our teachings]." (4:6) Again, "These things have I written unto you . . . that ye may know [be taught]." (3:13) He closes his epistle with a very important **teaching**, saying, "Little children, keep yourselves from idols [permit no person or thing to supplant God himself in your affections and reverence]."

Seeing then that the apostle cannot be understood as meaning that the Church has no need of human teachers—seeing on the contrary that he recognized human teachers as the agency employed by the Holy Spirit specially "set in the Church" for this very service, what can he mean by these words, "Ye need not that any man teach you," and "the same anointing teacheth you all things"? The proper answer to this query will be readily seen by examining the context in the light of facts already discussed.

This epistle is supposed by scholars to have been written in the year A. D. 90. By that date Christianity had attained considerable prominence in the world. It had gathered the "remnant" of fleshly Israel and drawn upon itself the hatred and persecution of the vast blinded majority of that people and been scattered everywhere throughout the then civilized world. Many things in Christianity commended it to the Greek philosophers of that time who sought to combine with it and to become philosophic Christians and Christian philosophers—still holding their philosophies which the Apostle Paul points out were "falsely so called." (1 Tim. 6:20) These philosophers were quite willing to acknowledge Jesus as a good man and a wise teacher but not as the Son of God who left a spirit nature, "a form of God," and was "made flesh," to thereby become man's Redeemer, and the author of eternal life to all who obey him. They were, however, teaching a future, eternal life and were glad to find Christians teaching the same: the difference being that the philosophers (Plato and others) taught that eternal life is a human quality, and inherent power in mankind—deathlessness, immortality, whereas the Christians taught that eternal life was not inherent in man but a gift of God through Christ, intended only for those who accept him.—Rom. 2:7; 5:15, 21; 6:23; 2 Cor. 9:15

These philosophers practically said to the Christians—We are glad to meet so respectable and sensible and free a people. Your great teacher, Jesus, surely did make you **free** from many of the customs and superstitions of the Jews and we congratulate you accordingly. But you are still in a measure of bondage: when you have investigated our philosophies you will have still **more liberty** and will find that much you still hold in common with the Jews—their hopes of a Messianic kingdom, their peculiar ideas of one God and your peculiar ideas that your Teacher, Jesus, was his only Son, etc., these things you will soon outgrow, with the aid of our philosophy.—2 Pet. 2:19; Jude 4

John's epistle is written to fortify Christians against these subversive doctrines. He exhorts them in this chapter (2:24) to hold fast the teachings heard by them from the beginning and to consider these philosophizing teachings as lies and all such false teachers representatives of the Antichrist which they had so often heard would be manifested in the Church. (2 Thess. 2:3-7; 1 John 2:18) He says, "These things have I written unto you concerning them that [seek to] seduce you [from Christ]."—Verse 26

Then comes the peculiar language of verse 27, now under discussion, which we paraphrase thus:—

But, dearly beloved, the true children of God can **not be seduced** by any such philosophies; with us no philosophy can take the place of Christ in our hearts—no theory could cause us to question the fullness and the correctness of the great message which we received as the Gospel of our Lord Jesus Christ —the Father's Beloved, the Father's Anointed. Besides the **reasonableness** of "the faith once delivered unto the saints," consider the marvelous effect of that message upon you: it was accompanied by miraculous "gifts" of "tongues," "miracles," etc., which these philosophers declare are duplicated by the fakirs of the East; but aside from this you have another testimony in your own new hearts—in the anointing which has transformed and renewed your minds. producing in your daily life **fruits** of the Spirit of holiness which the fakirs cannot duplicate and which the philosophers who would seduce you can**not deny.**

On these fundamentals of our holy religion—that Christ Jesus was not an impostor but the very Son of God and our Redeemer; and that eternal life can be obtained only through vital union with him—you have no need of instruction, neither from these false teachers nor from me. And so long as you have this Holy Spirit of love abiding in you, it will serve as a guard against all such blasphemous, antichristian theories. So long as you remember that "the peace of God which passeth all understanding" came to your hearts through an acceptance of Jesus as the Son of God and the only power of God unto salvation, so long will this spirit hold you firm, steadfast, on this point. And you will find this same test (of loyalty to the Holy Spirit of love received through the Father and the Son) helpful in proving all matters: for whatever contradicts or ignores this Spirit of love is an unholy spirit—a false teaching. And remember that its teaching is that if we would receive any reward we must "abide in him"—to abandon Christ is to abandon all.

GROANINGS WHICH CANNOT BE UTTERED

"The Spirit itself maketh intercession for us with groanings which cannot be uttered; and he that searcheth the heart, knoweth what is the mind of the Spirit."—Rom. 8:26, 27

This expression, intended to convey to God's people an understanding of the heavenly Father's love and care toward them, has been sadly misunderstood by many. They tell us that the Holy Spirit groans for them to the Father; and some attempt to give audible utterance to the groans themselves; and by some it is supposed that the amount of groaning which they do, somehow helps the Holy Spirit in the matter, compensating for the groanings which it cannot utter—though they cannot see just how. It would indeed be strange, if the Holy Spirit were a person, and, as the catechisms assert, "equal in power" with the Father and the Son, that he should find it necessary to address the Father and the Son on behalf of the Lord's people, with unutterable groans. Our Lord Jesus said that we might come direct to him and that we might come direct to the Father, assuring us, "The Father himself loveth you." Yet from this Scripture under consideration some have gotten the idea that we must needs go to the Father and to the Son through the Holy Spirit as a mediator, who would groan for us, and intercede for us, that we might be accepted of the Father and of the Son. This is in harmony with the prevailing confusion of thought respecting the Holy Spirit and its office.

The error of this interpretation is further noticeable when we consider that if the groans could not be uttered they would not be groans at all; for what is not uttered is not a groan. But this passage would appear equally strange and inconsistent, if we were to interpret it to mean that the Holy Spirit, the influence or power of Almighty Jehovah, is unable to express itself intelligently. We know that in past ages God's mind, will, Spirit, found abundant expression through the words and deeds of the prophets, and we cannot suppose that he has any less power or ability today. What, then, can this scripture signify—"The Spirit itself maketh intercession for us, with groanings which cannot be uttered"?

The mistake is in supposing that it is God's Spirit which supplicates. On the contrary, the Spirit which maketh intercession for us is **our own spirit**, the spirit of the saint, which supplicates God, and often fails to express itself properly. A glance at the text, with its connections, will make manifest the propriety of this interpretation. The apos**tle had just been writing of the sin-burdened humanity groaning in its fetters.** He assures us that it shall be granted liberty from the bondage, when the Church, the "sons of God," under the Captain of their Salvation, shall have been glorified. (Verses 19-21) He then passes from the **groanings** of the world to the present condition of the Church, in which **we groan**: "Ourselves also, which have the first fruits of the Spirit, even we groan within ourselves, waiting for the adoption, to

Supposed Objections Considered

wit, the deliverance of our body."—Verse 23

The renewed or transformed mind or spirit in the Church once worldly, is now holy and spiritual; but our bodies are still human, and have the Adamic imperfections. Hence we, as new creatures, are burdened by the flesh, and **groan** for the promised deliverance into Christ's likeness in the first resurrection. The apostle explains that we may by faith, reckon the earthly body dead, and think of ourselves as new creatures perfected, and thus realize ourselves **saved now**—"**saved by hope.**" (Verse 24) Then, having shown how we may reckon ourselves, he explains to us that from the divine standpoint we **are reckoned as "new" and "holy" and "spiritual"** beings: he shows that God, viewing us from this standpoint, recognizes not the flesh and its weaknesses and imperfections—but the spirit, the mind, the intentions, the will, the "new creature," devoted to his service. God knows when our holy spirit (new mind) is willing and the flesh weak, and he judges us not according to the flesh, but according to the spirit.

It was our begetting of the Spirit, our adoption of a new will, fully consecrated to the Lord, that brought us into a new relationship to God, and into these new hopes wherein we rejoice: and so "likewise the spirit [our new, holy mind] also helpeth [maketh up for] our [bodily] infirmities. For we know not [even] what we should pray for as we ought [much less are we always able to do as we would like]; but the spirit itself [our holy mind] maketh intercession [for us—omitted by oldest MSS] with groanings which cannot be uttered [in words]. And he that searcheth the hearts [God] knoweth what is the mind [Greek **phronema**—inclination] of [our] spirit, because he [or it—our spirit] maketh intercession for the saints according to the will of God."

In other words, God is pleased to accept the heart desires of his people, both in prayer and in service, notwithstanding the imperfection of their flesh—their earthen vessels. And he does accept these heart desires.

How fortunate for us, in our ignorance and weakness, that our heavenly Father accepts the intentions of our hearts instead of our words; for frequently his people have seriously asked amiss! We think of this whenever we hear God's people pray that God would baptize them with the Holy Spirit and with fire. The prayer is offered in a good conscience, and with a desire for a blessing only; but not understanding the passage of Scripture which he quotes, the petitioner really asks for a blessing to be followed by a curse. The prediction that Christ would baptize with the Holy Spirit and with fire was made by John the baptizer. The blessing portion of this came upon the waiting Church, at Pentecost, and subsequently upon all the faithful "remnant" of Israel, but its latter feature was fulfilled upon the rejected Jewish nation—in the baptism of fire, destruction, trouble, which wholly destroyed their polity in the year A. D. 70. But very graciously God does not answer his people's prayers according to their asking, but according to the intentions of the petitioner—he granting them blessing only.

Some have had the experience of being overtaken in a fault, and trapped by the adversary through some weakness of the fallen human nature: they felt almost disheartened as they approached the throne of the heavenly grace in prayer. They had no words for utterance, but merely groaned in spirit to God, **"being burdened."** But the Heavenly Father did not insist that they must formulate the petition in exactly proper language before he would hear them: instead he graciously answered their heart's desires, the unexpressed groans of their heart, which sought his forgiveness, his blessing and comfort. He answered the unuttered prayers, granted strength and blessing, with a blessed realization of forgiveness.

This is the apostle's argument in the whole connection, and it will be observed that he sums up the argument by saying, "What shall we say then? [In view of the fact that God has made every arrangement on our behalf, ignoring our weaknesses and imperfections, which are contrary to our wills, and

Supposed Objections Considered

not reckoning them as our deeds—and ignoring the lameness of our petitions, and our inability to express our desires, and on the contrary, making arrangements to bless us according to the spirit of our minds, as we are unable even to give utterance to our groans in our imperfect prayers, we will conclude]—If God be [thus] for us, who can be against us"?—Verse 31

HOW THE SPIRIT REPROVES THE WORLD

"When he [the Spirit of truth] is come he will reprove the world of sin and of righteousness and of judgment."—John 16:8

We have already considered the ground upon which the masculine pronoun is applied to the Spirit of truth—because it represents God who is masculine. We now examine this text, used by some as a proof that the Holy Spirit operates in sinners for their reformation. We contend that such a view is wholly incorrect—that the Scriptures, rightly understood, teach that the Holy Spirit is granted only to the consecrated believers; that it is not given to the unbelievers and consequently could not operate in them, after the manner generally claimed. Quite to the contrary, the children of this world have the spirit of the world; and only the children of God have the Spirit of God, the Holy Spirit, mind, disposition or will. "The spirit of the world," or "the carnal mind, is enmity against God." Neither can the carnally minded know the things of the Spirit of God, because they are spiritually discerned—can be discerned only by those who have the Holy Spirit. Hence it is, that wherever we find it, the Holy Spirit of harmony with God and obedience to his will and providence, evidences regeneration, begetting to newness of life. In harmony with this we read the apostle's words, "If any man have not the Spirit of Christ he is none of his." Those who have not the Spirit of Christ, and who are not of his, are the world in general—they are not Christ's, because they have not received of the Father's Spirit.

The Spirit of God, by means of its fruits and its

witnessing through the Word, is the evidence of our having been regenerated. It is evident to all that the Holy Spirit of God which is in the Church is not the same Spirit which is in the worldly—that the Spirit of God is in no sense in the worldly, carnally minded, who consequently in the Scriptures are designated "children of wrath," "children of this world" and "children of their father, the devil." Nevertheless, we should not forget that the "Spirit of truth," the "Spirit of love" has, to a considerable extent, modified the spirit of the world; so that while it is still a spirit of darkness, a spirit of selfishness, a carnal spirit, yet the world to some extent is copying, in a formal, outward manner, some of the graces of the Holy Spirit. It would be strange, indeed, if the beauties of the Spirit of holiness, as represented in gentleness, kindness and patience, made no impression upon the unregenerate.

Some people of the world cultivate these graces of the Spirit because they are styled part of the amenities of life, signs of good breeding, etc., and many whose hearts are wholly out of harmony with the principles of the Spirit of holiness, copy these graces as a gloss or surface gilding, to cover the baser metal of a depraved nature—unregenerate, unsanctified, selfish, out of harmony with the Lord and the Spirit of his holiness. We are, therefore, to closely distinguish between those who gild the surface of their conduct and those whose hearts have been transformed by the Spirit of the Lord. The latter only are the sons of God, who have his favor, and who will shortly be blessed and glorified.

The question then arises, If the Spirit of the Lord is communicated only to those who are his, through faith in Christ and consecration, what did our Lord mean by the above statement, that the Spirit of truth would reprove the world of sin, of righteousness, and of coming judgment?

The meaning of our Lord's words will be readily discernible when we remember his declaration, that his followers, upon whom his Spirit would come, and in whom it would dwell richly, in proportion to

Supposed Objections Considered

their faith and obedience, were to be the **light** of the world. It is this light of truth which shines forth from the truly consecrated Church, upon the world and the worldly minded of the nominal church, that tends to reprove their darkness. Our Lord said of himself, after he had been anointed with the Spirit of God, "I am the light of the world," and again, "As long as I am in the world I am the light of the world." (John 8:12; 9:5) And addressing his Church of this Gospel age, sanctified by the same Holy Spirit, he said, "Ye are the light of the world . . . Let your light so shine before men."—Matt. 5:14-16

The Apostle Paul, addressing the same body of Christ, says, "Ye were at one time darkness, but now are ye light in the Lord: walk as children of the light." (Eph. 5:8; 1 Thess. 5:5) Again he says, "For God [the Spirit of God, the Spirit of truth] hath shined **into our hearts**, to give the light of the knowledge of the glory of God." (2 Cor. 4:6) Thus we see that it is the light of God's truth, the Holy Spirit, mind or disposition, shining in our hearts, which shines **out upon the world;** and hence the exhortation, "Do all things without murmurings and disputings, that ye may be blameless and harmless, the sons of God, without rebuke, in the midst of a crooked and perverse nation, amongst whom ye shine as lights in the world."—Phil. 2:14, 15

Thus we see that the Holy Spirit shines upon the world—not directly but reflexly. It is not the Spirit of God communicated to them and operating in them, but the Holy Spirit of God operating in his people, who are sealed by it, which shines forth upon the darkness of the world.

The apostle gives us a clue as to how the world is to be reproved by the Spirit of holiness in the consecrated Church, saying, "Walk as children of the light . . . and have no fellowship with the unfruitful works of darkness, but rather **reprove** them. . . . All things that are reproved are made manifest [shown to be wrong] by the **light.**" (Eph. 5:8, 11, 13) The light of God's truth, which is the expressing of his mind or Spirit, as it shines through a sanctified life, is the Holy Spirit, reproving the darkness of the world showing those who see it what **sin** is, in contrast with **righteousness**. And from this enlightenment will come to them the conviction of a coming judgment, when righteousness will receive some reward, and sin some punishment. A godly life is always a reproof to the ungodly, even where no word of truth may be possible or proper.

It is because the Holy Spirit in God's people reproves the unholy and selfish spirit in those about them that the apostle urges the sanctified to remember that they are living epistles, known and read of all men. (2 Cor. 3:2) The justified and sanctified Church, following in the footsteps of Christ, has always been a light in the world, even though its light has not always had as much influence as it desired. Thus it was also with our Lord, who declared that all who were of the spirit of darkness hated him the more because their spirit of darkness was reproved by his Spirit of light. For this reason, not only the Lord, the great Light-bearer, was persecuted unto death, but similarly all the light-bearers who follow in his footsteps must be sharers also of his persecution and suffering.—John 16:3; Rom. 8:17, 18

While the chief mission of the Church has been her own development, "building up yourselves in your most holy faith," etc. (Jude 20), yet she has always had a secondary mission, that of witnessing to the truth, letting the light shine, reproving the world. And this reproving has necessarily been more toward nominal professors than toward the openly worldly, just as in our Lord's day his light was shed upon the professedly godly and holy, reproving their darkness. And our Lord warns us of the necessity of letting our light shine **continually**, saying, "If the light that is in thee be [become] darkness, how great is that darkness!" both to the individual soul in whom the light has gone out, and to the world, from whom the light is thus obscured. Satan achieves no greater triumph than when he seduces a soul which was once enlightened and sanctified by the truth. The influence of such an one for evil is more than doubled. "Let him that thinketh he standeth take heed lest he fall," and remember that to put his "light under a bushel" is a sure step toward darkness.

"HEREBY KNOW YE THE SPIRIT OF GOD" FROM THE SPIRIT OF ANTICHRIST
—— 1 John 4:2, 3; 2 John 7 ——

"Hereby know ye the Spirit of God: Every spirit that confesseth that Jesus Christ is come in the flesh is of God, and every spirit that confesseth not that Jesus Christ is come in the flesh is not of God: and this is that spirit of Antichrist."

Nothing should be plainer to any intelligent mind than that the apostle is not referring to a person, but to an influence, doctrine or teaching. The context (verses 1 and 3) shows beyond a doubt that the apostle's meaning is that the Lord's people must discriminate between doctrines presented to them as truth—they must "try the spirits," whether they be holy or evil, of God or of the Evil One—the Spirit of truth or the spirit of error. These both are introduced by prophets or teachers. Our Lord and the apostles and others following in their footsteps sowed the truth or "wheat" seed, begetting consecrated believers to newness of life and holiness of spirit. The enemy and his servants sowed error or "tare" seed, which has brought into the nominal church (or wheat field) multitudes of "tares"—having not the Holy "Spirit of Christ," but a modified, sugar-coated "spirit of the world." Hence every one presenting himself as a teacher and claiming to be a servant of the truth and to have holiness of spirit is to be tried, tested, as to whether he is preaching truth or error—inculcating the Spirit of truth or the spirit of error. The Word of God is to be the standard by which each is to be received as a true teacher or rejected as a false teacher: "for many false prophets are gone forth."

The apostle points out one general **test** respecting true and false faith, true and false teachers—the Spirit of truth and the spirit of error—the Holy Spirit of Christ guiding into all truth, and the unholy spirit of Antichrist, leading into all error, destructive to the faith once delivered to the saints and leading to a denial of the Lord's having **bought** us with his own precious blood. (2 Pet. 2:1) This **test** was the affirmation or denial of Messiah's having come in the flesh. And this was and still is a sure test—the **ransom test** stated in one of its forms: every doctrine that **denies** it is an active opponent of the truth, is anti-(against) Christ: every doctrine that **ignores** it is seriously wrong, not of God, however much of good may be blended with it; it is dangerous: every doctrine that **confesses** it is fundamentally correct—"of God," tending in the right direction.

Very early the Adversary began attacks on the true faith set forth by the Lord and the apostles from two standpoints, both of which denied that he came **in the flesh.**

(1) The heathen philosophies (against which **the** Apostle Paul also warned, 1 Tim. 6:20, 21) **claimed** that Jesus was indeed a great prophet, a great teacher, and ranked him with their own philosophers; but they insisted that he was not the Son of God more than the others—not the Messiah of the Jews, whose hopes and prophecies they accredited to narrowness and national pride and ambition to consider themselves the divinely favored nation. Thus they denied our Lord's pre-human existence—denied that he **came** in the flesh—denied that he was anything else than a member of the fallen race, though admitting that he was a bright specimen of it.

(2) According to his usual custom the Adversary early began to set one extreme of error against another extreme, that in the warfare between the two errors the truth between them might be left undefended and be forgotten. Hence he started the other extreme error on this subject, whose claim was and still is that Messiah was not a man at all—that he was the very God, the Father, who merely pretended to be flesh for a time, while really maintaining all his divine powers—using the body of flesh as a covering or disguise to hide his glory and to permit

Supposed Objections Considered

him to appear to weep and hunger and thirst and die. This view also denies that Messiah came in the flesh—that "he was **made flesh**."—John 1:14

As we look about us today we may well be astonished to find that the majority of Christian people hold one or the other of these false doctrines opposed to the Spirit of truth—of the spirit of antichrist; and the remainder are generally quite confused—bewildered—do not see the truth on this subject clearly, and accordingly are not firmly founded on the ransom. For all who fail to see clearly that "the Word [**Logos**] was **made flesh**," became "the man Christ Jesus," are as unable to see the ransom [**corresponding price**] as are those who see Jesus as an imperfect man, begotten of the flesh by an earthly father. Thus we see that the simple test set forth by the Holy Spirit through the apostle is still a test of doctrines—whether they be of God and the Holy Spirit, or of Satan and the spirit of antichrist.

While considering these texts we will note an objection raised against the translation of our common version Bibles to show that it is not valid—that the translation is a good one; that the fault lies in the critic who evidently has not a sufficient knowledge of Greek grammar rules on syntax to attempt a criticism. His claim is—

(1) That the Greek words in these two texts rendered **"has come"** signify **coming**.

(2) That with this change the apostle's words would signify that any teaching which denies that the **second advent** of our Lord will be **in the flesh** is an antichrist spirit.

We reply to this claim—

(1) It is true that the word **erchomai**, the root word from which is derived **eleluthota** (1 John 4:2) and **erchomenon** (2 John 7) signifies **coming** or **arrival**; but whether the **coming** referred to is a past or a future event must be determined by the construction of the sentence, just as we may use our English word "coming" in referring to matters past and future and say—"Faith in the first **coming** of

our Lord is general among Christians but not so general is the faith in his second coming." The context proves beyond peradventure that an occurrence of the past is referred to, for the record is "many deceivers **are gone forth**" or "went forth"; and the two statements quite evidently refer to the same thing.

(2) This claim is put forth by some who have an object in claiming that the text refers to a future event—they claim that our Lord is not "changed" to the divine nature, that he is still **flesh** and that he will continue to be a man, a human, fleshly being, and bear the scars of his human sufferings to all eternity. They deny, or at least ignore, the many Scriptural declarations to the effect that "Him hath God highly exalted"; "Now the Lord is that Spirit," and "Though we have known Christ after the flesh [yet] henceforth know we him [so] no more." (Phil. 2:9; 2 Cor. 3:17; 5:16) Their wish to find some Scriptural statements to support their unreasonable and unscriptural position deceives them as respects these passages. Indeed we may say that the vast majority of Christian people hold this erroneous view, among them nearly all who have ever had anything to do with translating the Scriptures.

But we will buttress our position by quoting the criticisms of these texts by Prof. J. R. Rinehart, Ph. D.. Professor of Languages in Waynesburg College (Cumberland Presbyterian). After quoting the text of 1 John 4:2 and 2 John 7, Prof. Rinehart says:—

(1) "The foregoing quotations are from the Emphatic Diaglott of Wilson, purporting to be from the original Greek text of the New Testament. The word **eleluthota** is the accusative, singular masculine, of the second perfect participle of the verb **erchomai,** having the same relation to this verb that any other perfect participle has to its verb. It stands with the verb **homolegei** in indirect discourse, and represents a finite, perfect tense, according to ordinary Greek syntax.—Goodwin's Greek Grammar, ††1588, 1288

"The following translation of the first quotation is, therefore, essentially correct. 'Every spirit that

Supposed Objections Considered

confesseth that Jesus Christ has come in the flesh, is of God.'

(2) "The word **erchomenon** in the second quotation is the accusative, singular, masculine, of the present participle of the verb **erchomai**, and is subject to the same rules of syntax as the word above. Its relation to **eiselthon** through **homologountes**, as well as the context, justifies its translation as of past time.—Ibid, †1289

"The translation of the second quotation, therefore, is properly given as follows: 'For many deceiv**ers went forth into the world—those who do not confess that Jesus Christ did come in the flesh.'**"

No Greek scholar, we believe, will ever be found to contradict this definition, even though he hold to the second coming of our Lord in flesh, and might thus have a preference for a construction favorable to his conceptions.

Finally, we notice that as a confession that Christ came in the flesh at his first advent is essential to a proper belief in the ransom, and a denial of that fact means a denial of the ransom (because otherwise he could not give a **corresponding price** for man), so all who believe that Christ is a **man** since his resurrection and that he will come a second time as a man, are thereby denying the ransom—for if our Lord is still a **man** he either did not give his manhood as our ransom, or, giving it for three days, **took it back again**—took back the redemption **price** and thus vitiated the purchase. But on the contrary the purchase was final: our Lord's humanity never was taken back: Him hath God highly exalted and given a name, and nature far above angels, principalities and powers and every name that is named (the Father's alone excepted). He is no longer a man nor in any sense like us: we if faithful shall be "changed" and made like him and "see him as he **is**."—1 John 3:2

HE IS ALTOGETHER LOVELY

Majestic sweetness sits enthroned
  Upon the Savior's brow;
His head with radiant glories crowned,
  His lips with grace o'erflow.

None other could with him compare
  Among the sons of men;
He's fairer too than all the fair
  Who fill the heavenly train.

He saw men plunged in deep distress,
  And flew to their relief;
For us he bore the shameful cross,
  And carried all our grief.

God's promises, exceeding great,
  He makes to us secure;
Yea, on this rock our faith may rest,
  Immovable, secure.

O! the rich depths of love divine,
  Of grace a boundless store!
Dear Savior, since I'm owned as thine,
  I cannot wish for more.

STUDY XII

THE SUBJECT OF THE ATONEMENT—MAN

What is Man?—The "Orthodox" Answer—The Scientific Answer—The Bible Answer—Man's Body—The Spirit of Man—The Human Soul—Confusion Through Mistranslation—The Propagation of Souls—What is "Sheol," "Hades," to which all Souls Go, in the Interim Between Death and Resurrection?—The Scriptural Statements Severally Considered.

"What is man, that thou art mindful of him? And the son of man, that thou visitest him? For thou madest him a little lower than the angels, and hast crowned him with glory and honor. Thou madest him to have dominion over the works of thy hands; thou hast put all things under his feet: all sheep and oxen, yea, and the beasts of the field, the fowl of the air and the fish of the sea."—Psa. 8:4-8

WHAT great being is man that the Creator of the universe has been so interested in his welfare as to make so bountiful a provision for his reconciliation —even through the sacrifice of his Son? We should know thoroughly, this highest of God's earthly creatures, so far as possible: and yet, so limited are our powers of judgment, and so circumscribed our knowledge, that on this subject we are dependent almost entirely upon what our loving Creator has made known to us in his Word. Although the saying has become proverbial that "The greatest study of mankind is man," yet, strange to say, there are few subjects upon which mankind is more confused than this one—What is man? There are two general views on the subject, neither of which, we hold, is the correct, the Scriptural one. Though both have certain elements of truth connected with them, both are grievously wrong and misleading; so that even those who are not wholly deluded by them are nevertheless so influenced and confused by these errors that many truths are robbed of their force and weight, and many fallacies are given an appearance of truth. Our subject, therefore, is important to all who would know the truth, and have the full benefit of the same in its influence upon their hearts and lives. The subject is of special importance in connection with the topic under discussion, the Atonement. He who has not a clear conception of what man is, will find it difficult if not impossible, to clearly comprehend the Scriptural teachings relative to the atonement for man's sin— its operation and results.

We will here consider the general and so-called orthodox view of the question, What is man? then the strictly scientific view, and finally the Bible view, which, we hold, is different from both, much more reasonable than either, and the only ground of proper harmony between the two.

ORTHODOXY'S VIEW OF MAN

The question, What is man? if answered from a so-called "orthodox theological" standpoint (which we dispute) would be about as follows: Man is a composite being of three parts body, spirit and soul; the body is born after the usual manner of animal birth, except that at the time of birth God interposes, and in some inscrutable manner implants in the body a spirit and a soul, which are parts of himself, and being parts of God are indestructible, and can never die. These two parts, spirit and soul, "orthodoxy" is unable to separate and distinguish, and hence uses the terms interchangeably at convenience. Both terms (spirit and soul) are understood to mean the real man, while the flesh is considered to be merely the outward clothing of the real man, in which he dwells for the years of his earthly life, as in a house. At death, they say, the real man is let out of this prison-house of flesh, and finds himself in a condition much more congenial.

In other words, "orthodoxy" claims that the real man is not an earthly being, but a spirit being wholly unadapted to the earth, except through its experi-

Man the Subject

ences in the fleshly body. When set free from the body by death it is theorized that a great blessing has been experienced, although the man, while he lived, made every effort to continue to live in the fleshly house, using medicines and travels and every hygienic appliance and invention to prolong the life in the flesh, which, theoretically, it is claimed is illy adapted to his uses and enjoyments. The "liberation" called "death" is esteemed to be another step in the evolutionary process: and in many minds such a future evolution from earthly to heavenly conditions, from animal to spiritual conditions, is regarded as a reasonable proposition and a logical outcome of the scientific conclusion that man was not created a man, but evolved, through long ages, from the protoplasm of prehistoric times to the microbe, from the microbe, by various long stages and journeys to the monkey, and from the monkey finally to manhood. It is further claimed that manhood, in its earliest stage, was very inferior to the manhood of the present time, that evolution has been bringing mankind forward, and that the next step for every human being is a transformation or evolution into spirit conditions, as angels and gods or as devils.

All this is very flattering to nineteenth century pride, for though, on one hand, it acknowledges an ancestry of the very lowest intelligence, it claims for itself today the very highest attainments, as well as a future exaltation. Nor is this view confined to the people of civilized lands: in a general way all heathen people, even savages, have practically the same thought respecting man, except that they do not usually trace back his origin so far. This view finds support in all the heathen philosophies, and to a considerable extent it is supported by the scientific theorizers of the present day, who, although they define the subject quite differently, nevertheless love to indulge in hopes of a future life along the lines of evolution, and experience a gratification of their vanity along lines which do not at all accord with their own scientific deductions respecting the spark of life in man.

MAN AS SEEN BY SCIENCE

The scientific answer to the question, What is man? stated in simple language, would be: Man is an animal of the highest type yet developed and known. He has a body which differs from the bodies of other animals, in that it is the highest and noblest development. His brain structure corresponds to that of the lower animals, but is of a better developed and more refined order, with added and larger capacities, which constitute man by nature the lord, the king of the lower creation. Man's breath or spirit of life is like that of other animals. Man's organism and spark of life are from his progenitors, in the same manner that the beasts receive their life and bodies from their progenitors.

Science recognizes every man as a soul or sentient being; but as to the future, the eternity of man's being, science has no suggestion whatever to offer, finding nothing whereon to base a conclusion, or even a reasonable hypothesis. Science, however, while it does not speculate, hopes for a future along the lines of evolution, which it believes it can trace in the past. Science is proud of the said evolutionary steps already accomplished by its god, natural law, and is hopeful that the same operations of natural law will (without a personal God) eventually bring mankind to still more godlike and masterful conditions than at present.

MAN FROM THE BIBLE STANDPOINT

The Bible view, while agreeing with both of the foregoing in some respects, controverts both most absolutely along some of their most important lines. The Bible does not speculate, but properly, as the voice or revelation of God, it speaks with authority and emphasis, declaring the beginning, the present and the future of man. The Bible view is the only consistent one, and hence the only **truly** scientific and orthodox view of this subject. But the Bible presentation does not pander to human pride; it does

Man the Subject

not make of man his own evolutor, nor does it commit this to a god of nature, which is no God. The Bible view respecting man gives God the glory for his original creation (Adam), in the divine likeness; and lays upon man the blame for failure to maintain that likeness, and for a fall into sin, and all the consequences of sin—mental and physical and moral impoverishment unto death. The Bible view honors God again, in revealing to us his mercy and magnanimity toward man in his fallen estate, in the provision for man's redemption and for his restitution to his original condition, at the hands of his Redeemer, during the Millennium.

A fruitful source of confusion in the minds of Christian people, when studying the nature of man, and particularly when attempting to obtain the Scriptural views upon the subject, is their failure to distinguish between mankind in general and the Church, the little flock, which God is selecting from amongst men during the present age, and fitting and preparing for new and super-human conditions—spiritual conditions. Failing to "rightly divide the word of truth" they apply to all men the statements and promises of the Scriptures, especially of the New Testament, which are addressed only to the Church class, and which have no bearing whatever upon the restitution hopes held out for all mankind. These "exceeding great and precious promises" are proportionately as untrue of the world as they are true of the Church. Thus, for instance, the apostle's words, "The body is dead because of sin, but the spirit is life because of righteousness" (Rom. 8:10), which apply only to the Church: thus the special and peculiar conditions of the call of the Church during this Gospel age, is interpreted to mean the same with respect to all humanity. Here the words "dead" and "life" are used in a relative sense, of those who after being justified through faith, by the grace of God, are at once reckoned as freed from death-condemnation, to the intent that they may present their bodies living sacrifices, reckoning their bodies and treating them as dead, so far as earthly rights and interests are concerned: and reckoning themselves as no longer fleshly or human beings, but as "new creatures," begotten to a new nature through the promises of God. As such, justified and sanctified believers (the Church) recognize themselves, from the divine standpoint, as having obtained a new spirit of life through the operation of faith in Christ and obedience to him. But such uses of the words "dead" and "life" in respect to the world would be wholly improper, for the world has no other nature than the one human nature; it has not, in any sense of the word, been begotten **again.**

Another text frequently misapplied to the world, which belongs to the Lord's consecrated people, says, "We have this treasure in earthen vessels, that the excellency of the power may be of God, and not of us." (2 Cor. 4:7) Here the Church alone is referred to—those who have received the treasure of the new mind, the new nature. They have this treasure, or new nature, in the natural body, which is reckoned as dead, and here denominated an "earthen vessel." The illustration is quite a correct one for the class to whom it is applied, the Church; but it is wholly incorrect to apply it to mankind in general, and to suppose that every human being has a heavenly treasure or new nature, and that thus every human body is an earthen vessel or receptacle for such new nature. The world has but one nature—the human nature: it has no new nature, either as a treasure or in any other sense; nor is there any promise that it will ever have. Quite to the contrary, the highest possible **aspiration ever to be opened to humanity, according to the divine Word of promise, is "restitution"—to be restored to the full perfection of the human nature, lost in Eden, redeemed at Calvary.**— Acts 3:19-23

Similarly we might discuss scores of statements of the New Testament, which are not applicable to mankind in general, but merely to the consecrated Church, begotten again, by the Holy Spirit to a new spirit nature. It will be profitable for all to notice carefully the salutations by which the apostles introduce their various epistles. They are not addressed, as is supposed by many, to mankind in general, but to the Church, "the saints," the "household of faith."

Be it remembered, therefore, that in discussing, What is man? in this chapter, we are not discussing what is the Church, the "new creature" in Christ Jesus, nor what is the spirit nature to which the Church is already begotten of the Spirit and if faithful shall be made partakers to the fullest extent in the first resurrection. On the contrary, we are discussing the first Adam and his children. We want to know who and what we are by nature, as a race, —What is man? Thus we can best understand from what man fell, into what man fell, from what man was redeemed, and to what man shall be restored, and other cognate subjects.

MAN—BODY, SPIRIT, SOUL

Accepting the standard definition of the word "animal"—"a sentient living organism," we need have no hesitation in classing man as one of and the chief and king over earth's animals, and thus far the Scriptures are in full accord with the deductions of science. Note the text which introduces this chapter: in it the Prophet David particularly points out that man, in his nature, is lower than the angels, and a king and head over all earthly creatures, the representative of God to all the lower orders of sentient beings.

The Scriptures nowhere declare, either directly or by implication, that a piece, part or spark of the divine being is communicated to every human creature. This is a baseless assumption on the part of those who desire to construct a theory, and are short of material for it. And this baseless hypothesis, that there is a portion of God communicated to every human creature at birth, has been made the basis of many false doctrines, grossly derogatory to the divine character—disrespectful to divine wisdom, justice, love and power.

It is this assumption, that a spark of the divine

being is communicated at birth to every human creature, which necessitated the theory of a hell of eternal torment. The suggestion is that if man had been created as other animals were created, he might have died as other animals die, without fear of an eternity of torture; but that God having imparted to man a **spark of his own life,** man is therefore eternal, because God is eternal: and that hence it is impossible for God to destroy his creature even though such destruction might become desirable. And if man cannot be destroyed it is held that he must exist to all eternity somewhere: and since the vast majority are admittedly evil, and only a "little flock" saintly and pleasing to God, it is held that the unsaintly must have a future of torment proportioned to the future of bliss accorded to the saintly few. Otherwise, it is admitted that it would be more to man's interest, more to God's glory, and more to the peace and prosperity of the universe, if the wicked could all be **destroyed.** The claim is that God, having the power to create, has not the power to destroy man, his own creation, because a spark of divine life was in some unexplained manner connected with him. We hope to show that this entire proposition is fallacious: that it is not only without Scriptural support, but that it is a fabrication of the Dark Ages, most positively contradicted by the Scriptures.

The Scriptures recognize man as composed of two elements, body and spirit. These two produce soul, sentient being, intelligence, the man himself, the being, or soul. The term "body" applies merely to the physical organism. It neither relates to the life which animates it, nor to the sentient being which is the result of animation. A body is not a man, although there could be no man without a body. The spirit of life is not the man; although there could be no manhood without the spirit of life. The word "spirit" is, in the Old Testament Scriptures, from the Hebrew word **ruach.** Its signification primarily is **breath;** and hence we have the expression **"breath of life,"** or **"spirit of life,"** because the spark of life once started is supported by breathing.

The words "spirit of life," however, signify more than merely breath; they relate to the spark of life itself, without which breath would be an impossibility. This spark of life we receive from our fathers, it being nourished and developed through our mothers.* It is quite untrue that the spark of human life is communicated in a miraculous way, any more than is the spark of brute life. The lower animals, the horse, the dog, cattle, etc., are begotten of the males and born of the females of their respective genera, in precisely the same manner as the human species is produced, nor does anything in Scripture suggest the contrary. It is purely human invention, designed to uphold a false theory, that claims divine interposition in the birth of human offspring. To suppose that God is the direct creator of every human infant born into the world is to suppose what the Scriptures contradict, for thus he would be the author of sin and of confusion and of imperfection, whereas the Scriptures declare, "His work is perfect." (Deut. 32:4) No, no! the mentally and physically and morally blemished and deformed are not God's workmanship. They are far removed, far fallen from the condition of their perfect progenitors, Adam and Eve, for whose creation alone God takes the responsibility. Those who claim that God directly creates every human being make out that God is responsible for all the idiocy and insanity and imbecility in the world: but both science and Scripture declare that the children inherit from their progenitors their vices and their virtues, their weaknesses and their talents. The apostle most explicitly declares, "By one man's disobedience sin entered into the world and death by [as a result of] sin: and thus death passed upon all men; because all men had [by heredity] become sinners." The Prophet refers to the same thing when he declares, "The fathers ate a sour grape [sin] and the children's teeth are set on edge"—they are all depraved.—Rom. 5:12; Jer. 31:29, 30; Ezek. 18:2

---

*See page 98.

But some one will inquire, Might it not be possible that God had implanted a spark of his immortal divinity in our first parents, and that thus that spark descends **nolens volens** to posterity? Let us examine the Scriptural statement respecting this subject, and in so doing let us remember that there is no other revelation than the account of the Scriptures open to any one else, hence we may know all there is to be known on the subject by anybody. What do we find in the Genesis account? We find indeed that man's creation is particularly mentioned, while that of the brute creation is not so particularly mentioned. We find, however, that the statements made are in very simple language, and that they contain no suggestion whatever of the impartation of some superhuman spark of being. Man's superiority over the beast, according to the account given in Genesis, consists not in his having a different kind of breath or spirit, but in his having a higher form, a superior body, a finer organism—endowed with a brain organism which enables him to reason upon planes far above and beyond the intelligence of the lower animals, the brute creation. We find that it is in these respects that man was created a fleshly likeness of his Creator, who is a spirit being.—John 4:24

THE SPIRIT OF MAN

As already seen* the word "spirit" in our Common Version Bibles translates the Hebrew word **ruach** and the Greek word **pneuma;** and hence to rightly appreciate the word **spirit** in God's Word we must keep always in memory the meaning attached to the originals, which it translates. As we have seen, "spirit" primarily means **wind,** and secondarily was made to apply to any **invisible power.** In connection with God we saw that it signifies that he is **powerful** but **invisible;** and used in reference to God's influence and operation, it implies that they are by an invisible power. It is applied to **mind** because it is a

---

*See page 172.

power that is invisible, intangible; **words** are also invisible, yet powerful; **life**, although all-important and all pervading, is an invisible power or quality, like electricity: hence the word "spirit" is applied to all of these various things. As a result, we have the Scriptures speaking of the spirit of our minds, the invisible power of the mind; the spirit of a man, a man's mental powers and will; the spirit of life, the power of living, which actuates our bodies and all creation; the Spirit of God, the power or influence which God exerts, either upon animate or inanimate things; the spirit of wisdom, a wise mind; the spirit of love, a mind or disposition actuated by love; a spirit of evil and of malice, a mind or disposition actuated by maliciousness; the spirit of truth, the influence or power exerted by the truth; the spirit of the world, the influence or power which the world exerts. Likewise, heavenly beings are described as spirit beings, that is, invisible beings, possessed of power, intelligence, etc. This is applicable, not only to God, the Father, of whom our Lord Jesus said, "God is a Spirit," but it is applicable also to our Lord Jesus since his resurrection, for of him it is declared, "Now the Lord is that Spirit." It is applied also to angels and to the Church, which is assured that in the first resurrection each overcomer shall have a spirit body. It is applied in the Scriptures also to Satan and his associates, spirit beings, invisible, yet powerful.

SPIRIT IN RE THE NEW NATURE IN THE NEW TESTAMENT

In considering the use of the word **spirit** in connection with **man**, we remark:—

(1) The words "spirit" and "spiritual" in the New Testament are often used to refer to (a) the **will**, especially to the **new mind** of the "saints," begotten by the Word and Spirit of God. The "new creatures in Christ" are called to a change of nature, from human to spiritual, and are promised that if faithful they shall in the resurrection have (b) **spirit bodies** like unto Christ's resurrection body, and like unto

the Heavenly Father's glorious person. In view of this, their future prospect, the hope of the Church is designated as (c) **spiritual** and **heavenly**, in contrast with the hopes and promises to which the world of mankind will become heirs during the Millennium. Spirit is also used (d) in referring to angels, who by nature are **spirit** beings—not flesh beings. But the thought of **invisibility** always attaches to the words "spirit" and "spiritual" whenever and wherever used.

A few illustrations of such uses of these words follow:—

(a) "Paul purposed in the **spirit** [**pneuma**—mind, will] . . . to go to Jerusalem."—Acts 19:21

(a) "Paul's **spirit** [**pneuma**—mind, feelings] was stirred in him when he saw the city wholly given to idolatry."—Acts 17:16

(a) "Paul was pressed in spirit [**pneuma**—in mind, he was mentally energized] and testified to the Jews that Jesus is the Christ."—Acts 18:5

(a) "[Apollos] was instructed in the way of the Lord; and being fervent in spirit [**pneuma**—of ardent mind] he spake and taught diligently."—Acts 18:25

(a) "God is my witness whom I serve with my **spirit** [**pneuma**—my new mind, my new heart, my renewed will] in the gospel of his Son."—Rom. 1:9

(a) "Glorify God in your body and in your **spirit** [**pneuma**—mind] which are God's."—1 Cor. 6:20

(a) "I verily, as absent in body, but present in spirit [**pneuma**—mentally] have judged already as though I were present."—1 Cor. 5:3

(a) "A meek and quiet **spirit** [**pneuma**—mind, disposition]."—1 Pet. 3:4

(b) "It is sown an animal body, it is raised a **spiritual** [**pneumatikos**] body."—1 Cor. 15:44

(b) "There is an animal body and there is a **spiritual** [**pneumatikos**] body."—1 Cor. 15:44

(b) "That was not first which is **spiritual** [**pneumatikos**]."—1 Cor. 15:46

(b) "Afterward that which is **spiritual** [**pneumatikos**]."—1 Cor. 15:46

Man the Subject

(c) "To be **spiritually** minded [pneuma—to have a mind controlled by God's Holy Spirit or will] is life and peace."—Rom. 8:6

(c) "Ye which are **spiritual** [pneumatikos—spirit begotten and possessed of the new mind] restore such an one in the **spirit** [pneuma—disposition] of meekness."—Gal. 6:1

(c) "The God and Father of our Lord Jesus Christ hath blessed us with all **spiritual** blessings [pneumatikos—blessings of a spirit kind] in heavenly privileges in Christ."—Eph. 1:3

(c) "Be filled with the **spirit** [pneuma—the holy Spirit of God] speaking to yourselves in psalms and hymns and **spiritual** songs [pneumatikos—songs in accord with your new spirit]."—Eph. 5:19

(c) "That ye might be filled with the knowledge of his will in all wisdom and **spiritual** understanding [pneumatikos—understanding of all matters connected with your new spiritual relationship to God and his plan]."—Col. 1:9

(c) "Ye are built up a **spiritual** household [pneumatikos—a family or household of a spirit order or kind]."—1 Pet. 2:5

(d) "A damsel possessed of a **spirit** [pneuma—an invisible power] of divination"—through fellowship with the fallen spirit-beings.—Acts 16:16

(d) "Paul . . . turned and said to the **spirit** [pneuma—the evil spirit-being possessing the woman] I command thee . . . to come out of her."—Acts 16:18

(d) "The evil **spirits** [pneuma] went out of them."—Acts 19:12, 13

(d) "And the evil **spirit** [pneuma] answered and said."—Acts 19:15

(d) "The Sadducees say that there is . . . neither angel nor **spirit** [pneuma—spirit being]."—Acts 23:8

(d) "If a **spirit** [pneuma] or an angel hath spoken to him let us not fight against God."—Acts 23:9

SPIRIT IN THE OLD TESTAMENT

(2) The word "spirit" is used of mankind in general, especially in the Old Testament; but always either with reference to (e) **the spirit of life,** the animating spark which God first enkindled in Adam and which thence (impaired) descended to all his posterity—which is an **invisible power** or quality; or (f) **the spirit of the mind,** the will—an invisible power which controls the life.

RUACH, PNEUMA—AN ANIMATING POWER

When speaking of man's creation it is the **spirit of life** that is understood—the breath of life. The Scriptures clearly show that this spirit of life is common to all God's creatures, and is not possessed exclusively by man, as the following Scripture quotations will clearly demonstrate.

(e) "All flesh wherein is **the breath of life** [**ruach**—the **spirit** or **breath** of life of all flesh]."—Gen. 6:17; 7:15

(e) "All in whose nostrils was the breath of **the spirit of life** [margin, **ruach**—the **spirit** or **power of life**]."—Gen. 7:22

(e) "The **spirit** of Jacob their father revived [**ruach**—the vital or **life powers** of Jacob revived]."—Gen. 45:27

(e) "And when he [Samson] had drunk, his **spirit** [**ruach**] came again and he revived [his strength, vigor, energy returned to him]."—Judges 15:19

(e) "In whose hand is . . . **the breath** [**ruach**] of all mankind. [The **spirit of life** of all mankind is in the divine power]."—Job 12:10

(e) "O God, the God of the **spirits** [**ruach**—life-power, spirit of life] of **all flesh,** shall one man sin and wilt thou be wroth with all the congregation?"—Num. 16:22

The theory that the distinction between man and beast consisted in a different spirit of life, a different kind of life, and that at death the one went up and the other down seems to have been very old amongst the world's philosophers; for we find Solomon, the wise man, querying:—

(e) "Who knoweth [who can prove] that the **spirit** [**ruach**—spirit of life] of man goeth upward and that the **spirit** [**ruach**—spirit of life] of the beast goeth downward to the earth?" (Eccl. 3:19-21) Solomon's own understanding he gives just previously, saying:—

(e) "That which befalleth the sons of men [death] befalleth beasts; even one [the same] thing befalleth them: as the one dieth so dieth the other; yea they have all one **breath** [**ruach**—spirit of life, breath of life]; so that a man hath no pre-eminence above a beast"—in this respect, in the matter of having a different kind of life—his pre-eminence must be sought and found elsewhere, as we shall see.

(e) "Into thine hand I commit my **spirit** [**ruach**—spirit of life or vital energy]."—Psa. 31:5

This was the prophetic declaration of our Lord Jesus' dying words. He had received the spirit of life from the Father as a gift: he had, in obedience to the Father's plan, become a man to be man's Redeemer: and when yielding up his **spirit of life** or vital energy, he declared his reliance upon God's promise to give the **spirit of life** again, by a resurrection.

Mankind received the **spirit of life** from God, the fountain of life, through father Adam. Adam forfeited his right to the power or spirit of life by disobedience, and gradually relinquished his hold upon it—dying slowly for nine hundred and thirty years. Then the body returned to the dust as it was before creation, and the spirit of life, the privilege of living, the power or permission of living, returned to God who gave that privilege or power: just as any contingent privilege or favor returns to the giver if its conditions are not complied with. (Eccl. 12:7) Nothing in this text implies that the spirit of life "wings its flight back to God," as some would represent; for the spirit of life is not an intelligence, nor a person, but merely a **power or privilege** which has been forfeited and hence reverts to the original giver of that **power or privilege. The** thought is that man having sinned has no further life-rights: the return of his forfeited life-rights to God, and the return of his flesh to dust, reduces his condition to exactly what it was before he was created.

But as our Lord Jesus had hope in the divine promise for a return of his "spirit of life" or life powers and rights under divine arrangement, so by reason of our Lord's redemptive sacrifice certain hopes and promises are opened to all mankind through "Jesus the mediator of the New Covenant." (Heb. 12:24) Hence believers "sorrow not as others who have no hope." Our Redeemer **purchased** the spirit of life-rights which father Adam had forfeited for himself and all his family. Now, therefore, believers can for themselves (and, by a knowledge of God's plan, for others also) commit their spirits (their powers of life) to God's hand also, as did our Lord and as did Stephen—full of faith that God's promise of a **resurrection** would be fulfilled. A resurrection will mean to the world a reorganization of a human body, and its vivifying or quickening with life-energy, the spirit of life (Hebrew, **ruach**; Greek, **pneuma**). To the Gospel Church, sharers in the "first [chief] resurrection," it will mean the impartation of the spirit of life or life-energy (Hebrew, **ruach**; Greek, **pneuma**) to a spirit body.—1 Cor. 15:42-45

In that graphic picture of earthly resurrection furnished us in Ezekiel's prophecy (37:5-10, 13, 14) the relationship of the body and the spirit of life, **"the breath,"** is clearly presented. It matters not that the prophet uses this merely as a **symbol**, it nevertheless shows (proves) that a human organism has no life until it receives the **ruach**—the breath of life—which, as elsewhere shown, is common to all animals, none of whom can live without it. Let us notice Ezekiel's statements very critically, as follows:—

(e) "I will cause **breath** [**ruach**—spirit of life, life-energy] to enter into you, and ye shall live."

(e) "And I will . . . bring up flesh upon you, **and** cover you with skin, and put **breath** [**ruach**—**spirit** of life, life-energy] in you, and ye shall live."

(e) "And when I beheld, lo, the sinews and the flesh came upon them, and the skin covered them above: but there was no **breath** [**ruach**—spirit of life, life-energy] in them."

(e) "And he said unto me, Prophesy unto the **wind** [**ruach**—spirit of life, life-energy—margin, breath] and say unto **the wind** [**ruach**—spirit of life, breath of life], Thus saith the Lord God, Come from the four **winds** [**ruach**] **O breath** [**ruach**—breath or spirit of life], and breathe upon these slain, that they may live."

(e) "So I prophesied as he commanded me, and **the breath** [**ruach**— spirit of life, breath of life, living energy] came into them, and they lived."

(e) "And ye shall know that I am the Lord, when I have opened your graves, O my people, and brought you up out of your graves, and shall put my **spirit** [**ruach**—spirit of life, breath of life] in you, and ye shall live."

This **spirit** of life or **power** of life given to Adam by his Creator he was privileged to **keep** forever if obedient. He forfeited this right by disobedience, and the **right to life** reverted to the great Giver; not as a person, nor as a thing, but as a right or privilege, the spirit of life returns or reverts to God, who gave that right or privilege conditionally, and whose conditions were violated.—Eccl. 12:7

(e) "No man hath power over the **spirit** [**ruach**—spirit of life, spark of life] to retain the **spirit** [**ruach**—spirit of life], breath of life."—Eccl. 8:8

By God's grace those forfeited life-rights or privileges which each man surrenders to God in **death** have all been purchased with the precious **blood**, and the purchaser is announced as the new Life-giver, regenerator or father for the race, who will give life, and that more abundantly, to all who will ultimately receive him.

We will give but one instance from the New Testament:—

(e) "The body without the **spirit** [**pneuma**—life—spark, breath of lives] is dead."—Jas. 2:26

RUACH, PNEUMA—THE MIND, THE WILL

Since the mind or will is an **invisible power** or influence, it is represented by the same words in the Hebrew and Greek languages, as the following examples will show:—

(f) "Hannah answered and said, No, my lord, I am a woman of sorrowful **spirit** [**ruach**—mind, disposition]."—1 Sam. 1:15

(f) "A fool uttereth all his **mind** [**ruach**—plans, thoughts, mind, purpose]."—Prov. 29:11

(f) "My **spirit** [**ruach**—mind, courage] was overwhelmed."—Psa. 77:3

(f) "My **spirit** [**ruach**—mind] made diligent search."—Psa. 77:6

(f) "He that is of a faithful **spirit** [**ruach**—disposition, mind]."—Prov. 11:13

(f) "All the ways of a man are clean in his own eyes; but the Lord weigheth the **spirits** [**ruach**—the mind, thoughts, motives]."—Prov. 16:2

(f) "Pride goeth before destruction, a haughty **spirit** [**ruach**—disposition, will, mind] before a fall."—Prov. 16:18

(f) "Better to be of an humble **spirit** [**ruach**—mind, disposition]."—Prov. 16:19

(f) "Vanity and vexation of **spirit** [**ruach**—mind]."—Eccl. 6:9

(f) "Patient in **spirit** [**ruach**—mind, disposition] . . . proud in **spirit** [**ruach**—mind, disposition] . . . hasty in thy **spirit** [**ruach**—mind, disposition]."—Eccl. 7:8, 9

A few illustrations from the New Testament:—

(f) "The child [John] grew and waxed strong in **spirit** [**pneuma**—mind, character]."—Luke 1:80

(f) "Not slothful in business, fervent in **spirit** [**pneuma**—mind, disposition, character] serving the Lord."—Rom. 12:11

(f) "Now you have received not the **spirit** [**pneuma**—disposition, mind] of the world."—1 Cor. 2:12

(f) "I had no rest in my **spirit** [**pneuma**—mind]."—2 Cor. 2:13

(f) "Be renewed in the **spirit** [pneuma—character, disposition] of your mind."—Eph. 4:23

(f) "The ornament of a meek and quiet **spirit** [pneuma—mind, disposition]."—1 Pet. 3:4

These Scriptural uses of these original words show that our English word **spirit** is a good equivalent, for we not only speak of the spirit of life, but also of a gentle spirit, a good spirit, an angry spirit or mood, a bitter spirit and a fiery spirit: and we also use these expressions in respect to the lower animals as well as man. The fact we are proving is abundantly demonstrated—namely, that the **spirit** is not the real man, nor another man, but that this word, when used in reference to man's creation, signifies simply the life-spark or life-power, which is common to all animals.

NESHAMAH—THE BREATH OF LIVES

Although the word **ruach** is sometimes translated "breath," the Hebrews had another word for breath, viz., **neshamah.** It occurs twenty-six times, and in nineteen of these it is translated "breath"—"inspiration" once, "spirit" twice, "souls" once, "blast" three times. As samples of the meaning of this word, and as proving that the word simply signifies life power, and in no sense of the word conveys any thought of everlasting life, or immortality, note the following uses of the word:—

"The Lord God formed man of the dust of the ground, and **breathed** [naphach—inflated, blew] into his nostrils the **breath** [neshamah] of **lives** [caiyah]."—Gen. 2:7

"All flesh died that moved upon the earth, both of fowl, and of cattle, and of beasts, and of everything that creepeth upon the earth, and every man: all in whose nostrils was the breath [neshamah] of life [caiyah] of all that was in the dry land died."—Gen. 7:21, 22

These first two occurrences of the word **neshamah** in the Bible are abundantly sufficient to prove our contention that the word has no reference to immortality, nor to an immortal principle, but simply refers to vitality, life power. This life power, we are told, was given to Adam, and the same life power, by the second text quoted, is declared to have been in all the dry land animals, fowl, cattle, beast and creeping things, as well as in man, and when deprived of this breath of life, the declaration is that all these souls or beings died as a result—man as well as the lower creatures. They died alike, except that there is a divine purpose respecting man, which in due time provided a ransom, and will in further due time provide the deliverance promised from the power of death by a resurrection of the being, of the soul.

A HUMAN SOUL

Many in reading the account of creation in Genesis have noted the fact stated that when God had formed man of the dust of the ground, and had communicated to him the breath (spirit) of life, the record is, "Man became a **living soul.**" This statement to the average reader taken in connection with his general misconceptions of the meaning of the word "soul," as misrepresented to him by those who should have instructed him properly, and should have understood the subject themselves, is sufficient to bewilder him and leads him to think that somehow there is some basis for the prevalent error which he does not comprehend, but which he supposes his chosen theological teachers have investigated and proven beyond peradventure.

Not comprehending the meaning of the word **soul,** many feel at liberty to use it in a reckless manner, and hence they reverse the Scriptural statement and instead of speaking of man as **being** a soul, they speak of man as **having** a soul, which is a very different thought. It is necessary, therefore, that each truth-seeker should, so far as possible divest his mind of prejudice on the subject, and especially with respect to things and features which he admits he **does not understand;** because it is the natural tendency to give attributes and powers to that which is mysterious and not comprehended. Thus the general

Man the Subject

idea of a soul is that it is wonderfully intelligent, possessed of wonderful powers, that it is indestructible, intangible, and incomprehensible.

A Methodist bishop is credited with having given the following definition of a soul, which certainly accords well with so-called "orthodox" theories, even if it is absurd when closely analyzed—"It is without interior or exterior, without body, shape, or parts, and you could put a million of them in a nutshell." These various things are predicated of a soul, to help fill out a theory which is wholly erroneous. The theory is that the soul is the real being, a spark of divinity, possessed of divine quality and intelligent life, etc., separate and apart from the body; and that it inhabits the human body for a time, and uses it for a house, and when the body is worn out or disabled abandons it. Inasmuch as no one ever saw a soul enter a body, and inasmuch as a soul cannot be found while it is in the body, by the most critical examination, and with all the improved appliances of the microscope, photograph and "X" rays, therefore it is supposed that it is "without a body, without shape, and without parts"; and since it is supposed to be so small that it cannot be distinguished by a microscope, it might as well be said that you could put fifty millions of them in a nutshell. Really, the bishop gave an excellent definition of **nothing;** and all will agree that a hundred millions of nothings could be put into the smallest kind of a nutshell and have room to spare.

But what foundation is there for such wild speculation? We answer, It is wholly unwarranted. It is the result of man's taking his own theory of a future life; and rejecting the divine theory and plan. Human theory says, There must be something which never dies, else there can be no future life. The divine theory says, The same God who created in the beginning is able to resurrect the dead. This is the conflict between the Word of God and all the human theories of earth amongst the civilized as well as amongst the barbarians: all human theories teach that man does not die, and hence has no need of a

Life-giver and a resurrection. The Bible theory is that man does die, and that without the Life-giver, and without a resurrection, death would indeed end all, and there would be no future life.

It is to support its theory that the world, and all its religious books (including, we are sorry to say, the majority of works on eschatology written by professed Christians), teach the doctrine of the immortality of the soul—that there is a soul in man, possessed of a separate life from his body, and that it is immortal, indestructible, and therefore destined to an eternity of pain or pleasure. We come then to the inquiry:—

WHAT IS A SOUL?

Examining this question from the Bible standpoint we will find that man has a body and has a spirit, but is a soul. Science concurs with the Scriptures in this. Indeed, one of the sciences, Phrenology, undertakes to treat the skulls of men and the lower animals as indexes and to read therefrom the natural traits and characteristics of the owners: and do not all men find themselves possessed of some ability in judging character physiologically? All can discern between the intellectual and the idiotic, between the kindly benevolent and the viciously brutal. Those who have not learned that **organism** (bodily form) is indissolubly connected with nature, character and disposition have made poor use of life's lessons and are unprepared to pass judgment on our topic or any other.

The word "soul," as found in the Scriptures, signifies **sentient being**; that is, a being possessed of powers of sense, sense-perception. With minds freed from prejudice, let us go with this definition to the Genesis account of man's creation, and note that (1) the organism or **body** was formed; (2) the **spirit of life**, called "breath of life," was communicated; (3) **living soul**, or sentient being, resulted. This is very simple, and easily understood. It shows that the **body** is not the soul, nor is the spirit or breath of life the soul; but that when these two were united by the Lord, the resultant quality or condition was living man, living being—a living soul, possessed of perceptive powers. There is nothing mysterious about this—no intimation that a spark of divinity was infused into humanity, any more than into the lower animals. Indeed, while the creation of the lower animals is passed over and not particularly described, we may know that with them, as well, the process must have been somewhat similar. We know that there could be no dog without a dog organism or body, nor without spirit or breath of life in that body. The body of the dog that had never been animated would not be a dog; it requires first the infusion of the spark of life, the breath of life, then doghood begins. The same would apply to all animals.

In full accord with this, we now call attention to a fact which will surprise many; viz., that according to the Scriptural account every dog is a soul, every horse is a soul, every cow is a soul, every bird and every fish are souls. That is to say, these are all **sentient** creatures, possessed of powers of sense-perception. True, some of them are on a higher and some on a lower plane than others; but the word **soul** properly and Scripturally applies to creatures on the lower planes as well as to man, the highest and noblest—to fish, reptiles, birds, beasts, man. They are all souls. Mark, we do not say that they **have** souls, in the ordinary and mistaken sense of that term, yet they all do **have** souls, in the sense of having **life, being, existence**—they **are** living souls. Let us prove this:

In the first, second and ninth chapters of Genesis the words "living soul" are applied in the Hebrew language to the lower animals nine times, but the translators (as though careful to protect the false but common vagary respecting a soul, derived from Platonic philosophy) sedulously guarded their work, so that, so far as possible, the English reader is kept in ignorance of this fact—that the word **soul** is common to the lower creatures, and as applicable to them as to man in inspired Scripture usage. How else could it happen that in all of these cases, and in many other instances throughout the Scriptures, they have carefully covered the thought, by using another English word to translate the Hebrew word, which, in the case of man, is rendered "soul"? So carefully have they guarded this point that only in one place in the Bible is this word translated "soul," in connection with the lower creatures, viz., in Num. 31:28, and there, very evidently, they were compelled to show the matter, by reason of the peculiar construction of the sentence—no other translation being reasonably possible. The passage reads:—

"Levy a tribute unto the Lord of the men of war which went out to battle: one soul of five hundred, both of the persons and of the beeves and of the asses and of the sheep." Here it will be noticed that the word "soul" is used respecting the lower creatures as well as in reference to man; and so it would appear elsewhere in the Scriptures, had the translators been free from the warp and twist of their false theories on this subject.

Let us now notice the nine texts in Genesis in which the Hebrew original of the word **soul (neh-phesh)** occurs in connection with the lower animals:

"God said, Let the waters bring forth abundantly the moving [creeping] creature **that hath life** [Heb., **neh-phesh**—soul],"—Gen. 1:20. Note that the marginal reading is **soul**; and that this was on the fifth creative day or period, long before man's creation.

"God created great whales, and every living **creature** [Heb., **neh-phesh**—living **soul**] that moveth, which the waters brought forth abundantly." (Gen. 1:21) This also was in the fifth "day,"—before man's creation. These were fish-souls.

"God said, Let the earth bring forth the living **creature** [Heb., **neh-phesh**—living **soul**] after his kind—cattle and creeping thing and beast." (Gen. 1:24) These were dry-land souls, higher than the fishes—but man, human soul or being, had not yet been created.

Man the Subject

"And God said . . . To every beast of the earth and to every fowl of the air, and to everything that creepeth upon the earth, wherein there is **life** [living **soul—neh-phesh**] I have given every green herb for meat." (Gen. 1:30) Here the lower animals are specified, and it is distinctly declared that they are all living souls—in exactly the same terms that refer to man.

"Out of the ground the Lord God formed every beast of the field, and every fowl of the air; . . . and whatever Adam called every living **creature** [Heb., living **soul—neh-phesh**], that was the name thereof." (Gen. 2:19) Comment here is unnecessary: there can be no question that **soul** is not **exclusively a human** part or quality, but rightly understood is applicable to all **sentient creatures** from the lowest to the highest—all creatures possessed of **sensibilities.**

"Every moving thing that liveth shall be meat for you . . . but flesh **with the life thereof** [Heb., flesh, **soul—neh-phesh**] which is the blood thereof, shall ye not eat." (Gen. 9:3, 4) Here the animals which man may eat are not only declared to possess soul or **being,** but their **blood** is said to represent their **existence, being** or **soul,** and hence man is forbidden to use blood as food—forbidden to cultivate blood-thirstiness.

"Behold I establish my covenant with you [Noah] and with your seed after you; and with every living **creature** [Heb., living **soul—neh-phesh**] that is with you, of the fowl, of the cattle, and of every beast of the earth." (Gen. 9:9, 10) A very plain statement that all living creatures are souls as well as man—though inferior to him in nature, organism, etc.

"This is the token of the covenant which I make between me and you and every living **creature** [Heb., living **soul—neh-phesh**]." (Gen. 9:12) What could be more explicit than this?

"I will remember my covenant which is between me and you and every living **creature** [Heb., **every** living **soul—neh-phesh**] of all flesh."—Gen. 9:15

The same expression exactly is repeated in verse 16. And there is no room for cavil as to the meaning when the veil of mistranslation is lifted and we catch the thought God wished us to receive from his Word.

We might similarly proceed through other books of the Bible, but we have quoted sufficient to establish our contention before any reasonable mind—that soul in Scriptural usage as properly applies to the lower animals as to man; and hence that all claims or theories built upon the idea that man's hopes of a future life and his present superiority over lower animals result from his being a **soul** and they not, is a false theory and needs radical reconstruction if we would see matters from the true standpoint of divine revelation.

But let no one misunderstand us to teach that because all living, moving creatures, from a mite to an elephant and from a tadpole to a whale are **living souls**, therefore all these must have a future life, either by a transfer to spirit conditions or by a resurrection future. Such a thought would be arrant nonsense—insanity—without a shadow of reason. Billions of living **souls** on these lowest planes of animal nature are born every minute while other billions die every minute.

Our argument is that man is a **soul** or **being** of the highest order—the king and lord over the lower orders of souls or sentient beings, yet one of them—an earthly, human animal soul; and yet so grandly constituted originally (Adam) that he was properly described as in the **likeness** of God—the image of him that created him.

Man as a soul is differentiated from the lower animals or souls by reason of his higher **organism:** not merely is his superiority indicated by his upright form; it is witnessed to by his superior mental endowments, which are God-like and are reflected in his countenance. It is in his mental and moral endowments rather than in physical form that man was created in divine likeness. While many of the lower orders of animal soul or being possess **reasoning powers** and demonstrate them in thousands of ways, yet each has a level beyond which no progress can be made; but man's reasoning powers are almost unlimited, because he was created an **"image of God,"** "the likeness of him that created him." And notwithstanding man's fall into sin and his thousands of years of gross darkness and degradation we can still see God-likeness—especially in those who have accepted Christ's ministry of reconciliation to God, and have again become "sons of God," and who are seeking to be conformed to the image of God's dear Son.

To illustrate: horses, dogs and birds may be taught the meaning of many words so as to be able to understand many things pertaining to life's affairs. They often demonstrate their reasoning powers, and some are able to count—as high as twenty: but who would attempt to teach a horse or a dog or a bird algebra or geometry or astronomy? The highest of the lower animals can be taught a certain degree of moral honesty and obligation to their masters—not to kill sheep, not to bite, kick, etc., but who would attempt to teach his dumb brutes the Decalogue? They may be taught a certain kind of love for their master and his friends, but who would think of teaching them to love or worship God, or more than mere endurance of enemies who had despitefully used them?

The point to be noticed is that all these differences are not by reason of the lower animals having a different kind of **breath** or spirit of life, for as we have seen, "they have all **one breath**" (Eccl. 3:19); nor because man is a soul and the brute beast is not, for as we have seen they are all souls. But as we have found, and as all men are witnesses, each has a **different** bodily organism which gives to each his different characteristics, and which alone constitutes one higher and the other lower in the scale of intelligence. Notice, too, that not size and weight give excellence and superiority, else the elephant and whale would be the lords of earth; the excellence is in the **"organic quality"** represented chiefly in brain-structure and functions.

Man, therefore, is the highest type of earthly creature—"of the earth, earthy"—and his excellence consists in the superiority of his mental endowment—not a development, but a gift from his Creator.

"THE SOUL THAT SINNETH, IT SHALL DIE"

It is quite in harmony with the foregoing, but quite out of harmony with the usual thought on the subject, that we find the Scriptures declaring repeatedly the death of the soul, which human philosophy and hymn-book theology most emphatically declare to be indestructible. We read, for instance, that our Lord, when he became our ransom-price, "poured out his **soul** [being] unto death." "He made his **soul** an offering for sin." (Isa. 53:10, 12) This was necessary because it was Adam's **soul** that was sentenced to death, and the promise to mankind is a redemption of **soul** or being from the power of death. "God will redeem my **soul** from the grave [**sheol**—the condition of death]." (Psa. 49:15) And, as we have seen, it is because all souls are thus redeemed in the one redemption that all our friends—all mankind—are said to "sleep in Jesus."—1 Thess. 4:14

We remark here that the apostle could not, in this expression, refer merely to the saints, as when he speaks of those who are "in Christ"; for those referred to as "new creatures" are those only who are begotten of God through the Spirit, to joint-heirship with Christ, as his Church, the members of his body. But "those who sleep in Jesus" include the entire race, for our Lord Jesus was a propitiation for our sins, and not for ours only, but also for the sins of the whole world, and he is by virtue of that sacrifice our Life-giver, and not only ours, but also the Life-giver for the whole world—the testimony and the opportunity for acceptance being, with the majority, still future.—1 John 2:2; 1 Tim. 2:4-6

That the apostle has this thought in mind is manifest from this context: he is here exhorting believers to sorrow not as others who have no hope; and gives as the reason of the hope this fact, that Jesus died for man's sin, and rose again to be man's justifier, and hence that all "sleep in Jesus," or are legally freed from the death sentence, and amenable to Jesus, to be brought from the dead by the divine power. Had the apostle said or been understood to mean that merely the saints would be thus blessed through Jesus, we can readily see that believers then and since would have very little consolation in his words, because the vast majority of the friends of believers, then and since, cannot be termed saints: and if the awakening from the sleep of death is a blessing intended only for the saints, the thought, instead of being consolation, would be the reverse, an anguish, a distress. But the apostle refers to the whole world as being thus **asleep** in Jesus, although none knows it from this standpoint except the Heavenly Father and his consecrated people, whom he has instructed respecting his future gracious plans, through the Word of truth, that they may rejoice in the lengths and breadths and heights and depths of divine goodness, and "sorrow not, even as others that have no [such substantial] hope."

As the natural sleep, if sound, implies total unconsciousness, so with death, the figurative sleep—it is a period of absolute unconsciousness—more than that, it is a period of absolute non-existence, except as preserved in the Father's purpose and power. Hence the awakening from death, to those restored, will mean a revival of consciousness from the exact moment and standpoint where consciousness was lost in death. There will be no appreciation of time, as respects the interim. The moment of awakening will be the next moment after the moment of death so far as conscious appreciation is concerned.

This same condition has been noted in connection with persons who have sustained injuries which have caused pressure upon the brain, and thus temporarily suspended consciousness, without extinguishing life. In cases of this kind, when the pressure upon the brain has been removed by trepanning, the subject suddenly coming to consciousness has in numerous instances been known to complete a sentence which had been interrupted by the concussion which interrupted thought; for divine power will thoroughly duplicate every convolution of every brain and vivify them. Thus in the awakening-time the world of mankind in general will revive with the same words and thoughts with which they expired. But let it not be forgotten that we here refer to the world in general, not to the elect and special class selected out of the world, namely, the Church, the body of Christ, which will have part in the first resurrection, and in many respects know a different experience.

But while, as the Adamic death has been turned, by reason of the divine plan and the ransom, from being a **destruction** to a **suspension** of existence, called sleep, nevertheless we find that the Scriptures very distinctly assert that after the revival or awakening from the death-sleep, it will depend upon each individual whether he shall go on unto perfection and life, under the guidance, government and tutelage of the glorious Christ, or whether he will wilfully, deliberately and stubbornly choose the way of sin. If he choose the latter he will get the punishment originally designated for father Adam, viz., death, but no longer Adamic death, the penalty of Adam's sin: this is styled Second Death. This Second Death is nowhere spoken of as a **sleep,** nor is there the slightest intimation anywhere given that there will be any awakening from it. On the contrary, it is designated "everlasting destruction from the presence of the Lord."—2 Thess. 1:9

Of this redeemed and awakened class, which in general shall have its trial during the Millennial age, the Scriptures declare, "The soul that sinneth it shall die." (Ezek. 18:20) That this Scripture is not generally applicable at the present time is evident from three considerations:

(1) It would be meaningless, at the present time, when all die—saints and sinners.

(2) It is expressed in the form of a second sentence, and based upon the individual action, and this

could not be applicable in the present time, because now we all die because of "one man's disobedience," and the sentence of death which came upon **him,** and indirectly affects all his race.—Rom. 5:12

(3) The context shows that this passage refers particularly to those who have gotten free from Adamic sin which prevails in general today. Its special applicability, therefore, must belong to the next age, the Millennial age. Note the connections, not forgetting that the law covenant of the Jewish age was analogous to the covenant of the Millennial age, except that the latter will have a better Mediator, able and willing to succor and to help all who shall seek to walk righteously, not imputing unintentional short-comings.

The context declares: This shall no more be a proverb in Israel, The fathers have eaten sour grapes, and the children's teeth are set on edge. But, on the contrary, each soul shall be responsible to God for itself, and "**the soul that sinneth** it shall die. The son shall not bear the iniquity of the father, neither shall the father bear the iniquity of the son: the righteousness of the righteous shall be upon him, and the wickedness of the wicked shall be upon him." (Ezek. 18:2, 4, 20) It is evident that this time has not yet come. The children still have their "teeth set on edge," by reason of the sour grapes of sin which their fathers have eaten; we are still under the law of heredity; all still die for Adam's sin, and not for individual sin. In proof of this note the indisputable fact that nearly one-half of the human family die in infancy, without having reached years of discretion or responsibility on their own account. Who cannot see that the agonizing and dying infant of a few days or a few months old is not dying for **its own sins,** but that it is dying because it is a member of the Adamic race, which is still under the curse pronounced against our father Adam, "Dying thou shalt die"? It has inherited a share of the curse, and will also inherit a share of God's blessing through

Christ in the coming awakening, secured through the merit of the great Atonement finished at Calvary.

If we turn to Jeremiah 31:29-34, we find another reference to exactly the same conditions mentioned by Ezekiel, only that in Jeremiah we are furnished with more explicit details, which show that this condition belongs not to the present age, but to a future age. Jeremiah declares:—

"**In those days** they shall say no more, The fathers have eaten a sour grape, and the children's teeth are set on edge. But every one [who dies] shall die for his own iniquity: every man that eateth the sour grape his teeth shall be set on edge."

The words "In those days" clearly refer to the future times of restitution, under the reign of Christ, and not to the present time of the reign of sin and death. Notice that the Prophet proceeds to describe other features of the Millennial age, telling about the New Covenant which is to be confirmed to Israel and Judah, the everlasting covenant, under which they shall obtain their long-looked-for portion of the Abrahamic blessings and promises.—Compare Rom. 11:26-31

This same thought, that death will again be the penalty for sin, to all redeemed from the Adamic death, if after they come to a knowledge of the grace of God, they receive that grace in vain, is shown by our Lord's own words, "Fear not them which kill the body but are not able to kill the soul [fear not them which take away the present life, which is already under sentence of death, anyway; but remember that you have been redeemed, and that a future life is a possibility to you, and that no man can rob you of that which God has provided for you through the redemption in Christ Jesus], but fear him that can destroy both soul and body in Gehenna." (Matt. 10:28) Here the power of God to destroy the soul is positively asserted, and that by an unquestionable authority. We are aware that a crooked theology has sought to wrest the Scriptures, and therefore asserts that this signifies that God is able to **destroy** the happiness of the soul in Gehenna, but that he is unable to destroy the soul itself. We reply, that this is a wresting of the Scriptures, and their perversion in a manner which cannot fail to bring evil consequences upon those who "handle the word of God deceitfully." We elsewhere show* that the word "Gehenna" here used signifies "the Second Death"—utter destruction—to all souls which will not hear God's great Prophet when, in due time, he shall speak plainly unto all people, as he now is speaking under parables and dark sayings, expounded only to the Church.—Acts 3:23; Matt. 13:11

We claim, therefore, that the Scriptures unquestionably declare that **man** is a soul or being; that his right to existence under divine arrangement was forfeited by sin, and that he is now under the curse or penalty of the divine sentence, **death;** that man's privileges and rights were all purchased by the man Christ Jesus, who gave himself a ransom for all; that as a consequence death is not to be accounted as death, utter destruction, but merely as a temporary "sleep," from which the world of mankind will be awakened by their Redeemer in the resurrection morning of the Millennial age.

CONFUSION THROUGH MISTRANSLATIONS

It should not surprise us when we find that, holding grossly erroneous views respecting what is the soul, what is the spirit, what is the real man, the translators of our Common Version English Bible have been sorely perplexed: and in their endeavor to force the translation into harmony with their preconceived ideas on this subject, they have confused the ordinary English reader tenfold. They have so covered and twisted the meaning of words as to make it extremely difficult for the English reader to see through the now double difficulty, (1) the false teaching on the subject, and (2) the mistranslations which support that false teaching.

---

*"The Truth About Hell." Price 10 cents.

However, in divine providence, we are now living in a day provided with helps of every kind, so that man or woman of even ordinary education, with the helps before him, can get a better view of the entire subject than the translators themselves had. There are now three works which give the English reader a tolerably clear insight into the Common Version English Bible, and show exactly how it has translated the Hebrew and Greek originals. (1) The Englishman's Hebrew and Greek Concordance of the Holy Scriptures [unsectarian]. (2) Professor Young's Analytical Concordance to the Bible [Presbyterian]. (3) Dr. Strong's Exhaustive Concordance [Methodist]. All three of these give each word of the Scriptures, and show the original from which it is derived. Although we have mentioned the denominations represented in these different Concordances, it is but fair to say that, so far as we have yet observed, denominational prejudices have not been permitted to interfere with the accuracy of any of them. Although gotten up on somewhat different lines, their testimony is harmonious and accurate, the differences between them being those of convenience and utility.

Examining these standard works what do we find? This: that the Hebrew word **neh-phesh**, which is generally rendered "soul" (436 times) throughout the Old Testament, and which has the signification of "sentient being," is translated in thirty-six different ways, as follows: "any," 4 times; "appetite," 2; "beast," 1; "body," 4; "breath," 1; "creature," 9 [see Gen. 1:21, 24; 2:19; 9:10, 12, 15, 16; Lev. 11:46, twice]; "dead," 5; "deadly," 1; "desire," 3; "discontented," 1; "fish," 1; (Isa. 19:10; "ghost," 2; "greedy," 1; "hath," 1; "he," 1 (Psa. 105:18); "heart," 15; "hearty," 1; "herself," 1; "her," 1; "himself," 4; "life," 100; "lust," 2; "man," 2; "me," 3 (Num. 23:10; Judges 16:30; 1 Kings 20:32); "mind," 15; "mortally," 1; "myself," 1 (Psa. 131:2); "one," 1 (Lev. 4:27); "own," 1 (Prov. 14:10); "person," 24 (Gen. 14:21; 36:6; Num. 31:19; 35:11, 15, 30; Deut. 10:22; 27:25; Josh. 20:3, 9);

"pleasure," 3; "self," 21; "slay," 1; "thing," 2 (Lev. 11:10; Ezek. 47:9); "will," 3; "your," 3.

The Greek word, **psuche** [sentient being], of the New Testament corresponding to **neh-phesh**, is translated "soul," fifty-six times; is also translated "mind" three times (Acts 14:2; Phil. 1:27; Heb. 12:3); "heart," once (Eph. 6:6); "life," forty-one times.

Amongst these variations in translation none has served to obscure the truth more than the last. It has tended to give the impression that the **life** is one thing, and **soul** or being another thing; and has fostered the idea that a man might lose his life, without losing his soul, his being. The following are the instances in which the word **psuche** is translated **life**, but would better have prevented confusion if translated **being** or **soul**:—

"Which sought the young child's **life** [**psuche**—soul, being]."—Matt. 2:20

"Take no thought for your **life** [**psuche**—soul, being], what ye shall eat."—Matt. 6:25

"Is not the **life** [**psuche**—soul, being] more than meat?"—Matt. 6:25

"He that findeth his **life** [**psuche**—soul, being] shall lose it, and he that loseth his **life** [**psuche**—soul, being] for my sake shall find it."—Matt. 10:39

"Whosoever will save his **life** [**psuche**—soul, being] shall lose it, and whosoever will lose his **life** [**psuche**—soul, being], for my sake shall find it."—Matt. 16:25

"The Son of man came . . . to give his **life** [**psuche**—soul, being] a ransom for many."—Matt. 20:28

"Is it lawful to save **life** [**psuche**—soul, being] or to kill?"—Mark 3:4

"Whosoever will save his **life** [**psuche**—soul, being] shall lose it, but whosoever shall lose his **life** [**psuche**—soul, being] for my sake and the Gospel's, the same shall save it. For what shall it profit a man if he gain the whole world and lose his own **soul** [**psuche**—life, being], or what shall a man give in exchange for his **soul** [**psuche**—life, being]?" [How few English readers are aware that "life" and "soul," each used twice in this Scripture, are from the same

Greek word **psuche**.]—Mark 8:35-37

"The Son of Man came to give his **life** [**psuche**—soul, being] a ransom for many."—Mark 10:45

"Is it lawful to save **life** [**psuche**—soul, being] or to destroy it?"—Luke 6:9

"Whosoever will save his **life** [**psuche**—soul, being] shall lose it, but whosoever will lose his life [**psuche**—soul, being] for my sake the same shall save it. For what is a man advantaged if he gain the whole world and lose himself, or be cast away?"—Luke 9:24

"The Son of Man is not come to destroy men's **lives** [**psuche**—souls, beings] but to save them."—Luke 9:56

"Take no thought for your **life** [**psuche**—soul, being] what ye shall eat, neither for the body, what ye shall put on. The life is more than meat, and the body is more than raiment."—Luke 12:22, 23

"If any man come to me, and hate not [love not less] his father and mother and wife and children and brethren and sisters, yea, and his own **life** [**psuche**—soul, being] also, he cannot be my disciple."—Luke 14:26

"Whosoever shall seek to save his **life** [**psuche**—soul, being] shall lose it, and whosoever shall lose his **life** [**psuche**—soul, being] shall preserve it."—Luke 17:33

The thought in this last text, and in several preceding it, is that the Lord's people are to remember that their present existence or being is under sentence of death anyway; but that divine grace has provided redemption—not a continuance of being, but a resuscitation, a resurrection, a living again. The call of this Gospel age is to lay down our lives in the Lord's service, as living sacrifices, following the example of our Redeemer—the promise being that all believers in Christ who so do, faithfully, shall be granted a share with him in the divine nature, through the operation of the first resurrection. Thus they will get back again their soul, being, existence—with **"life** [**zoee**] more abundantly."—John 10:10

"The good Shepherd giveth his **life** [**psuche**—soul,

Man the Subject

being] for the sheep [our Lord "poured out his **soul** unto death; he made his **soul** an offering for sin."—Isa. 53:10, 12].—John 10:11

"I lay down my **life** [**psuche**—soul, being] for the sheep."—John 10:15

"I lay down my **life** [**psuche**—soul, being] that I might receive it again [according to the divine promise and power, through the resurrection]."—John 10:17

"He that loveth his **life** [**psuche**—soul, being] shall lose it; and he that hateth his **life** [**psuche**—soul, being] in this world shall preserve it unto life eternal."—John 12:25

The thought here is, that faithfulness to God under present evil conditions necessarily means dissatisfaction with present conditions, and a willingness to sacrifice them all in the service of God and righteousness and our fellow creatures—and thus, according to the divine provision, to be accounted worthy of **existence** [soul, being] under the more favorable conditions of the dispensation to come. He who loves the present conditions of things, and who values the enjoyments and pleasures of the present time higher than he values righteousness and obedience to God, will thus be proving himself unworthy of the future existence God has proffered us, unworthy to have his soul, his being, restored in the first resurrection.

"Wilt thou lay down thy **life** [**psuche**—soul, being] for my sake?"—John 13:38

"Greater love hath no man than this, that a man lay down his **life** [**psuche**—soul, being] for his friends."—John 15:13

"Men that have hazarded their **lives** [**psuche**—souls, beings]."—Acts 15:26

"Trouble not yourselves, for his **life** [**psuche**—soul, being] is in him [he has not expired, or breathed out existence]."—Acts 20:10

"Neither count I my **life** [**psuche**—soul, being, existence] dear unto myself, so that I might finish my course with joy."—Acts 20:24

The apostle had learned to rightly view the present existence as of small value in comparison to the future one promised in the resurrection. He did not count it "dear," precious, in the sense of valuing it more than the Lord and the Lord's favor, and the opportunities for serving the Lord's cause. He was willing to spend and be spent in the Master's service, in hope of attaining to the first resurrection, as he explicitly tells us in Phil. 3:8-11.

"Sirs, I perceive that this voyage will be with hurt and much damage, not only of the lading and ship, but also of our **lives** [**psuche**—souls, beings]." – Acts 27:10

"There shall be no loss of any man's **life** [**psuche**—soul, being]."—Acts 27:22

"I am left alone, and they seek my **life** [**psuche**—soul, being]."—Rom. 11:3

"Who have for my **life** [**psuche**—soul, being] laid down their own necks."—Rom. 16:4

"Because for the work of Christ he was nigh unto death, not regarding his **life** [**psuche**—soul, being], supplying your lack of service toward me."—Phil. 2:30

"Because he laid down his **life** [**psuche**—soul, being—"he poured out his soul unto death; he made his soul an offering for sin"] for us; and we ought to lay down our **lives** [**psuche**—souls, beings] for the brethren."—1 John 3:16

"The third part of the creatures which were in the sea, and had **life** [**psuche**—soul, being], died."—Rev. 8:9

"They loved not their **lives** [**psuche**—souls, beings] unto death."—Rev. 12:11

Once we get our minds clear upon this subject of the soul and obtain a clear understanding of just how the words **neh-phesh** and **psuche** are used throughout the Scriptures, by the inspired writers, it removes all the mystery that has heretofore been shrouded under the obscure words, **soul** and **ghost,** which, not only to the ignorant, but also to many of the educated, have meant something indefinite, indescribable and incomprehensible.

But let none get the thought that the body is the

soul: this is an error, as our Lord's words clearly show—"God is able to destroy **both** soul and body." But on the other hand there can be no soul, no sentient being without a body—heavenly or earthly, spiritual or animal.

Going to the Genesis record of man's creation we see that the body was formed first, but it was not a man, soul or being, until animated. It had eyes, but saw nothing; ears, but heard nothing; a mouth, but **spoke nothing; a tongue, but no taste; nostrils, but no sense of smell; a heart, but it pulsated not;** blood, but it was cold, lifeless; lungs, but they moved not. It was not a man, but a corpse, an inanimate body.

The second step in the process of man's creation was to give vitality to the properly "formed" and in every way prepared body; and this is described by the words "blew into his nostrils the breath of life." When a healthy person has been drowned and animation is wholly suspended, resuscitation has, it is said, been effected by working the arms and thus the lungs as a bellows, and so gradually establishing the breath in the nostrils. In Adam's case it of course required no labored effort on the part of the Creator to cause the perfect organism which he had made to breathe the life-giving oxygen of the atmosphere.

As the vitalizing breath entered, the lungs expanded, the blood corpuscles were oxygenized and passed to the heart, which in turn propelled them to every part of the body, awakening all the prepared but hitherto dormant nerves to sensation and energy. In an instant the energy reached the brain, and thought, perception, reasoning, looking, touching, smelling, feeling and tasting commenced. That which was a lifeless human **organism** had become a **man**, a sentient being: the **"living soul"** condition mentioned in the text had been reached. In other words, the term "living soul" means neither more nor less than the term "sentient being"; i. e., a being capable of sensation, perception, thought.

Moreover, even though Adam was perfect in his organism, it was necessary for him to **sustain** life, **soul** or sentient being, by partaking of the fruits of the trees of life. And when he sinned, God drove him from the garden, "**lest** he put forth his hand, and take also of the tree [plural **trees** or **grove**] of life, and eat, and **live forever** [i. e., by eating continuously]." (Gen. 3:22) How the fogs and mysteries scatter before the light of truth which shines from God's Word!

Although, because of his fall into sin and death, man's condition is far from what it was in its original perfection when pronounced "very good" by the highest Judge, so that some, by the cultivation of the lower organs of thought and a failure to use the higher intellectual faculties, have dwarfed the organs of the brain representing these higher faculties, yet the **organs** are still there, and are capable of development, which is not the case with the most nearly perfect specimen of the brute creation. So then it is in that the Creator has endowed man with a higher and finer **organism**, that he has made him to differ from the brute. They have similar flesh and bones, breathe the same air, drink the same water, and eat similar food, and all are souls or creatures possessing intelligence; but man, in his **better body**, possesses capacity for higher intelligence and is treated by the Creator as on an entirely different plane. It is in proportion as sin degrades man from his original likeness of his Creator that he is said to be "brutish"—more nearly resembling the brutes, destitute of the higher and finer sensibilities.

Those whose eyes of understanding begin to open to this subject, so that they see that the word "soul" signifies intelligence, being, and the word "breath" or "spirit of life" signifies the divine power to live, can readily see, from the foregoing, that every creature which possesses life-consciousness has, first of all, a body or organism; secondly, the spirit of life animating it, and thirdly, existence, being, soul, as a result. An illustration which helps some to grasp the proposition is the similarity between heat and soul. If a lump of coal is placed under favorable conditions, giving access to the oxygen of the air, and then ignited, a new thing will be produced—**heat**. The coal is not heat, though it possesses some of the qualities which, under favorable conditions, would produce heat; neither is the oxygen heat, yet it also, under favorable conditions, may be an element in producing heat. So, to carry the analogy, the body is not the soul, though the body possesses the qualifications necessary to soul; neither is the breath or spirit of life the soul—it is the power which came from God, and which is necessary to the production of the sentient creature. The body, when properly united with the breath or spirit of life, produces a new thing—a being, a soul, a sentient creature.

And the process of dissolution, death, is in harmony with these facts. If the breath or spirit of life be withdrawn, death results. Now the question is, what dies? Does the breath or spirit of life die? Surely not; it never had sentient being, it is a principle or power, like electricity; it has no thought, no feeling; it could not die. Does the body die? We answer, No. The body may lose the life with which the Father animates it, but the body of itself, apart from the breath or spirit of life, had no consciousness, no feeling, no sense, and could not, therefore, be said to die; it was **inanimate** before the breath or spirit of life came into it; it was **animate** while the breath or spirit of life was in it; it becomes **inanimate** again, or dead, when the spirit of life is withdrawn.

What, then, dies? We answer that it is the soul that dies—the sentient being ceases. Let us remember that the sentient being was produced by the union of the breath or spirit of life with an organism, and that the separation or dissolution of these two causes the cessation of the being, the soul— death. That this is true of the lower animals, none would for a moment question; but is it not equally true of man, the highest animal, created in the intellectual image and moral likeness of God? It is no less true, and should be equally evident to every reasoning mind. We are aware that some few Scriptures might be twisted and misunderstood to contradict this proposition, but in due course they will have consideration and will be found in most absolute accord with these presentations.

Take another illustration of the relationship between the human or animal body, spirit and soul: an unlighted candle would correspond to an inanimate human body or corpse; the lighting of the candle would correspond to the spark of life originally imparted by the Creator; the flame or light corresponds to sentient being, or intelligence, or soul quality; the oxygenized atmosphere which unites with the carbon of the candle in supporting the flame corresponds to the **breath** of life or spirit of life which unites with the physical organism in producing soul or intelligent existence. If an accident should occur which would destroy the candle, the flame, of course, would cease; so if a human or animal body be destroyed, as by disease or accident, the **soul**, the **being**, intelligence, personality, **ceases**. Or if the supply of air were cut off from the candle flame, as by an extinguisher or snuffer, or by **submerging the candle in water, the light would be extinguished even though the candle remained** unimpaired. So the **soul**, life, existence, of man or animal would cease if the breath of life were cut off by drowning or asphyxiation, while the body might be comparatively sound.

As the lighted candle might be used under favorable conditions to light other candles, but the flame once extinguished the candle could neither relight itself nor other candles, so the human or animal body while alive, as a living soul or being can, under divine arrangement, start or **propagate** other souls or beings—offspring: but so soon as the spark of life is gone, soul or being has ceased, and all power to think, feel and propagate has ceased. In harmony with this we read in the Scriptures of Jacob's children: "All the **souls** that came out of the loins of Jacob were seventy **souls**." (Exod. 1:5) Jacob received his spark of life as well as his physical organism, and hence the united product of these, his soul or **intelligent being**, from Isaac, and hence from Adam, to whom alone God ever directly imparted life. And Jacob passed on the life and organism and soul to his posterity, and so with all humanity.

A candle might be relighted by any one having the ability; but by divine arrangement the human body bereft of the spark of life, "wasteth away," returns to the dust from which it was taken, and the spark of life cannot be re-enkindled except by divine power, a miracle. The promise of **resurrection** is therefore a promise of a relighting, a re-enkindling of animal existence or soul; and since there can be no being or soul without a body and restored life-power or spirit, it follows that a promised resurrection or restoration of soul or being **implies** new bodies, new organisms. Thus the Scriptures assure us that human bodies, which return to dust will not be **restored**, but that in the resurrection God will give such new bodies as it may please him to give.—1 Cor. 15:37-40

The apostle here declares that in the resurrection there will be a special class accounted worthy of a new nature, spiritual instead of human or fleshly: and, as we should expect, he shows that this great change of nature will be effected by giving these a **different kind of body**. The candle may here again serve to illustrate: suppose the fleshly or human nature to be illustrated by a tallow candle, the new body might be illustrated by a wax candle of a brighter flame, or indeed by an electric arc-light apparatus.

With any power and wisdom less than that of our Creator guaranteeing the resurrection, we might justly fear some break or slip by which the **identity** would be lost, especially with those granted the great change of **nature** by a share in the first (chief) resurrection to **spirit being**. But we can securely trust this and all things to him with whom we have to do in this matter. He who knows our very thoughts can reproduce them in the new brains so that not one valuable lesson or precious experience shall be lost. He is too wise to err and too good to be unkind; and all that he has promised he will fulfil in a manner exceedingly abundantly better than we can ask or think.

Many suppose that the bodies buried are to be restored atom for atom, but, on the contrary, the apostle declares, "Thou soweth [in death] not that body which shall be." It is the **soul**, the sentient being, that God proposes to **restore** by resurrection power; and in the resurrection he will give to each person (to each soul or sentient being) such a body as his infinite wisdom has been pleased to provide; **to the** Church, the "bride" selected in this age, **spirit** bodies; to the restitution class, human bodies, but not the ones lost in death.—1 Cor. 15:37, 38

As in Adam's creation, the bringing together of an **organism** and the **breath of life** produced a **sentient being or soul,** so the dissolution of these, from any cause, puts an end to sentient being—stopping thoughts and feelings of every kind. The soul (i. e., sentient being) ceases; the body returns to dust as it was; while the spirit or breath of life returns to God, who imparted it to Adam, and to his race through him. (Eccl. 12:7) It returns to God in the sense that it is no longer amenable to human control, as in pro-creation, and can never be recovered except by divine power. Recognizing this fact, the Lord's instructed ones commit their hope of future life by resurrection to God and to Christ, his now exalted representative. (Luke 23:46; Acts 7:59) So, then, had God made no provision for man's future life by a ransom and a promised resurrection, death would have been the end of all hope for humanity.—1 Cor. 15:14-18

But God has thus made provision for our living again; and ever since he made known his gracious plan, those who speak and write intelligently upon the subject (for instance, the inspired Scripture writers), as if by common consent, speak of the unconscious interim between death and the resurrection morning, in which sensibility (sentient being) is suspended, as a **"sleep."** Indeed, the illustration is an excellent one; for the moment of awakening will seem to them like the moment after the moment of their dissolution. For instance, we read that speaking of Lazarus' death our Lord said, **"Our** friend Lazarus **sleepeth,** I go that I may **awake him out of sleep."** Afterward, because the disciples were slow to comprehend, he said, "Lazarus is dead." (John 11:11) Were the theory of consciousness in death correct, is it not remarkable that Lazarus gave no account of his experience during those four days? None will claim that he was in a "hell" of torment, for our Lord called him his "friend"; and if he had been in heavenly bliss our Lord would not have called him from it, for that would have been an unfriendly act. But as our Lord expressed it, Lazarus slept, and he awakened him to life, to consciousness, to his **sentient being**, or **soul** returned or revived; and all this was evidently a favor greatly appreciated by Lazarus and his friends.

The thought pervades the Scriptures that we are now in the night of dying and sleeping as compared with the morning of awakening and resurrection. "Weeping may endure for a **night,** but joy cometh in the **morning**" (Psa. 30:5)—the resurrection morning, when the sleepers shall come forth from the tomb, as expressed by the Prophet: "Awake and sing, ye that dwell in the dust [of the earth]."—Isa. 26:19

The apostles also frequently used this appropriate, hopeful and peaceful figure of speech. For instance: Luke says of Stephen, the first martyr, **"he fell asleep"**; and in recording Paul's speech at Antioch he used the same expression, "David **fell on sleep.**" (Acts 7:60; 13:36) Peter uses the same expression, saying, "The fathers **fell asleep.**" (2 Pet. 3:4) And Paul used it many times as the following quotations show:

"If her husband be dead [Greek, **fall asleep**]."—1 Cor. 7:39

"The greater part remain unto this present, but some are **fallen asleep.**"—1 Cor. 15:6

"If there be no resurrection, . . . then they also which are **fallen asleep** in Christ are perished."—1 Cor. 15:13-18

"Christ is risen from the dead and become the firstfruits of them that **slept.**"—1 Cor. 15:20

"Behold, I show you a mystery, we shall not all sleep."—1 Cor. 15:51

"I would not have you to be ignorant, brethren, concerning them that **are asleep**."—1 Thess. 4:13

"Them that **sleep** in Jesus, will God bring [from the dead] with [by] him."—1 Thess. 4:14

When the Kingdom, the resurrection time, comes, "we who are alive and remain unto the **presence** of the Lord shall not **precede** them that are **asleep**."— —1 Thess. 4:15

The same thought is presented by the Prophet Daniel: describing the resurrection he says—"Many that **sleep** in the dust shall awake"—and the description shows that these sleepers include both the good and bad. (Dan. 12:2) They "fell asleep" in peace, to await the Lord's day—the day of Christ, the Millennial Day—fully persuaded that he (Christ) is able to keep that which they committed unto him against that day. (2 Tim. 1:12) This same thought runs through the Old Testament as well—from the time that God first preached to Abraham the Gospel of a resurrection: the expression, "He slept with his fathers," is very common in the Old Testament. But Job puts the matter in very forcible language, saying, "Oh that thou wouldest hide me in the grave, that thou wouldest keep me secret until thy wrath be [over] past!" The present dying time is the time of God's wrath—the curse of death being upon all, because of the original transgression. However, we are promised that in due time the curse will be lifted and a blessing will come through the Redeemer to all the families of the earth; and so Job continues, "All the days of my appointed time will I wait, until my change come; [then] thou shalt call (John 5:25) and I will answer thee; thou shalt have a desire to the work of thine hands." (Job 14:14, 15) And we of the New Testament times read our Lord's response, "All that are in the graves shall hear the voice of the Son of God [calling them to awake and come to a full knowledge of God and to a full opportunity of everlasting life]."—John 5:25, 28, 29

This death-"sleep" is so absolutely a period of unconsciousness that the awakened ones will have no knowledge of the lapse of time. Indeed, "sleep" is merely an accommodated term, for really the dead are dead, utterly destroyed, except as God's wisdom preserves their identity, and has decreed through Christ their awakening—their reorganization and resuscitation. And this, indeed, will be a **re-creation** —a still greater manifestation of divine power than was the original creation of Adam and Eve. It will be the re-creation of fifty billions instead of two persons. It will be the reproduction of infinite varieties instead of one. Only our God possesses such omnipotent wisdom and power; he is both able and willing to perform. It is to be one of the benefits resulting from the permission of evil that its eradication will manifest all the features of divine character as they could not otherwise be manifested and known. Before both angels and men divine **justice** will shine, so will divine **love**, so will divine **power**, and finally the divine **wisdom** in preparing and permitting such an exhibition of God's character will be seen and owned by all his creatures also.

The Scriptural testimony regarding the necessity for a resurrection of the dead is most clear and explicit—and how could there be a resurrection of the **dead** if none are **dead**, but, as some maintain, "all who seem to die are more alive than they ever were"; thus contradicting the five senses of every intelligent being as well as the positive declaration of Scripture that "To all the living there is hope: for a living dog is better than a dead lion. For the living [even the least intelligent] know that they shall die, but the dead **know not anything,** neither have they any more a reward; for the memory of them is [very generally] forgotten. Also their love, and their hatred and their envy, is now perished; neither have they any more a portion [interest] forever [Hebrew, **olam**—for a long indefinite period] in anything that is done under the sun . . . Whatsoever thy hand findeth to do, do it with thy might; for there is no work. nor device, nor knowledge, nor wisdom, in the grave* whither

---

*Sheol—the state or condition of death as respects the soul, in contrast with grave, a tomb for a dead body which

thou [the **soul,** the sentient being] goest."—Eccles. 9:4-10; Isa. 26:14

"Thou destroyest the hope of man [in himself]. Thou prevailest forever against him, and he passeth: thou changest his countenance and sendest him away. His sons come to honor and he knoweth it not; and they are brought low, but he perceiveth it not of them."—Job 14:19-21; Isa. 63:16

Note the significance of the apostle's words in his celebrated treatise on the resurrection in 1 Cor. 15: 12-54. He says:—

"If Christ be preached that he rose from the dead, how say some among you that there is no resurrection of the dead?"

If the dead are not dead, but more alive than ever, then none are dead, and surely there could be no resurrection of the dead. The apostle held no such theory, but the very contrary, that the dead are **perished** like brute beasts unless God will resurrect them; and that our hopes for them are vain hopes except they be resurrection hopes. Mark well every word of this forceful argument by one of earth's greatest logicians. He says:—

"If there be no resurrection of the dead, then is Christ not risen [but is still dead]: And if Christ be not risen [but still dead], then is our preaching vain, and your faith is also vain [because a dead Christ could know nothing and could help nobody]. Yea, and we are found false witnesses of God [we are wicked deceivers instead of divinely appointed ambassadors]; because we have testified of God that he raised up Christ: whom he raised not up—if so be [if it be true] that the dead rise not. For if the dead rise not then is Christ not raised."

---

in the Hebrew is **qebar.** See Psa. 30:3; 49:15; 89:48; where **sheol** is rendered grave. See 2 Chron. 34:28; Job 10:19 Psa. 88:5; where **qebar** is grave. Our Lord's **soul** went to **sheol** the condition of death (Psa. 16:10; Acts 2:27), but "**he** made his grave **[qebar,** tomb] with the wicked and rich."—Isa. 53:9

Man the Subject

It should be observed that the apostle is not pressing his argument as respecting a resurrection of the **body**, but as respects a resurrection of being, or **soul**; —"that his **soul** was not left in **sheol, hades**." (Acts 2:31, 32) Had Paul the popular theory of our day respecting resurrection, he would have said something like this: Some of you speak of a resurrection of the **body** as though it were a matter of importance; but really the body is a "clog," a hindrance, a "prison house" for the soul, which is far better off when "set free." The resurrection of the body, whenever it comes, will be a calamity and imply the "refettering" of the soul and a limitation of its powers.

The apostle said nothing of the kind because it would have been the reverse of the truth. He taught a resurrection of the soul or sentient being from unconsciousness, from death; but denied the resurrection of the body which died, saying "Thou sowest **not** that body which shall be: . . . [in the resurrection of the soul or being] God giveth it a [new] **body**, as it hath pleased him, and to every [kind of] **seed** his own [appropriate kind of] body." (1 Cor. **15:37, 38**) The masses of mankind of human seed or **kind** will receive human bodies; but not the same **bodies** which mouldered to dust and whose fragments **or** atoms have passed into vegetable and animal organisms infinitesimal. The Church will receive spirit bodies like to that of their risen Lord and wholly unlike their earthly bodies—so much so that the apostle declares, "It doth not yet appear what **we** shall be, but we know that when he shall appear **we** shall be like him; for we shall see him as he is"—not **as** he was.—1 John 3:2

But let us follow the apostle's argument further, He declares:—

"If Christ be not raised, your faith is vain: ye are yet in your sins. Then they also that are fallen asleep in Christ are **perished**."—Verses 17, 18

Those who claim that the soul cannot die and therefore does not die and who therefore deny the resurrection of the soul or sentient being, and who in consequence are forced by their argument to claim that Scriptural references to resurrection refer merely to the body, are in a quandary what to do with these words of the inspired apostle. If they claim that our Lord was alive, "more alive than ever," during the three days the Scriptures declare he was dead, and think of his resurrection body as the one that lay in Joseph's tomb wounded and scarred, how could they claim that faith in a Christ who did not die (but who merely shed off his body for three days) is a "**vain**" faith? How can they acknowledge that such a faith does not release from condemnation? How could they claim that the "more-alive-than-ever" Christ "freed" from his body of flesh could not save sinners and hence that all that have fallen asleep in Christ have "**perished**"?

Their entire **theory** is in conflict with the Scriptural presentation of the **facts**. They deny that any soul could **perish** [Greek **apolloomee**—be destroyed] while the apostle says it could; and so says our Lord —"God is able to destroy both soul and body." They deny also that any "are fallen **asleep** in Christ" denying that death is a sleep, awaiting a resurrection morn awakening, while the apostles, our Lord and all the holy prophets unitedly declare it to be a "sleep" from which God's power alone can awaken to consciousness, soul, sentient being, on any plane of existence. For be it noted that those who experience the "change" of the first resurrection to the divine nature will be **souls** as truly as they were in their earthly nature. God is declared to be a **soul**, the same word **psuche** being used—"If any man draw back, my **soul** [**psuche**—sentient being] shall have no pleasure in him."—Heb. 10:38

The Platonic philosophy (that man does not and cannot die, but merely appears to do so) prevailed throughout Greece at the time of the first advent, **and constituted the great obstacle to the progress of** the gospel among the Gentiles. For instance, we read that when Paul preached at Athens he was listened to as a great teacher by the philosophers until he touched on the resurrection of the dead—that was enough; they had no further interest; they considered themselves far in advance of the Jewish idea that the dead can have no future existence except by a resurrection. "And when they heard of the resurrection of the **dead** [and thus discerned that Paul disagreed with their theory that the dead are more alive than ever] some mocked" and others said, That's enough at present.—Acts 17:32

The heathen idea, that death is not death, but a step into broader conditions of life, had not to any extent permeated Jewish thought up to the time of the first advent. The Pharisees were the principal sect of the Jews, and our Lord declares them the successors and representatives of the Mosaic law, saying, "The scribes [writers] and Pharisees sit in Moses' seat." (Matt. 23:2) The Sadducees, much less numerous than the Pharisees, were next as a sect in point of influence: they were really unbelievers, infidels. They denied entirely a future life, holding that man dies exactly as does the brute, and that there will be no resurrection of the dead. They were disbelievers in all the Messianic promises, deniers also of the superhuman intelligences, such as angels, etc. True, Josephus does call attention to a sect called the Essenes, which he declares held the Platonic theory prevalent amongst the Gentiles, to the effect that man never really dies, but merely takes a progressive step in life development, at the crisis termed death. But we are to remember that Josephus wrote his history of the Jews while at the Roman court, and that he wrote it with a view of influencing the minds of the emperor and his court in favor of the Jews. The Romans had come to regard the Jews, as the Scriptures declare them to have been, "a stiff-necked and rebellious people," and naturally had concluded that the cause of this rebellious disposition lay somehow or other in their religion. This was a true supposition; it is undoubtedly a fact that the truths of divine revelation tend to produce a spirit of liberty wherever they are applied—breaking down the wide distinctions as between priests and people, kings and subjects, teaching that all are amenable to one great Judge and King. But Josephus wished to counteract this correct estimate of the Jewish people, and the Jewish religion; and hence he stretched the truth in his endeavor to make out a case, and to show the Roman court that the Jews' religion was practically the same as the various heathen religions, (1) in respect to consciousness of the dead, and (2) a belief in eternal torment.* To make out his case, he cites the sect of the Essenes, as though they were the chief religious sect amongst the Jews. On the contrary, they were so insignificant that they are not so much as mentioned in the New Testament, and evidently never came in conflict with either the Lord or the apostles, whereas the Pharisees and the Sadducees are continually and frequently referred to.

"ALL LIVE UNTO HIM"—Luke 20:37, 38

It was after our Lord had answered the doctors of the law and the scribes and Pharisees, and had discomfited them, that the Sadducees put in an appearance, thinking that they could show the superiority of their infidel position, by refuting our Lord's doctrines. To these Sadducees, who claimed that the dead were forever dead, our Lord said, "And now that the dead are [to be] raised, even Moses showed at the bush, when he calleth the Lord the God of Abraham, and the God of Isaac, and the God of Jacob. For he is not a God of the dead, but of the living: for all live unto him."—Luke 20:37, 38

Our Lord suggests that this of itself is a proof "that the dead are [to be] raised," because God would surely not refer thus to beings totally and forever blotted out of existence. He then shows that

---

*Eternal torment never was the Jewish belief except of the very few; but the Roman Emperors favored this theory, for it increased the imperial influence over the common people. Later the Emperors adopted the title, "Pontifex Maximus,"—chief religious ruler—later still adopted by Papacy for the popes.

God's plan for a resurrection is fixed, and that those whom men call "dead" "all live unto Him"—from God's standpoint they only "sleep." God's Word, therefore, speaks of these as "asleep" and not as destroyed. Though the original sentence was to destruction it is now offset by the ransom. So Moses says: "Thou turnest man to destruction, and sayest [in resurrection], Return, ye children of men." (Psa. 90:3; 103:4) In saying, "I am the God of Abraham," God speaks not only of things past as still present, but also of things to come as if already come to pass. —Rom. 4:17

THE BODY, SPIRIT AND SOUL OF THE CHURCH
—1 Thess. 5:23—

The terms body, soul and spirit are figuratively used of the Church collectively. For instance, the apostle says: "I pray God [that] your whole spirit, soul and body be preserved blameless, unto the coming of our Lord Jesus Christ." This prayer must be understood to apply to the Church as a whole—the elect Church whose names are written in heaven. The true **spirit** has been preserved in the little flock. Its body is discernible today, also, notwithstanding the multitude of tares that would hide as well as choke it. And its **soul**, its activity, its intelligence, its sentient being, is in evidence everywhere, lifting up the standard for the people—the cross, the ransom.

In no other way could we apply the apostle's words; for, however much people may differ respecting the preservation of the individual spirits and souls of the people addressed, all will agree that their **bodies have not been preserved**, but have returned to dust, like those of others. Besides, the words body, soul and spirit are in the singular, not in the plural.

WHAT IS SIGNIFIED BY "SHEOL" OR "HADES" TO WHICH ALL SOULS GO?

It is held that since souls are said to go to **sheol, hades**, therefore the soul of man must be something tangible and conscious after dissolution—after the separation of the spirit of life from the organism or body. It is therefore proper that we examine the Word of the Lord on this line, and see—What is **sheol, hades?**

The Hebrew word **sheol** occurs sixty-five times in the Old Testament Scriptures. It is three times translated **pit**, thirty-one times translated **grave**, and thirty-one times translated **hell**. These are all faulty translations, if measured by the present general use of the words, hell, grave and pit.

The meaning of the Hebrew word **sheol** (**hades** is its Greek equivalent) can scarcely be expressed by any one English word: it signifies **hidden or extinguished**, or **obscure**—the condition or state of death: it is not a place but a condition, and perhaps the word **oblivion** would more nearly than any other in our language correspond with the word **sheol** of the Hebrew and **hades** of the Greek. Nothing in the word **sheol** signifies joy or misery, or any feeling; the connections must guide us in this. Let us therefore examine uses of the words **sheol** and **hades** and ascertain from the connection all we can respecting "hell." We will find it clearly stated in the Scriptures that **sheol, hades, oblivion**, receives all mankind, good and bad alike; that it has no light, no knowledge, no wisdom, no device; that no tongue there praises the Lord, neither blasphemes his name; that it is a condition of absolute silence, and in every way an undesirable condition, except that it has attached to it a hope of resurrection.

It will be noticed also that it is "souls," both good and bad, that go to this condition—**sheol, oblivion**—to await the summons of the Life-giver in the morning of the Millennial age. It cannot be denied that the translators of our Common Version English Bible have been at times inconsistent, but we urge that this be not charged wholly to dishonesty, even though in many instances it may appear to be little short of this: rather let us believe that it was the result of a confusion of mind on this subject, superinduced by long centuries of false teaching, handed down from the "dark ages." Another thing that can be said in extenuation of the work of the translators is, that in the "old English" the word **hell** had no such meaning as it has in modern English language. It, in no sense of the word, signified or implied a place of flames or torture or trouble or pain, but more the thought of grave—hidden condition, **oblivion**. The translators in using the word **hell** probably partially justified themselves, on the ground of its ancient significance, its primary meaning, as given in unabridged English dictionaries.

In examining the following occurrences of the word **sheol**, the reader is urged to note what would be the sense of the passage, if the word **sheol** were translated in each case "hell fire," or "place of torment," and then also to note how, in every instance, the translation would be thoroughly smooth and consistent with the context if it were translated **oblivion**. These prove conclusively that "souls" go to **sheol**, **oblivion**, and that they are not in torment there, nor have they any knowledge or wisdom or work or joy or pain or feeling of any kind, but simply wait in **oblivion** for "the voice of the archangel and the trump of God."

"I will go down **into the grave** [into **sheol**, into **oblivion**] unto my son, mourning."—Gen. 37:35

Thus did Jacob mourn for his son Joseph, whom he supposed had died a violent death.

"If mischief shall befall him [Benjamin] by the way in which ye go, then shall ye bring down my gray hairs with sorrow to **the grave** [to **sheol**, to **oblivion**]."—Gen. 42:38

These were the words of Jacob, when parting with Benjamin, and fearful lest he should be killed, as he supposed Joseph had been.

The same words identically are repeated under similar circumstances, in chapter 44:29, when the brethren of Joseph are relating to him the parting injunction of their father respecting Benjamin. And in the 31st verse the brethren again state the matter as for themselves, saying, "Thy servants shall bring down the gray hairs of thy servant our father **to the grave** [to **sheol**, to **oblivion**]."

Here are four instances in which the word **sheol** has been translated "grave," and we invite all to consider how inappropriate it would have been to have used the word **hell**, attaching to it the usual, ordinary thought of fire, torment and anguish. The translators were evidently quite positive that the word **hell**, as ordinarily understood, would give very false ideas of the expectation of Jacob for himself, and of his sons respecting him: hence they here translated the word "grave." Nevertheless, they did not believe, nor do the majority of people believe, that Jacob went into the grave, or had any thought of going into the grave. Nor was the patriarch thinking of the burial of his body in a tomb, for then doubtless he would have used the same Hebrew word for grave which he used in speaking of Rachel's grave, viz., **qeburah** (Gen. 35:20), or else he would have used the same word which his son Joseph used (**qeber**), when speaking of Jacob's grave, which Jacob himself had already caused to be prepared before he died. (Gen. 50:5) On the contrary, we see that Jacob was speaking about **himself**, as a soul or being —that the disappointment of the loss of Benjamin would bring **him** down to **oblivion**, to the state of death, in his now old age and feeble health.

"If the Lord make a new thing, and the earth open her mouth, and swallow them up . . . and they go down quick **into the pit** [into **sheol**, into **oblivion**]." —Num. 16:30

"They . . . went down alive **into the pit** [**sheol, oblivion**], and the earth closed upon them and they perished from among the congregation."—Num. 16:33

These two texts referring to Korah, Dathan and Abiram, showing how they were destroyed, could not have been consistently translated "into **hell**," for fear of proving that the claimed place of torture is under the surface of this earth. But how simple the statement when rightly understood: the earth opened her mouth and swallowed them up, and they went down from the midst of life's activities into oblivion, unconsciousness.

"A fire is kindled in mine anger, and shall burn unto the lowest hell [sheol, oblivion], and shall consume the earth with her increase, and set on fire the foundations of the mountains."—Deut. 32:22

Here certainly is a mention of fire, but not of literal fire. The entire context shows that it is the fire of God's jealousy, and the statement follows, "They shall be burnt with hunger, and devoured with burning heat and bitter destruction . . . the sword without and terror within shall destroy." We are not left to conjecture respecting how this prophecy was fulfilled; for the Apostle Paul, speaking under the inspiration of the Holy Spirit, refers to this passage, and applies it to fleshly Israel, and to the trouble which came upon them as a nation, when they rejected the Lord Jesus, and in turn were themselves rejected of the Lord. The apostle declares that wrath came upon them to the uttermost (1 Thess. 2:16): divine anger burned against them and did continue to burn against them until, as a people, they had suffered for their national sins. After divine wrath has burned out their national transgression, even searching them out to the very lowest oblivion (**sheol**) he will then speak peaceably toward them, saying to the Church, "Comfort ye, comfort ye my people; speak ye comfortably to Jerusalem, and cry unto her that her warfare is accomplished, that her iniquity is pardoned; for she hath received of the Lord's hands double for all her sins." (Isa. 40: 1, 2) Then also shall come the deliverance of Jacob predicted by the Apostle Paul, on the strength of the divine statement, "For this is my covenant unto them, when I shall take away their sins." (Rom. 11: 26, 27) The same thought that this burning of divine wrath against Israel, to the very lowest oblivion, will be followed by divine blessing, is shown in the context.—See Deut. 32:26-43

"The Lord killeth and maketh alive: he bringeth

down to **the grave** [to **sheol**, to **oblivion**], and bringeth up [by a resurrection out of **oblivion**, out of **sheol**]."—1 Sam. 2:6

"The sorrows of **hell** [**sheol, oblivion**] compassed me about."—2 Sam. 22:6

The prophet David here expressed the fact that his life was in jeopardy, but that God delivered him from the hand of Saul. The context, however, shows quite clearly that the Psalmist speaks prophetically of the Christ, and the time of the full deliverance of the body of Christ, which is the Church, from the present evil world, into the glories of the world to come, showing (verses 8-18) that the deliverance of the body of Christ would be just before a great time of trouble, and manifestation of divine power and indignation against wickedness.

"Let not his hoar head go down to **the grave** [**sheol, oblivion**] in peace . . . but his hoar head bring thou down to **the grave** [**sheol, oblivion**] with blood."—1 Kings 2:6, 9

David was the speaker, pointing out to Solomon his son that Joab was a dangerous man, a man of blood, justly deserving of some retribution before he died. The translators evidently thought that, although Joab was a bad man, it would not do here to translate the word **sheol** by the word **hell**, because the context speaks of gray hairs, while their theory asserts that the hairs and all the remainder of the physical body are buried, and that the naked soul or spirit goes to hell. Hence they preferred here to render **sheol** by the English word **grave**. But with the proper thought in mind, there is no difficulty about having Joab's gray hairs and also Jacob's gray hairs go down into **sheol**, oblivion, the state of death, together. The words "gray hairs" and "hoar head" are simply figures of speech signifying aged.

"As a cloud is consumed and vanisheth away, so he that goeth down to **the grave** [**sheol—oblivion**] shall come up no more."—Job 7:9

Job here points out the utter destruction of man's

soul, or being, in death. Nevertheless in verse 21 he concludes the argument with the declaration, "I shall sleep and thou shalt seek me in the morning, but I shall not be." Here the interim of death is referred to as a sleep, as the Millennial age is referred to as the morning, and the present age as the night of weeping and trouble, dying and crying. The Lord will seek Job in the morning, in resurrection power, and though he shall not be, though death shall have worked utter destruction, nevertheless the case is not beyond divine power, and hence, when the Lord's time shall come "he shall have a desire unto the work of his hands," when the day of the Lord's vengeance shall have passed, and the times of refreshing shall have come—then he shall call, and Job and all others will answer him.—See Chap. 14:14, 15

"It is as high as heaven; what canst thou do? Deeper than **hell** [**sheol, oblivion**]; what canst thou know?"—Job 11:8

These words are by Zophar, one of Job's mistaken comforters, whom the Lord reproved. By this statement he is attempting to show Job that the divine principles of government are inscrutable to humanity: as an illustration of man's utter lack of knowledge of God he refers to **sheol**, and compares the two; as there is no knowledge in **sheol**, equally, he claims, there can be no knowledge of the divine wisdom and plan.

"O that thou wouldst hide me in **the grave** [**sheol, oblivion**], that thou wouldst keep me in secret until thy wrath be past, that thou wouldst appoint me a set time and remember me."—Job 14:13

Here is the most simple and most explicit statement of Job's hope. He was not anxious for a perpetuation of the present conditions of sin and sorrow and trouble and pain; he was quite willing to be hidden in oblivion until the time when the curse, "wrath," shall be lifted from the earth, and the times of refreshing instead shall come. But he does not wish to be blotted out forever. Oh no! having confidence in the divine provision for a future life, through a resurrection, he prays that God in due time, after the curse of sin has been rolled away, will remember him, and call him out of oblivion into being again, by the restitution powers then to be exercised through the Christ.—See Acts 3:19-21

"If I wait, **the grave** [sheol, oblivion] is my house: I shall make my bed in the darkness. I have cried to corruption, Thou art my father; to the worm, Thou art my mother and my sister."—Job 17:13, 14

How expressive this language! Oblivion is the house or is the bed, and it is full of darkness—Job's soul, his being, sleeps, is inanimate, waiting for the morning of the resurrection, while his body turns to corruption.

"Where is now my hope? As for my hope, who shall see it? They shall go down to **the bars of the pit** [to **sheol, oblivion,** separately]. Truly in the dust alone there is rest for all."—Job 17:15, 16

The servant of God expresses his own hope or confidence, but questions how many can have such a confidence. He has already expressed the hope that his death will be merely a sleep, from which he shall awake in the morning. But although each separately goes down to **sheol,** to oblivion, whether they have this hope or not, all find rest in the dust.

"They spend their days in wealth and in a moment go down into **the grave** [sheol, oblivion]."—Job 21:13

Job is here describing the prosperous course of some who are not the Lord's people—contrasting the same with the tribulations experienced by some who are the Lord's people, and come under the rod of divine correction, to fit and prepare them for better things hereafter.

"Drought and heat consume the snow waters: so doth **the grave** [sheol, oblivion] those which have sinned."—Job 24:19

All mankind has sinned, and hence all mankind is subject to death, and goes down to oblivion. The only hope is in him who redeemed us from death,

Man the Subject

and who, "in the morning," will bring us out of oblivion, according to his own gracious promise. Job, however, in this instance is specially referring to evil doers, who hasten their death by an evil course.

"Hell [sheol, oblivion] is naked before him, and destruction hath no covering."—Job 26:6

Here Job points out the all-wisdom of the Creator, who not only knows the end from the beginning, but every secret thing of oblivion is open to his inscrutable gaze.

"For in death there is no remembrance of thee; in the grave [sheol, oblivion] who shall give thee thanks?"—Psa. 6:5

What a clear, positive statement we have here, proving the unconsciousness of man in death! It should be noticed also that the statement is not with reference to the wicked, but with reference to God's servants who desire to thank and to praise him for his mercies. Note also that the reference is not to the dead **flesh** which is buried in **qeber,** but to the **soul** which goes to **sheol,** oblivion.

"The wicked shall be [re-] turned into hell [sheol, oblivion] and all nations that forget God."—Psa. 9:17

The Hebrew word **shub** in this text is properly translated "returned." This gives the thought of one recovered from **sheol,** oblivion, and that some thus recovered will be returned to oblivion on account of wickedness and forgetfulness of God. The deliverance of mankind in general from **sheol** will occur during the Millennial age, as a result of the ransom price finished at Calvary. However, those once awakened and brought to a knowledge of the truth, who then are wilfully perverse, will be returned again to oblivion—"the Second Death," from which there is to be no ransom and no restitution. That this passage is not applicable to the masses of mankind (the heathen) who have never known God, is very evident—from its own statement it refers to those who **forget** God after they have been brought to clear knowledge of him, and to corresponding responsibility.

"Thou wilt not leave my soul in **hell** [**sheol, oblivion**]; neither wilt thou suffer thine Holy One to see corruption."—Psa. 16:10

The Apostle Peter, speaking on the day of Pentecost, under the plenary influence of the Holy Spirit, expounds to us the true significance of this statement, pointing out that it could not possibly be true of David himself; because David's soul was left in **sheol**, and his flesh did see corruption. He declares of David, "He is both **dead** and buried, and his sepulcher is with us unto this day." "David is not ascended into the heavens."—Acts 2:27-34

The apostle's words are emphatic and thoroughly convincing on two points, (1) that the soul of David went to **sheol**, oblivion, and still remained there and up to the time of Peter's discourse had not gone to heaven; (2) that the soul of Christ Jesus went to **sheol**, oblivion, also, but did not remain because resurrected the **third day**—and subsequently ascended to heaven.

These plain statements from an inspired source should clarify this subject to all genuine truth seekers. They set before us the following facts: (1) The soul (being) of our Lord Jesus went to oblivion, to **sheol**, at death. (2) He was dead parts of three days. (3) He arose, was quickened, brought out of oblivion, to the divine nature, on the third day, by the power of the Holy Spirit of God, and became "the first fruits of them that **slept**." Our Lord's being or soul was non-existent during the period of death: "He poured out his soul unto death; he made his soul an offering for sin." But his soul [being] was revived in resurrection, being granted a new spiritual body.*

"The bonds of **hell** [**sheol, oblivion**] encircle me; the snares of death seize me."—Psa. 18:5—Leeser

A figurative expression of deep anguish and fear of death.

---

*Vol. II, p. 108.

"O Lord, thou hast brought up my soul from **the grave [sheol, oblivion]**: thou hast kept me alive."—Psa. 30:3

This is a thanksgiving for recovery from severe illness, which threatened death.

"Let the wicked be ashamed, let them be silent in **the grave [sheol, oblivion]**; let the lying lips be put to silence."—Psa. 31:17, 18

Here, as elsewhere, the Psalmist longs for the cleansing of the earth from those who love and practice wickedness. This has no reference whatever to a future life, nor does it imply a hope of resurrection. When the Kingdom is the Lord's and he is the governor amongst the nations, and the laws of righteousness and truth are established, and when mercy and love shall bring to every creature fullest opportunity of knowledge and recovery from sin, it may be that some who are now wicked will seek righteousness, seek justice, and be hidden under the mercy of Christ's righteousness, and eventually attain to eternal life through him. Neither the prophet David nor any one else could offer objections to such a reformation, nor to the giving of eternal life to those thoroughly reformed and brought back to harmony with God.

"Like sheep they are laid in **the grave** [sheol, oblivion]; death shall feed upon them, and the upright shall have dominion over them in the morning; and their strength shall consume, **the grave [sheol, oblivion]** being an habitation to every one of them. But God will redeem my soul from the power of **the grave [sheol, oblivion]**."—Psa. 49:14, 15

That **sheol** does not signify grave in the ordinary sense, but as we translate it, oblivion, is clearly manifested from this text; for sheep are not buried in graves, though all sheep go into oblivion, are forgotten, are as though they had not been. The Prophet is here pointing out his own confidence in the resurrection, that God would redeem his soul from **sheol**, oblivion. This is in full harmony with the Apostle Peter's statement that "David is not ascended into the heavens." David's soul went to sheol, to oblivion, and David's only hope is in the redemption of his soul from **sheol**, from oblivion, to life, by the Redeemer in the resurrection. Moreover, even those who go into oblivion like the sheep are to come out of oblivion again, for this passage distinctly declares that "in the morning" of the resurrection, the Millennial morning, the righteous shall "have dominion" over these, shall rule them, shall control them, shall judge them in righteousness. So also saith the apostle, "The saints shall judge the world."—1 Cor. 6:2

"Let death seize them, and let them go down quick into **hell** [**sheol, oblivion**]: for wickedness is in their dwellings."—Psa. 55:15

This Scripture, as ordinarily misunderstood, has been a great stumbling block to many of God's people. They have said, how could it be that a good man like David should pray for his enemies to go down into **hell**—into everlasting torture. A good man would not so pray, nor was this the tenor of David's prayer. As we have seen, and are seeing, the word **sheol** contains no thought whatever of fire or blaze or torment or anything of the kind, but simply signifies oblivion, the extinguishment of life. It follows, then that David's prayer or desire for his enemies, the opponents of righteousness, was a perfectly proper desire, in fullest harmony with the laws of the most civilized peoples in this day of greatest enlightenment. Today the laws of civilized nations declare that all murderers shall be executed, and they generally stipulate the supposedly easiest and least painful methods of execution. The law is thus saying, as did David, Let these culprits go to **sheol**, oblivion—let them die. Nevertheless, God in his mercy, has redeemed, by the precious blood of Christ, the vilest sinner as well as the least vile, for "Jesus Christ, by the grace of God, tasted death for every man." "He gave himself a ransom for all, to be testified in due time." If some of our fellow-creatures are more perverse than ourselves, it may, for aught we know to the contrary, be because of the specially blinding influences of the Adversary upon them (2 Cor. 4:4); or because of a more evil heredity. In any case, God's provision is that each individual of the race shall have a full, fair, impartial opportunity of deciding his choice for righteousness and life, or for unrighteousness and the Second Death—to be returned to sheol. All this is fully guaranteed to us in the New Covenant secured and sealed to us through the merit of the precious blood of Christ.

"Great is thy mercy toward me: thou hast delivered my soul from the lowest hell [sheol, oblivion]."—Psa. 86:13

The words "lowest hell" here would signify depth of oblivion. We may not improperly consider that the Prophet is here personating the Lord Jesus, as he does in many of his Psalms. If so, the words "depth of oblivion" would have a peculiar applicability. In the case of the world of mankind death is but a sleep, and its oblivion but a temporary one, from which there shall come an awakening in the resurrection, as a result of the redemption. But in the case of our Lord Jesus it was different: inasmuch as he took the place of the sinner (Adam), death to him must have meant the extreme penalty of sin, viz., a perpetual oblivion, except as, by the Father's grace and power, he should be raised from the dead, and become the Deliverer of those whom he redeemed.

"My soul is full of troubles, and my life draweth nigh unto the grave [sheol, oblivion]."—Psa. 88:3

Here, again, sorrow nigh unto death is briefly and poetically described.

"What man is he that liveth and shall not see death? Shall he deliver his soul from the hand [power] of the grave [sheol, oblivion]?"—Psa. 89:48

How consistent this inquiry and its implied answer, with all the facts of the case as we have thus far seen them, and how inharmonious are these words with the common thought upon the subject discussed! The common thought is that no man, no soul, experiences death; that the moment of dying is the moment of an increase of life; hence that the soul is quite superior to the powers of sheol, oblivion—that the soul cannot die: so far from it being a question whether it could deliver itself from the power of **sheol**, it passes unquestioned that **sheol** has no power whatever to touch the soul. How consistent the Scriptures and the truth! How inconsistent the commonly accepted Platonic philosophy!

"The sorrows of death compassed me, and the pains of **hell** [**sheol, oblivion**] gat hold upon me; I found trouble and sorrow."—Psa. 116:3

Here, again, fear of death is graphically portrayed.

"Whither shall I go from thy spirit [power—to escape or be hidden from divine power], or whither shall I flee from thy presence? If I ascend up into heaven, thou art there: if I make my bed in **hell** [**sheol, oblivion**] behold, thou art there."—Psa. 139: 7, 8

According to the prevalent idea, this would mean that God is a permanent resident of the awful torture chamber which **sheol** is represented to be. On the contrary, the Prophet is taking a large view of the divine power, and telling us the result of his researches, that there is no place in all the universe that is not accessible to divine power. Even the oblivion of death is subject to our Lord who declares, "I have the keys of death and of **hades** [oblivion]." It is our confidence in God—in his omnipotence—that constitutes the basis of our faith in a resurrection of the dead.

"Our bones are scattered at the **grave's** [**sheol, oblivion**] mouth, as when one cutteth and cleaveth upon the earth."—Psa. 141:7

The significance of this passage is very obscure, but in any event, it has nothing in it favorable to the common idea of a hell of torment. Young's translation renders this verse—"As one tilling and ripping up the land, have our bones been scattered at the command of Saul."

"Let us swallow them up alive, as **the grave** [**sheol, oblivion**]."—Prov. 1:12

This purports to be the language of murderers, who would destroy their victims quickly, and have them lost from sight and from memory—in oblivion.

"Her feet go down to death; her steps take hold on

hell [**sheol, oblivion**]."—Prov. 5:5

Here the temptations of an evil woman, and their baneful results, are poetically set forth: her ways lead to destruction, to death, to oblivion.

"Her house is the way to **hell** [**sheol, oblivion**], going down to the chambers of death."—Prov. 7:27

A similar expression to the one preceding, but giving evidence that the hell referred to is not ablaze; not a place of torment, but the dark chambers of death, nonentity, oblivion.

"Her guests are in the depths of **hell** [**sheol, oblivion**]."—Prov. 9:18

Here, in hyperbolic language, the harlot's guests are represented as dead, as having lost self-respect, and all the dignity of manhood—undoubtedly they are in the way of death, for the way of licentiousness hastens disease and death. They are in the way of oblivion, not only in the physical sense, but also in the sense of losing their respect and influence amongst men.

"**Hell** [**sheol, oblivion**] and destruction are before the Lord: how much more, then, the hearts of the children of men?"—Prov. 15:11

It should be noted that there is no intimation here of torture, but quite the reverse, **sheol**, oblivion, is associated with destruction.

"The way of life is above to the wise, that he may depart from **hell** [**sheol, oblivion**] beneath."—Prov. 15:24

Our translators have very nearly made this text favor their theory that the righteous go **up** to heaven, and the unrighteous go **down** to hell. Notice the Revised Version's rendering—"To the wise the way of life goeth upward that he may depart from sheol [margin, the grave] beneath." The correct thought might properly be rendered thus—The path of life for the wise is an upward one toward righteousness, that they may be delivered by resurrection power from oblivion.

"Thou shalt beat him with the rod, and shalt deliver his soul from **hell** [**sheol, oblivion**]."—Prov. 23:14

It is, perhaps, unnecessary to explain that this passage does not teach that after death the corpse should be beaten, in order that the soul might be gotten out of a hell of torment. The meaning is clearly indicated by the context. The injunction is that the child shall not be spared the rod, if it needs it, for in so doing years of usefulness may be added to its life— its soul (being) shall be kept back from a premature oblivion, and possibly be saved from the Second Death—from being returned to oblivion.

"**Hell** [**sheol, oblivion**] and destruction are never full; so the eyes of man are never satisfied."—Prov. 27:20

So far from this signifying a burning hell, of so immense proportions that it never can be filled, it merely signifies that there is no limit to the capacity of death—oblivion and destruction cannot be overcrowded.

"There are three things that are never satisfied; yea, four things say not, It is enough: **the grave** [**sheol, oblivion**]; the barren womb; the earth that is not filled with water, and the fire that saith not, It is enough."—Prov. 30:15, 16

In this text, as in the one preceding it, death, oblivion, is said to have no end of capacity, and cannot be over-filled.

"Whatsoever thy hand findeth to do, do it with thy might; for there is no work, nor device, nor knowledge, nor wisdom in **the grave** [**sheol, oblivion**] whither thou goest."—Eccl. 9:10

Here is a most positive statement respecting hell, **sheol**, oblivion. It is applicable not merely to the wicked, but also to the righteous—to all who enter death. There is neither good work nor bad work, neither praising God nor cursing God, neither thinking good nor thinking ill, neither holy knowledge nor unholy knowledge, neither heavenly wisdom nor other wisdom, in **sheol**, in the oblivion of death. How could the matter be more clearly or more emphatically stated?

"Jealousy is cruel as **the grave** [**sheol, oblivion**]."
—Sol. Song, 8:6

Man the Subject

Here the death state, oblivion, is represented as the very personification of relentlessness. It swallows up the entire human family, making no exceptions, either of character or condition.

"Therefore **hell** [**sheol, oblivion**] hath enlarged herself and opened her mouth without measure."—Isa. 5:14

The Prophet here uses the word **sheol**, oblivion, to describe the loss of prestige, the ignominy, the dishonor upon Israel. They had become as though dead, they had passed into oblivion in large numbers. The passage has no reference to a literal grave, nor to a lake of fire.

"**Hell** [**sheol, oblivion**] from beneath is moved for thee to meet thee at thy coming."—Isa. 14:9

This is highly symbolic language. It is applied to Babylon. Its fulfilment, we believe, is still future, and is now close at hand. Great Babylon is to be swallowed up; as a stone cast into the sea, it shall be utterly lost sight of and forgotten—it will go to oblivion, **sheol**. (Rev. 18:21) This is shown by the context, which declares, "How hath the oppressor ceased, the golden city ceased!"—See verses 4-8

"Thy pomp is brought down to **the grave** [**sheol, oblivion**]."—Isa. 14:11

This is a continuation of the same symbolical picture of the **destruction** of mystic Babylon, whose greatness will soon be a thing of the past—buried in oblivion, not in a burning hell.

"Ye have said, We have made a covenant with death, and with **hell** [**sheol, oblivion**] are we at agreement."—Isa. 28:15

Here the Lord predicts direful trouble, stumbling, and falling amongst those who, through false doctrines, have come to disregard the Scriptural teaching that death is the wages of sin. This time of retribution upon those who have handled the Word of God deceitfully, and who, instead of being sanctified by the truth, are preferring the error, is near at hand. Our great adversary, Satan, is taking advantage of the prevalent misbelief on this subject to ensnare the world with various false doctrines presented upon this false premise. Already he has misled the Papists and the entire heathen world into prayers and masses for the dead, who are believed to be not dead, but very much alive in the torments of purgatory. And now, through Spiritualism, Theosophy and Christian Science, the same Adversary is making special attacks upon Protestants, who because of their belief that the dead are not dead, are very susceptible to these deceiving influences.

Christians of various denominations have "made a league with death," and declare that it is a friend, whereas the Scriptures declare that it is man's greatest enemy, and the wages of his sin. With the grave nominal Christians are in agreement; they consider it to be nothing but a storehouse for the earthly body, which they declare themselves well rid of. Failing to **see that death (oblivion) is the wages of sin, they are ready to believe Satan's falsehood, that eternal torment is the wages of sin.** Failing to believe that death is the wages of sin they are ready to deny that the death of Christ was the remedy, the corresponding price, for man's release, and thus all the gracious features of the divine plan of the ransom and restitution are **more or less obscured** from their view, and made difficult of apprehension.

"Your covenant with death shall be disannulled, and your agreement with **hell [sheol, oblivion]** shall not stand."—Isa. 28:18

Thus the Lord declares that he will ultimately convince the world of the truth of the Scripture statements respecting death and the oblivion condition; but it shall be through a great time of trouble and confusion to those who are under this deception, and who refuse to hearken to the voice of the Word of the Lord on this subject.

"I said, in the cutting off of my days, I shall go to the gates of **the grave [sheol, oblivion]**: I am deprived of the residue of my years."—Isa. 38:10

These are the words of Hezekiah, the good king of Judah, on whose behalf a miracle was wrought, prolonging his days. In these words he is telling what were his thoughts at the time of his sickness. He certainly did not mean that he expected to have gone down to a hell of eternal torment, and the translators were wise enough to see that if in this instance they had translated **sheol** with the word **hell,** it would have aroused questionings and investigations on the part of the readers, which would the sooner have brought the truth on this subject to general attention. The king simply declares that he felt himself near to death, to oblivion, and that he was about to be deprived of the residue of his days, that he might reasonably have expected to enjoy.

"The grave [**sheol, oblivion**] cannot praise thee: death cannot celebrate thee."—Isa. 38:18

These are the words of Hezekiah, a part of the same description of his sickness, his fear of death, his record of the Lord's goodness and mercy in prolonging his life, and his thanksgiving to the Lord. He declares, "Thou hast in love of my soul [being] delivered it from the pit of corruption." The translators did not render this, "Hell cannot praise thee," else those of inquiring mind would have been asking what kind of a hell would be referred to. Hezekiah associates the thought of death, with oblivion, **sheol,** and uses them synonymously, and then he declares, "The living, the living, he shall praise thee, as I do this day." In other words, a living man can praise the Lord, but if a man be dead, if his soul be gone to **sheol,** to oblivion, he cannot praise the Lord, nor in any sense recount his mercies—until, in the morning of the resurrection, as Job declares, the Lord will call, and all will answer him.

"Thou wentest to the king with ointment . . . and didst debase thyself even unto **hell** [**sheol, oblivion**]."
—Isa. 57:9

This is a figurative expression. It does not refer to a hell of torment, nor to a literal grave. It represents Israel as a woman, negligent of her husband, the Lord, seeking alliance with the kings of the earth, to oblivion—to the extent of becoming figuratively dead, oblivious to the Lord and to the principles of his truth and the righteousness which is of faith.

"In the day when he went down to **the grave,** [**sheol, oblivion**] I caused a mourning . . . I made the nations to shake at the sound of his fall, when I cast him down to **hell** [**sheol, oblivion**] . . . they also went down into **hell** [**sheol, oblivion**] unto them that were slain with the sword."—Ezek. 31:15-17

Here the Lord, through the Prophet, is in figurative language describing the fall of Babylon. As heretofore seen, the fall of Babylon, and the extravagant descriptions of it, were in part applicable to literal Babylon, and in greater part are yet to be applied in the complete fall and collapse of mystic Babylon. The old-time nation of Babylon was overthrown by the Medes and Persians, and went down into oblivion, into the death state as a nation: modern mystic Babylon is similarly to fall into oblivion, to rise no more.

"The strong among the mighty shall speak to him, and them that help him, out of the midst of **hell,** [**sheol, oblivion**]."—Ezek. 32:21

Here the passing of the nation of Egypt into oblivion, and the other strong nations which went down into oblivion prior to the fall of Egypt, are represented as speaking to Egypt in respect to its fall. Thus we say that history **tells us** certain things— that history repeats her lessons.

"They shall not lie with the mighty that are fallen of the uncircumcised which are gone down to **hell** [**sheol, oblivion**] with their weapons of war."— Ezek. 32:27

The Prophet is here foretelling the destruction of Meshech and Tubal, how they also will go down to oblivion with their weapons of war. The weapons of war can, indeed, go down into oblivion, and we thank the Lord that no provision has been made for their restoration, in the glorious age that is to come, when Emmanuel shall have established his Kingdom, for the positive promise is, "He shall make wars **to cease unto the ends of the earth.**"—Psa. 46:9

Man the Subject

"I will ransom them from the power of the grave [sheol, oblivion]; I will redeem them from death: O death, I will be thy plagues, O grave [sheol, oblivion] I will be thy destruction: repentance shall be hid from my eyes."—Hos. 13:14

Whoever has not already been convinced that **sheol** does not signify a place of torture can at least take comfort from this text, in which the Lord declares unqualifiedly that **sheol shall be destroyed.** If, therefore, anyone still believes and contends that it is a place of torture, let him also at least admit that it will not endure to all eternity, because the Lord himself has decreed its destruction.

But how beautifully clear and harmonious is this entire statement from the true standpoint! The ransom price has already been paid by our dear Redeemer, and the work of delivering mankind from **sheol**, from the oblivion of death, merely waits until the Church, the Body of Christ, has been selected from amongst mankind, and glorified with her Lord and Head, Christ Jesus. As soon as the resurrection of the Church is complete (the chief or first resurrection) **then,** declares the apostle, "shall be brought to pass the saying that is written, Death is swallowed up in victory. O death, where is thy sting? O grave, where is thy victory?"—1 Cor. 15:54, 55

The swallowing up of death in victory will be the work of the Millennial age, and a gradual one, just as the swallowing up of mankind by death has been a gradual one. Eventually the death sentence which now rests upon mankind, and **sheol,** the oblivion which it enforces upon mankind, shall completely pass away, because all have been redeemed from its power. Under the new conditions, under the New Covenant, with its abundant provision, no one shall enter death (oblivion) again, except such as will be intentional sinners on their own behalf. This will be the Second Death, from which there will be no hope of recovery.

The Atonement

"Though they dig into **hell [sheol, oblivion]** thence shall my hand [power] take them."—Amos 9:2

In this strongly figurative language the Lord declares the completeness of his power and control over mankind, referring in particular to Israel. As a nation, no more than as individuals, could they escape from the divine judgments, and though they should go down into death, individually and nationally, still all of God's promises, and threats as well, shall be fulfilled. Nevertheless, after declaring their utter overthrow and scattering amongst all nations of earth, as we see it fulfilled today, the Lord's promise is (verse 11-15), "In that day [in the dawning of the Millennial day] I will raise up the tabernacle of David that is fallen . . . and I will bring again the captivity of my people, Israel . . . and they shall no more be pulled out of the land which I have given them, saith the Lord thy God." None would think of digging his way into a place of eternal torment but Israel as a nation did dig its way toward national oblivion. Yet God shall prevent this.

"Out of the belly of **hell [sheol, oblivion]** cried I, and thou heardest my voice."—Jonah 2:2

The belly of hell, in which Jonah was, and from which he cried to the Lord, and from which he was delivered, was the belly of the great fish which had swallowed him. It was the belly of oblivion, destruction, death to him, had he not been delivered from it.

"Yea also, because he transgresseth by wine, he is a proud man, neither keepeth at home, who enlargeth his desire as **hell [sheol, oblivion]**, and is as death, and cannot be satisfied, but gathered unto him all nations, and heapeth unto him all people."—Hab. 2:5

Here apparently, an ambitious nation is referred to, an aggressive nation. It might be very fitly applied to the nations of the present time, which are scouring the world to bring smaller and less civilized nations under their control and patronage. Or it might refer to the Man of Sin, and his world-wide influence, through which he draws his revenues from all nations under the sun. In any case, the thought is that

Man the Subject

covetousness is like death (oblivion), in that it never has enough; its capacity cannot be satisfied.

"HADES" IN THE NEW TESTAMENT

In the New Testament the Greek word **hades** is the exact equivalent of the Hebrew word **sheol**. We have the most absolute proof of this from the fact that the apostles, in quotations from the Old Testament, render **sheol** by the word **hades**. The following are all the instances in the New Testament in which the word **hades** occurs:—

"Thou, Capernaum, which art exalted unto heaven, shalt be brought down to **hell [hades, oblivion]**."—Matt. 11:23

It certainly was not true that the city of Capernaum went into eternal torment, neither was it true that it went into a grave, in the ordinary sense of that word, but it was most absolutely true that Capernaum did go into oblivion, into destruction.

"I say unto thee, Thou art Peter, and upon this rock I will build my Church, and the gates of **hell [hades, oblivion]** shall not prevail against it."—Matt. 16:18

Peter had just made confession of the Lord Jesus as being the Anointed, the Son of the living God, the Messiah. This truth is the mighty rock upon which the entire Church of Christ, as living stones, must be built, for there is no other name given whereby we must be saved. Our Lord declares Peter to be one of these **living stones**, and Peter declares (1 Pet. 2:5), that all consecrated believers are similarly **living stones**, built upon this great foundation rock, Christ, the Anointed. These living stones are being built up for a habitation of God, through the spirit, to be a glorious temple for his indwelling, and through which he will bless all the families of the earth. Notwithstanding this fact, that God has accepted believers in Christ and is counting them as members of this future temple, he is permitting death to prevail against his people now: they go down into death (oblivion), apparently as do others: they therefore have need of the Lord's encouraging assurance that death shall not prevail against them, that the doors of oblivion shall not forever remain closed; that as he symbolically burst the bars of death, and came forth in resurrection through the Father's power, so also his Church shall be delivered from the power of death—from oblivion, and shall have share in his resurrection, "the first resurrection." Surely this is in harmony with all Scriptural testimony, and surely no other interpretation of our Lord's words would make the least sense.

"Thou, Capernaum, which art exalted to heaven, shalt be thrust down to **hell [hades, oblivion]**."—Luke 10:15

Capernaum was highly exalted, highly privileged, in that it had our Lord as a resident for some time, enjoyed the privileges of his teaching, and witnessed many of his mighty works; and this hyperbolically is termed **exaltation to heaven**. But in consequence of a failure to rightly use these high privileges and opportunities, our Lord declares that the city would suffer corresponding depression, overthrow, death, as a city—be cast down to oblivion. And this has been fulfilled.

"In **hell [hades, oblivion]** he lifted up his eyes being in torments."—Luke 16:23

This is the only passage of the Scriptures in which there is the slightest intimation of the possibility of thought, feeling, torture or happiness in **hades** or **sheol**. At first it seems to be opposed to the declaration that there is no work, nor knowledge, nor device in **sheol**, and it can only be understood from the one standpoint, viz., that it is a parable. Elsewhere we discuss it in its details,* and show that the rich man who went into oblivion, and yet was tortured while in oblivion, is the Jewish nation. Israel certainly has gone into oblivion; as a nation it is dead, yet as

---

*See "The Truth About Hell."

a people scattered amongst all the nations, Israel lives and has suffered torments since the rejection of Messiah, and will so continue to do until having filled her measure of tribulation she shall be restored to divine favor, according to the conditions of the divine covenant.—Rom. 11:26-29

"Thou wilt not leave my soul in hell [hades, oblivion]."—Acts 2:27

This is the quotation from the Psalms with which we started our present examination—to ascertain whether it is the soul, or merely the body, that goes to hades, to sheol, to oblivion. This text most emphatically teaches that our Lord's soul went to hades, oblivion, and that it was delivered therefrom by a resurrection. The context proves that David's soul also went to sheol, but that it has not yet been delivered from sheol—nor can it be delivered, according to the divine arrangement, until after all the Church, which is the body of Christ, has first been delivered, and until the first resurrection is complete. —See vss. 29, 34; Heb. 11:32, 39, 40

"David, seeing this before, spake of the resurrection of Christ, that his soul was not left in hell [hades, oblivion]."—Acts 2:31

This positive statement is a further confirmation of what we have just seen.

"O death, where is thy sting? O grave [hades, oblivion] where is thy victory?"—1 Cor. 15:55

The apostle gives this as a quotation from the Old Testament, in corroboration of his argument that the only hope for the dead is a resurrection—not in a resurrection of the body, for he distinctly states that the body buried will not be the one resurrected— (see verses 37, 38): the resurrection hope is for the soul, the being, regardless of what kind of body God may be pleased to give it. It is not, "If your body rise not . . . your faith is vain," but "If the dead rise not . . . your faith is vain . . . then they also which are fallen asleep in Christ are perished." (Verses 16-18) It is that which falls asleep, not that which turns to corruption, that is to be awakened, resurrected.

"I am he that liveth and was dead; and behold I am alive forevermore, amen; and have the keys of **hell [hades, oblivion]** and of death."—Rev. 1:18

This passage is given as an encouragement to God's people, hence surely **hell, hades,** here cannot mean a place of torment: otherwise, what would be the force of this expression? These words imply that the Lord's people go to **hades** (oblivion), whoever else may go there, and that the hope of the Lord's people, when going down to **hades,** to oblivion, is that in due time our great Redeemer shall unlock this figurative prison-house of death, and bring forth the captives from the tomb, from **sheol, hades,** oblivion. This is the significance of the statement that he has the keys, that is, the power, the authority—he can open and he can shut; all power is given into his hand.

In preaching at his first advent, he quoted the prophecy of Isaiah respecting himself, which declares that he will open the prison-house, and set at liberty the captives, and declared this to be the Gospel, (Isa. 61:1; Luke 4:18) It is the Gospel of the resurrection, the message, the good tidings of deliverance of all the captives from the oblivion of death, from the power of the Adversary, "him that hath the power of death, that is, the devil." How full of meaning are these Scriptures, when viewed from the proper standpoint; how confusing and absurd when viewed from any other standpoint, except when the ignorance is so dense as to cover and hide the inconsistencies!

"And his name that sat on him was death, and **hell [hades, oblivion]** followed with him: and power was given unto them over the fourth part of the earth, to kill with the sword, and with hunger, and with death, and with the beasts of the earth."—Rev. 6:8

It would require a very strong imagination to harmonize this statement with the commonly accepted **view that hades is a place of torment of such im-**

Man the Subject

mense size as to be capable of receiving and torturing the fifty thousand millions of the earth's population. Nor could any one see the slightest consistency in using a symbol representing such a place of torment riding on horseback. But the reasonableness of the symbols, death and the state of death, destruction, **oblivion, unconsciousness,** stalking through the earth and sweeping off large proportions of the human family, is entirely consistent. We content ourselves here with merely showing this reasonableness, without offering any explanation of the symbols.

"Death and **hell** [hades, oblivion] delivered up the dead which were in them: and they were judged, every man according to their works."—Rev. 20:13

As a result of the first trial in Eden, the death sentence passed upon all men. Probably fifty thousand millions have already gone into **sheol, hades, oblivion;** and hundreds of millions whom we still call alive are not, in the true sense of the word, alive, but are nine-tenths dead, under the operation of the death sentence. As a result of the ransom price paid at Calvary, an opportunity for a new trial is to be granted to each member of the human family; and only a favored minority get such opportunity and trial during this age appointed for the selection of the Church. This means the rolling back of the original sentence of death, and the bringing of all mankind into a condition of judgment or trial for eternal life, on the basis of his own works of obedience or disobedience. This Scripture shows us that at the proper time not only will the dead (those under sentence of death, who have not yet gone into the tomb) be granted a full trial or judgment, to determine their worthiness or unworthiness of life everlasting, but also all of those who have gone into **sheol, hades, oblivion,** shall also come forth from unconsciousness, from the sleep of death, to be judged. This scene of judgment is located in the Millennial age, which is the "day of judgment" for the world, as the Gospel age is the day of judgment for the **Church.**

"And death and **hell** [**hades**, oblivion] were cast into the lake of fire—this is the Second Death."—Rev. 20:14

Great confusion must necessarily come to all who would attempt to interpret **hades** as meaning a place of eternal torment, when considering this passage of Scripture, but how reasonable and harmonious it is from the correct standpoint! The lake of fire (**gehenna**) represents utter destruction, the Second Death, which shall utterly destroy all evil things. The "death and **hades**" here pictured as destroyed in the Second Death are the same as we have just described in connection with the preceding 13th verse. The present state of condemnation, the result of Adam's transgression, is styled "death and **hades**" —the dying condition of those now called the living and the oblivious sleep of the fully dead.

As the 13th verse declares that all men shall be brought out of these conditions in due time for trial, so this verse declares that Adamic death, and the sleep in oblivion, consequent to it, shall be no more, after the Millennial age; and it explains why, viz., because they shall be merged into or swallowed up by the Second Death condition. In the future no one will die for Adam's sin: it will be out of consideration as a factor in the trial of the future. The only death thereafter will be the Second Death, which will affect only the sinner who commits the sin, not the parents, not the children. In that day he that dies shall die for his own sin. "The soul that sinneth it shall die." Although such will have weakness of the Adamic nature from which they will never recover, because of refusal to use the means and opportunities placed within their reach during the Millennium by the Mediator of the New Covenant, yet under that New Covenant those inherited weaknesses will not be reckoned against them, being fully offset by their Redeemer's sacrifice. Hence from and after the time when this full opportunity of the Millennial age is offered to each individual, although Adamic weaknesses and imperfections will still be upon them, their death will not be counted as being a part of Adamic death, but as being a part

Man the Subject

of the Second Death—because their failure to make progress will be the result of **their own** wilfulness, and not the result of Adam's transgression, nor of their own heredity to its weaknesses.

We have now examined every text of Scripture containing the words **sheol** and **hades**, and have ascertained that it is the souls of men that at death pass into this condition, and that it is a state or condition, and not a place, although sometimes figuratively spoken of as a place, a prison-house, from which all prisoners shall come forth in the resurrection morning. We have found that it is figuratively described as dark, silent, and the statement freely made that there is no knowledge, nor device, nor wisdom, nor work, nor cursing, nor praise to God on the part of any who enter this state or condition of oblivion. Their only hope is in the Lord—that having redeemed their souls (beings) from destruction by the sacrifice of his own soul, he shall in due time deliver them, call them forth from oblivion, in such bodies as may please him, and to more favorable conditions than the present, when his wrath, the curse, is passed away and the Millennial era of blessing has been ushered in.

It is not surprising that the translators of our Common Version English Bible, and most commentators, being influenced by erroneous views respecting the nature of man, and the time and place of his reward and punishment, and misapprehending his condition in the interim of death, have rendered and glossed certain passages of the Scriptures, in harmony with their misconceptions, which are to some extent stumbling-blocks to those seeking the truth. It is proper, therefore, that we consider some of these stumbling-blocks, and remove them from our path; but as we must not interrupt our subject proper, these will be left for examination, with other popular misconceptions of Scripture, in our next volume of the **Scripture Studies** series.

A LITTLE LIGHT

'Twas but a little light she bore,
While standing at the open door;
A little light, a feeble spark,
And yet it shone out through the dark
With cheerful ray, and gleamed afar
As brightly as the polar star.

A little light, a gentle hint,
That falls upon the page of print,
May clear the vision, and reveal
The precious treasures doubts conceal,
And guide men to an open door,
Where they new regions may explore.

A little light dispels the gloom
That gathers in the shadowed room,
Where want and sickness find their prey,
And night seems longer than the day,
And hearts with many troubles cope
And feebler glows the spark of hope.

O, sore the need that some must know
While journeying through this vale of woe!
Dismayed, disheartened, gone astray,
Caught in the thickets by the way,
For lack of just a little light
To guide their wandering steps aright.

It may be little we can do
To help another it is true;
But better is a little spark
Of kindness, when the way is dark,
Than one should walk in paths forbidden,
For lack of light we might have given.

STUDY XIII

HOPES FOR LIFE EVERLASTING AND IMMORTALITY SECURED BY THE ATONEMENT

The Earnest Expectations or Hopes of the Groaning Creation—Are not Proofs—The Promises and the Outworking of Atonement, as Proofs—A Distinction and a Difference—Is the Human Soul Immortal, or has it a Hope of Becoming Immortal?—Are Angels Immortal?—Is Satan Immortal?—The Life and Immortality Brought to Light Through the Gospel—The Greek Words Rendered Immortal and Immortality in the Scriptures—Wherein the Hope of the Church and the Hope for the Saved World Differ.

"If a man die shall he live again? All the days of my appointed time will I wait till my change come."—Job 14:14

"Our Savior Jesus Christ . . . hath abolished death and brought life [everlasting] and immortality to light through the Gospel."—2 Tim. 1:10

THERE is a longing hope within men that death does not end all existence. There is an undefined hope that, somehow and somewhere, the life now begun will have a continuation. In some this hope turns to fear. Realizing their unworthiness of a future of pleasure, many fear a future of woe; and the more they dread it for themselves and others the more they believe in it.

This undefined hope of a future life and its counterpart, fear, doubtless had their origin in the Lord's condemnation of the serpent after Adam's fall into sin and death, that eventually the seed of the woman should bruise the serpent's head. This was no doubt understood to mean that at least a portion of the Adamic family would finally triumph over Satan, and over sin and death, into which he had inveigled them. No doubt God encouraged such a hope, even though but vaguely, speaking to and through Noah, and through Enoch who prophesied, "Behold the Lord cometh with ten thousand of his saints." But the **gospel** (the good tidings) of a salvation from death, to be offered to all mankind in God's due time, seems to have been first clearly stated to Abraham. The apostle declares: "The **gospel** was preached before to Abraham—saying, 'In thy seed shall all the families of the earth be blessed.'" This at least was the basis of the Jewish hope of a resurrection; for since many of the families of the earth were dead **and dying, the promised blessing of all implied a future life.** And when, centuries after, Israel was scattered among the nations at the time of the Babylonian captivity, they undoubtedly carried fragments of God's promises and their hopes everywhere they went.

Sure it is, that whether it came as a result of an admixture of Jewish thought, or because hope is an element of man's nature or both, the whole world believes in a future life, and almost all believe that it will be everlasting. This the apostle designates, "The earnest expectation of the creature"—the groaning creation. But such **hopes** are not **proofs** of the doctrine; and the Old Testament promises, made to the Jews, are too vague to constitute a groundwork for a clear faith, much less for a "dogmatic theology," on this subject.

It is not until we find, in the New Testament, the clear, positive statements of our Lord, and afterwards the equally clear statements of the apostles on this momentous subject of **Everlasting Life** that we begin to exchange vague hopes for positive convictions. In their words we not only have positive statements to the effect that the possibilities of a future life have been provided for all, but the philosophy of the fact and how it is to be attained and maintained are set forth there as nowhere else.

Many have not noticed these points, and hence are "weak in faith." Let us see what this philosophy is

Life and Immortality

and be more assured than ever that future life, everlasting life, is by our great wise Creator's provision made a possibility for every member of the human family.

Beginning at the foundation of this New Testament assurance of Life Everlasting, we find to our astonishment that it first of all admonishes us that in and of ourselves we have nothing which would give us any hope of everlasting life—that the life of our race was forfeited by the disobedience of our father Adam; that although he was created perfect and was adapted to live forever, his sin not only brought to him the wages of sin—death—but that his children were born in a dying condition, inheritors of the dying influences. God's law, like himself, is perfect, and so was his creature (Adam) before he sinned; for of God it is written, "His work is perfect." And God through his law approves only that which is perfect, and condemns to destruction everything imperfect. Hence the race of Adam, "born in sin and shapen in iniquity," has no hope of everlasting life except upon the conditions held out in the New Testament and called **The Gospel**—the good tidings, that a way back from the fall, to perfection, to divine favor and everlasting life, has been opened up through Christ and for all of Adam's family who will avail themselves of it.

The key-note of this hope of reconciliation to God, and thus to a fresh hope of life everlasting, is found in the statements (1) that "Christ died for our sins" and (2) that he "rose again for our justification"; for "the man Christ Jesus gave himself **a ransom** [a corresponding price] for all." Adam and his race, which when he sinned was yet in him and shared his sentence naturally, have been **"redeemed** [bought] by the precious blood [death] of Christ."—1 Pet. 1:19

But although the Lord's provision is abundant **for all**, it is not applicable **to any** except on certain conditions; namely, (1) that they accept Christ as their Redeemer; and (2) that they strive to avoid sin and to live thenceforth in harmony with God and righteousness. Hence we are told that "Eternal Life is the gift of God **through** Jesus Christ our Lord." (Rom

6:23) The following Scriptural statements are very clear on this subject:—

"He that hath the Son hath life [a right or privilege or grant of life as God's gift]; but he that hath not the Son shall not see [perfect] life."—John 3:36; 1 John 5:12

None can obtain everlasting life except from Christ the Redeemer and appointed **Life-giver;** and the truth which brings to us the privilege of manifesting faith and obedience, and thus **"laying hold** on eternal life," is called the "water of life" and the "bread of life."—John 4:14; 6:40, 54

This everlasting life will be granted only to those who, when they learn of it and the terms upon which it will be granted as a gift, seek for it, by living according to the spirit of holiness. They shall **reap** it as a gift-reward.—Rom. 6:23; Gal. 6:8

To gain this everlasting life we must become the Lord's "sheep" and follow the voice, the instructions, of the Shepherd.—John 10:26-28; 17:2, 3

The gift of everlasting life will not be forced upon any. On the contrary, it must be desired and sought and laid hold upon by all who would gain it.—1 Tim. 6:12, 19

It is thus a **hope,** rather than the real life, that God gives us now: the hope that we may ultimately attain it, because God has provided a way by which he can be just and yet be the justifier of all truly believing and accepting Christ.

By God's grace our Lord Jesus not only bought us by the sacrifice of his life for ours, but he became our great High Priest, and as such he is now the "author [source] of eternal salvation to all that **obey him."** (Heb. 5:9) "And this is the promise which he hath promised us, even eternal life."—1 John 2:25

"And this is the record, that God hath given to us eternal life [now by faith and hope, and later actually 'when he who is our life shall appear'], and this life is in his Son. He that hath the Son hath life: and he that hath not the Son of God hath not life."—1 John 5:11. 12

Life and Immortality

This everlasting life, made possible to Adam and all his race by our Creator through our Redeemer, but intended for, and promised to, only the faithful and obedient, and which at present is given to these only as a **hope**, will be **actually** given to the faithful in the "resurrection."

It will be noticed that the explicit promises of God's Word differ widely from the worldly philosophies on this subject. They claim that man must have a future everlasting life **because he hopes for it,** or in most cases fears it. But hopes and fears are not reasonable grounds for belief on any subject. Neither is there basis for the claim that there is **something** in man which must live on and on forever—no such part of the human organism is known, or can be proved or located.

But the Scriptural view of the subject is open to no such objections: it is thoroughly reasonable to consider our existence, soul, being, as therein presented—as a "gift of God," and not an inalienable possession of our own. Furthermore, it avoids a great and serious difficulty to which the idea of the heathen philosophies is open; for when the heathen philosopher states that man cannot perish, that he **must** live forever, that eternal life is not a **gift** of God, as the Bible declares, but a natural quality possessed by every man, he claims too much. Such a philosophy not only gives everlasting existence to those who would use it well and to whom it would be a blessing, but to others also who would not use it well and to whom it would be a curse. The Scriptural teaching, on the contrary, as we have already shown, declares that this great and inestimably precious **gift** (Life-Everlasting) will be bestowed upon those only who believe and obey the Redeemer and Life-giver. Others, to whom it would be an injury, not only do not possess it now, but can never get it. "The wages of sin is death; but the gift of God is eternal life through Jesus Christ our Lord." (Rom. 6:23) The wicked (all who, after coming to a clear knowledge of the truth, still wilfully disobey it) shall be cut off from among God's people in the Second Death. They "shall be as though they had not been." "They shall utterly perish." "Everlasting destruction" shall be their doom—a destruction which will last forever, from which there will be no recovery, no resurrection. They will suffer the loss of everlasting life, and all of its privileges, joys and blessings—the **loss** of all that the faithful will **gain.**—Acts 3:23; Psa. 37:9, 20; Job 10:19; 2 Thess. 1:9

God's gift of life eternal is precious to all his people, and a firm grasp of it by the hand of faith is quite essential to a well-balanced and consistent life. Only those who have thus "laid hold on eternal life," by an acceptance of Christ and consecration to his service, are able to properly and profitably combat the tempests of life now raging.

A DISTINCTION AND A DIFFERENCE

But now, having examined the hope of immortality from the ordinary understanding of that word (everlasting life), and having found that everlasting life is God's provision for all those of Adam's race who will accept it in "due time" under the terms of the New Covenant, we are prepared to go a step further and to note that everlasting life and immortality are not synonymous terms, as people in general suppose. The word "immortal" means more than power to live everlastingly; and, according to the Scriptures, millions may ultimately enjoy **everlasting life,** but only a very limited "little flock" will be made **immortal.**

Immortality is an element or quality of the divine nature, but not of human or angelic or any other nature than the divine. And it is because Christ and his "little flock," his "bride," are to be **"partakers of the divine nature"** that they will be exceptions to all other creatures either in heaven or on earth.—2 Pet. 1:4

IS THE HUMAN SOUL IMMORTAL, OR HAS IT A HOPE OF BECOMING IMMORTAL?

We have seen that a human soul (sentient being)

results from a union of breath of life (**ruach—pneuma**) with a human organism or body; exactly the same as in the cases of lower animal souls (sentient beings) except as man is endowed with a higher organism, a superior body possessed of superior powers and qualities. Our present inquiry then is, Are all animals immortal? And if this be answered negatively, we must inquire, What does man possess above the lower animals which gives hope for his immortality?

Solomon's declaration as well as our own observations attest that man like the lower animals is subject to death—"As the one dieth so dieth the other. Yea, they have all one [kind of] **breath** [spirit of life—**ruach**]." (Eccl. 3:19) On every hand the crape, the casket, the hearse, the cemetery, all testify that man does die and hence that he is not **immortal**, for the word "immortal" signifies death-proof, that which **cannot die**. Whatever man's hope of immortality, it is not a present possession and can at very most be a **hope** in some divine provision, future.

Before probing this question further it will be profitable for us to consider the meaning of the words "mortal" and "immortal," for a gross misunderstanding of the significance of these words is very prevalent and often leads to confusion of thought.

The word **Immortal** signifies not mortal—death-proof, incorruptible, indestructible, imperishable. Any being whose existence is dependent in any manner upon another, or upon conditions such as food, light, air, etc., is not immortal. This quality originally inhered in Jehovah God alone, as it is written—"The Father hath life **in himself**" (John 5:26); i. e., his existence is not a derived one, nor a sustained one. He is the King eternal, immortal, invisible. (1 Tim. 1:17) These Scriptures being decisive authority on the subject, we may know beyond peradventure that men, angels, archangels, or even the Son of God, before and during the time he "was made flesh and dwelt among us"—were not immortal—all were **mortal**.

But the word "mortal" does not signify **dying, but** merely **die-able**—possessing life dependent upon God for its continuance. For instance, angels not being immortal are mortal and could die, could be destroyed by God if they became rebels against his wise, just and loving government. In him (in his providence) they live and move and have their being. Indeed, of Satan, who was such an angel of light, and who did become a rebel, it is distinctly declared that in due time he will be destroyed. (Heb. 2:14) This not only proves that Satan is **mortal,** but it proves that angelic nature is a **mortal** nature—one which could be destroyed by its Creator. As for man, he is a "little lower than the angels" (Psa. 8:5), and consequently **mortal** also, as is abundantly attested by the fact that our race has been dying for six thousand years and that even the saints in Christ are exhorted to **seek** immortality.—Rom. 2:7

The common definition of mortal is **dying,** and **of** immortal **everlasting**—both wrong. To demonstrate the falsity of these general definitions let us propound a simple question—

WAS ADAM CREATED MORTAL OR IMMORTAL?

If the answer be—"Adam was created **immortal,**" we respond, How then was he threatened with, and afterward sentenced to, death: and how could he die if he were death-proof? And why did God in punishing him drive him out of the Garden of Eden away from the life-sustaining grove or trees of life, lest he **by eating** live forever?—Gen. 3:22

If the answer be that man was created **mortal** (according to the erroneous common definition, **dying**) we inquire, How could God sentence man to death after his disobedience if he were already a **dying** creature and never had been otherwise? And if Adam was created **dying** how could God declare that his **death came by his sin?**

Life and Immortality

Confusion is unavoidable unless the true definitions of mortal and immortal be clearly recognized as follows:

Immortal—the state or condition in which death is impossible—a death-proof condition.

Mortal—a state or condition in which death is possible—a condition of liability to death, but not necessarily a dying condition unless a death sentence has been incurred.

From this standpoint we can see at a glance that Adam was created **mortal**—in a condition in which death was a possibility or everlasting life a possibility; according as he pleased or displeased his wise, just, and loving Creator. Had he remained obedient he would have continued living until now—and forever—and yet all the while he would have been **mortal**, liable to death if disobedient. Nor would such a condition be one of uncertainty; for God with whom he had to do is unchangeable: hence Adam would have had **full assurance** of everlasting life so long as he continued loyal and obedient to his Creator. And more than this could not reasonably be asked.

Adam's life condition previous to his disobedience was similar to that now enjoyed by the holy angels: he had life in full measure—lasting life—which he might have retained forever by remaining obedient to God. But because he was not **death-proof**, because he did not have "life in himself" but was dependent for continuance upon conditions subject to his Creator's pleasure, therefore God's threat that if he disobeyed he should die, meant something. It meant the loss of the spark of life, "the breath of life," without which the body would moulder into dust and the living **soul** or sentient **being** would cease. Had Adam been **immortal**, undie-able, death-proof, God's sentence would have been an empty threat. But because **Adam was mortal, die-able,** liable to death **except as sustained by his Creator's provisions,** therefore, as declared, he died "in the day" of his disobedience.—See 2 Pet. 3:8

To those who think that the Bible abounds with such expressions as **immortal soul, undying soul, never-dying soul**, etc., we can offer no better advice than that they take a Bible concordance and look for these words and others of similar import. They will find none; and thus the sincere truth-seekers will most quickly convince themselves that Christian people in general have for centuries, in thought at least, been **adding to** the Word of God, much to their own confusion.

According to the Scriptures the angels are enjoying life-everlasting but are **mortal**: that is to say, the everlastingness of their angelic existence is not because they are immortal or death-proof and so could not be destroyed by their Creator; but because he desires that they shall live so long as they will use their lives in accord with his just and loving arrangement. This is easy of demonstration; for was not Satan one of the holy angels before he by pride and ambition sinned? And did he not thus become one of the wicked (willingly, intentionally opposing God) of whom it is written, "All the wicked will God **destroy**"—"who shall be punished with everlasting destruction"? (Psa. 145:20; 2 Thess. 1:9) Note the explicit declaration respecting Satan's destruction, applicable in principle to all who follow his evil way and reject divine arrangements knowingly, intentionally.—Heb. 2:14

While the Scriptures do speak of the mortality of man, and indeed in nearly all particulars confine themselves to man's relationship to God, yet they no less positively teach in another way the mortality of angels, by declaring that Christ "only hath immortality" (1 Tim. 6:16)—the Father as always being excepted. (1 Cor. 15:27) And as we have already seen, our Lord Jesus received **immortality** (which is an element or quality of "divine nature," only) at his resurrection, and as a reward for his faithful obedience to the Father's will to the extent of self-sacrifice—"unto death, even the death of the cross—wherefore him hath God **highly exalted**." Although always superior to all others as "the only

Life and Immortality

Begotten," this **exaltation** raised him, as the apostle declares, **far above** angels and principalities and powers and every name that is named in heaven and in earth.—Eph. 1:21

Thus it appears clear, from God's own revelation on the subject, that only Himself and his Only Begotten Son possessed this quality of immortality at the time the apostles wrote their epistles. Indeed, had the Only Begotten been **immortal** sooner than at the time of his exaltation he could not have been the Savior of the world—because he **could not have died;** and under divine arrangement to be our Redeemer he must die: the record is, "Christ died for our sins" and was exalted to immortality afterward.

Hopes of a future everlasting life are held out vaguely in the Old Testament; but immortality is not so much as mentioned. Indeed, the inspired apostle declares of our Lord Jesus, that he "abolished death [broke its hold on man] and brought **life** and **immortality** to light through the gospel." (2 Tim. 1:10) This shows two things: (1) That **life** in perfection, lasting life, is separate and distinct from **immortality**, indestructibility. (2) It shows that neither of these great blessings had been disclosed or made accessible previous to the gospel—the "great salvation which **began** to be preached by our Lord." —Heb. 2:3

And what did our Lord's gospel bring to **"light"** respecting these two great blessings—life and immortality?

(a) It shows that by divine grace our Lord purchased the whole world of Adam's posterity and thus secured for each and every member of the race an opportunity to **return** from **death** to life—in other words it declares coming "times of **restitution** of all things which God hath spoken by the mouth of all the holy prophets since the world began." Restitution in its highest and ultimate sense will be the bringing of the restored ones not only out of the tomb, but out of the various degrees of death (represented in sickness and imperfection) up to **life**—

lasting life as Adam enjoyed it before his disobedience. The gospel of Christ assures us that a full opportunity to attain this life blessing shall be granted to all under the reasonable terms of the New Covenant—"in due time."—1 Tim. 2:6

(b) The "light" of Christ's gospel shows a special provision in the divine plan for a special calling, testing and preparing of a small number of his creatures to more than a moral and rational likeness to himself—an invitation so to conform themselves to the Father's will and so to prove their loyal obedience to him, that he might make of them, "new creatures," "the express image of his person," and "partakers of the divine nature"—a prominent constituent element of which is **immortality.** This our Lord Jesus broached, brought to light, in his gospel of God's grace.

With amazement we inquire—To whom of God's holy ones—angels, cherubim or seraphim—is so high a call extended? The reply of the gospel of Christ is that it is not extended to the angels at all, but to the Son of Man and his "bride" to be chosen from among those whom he redeemed with his own precious blood.

Consider him, who, for the joy set before him, endured the cross, despising the shame, and is now in consequence set down at the right hand (place of favor) of the throne of God. He was rich, but for our sakes he became poor. Inasmuch as the man and race to be redeemed were human, it was needful that he become human so as to give the ransom or corresponding price. He therefore humbled himself and took the bondman's form; and after he found himself in fashion as a man, he humbled himself even unto death—even unto the most ignominious form of death—the death of the cross. Wherefore, God hath highly exalted him [to the promised divine nature, at his resurrection], and given him a name that is above every name [Jehovah's name excepted —1 Cor. 15:27]."—Heb. 12:3, 2; 2 Cor. 8:9; Phil. 2:8, 9

Life and Immortality

"Worthy is the Lamb that was slain **to receive** power, and riches, and wisdom, and strength, and honor, and glory, and blessing."—Rev. 5:9-12

The opulence of divine favor might well have stopped with the exaltation of this great and worthy One: but no; God, the Father, has arranged that Christ Jesus, as the Captain, shall lead a company of Sons of God to "glory, honor and immortality" (Heb. 2:10; Rom. 2:7), each of whom, however, must be a spiritual "copy" or likeness of the "First Begotten." As a grand lesson of the divine sovereignty, and as a sublime contradiction to all evolution theories, God elected to call to this place of honor (as "the bride, the Lamb's wife and joint-heir"—Rev. 21:2, 9; Rom. 8:17), not angels and cherubs, but some from among the sinners redeemed by the precious blood of the Lamb. God **elected the number** to be thus exalted (Rev. 7:4), and **predestinated** what must be **their characteristics** if they would make their calling and election sure to a place in that company to be so highly honored; and all the rest is left to Christ, who worketh now as the Father worked hitherto.— John 5:17

The Gospel age, from Pentecost to the setting up of the Kingdom at the second advent, is the time for the selection of this elect Bride of Christ class variously termed "the Church," "the body of Christ," the "royal priesthood," the "seed of Abraham" (Gal. 3:29), etc.; and the continued permission of evil is for the purpose of developing these "members of the body of Christ" and to furnish them the opportunity of sacrificing their little and redeemed **all,** in the service of him who bought them with his precious blood; and thus of developing in their hearts his spiritual likeness, that when, at the end of the age, they are presented by their Lord and Redeemer before the Father, God may see in them "the image of his Son."—Col. 1:22; Rom. 8:29

As the reward of "glory, honor and immortality," and all the features of the divine nature, were not conferred upon the "First Begotten" until he had finished his course by completing his sacrifice and obedience in death, so with the Church, his "bride"—counted as one and treated collectively. Our Lord, the First Born and Captain, "entered into his glory" at his resurrection: he there became partaker of the divine nature fully, by being "born from the dead," "born of the Spirit:" he there was highly exalted to the throne and highest favor ("right hand" of God); and so he has promised that his Church, his "bride," shall in resurrection be changed, by divine power, from human nature to the glory, honor and immortality of the divine nature.—Heb. 13:20; 2 Pet. 1:4

And so it is written respecting "the resurrection" of the Church: "It is sown in corruption; it is raised in incorruption [immortality]: it is sown in dishonor; it is raised in glory: it is sown in weakness; it is raised in power: it is sown a natural [animal] body; it is raised a spiritual body."—1 Cor. 15:42-44, 49

The conditions imposed upon all who would make their calling and election sure to this favored position are **exacting**, though nevertheless "a reasonable service"; and in offset the faithful are promised the "glory, honor and **immortality**" of "the divine nature"—that thus they shall share the Redeemer's high exaltation "far above angels," if they share his ignominy by walking in his footsteps, following his example in this present time while evil is permitted to triumph.

Note well the fact that every promise or suggestion of hope of immortality in the Lord's Word is to this special elect Church. This is the inherent life referred to by our Lord, saying—"As the Father hath **life in himself** [a life not requiring sustenance—**immortality**] so hath he given unto the Son that he should have **life in himself** [immortality]" and that he should give it unto whomsoever he would—**his bride, his Church**—"members of his body."—John 5:26; Eph. 3:6

Two Greek words are translated **immortality**:—

(1) **Athanasia**, which Strong defines as **"deathless-**

Life and Immortality

ness." This word is found in the following Scriptures only:—

"This mortal must put on **immortality** [**athanasia**—deathlessness]"—referring to the first resurrection shared in only by the Church.—1 Cor. 15:53

"When this mortal shall have put on **immortality** [**athanasia**—deathlessness]"—referring to the same first resurrection of the Church."—1 Cor. 15:54

"Who only hath **immortality** [**athanasia**—deathlessness]—referring to our Lord Jesus and excepting the Father from comparison, as always.—1 Tim. 6:16

(2) **Aptharsia** and **apthartos** (from same root) are rendered **immortality** twice and **immortal** once, but would more properly be rendered **incorruption** and **incorruptible**, and are generally so rendered by lexicographers. All the occurrences of these words in the Bible follow:—

"To those who seek for glory, honor and **immortality** [**aptharsia**—incorruption]."—Rom. 2:7

"It is sown in corruption, it is raised in **incorruption** [**aptharsia**]."—1 Cor. 15:42

"Flesh and blood cannot inherit the Kingdom of God; neither doth corruption inherit **incorruption** [**aptharsia**]."—1 Cor. 15:50

"This corruptible must put on **incorruption** [**aptharsia**]."—1 Cor. 15:53

"When this corruptible shall have put on **incorruption** [**aptharsia**]."—1 Cor. 15:54

"Grace be with all them that love our Lord Jesus Christ in **sincerity** [**aptharsia**—incorruptly]."—Eph. 6:24

"Jesus Christ who hath brought life and **immortality** [**aptharsia**—incorruptible] to light through the gospel."—2 Tim. 1:10

"In doctrine showing uncorruptness, gravity, **sincerity** [**aptharsia**—incorruption]."—Titus 2:7

"The glory of the **uncorruptible** [**apthartos**—incorruptible] God."—Rom. 1:23

"They do it to obtain a corruptible crown; but we an **incorruptible** [**apthartos**]."—1 Cor. 9:25

"The dead [Church] shall be raised **incorruptible** [apthartos]."—1 Cor. 15:52

"The King eternal, **immortal** [apthartos—incorruptible], the only wise God."—1 Tim. 1:17

"An inheritance **incorruptible** [apthartos], undefiled, and that fadeth not away, reserved in heaven for you."—1 Pet. 1:4

"Being born again, not of corruptible seed but of **incorruptible** [apthartos]."—1 Pet. 1:23

"That which is not **corruptible** [apthartos] even the ornament of a meek and quiet spirit."—1 Pet. 3:4

The thought in this word is— that which cannot corrupt, cannot decay, cannot lose value: **aptharsia** is thus in many respects the equivalent of **athanasia** or **deathlessness** when applied to sentient beings; for that which having life is death-proof, may truly be styled incorruptible.

MANKIND'S HOPE FOR EVERLASTING LIFE

The boldest and ablest scientists and evolutionists have attempted to show that man's life was not a gift from the Creator. Theoretically they have brought man and all the lower animals up, by evolution process, from a microscopic germ; yea, from protoplasm, which Prof. Huxley called "the physical basis of life"; and they fain would in some way ignore the Creator and Life-giver entirely: but, as a matter of fact, they have been unable to suggest any way that even protoplasm could get life from inert matter. To this extent, therefore, they are obliged to recognize a first great cause of life. But the reverent Bible student should not have the slightest difficulty in accepting the statement of the Scriptures that God himself alone is the First Great Cause, the fountain of life, from whom has proceeded all life on every plane; as says the apostle, All things are **of** the Father, and all things are **by** the Son, and we by him. (1 Cor. 8:6) The Christian not only finds the evidences of a Creator in the book of Nature, but he

Life and Immortality

finds in the Bible the express and particular revelation of that Creator, and of that creation. He accepts as a fact the statement that God created our first parents, and bestowed life upon them, and provided for their propagation of a race of sentient beings, souls, of their own kind, just as he provided for a similar process in the brute creation.

Looking back to Eden we see Adam and Eve in their perfection, possessed of moral and inteNectual powers, in the likeness of their Creator, and therefore far superior to their subjects, the brute creation —souls of a higher order, the result of a higher and finer organism; and we inquire, What was the purpose of God respecting man in his creation? We see that so far as the brute creation is concerned, the Lord's evident design was that they should live a few years and then die, giving place to others of the species; and that thus they should minister as servants to the pleasure and convenience of man, their master, who in his perfection was a gracious master. But how about man? Was man born to die like the beasts? We have just seen that he had no undying quality bestowed upon him, but we find abundant testimony of God's provision for the **everlasting life** of all who attain to approved conditions: that provision consisted not in the bestowment of immortal powers and qualities, but in the good will and purpose of his Creator, under which alone he "lives, moves and has his being."

Occasionally a shallow thinker will argue that man is immortal, indestructible, because science has determined that **"matter is** indestructible." But, as already pointed out, **matter** is not **man,** nor is the soul, or being, matter. The body is matter, but to be the body of a man matter must have a special peculiar organization, and then spirit of life must be added before it becomes man or soul. No one will argue that an **organism** is indestructible, and hence any one of reasoning ability can see that the **being** or **soul** based upon and dependent on organism can be destroyed. Besides, this absurd reasoning or rather failure to reason would be forced by analogy to claim that all insects and creeping things have immortality, are indestructible. There is an immense difference between destroying inert matter and destroying being.

God declared to our father Adam, according to the record, that his life was secure, and would be continuous so long as he continued an obedient son of God; that only disobedience would expose **him** (the being, the soul) to death. The same Scriptures tell us of the disobedience of our first parents, and of the divine pronouncement of the sentence of death, as the penalty for sin. And we should notice carefully the language of our Lord, in respect to this sentence. God did not address his language to the senseless body, before it had been vitalized; neither did God address himself to the breath or spirit of life, which is an unintelligent vitalizing power merely. He addressed Adam, the **soul**, the intelligent or sentient **being**, after he had been fully created. And we all agree that this was the reasonable and only proper course—that the soul or being alone should be addressed. Now mark the Lord's words: "In the day that **thou** eatest thereof, **thou** shalt surely die."

When Adam transgressed the divine law and came under the sentence thereof, that his soul should die, the Lord might have executed his penalty in an instantaneous death; but instead he merely withdrew his special provision for his continuance of life, and thus let Adam die gradually. The conditions of life are explained to us as having been a special grove of life-giving trees, by the eating of which man's life would have continued, making good daily its wastes, and suffering no decay. As soon as man became a transgressor, he was restrained from access to these trees of life, or orchard of life, and thus, like the lower animals of his dominion, became subject to death. In man's case, however, death is said to be a "curse," because it came as a result of the violation of the divine regulations, and incidentally, through the curse upon earth's king, a curse rests upon his dominion and upon all his subjects, the lower animals; for the king having lost his perfection, the entire dominion fell into disorder.

Life and Immortality

Moreover, the children of Adam could not obtain from him, as their progenitor, rights or privileges or physical perfections, which he had forfeited and was losing; hence, as the Scriptures show, the entire race of Adam fell with him under the curse—into death, and hence, as creatures in the image of God, possessed of powers of intelligence appreciative of everlasting life, we look up to God to see whether or not infinite wisdom, infinite love, infinite justice and infinite power can unitedly produce a plan of salvation for man, under which God can be just, and yet be the justifier of him that believeth in Jesus.—Rom. 3:26

Nor is the hope a vain one. God's provision, through Christ, as revealed in the Scriptures, is for a resurrection of the dead, a restitution of man to his former estate. True, there are limitations and conditions, and not all shall return to the divine favor, but an opportunity to return shall be granted to all, with the strong probability, we believe, that a majority of Adam's posterity shall, when they know the truth, gratefully accept of God's grace through Christ, and conform their lives to the law of the New Covenant, through faith in the Redeemer.

It is not, however, for us or anyone to answer the query which our Lord refused to answer, viz., "Are there few that be saved?" (Luke 13:23) The most we are privileged to do is to point out that "a ransom for all" has been given by our Lord and the promise that in "due time" all shall come to a knowledge of this great truth and to opportunity to attain everlasting life from him, the great Light who shall yet "lighten every man that cometh into the world." (1 Tim. 2:4-6); John 1:9) We should and do repeat during this age to all who have "ears to hear" the Master's words: "Strive to enter in at the straight gate: for many shall seek to enter in and shall not be able, when once the Master of the house has risen up and shut the door." (Luke 13:24, 25) In other words the call, the only call of this Gospel age, is to the narrow way of self-sacrifice: and no distraction of interest should slack our running for the great prize of immortality now offered. When the number of the "elect" is filled full and the great tribulation of the end of this age gives notice that the Church is completed and glorified, there will be many to take a different view of the worldly trifles which now hinder their fulfilment of their consecration pledges.

God's plan of salvation for the general race of Adam is to extend to each member of it, during the Millennium, the **offer of eternal life u**pon the terms of the New Covenant sealed for all with the precious blood of the Lamb. But there is no suggestion anywhere that immortality, the Divine Nature, will ever be offered or granted to any except the "elect Church of the Gospel age—the "little flock," "the Bride, the Lamb's wife." For the others of Adam's race the offer will be "restitution" (Acts 3:19-21) to life and health and perfection of **human** nature—the same that Adam possessed as the earthly image of God before his fall from grace into sin and death. And when at the close of the Millennial age all the obedient of mankind shall have attained all that was lost in **Adam and redeemed by Christ**—then all, armed with complete knowledge and experience, and hence fully able to stand the test, will be tested severely (as was Adam), but individually (Rev. 20: 7-10), and only those found in fullest heart-sympathy, as well as in outward harmony, with God and his righteous arrangements, will be permitted to go beyond the Millennium into the everlasting future or "world [age] without end." All others will be destroyed in the Second Death—"destroyed from among the people."—Acts 3:22

But although there shall be no more death, neither sighing nor crying, it will not be because the victors of the Millennial age will be crowned with immortality, but because, having learned to judge between right and wrong and their effects, they shall have formed characters in full accord with God and righteousness; and because they will have stood tests which will demonstrate that they would not wish to sin if the way were opened and no penalties attached. They will not have life in themselves, but will still

Life and Immortality

be dependent upon God's provision of food, etc., for the sustenance of life.—Compare Rev. 21:4, 6, 8; 7:16; Matt. 5:6

As the curse brought the death of mankind, so the removal of the curse means the removal of all legal objections to man's return to all the original blessings bestowed upon him in Eden. But man, now degraded and imperfect mentally, morally and physically, is not fit, as Adam was, to enjoy the perfections of an Eden or Paradise condition; hence the divine purpose is that in the "restitution times," during the Millennial age, mankind, whose sins have been atoned for by the death of the Lord Jesus, may be brought back by him, the Life-Giver and Deliverer, from the bondage of sin and death, to all the fullness of the perfection of the original likeness of God. Not only so, but the divine plan we find is that man's experience with sin shall constitute a lesson which will have an everlasting influence upon some, giving them to know, by personal experience, something of the "exceeding sinfulness of sin," and of its sure reward or penalty, death: so that when, during the Millennial age, these shall be brought to a knowledge of righteousness, truth, goodness, love, and all the graces and qualities of divine character, the willing and obedient shall know and appreciate the privilege of eternal life in a way that Father Adam never would have known it, and never could have appreciated it.

To this end the dying has been a **gradual** process with the race in general, and to the same end the resurrection is to be a gradual process: inch by inch, as it were, mankind will be raised up, up, up out of the mire of sin, out of the terrible pit of degradation and death, to the grand height of perfection and life from which he fell in the person of father Adam. The only exception to this general program for the world, as presented to us in the Scriptures, being the few brought into harmony with God in advance, the seed of Abraham, natural and spiritual.—Gal. 3:29; Heb. 11:39, 40

Seen in this, the Scriptural light, the subject of immortality shines resplendently. It leaves the way clear for the general "gift of God, eternal life," to be extended to all whom the Redeemer shall find willing to accept it upon the only terms upon which it could be a blessing; and it leaves the unworthy subject to the just penalty always enunciated by the great judge of all, viz.:—

"The wages of sin is **death**."—Rom. 6:23

"The **soul** that sinneth it shall **die**."—Ezek. 18:4, 20

"He that believeth not the Son shall not see life; but the wrath of God [the curse, **death**] abideth on him."—John 3:36

Thus we find, on this subject as on others, that the philosophy of the Word of God is deeper as well as clearer, and more rational by far, than the heathen systems and theories. Praise God for his Word of Truth and for hearts disposed to accept it as the revelation of the wisdom and power of God!

But does doubt cry out, How could God in resurrection reproduce the millions of earth completely so that each will know himself and profit by the memory of present life experiences? We answer that in the phonograph cylinder even man is able to preserve his own words and reproduce them; much more is our Creator able to reproduce for the entire race such brain organisms as will perfectly reproduce every sentiment, thought and experience. David seems to refer to the power of God in a manner that might be applicable either prophetically to the resurrection or reflectively to the first birth. He says:—

"I will praise thee; for I am fearfully and wonderfully made. My substance [organism] was not hid from thee when I was made in secret, curiously wrought in the lower parts of the earth. Thine eyes did see my substance being yet imperfect; and in thy book all my members were written which in continuance [gradually] were fashioned when as yet there was none of them."—Psa. 139:14-16

STUDY XIV

THE NECESSITY FOR THE ATONEMENT—THE CURSE

The "Curse" a Present and Not a Future Evil—Where and Why the Blight Came Upon All—When this "Wrath" of God Against Sin Will Cease—"Escape" Now and in the Future—Atonement Necessary, Because of the Plan adopted by God—Man an Example for Angels and for Future Creations.

"And there shall be no more curse."—Rev. 22:3

OUR text is in full accord with the general tenor of the Scriptures, that the time is coming when the work of Atonement shall be fully accomplished, and when, as a result, the curse will be completely lifted from man, and from the earth, his dominion. But this implies that the curse is not yet lifted, that it still rests upon the earth and upon mankind. Moreover, it implies that there was a certain time when this curse came upon all, when it was first inflicted upon mankind and the earth. Whoever will take the trouble to investigate the matter will find so wonderful a harmony in the Scriptures upon these three points as will probably astound him, and convince him that the Scriptures are not of human origination, but that although written by various persons, and at various periods, during two thousand years, they are a unit in their testimony; and upon no subject is their testimony more positive, consistent and conclusive than on this subject of the curse, its effects upon man, the redemption from it, and its ultimate removal.

The curse upon mankind, as it is generally understood and preached, is a future curse of eternal torment—not a present curse. But according to the Scriptures it is a present curse, viz., death, which will be lifted in the future. Nor are we to think of this death-curse in the usual limited manner—as affecting a dying moment or a few dying hours, or days, or a few moments, at the time we expire or breathe out or lose the breath of life. On the contrary, to realize what this death-curse is, we would require to have before the mind's eye the first perfect man, with all his powers of mind and body—the image of his Creator in his mental qualities, and physically, as well as mentally and morally, "very good"; so pronounced by the very highest authority on the subject.—Gen. 1:31

The very brief scrap of history furnished us in Genesis, together with the fact that the flood completely obliterated all evidence of the genius and handiwork of the father of our race, and his earliest progeny, gives us no basis of calculations respecting his mental and physical abilities. For information we are thrown upon the fact that all God's work is "perfect," his own declaration (Deut. 32:4); and his further declaration that man "sought out many inventions," and defiled himself (Eccl. 7:29); and the fact that even under the curse, and under the unfavorable conditions in which man lived after being thrust out of the Garden of Eden—despite all these unfavorable conditions, so grandly perfect was this human organism that the father of humanity was sustained for the long period of nine hundred and thirty years.—Gen. 5:5

It is when we compare this physical vitality, unaided by large experience in the development of medicines and sanitary arrangements, with present conditions, and discern that with all of our advancement in science, under the light and experience of centuries, nevertheless today one-half of the population die under ten years, and as a whole the average of life is about thirty-three years, that we may judge how much physical vitality we have lost since the fall—how much the "curse" has affected us physically. And since we know that mental and physical powers are largely co-ordinated in man, so that the sounder the physical organism, all things being equal, the stronger and the truer should be the mental power and faculties, we may from this gain quite a respectful view of the mental caliber of father Adam, whom the great Creator pronounced very good, and considered worthy to recognize as his son, his mental and moral likeness.—Luke 3:38

And mental and physical perfection, under the conditions presented in the divine account of the creation, clearly and positively imply moral **perfection;** for we are to remember that, according to the Scriptures, moral obliquity and consequent degradation had not set in. Nor is it supposable that man, without moral elements to his mental development, would be described in the Scriptures as a "very good" man, or as an image of his Creator. To have created Adam perfect physically and perfect mentally, except in moral qualities, would have been to make him a very bad man, on the principle that the greater the abilities the greater the villain, unless the abilities be under moral control.

The death sentence, or "curse," pronounced against Adam, viz., "Dying thou shalt die" (Gen. 2:17, margin), was not merely against his muscles and physical frame—it included the entire man, the mental as well as the physical; and this also included the moral qualities, because they are a part of the mental. It is in full confirmation of this that we see today the man is a fallen being in every sense of the word; physically he is degenerated, and his average of life has fallen, under most favorable conditions, to thirty-three years; mentally and morally we also see that he is very deficient, yet possessing organs capable of much higher development than his short life will permit. Speaking of man's moral abilities the apostle declares, "There is none righteous, no, not one; . . . all have sinned and come short of the glory of God"—all are sharers of the original sin and its consequences.—Rom. 3:10, 23

Further, the apostle points out that father Adam,

when tried at the bar of God, was a wilful transgressor, and not a deceived one. (1 Tim. 2:14) He thus shows us that in moral quality he was capable of obedience to the divine requirements, for it would have been unjust on God's part to have tried and to have condemned for failure a being who, through defective creation, was incapable of standing the trial successfully, rendering obedience to his commands. The fact that Adam had a trial in which the issues were life and death everlasting, and the fact that his failure under that trial was wilful, and justly drew upon him the sentence of the great Judge to the full penalty of the law, must prove to every unbiased, logical mind that Adam was in every sense of the word perfect, and properly susceptible of trial.

And the fact that God, even after the ransom price has been paid, refuses to try mankind again before the same supreme and unimpeachable Court, and declares the reason to be that in a fallen condition we are incapable of a trial at his bar of absolute justice, and that by our best deeds none could be justified before him—all this proves conclusively, not only that the race has grievously fallen, but also proves that God would not have tried Adam at all had he not been much better than we are, and thoroughly fit for trial—a perfect man. It is in full accord with this thought that God proposes the judgment of the Church during this Gospel age, for the prize of eternal spirit being; and the judgment of the world during the Millennial age, for the prize of everlasting human perfection. "For the Father judgeth no man, but hath committed all judgment unto the Son."—John 5:22

Viewing man as a whole (mentally, morally and physically one) as the Scriptures do, we can see that the curse, the sentence of death, is in operation against every part and element of his being; and looking about us throughout the world, we find corroboration of this on every hand. As in the decay of physical powers, the weakest point with some is the stomach, with others the muscles, with others

Its Necessity—the Curse

the bones, so in viewing man as a whole, we find that in some the greatest loss, decay, depravity, has been mental, with others moral, with others physical, yet all are blemished in all respects; all were hopelessly "lost" under this curse. There can be no hope to any that he ever could recover himself out of these bonds of corruption in which we are born, as it is written, "I was shapen in iniquity, and in sin did my mother conceive me." (Psa. 51:5) This death-curse rests upon us from the moment of birth, and hence demonstrates the fact that it is not the result of our individual sins, but of inherited sins—a curse or blight which has reached us from father Adam by heredity.

It has been said that we are "born dying"; and how true this is all can testify; **dis**-ease, decay, aches and pains, weakness and sickness, are but the elementary processes of death working in us. Thus, if it were not for the blindness superinduced by Satan's deceptive misrepresentations of the divine plan, men would on every hand readily see clear manifestations of the fact of the curse, and the apostle declares, "The wrath of God **is revealed** against all unrighteousness," for the least unrighteousness is sin. (Rom. 1:18) The apostle does not say that in a future life and in flames of torment the wrath of God will be revealed, but he correctly states it as of the present life and of the present time, and to be seen by all whose eyes are open to see the true facts of the case. The wrath of God is revealed by every physician's sign, which indicates disease and death working in the race. The wrath of God is revealed by every undertaker's sign, which calls our attention to the fact that mankind is dying, that the wrath, the curse of God is resting upon the race. The wrath of God is revealed by every funeral procession, every hearse, every graveyard, every tombstone, and by every piece of crape and every badge of mourning. The wrath of God is not only revealed against the grossest of sinners, but against all unrighteousness, even the slightest. Hence there is no escape, for there is none righteous, no not one; and hence the infants as well as the gray-haired are subject to this "wrath," this "curse."

The Prophet Job, in his distress under the curse, the wrath, cried out, "O that thou wouldest hide me in sheol [oblivion] **until thy wrath be past** [over; then] thou shalt call and I will answer thee, for thou wilt have respect unto the works of thy hands." (Job. 14:13, 15) This time of wrath which has now lasted for six thousand years is to be brought to a close by the great Day of Vengeance, in which Justice prescribes that there shall be additional trouble upon mankind, because of the rejection of greater opportunities and privileges, and a failure to obey the laws of righteousness, to the extent that these laws have been discerned by Christendom. Hence this Day of Vengeance and of special wrath, additional to that which has prevailed previously, it is declared, will be "A time of trouble such as was not since there was a nation." The saints of God are assured that they shall be accounted worthy to escape all those things coming upon the world, and to stand before the Son of Man. They shall escape this special wrath, but they do not escape the general wrath which is revealed from heaven against all unrighteousness. They share this with the world, in many respects, and yet there is this finely drawn distinction, which the Scriptures clearly point out, viz:—

Those who accept Christ during this Gospel age, and who make full consecration of themselves to him, are reckoned as having passed from death unto life; as having escaped the wrath, the curse, "escaped the corruption that is in the world." (2 Pet. 1:4; 2:18, 20) True, they are still in the world, still subject to death, and may still share with the world the sickness, pain, sorrow, and trouble incidental to the curse, and from the worldly standpoint there is no difference; but from the divine standpoint, which is to be the believer's standpoint, there is a wide difference. Such are not reckoned any longer as dying because of divine "curse" or "wrath," but in view of their justification and subsequent presentation as living sacrifices their death is reckoned as a part of Christ's sacrifice. As the apostle expresses it, such are reckoned in death as dead with Christ, sharers in his sacrifice, and not as dying with Adam, like the remainder of the race. "If we be dead with Christ we believe that we shall also live with him." —Rom. 6:8

Likewise, our share in physical troubles and pains is the result of physical weaknesses, heredity, etc. The Lord assures us that whatever of this kind shall be permitted in the case of such, should not be regarded as manifestations of his wrath; but that all evils permitted to come against these shall by divine wisdom and love and power be overruled for their good, as disciplines to develop in them more abundantly his Spirit, and thus ultimately, as his children, to fit and prepare them for glory, honor and immortality—by working out in them the peaceable fruits of righteousness, and thus preparing them for a far more exceeding and eternal weight of glory. (Phil. 2:13; Rom. 2:7; Heb. 12:11; 2 Cor. 4:17; 2 Pet. 1:4-11) Nevertheless, in all these respects these walk by faith, not by sight. So far as outward sight is concerned, they have nothing more than the world; indeed, God's people may sometimes appear to have more difficulties, more trials, more troubles, more pains, than the natural man, with whom God is not yet dealing, because not yet brought into a condition of reconciliation and at-one-ment with him. Even this increased requirement of faith is of itself a blessing, a discipline, a development of character, a good fruit of the Spirit.

But we are viewing our subject—the necessity for atonement—from the standpoint of the world in general, all mankind. The curse, sentence, or verdict of the divine law against all imperfection is destruction. God created all things very good, and that is the only condition in which anything will ever be wholly satisfactory to him. The fact that for the time being he permits imperfect things—imperfect beings, and imperfect conditions—is no proof of a change of plan on the divine part: this period of imperfection is permitted, because divine wisdom has foreseen the possibility of a glorious outcome, and to this end God is "working all things after the counsel of his own will." (Eph. 1:11) He could, for instance, **have destroyed Satan, the** moment he became a transgressor—likewise the angels that fell, and man; and thus the generation of an imperfect race would have been avoided. But the divine plan, on the contrary, has been to permit the imperfect **and sinful for a time to take their own course in matters which shall not interfere with the grand outcome of the divine arrangement, that thus an illustration might be presented of the downward, degrading tendencies of sin, in Satan, the fallen angels and in mankind.**

The fall of mankind under the just penalty of death, destruction, was indirectly the result of Eve's lack of knowledge and her consequent deception, and involves, through heredity, many who have not wilfully and intelligently violated the divine law. This fact left the opportunity open for the exercise of divine love and clemency, and incidentally gave an illustration of the operation and co-ordination of the divine attributes, which could not have been so thoroughly manifested and exemplified in any other manner of which we can conceive. It was, therefore, a part of the original design of the Creator to reveal himself, the attributes of his character, to his creatures—not only to mankind, but also to the angelic hosts. Unquestionably, when the great plan of salvation shall be fully consummated, the heavenly angels as well as the reconciled of the world shall know of the divine character—wisdom, justice, love and power—in a much larger degree than was ever before appreciated, or than could have been appreciated, without the great lessons now being taught through the permission of sin, and the redemption promised under the divine plan, through Christ. This is intimated by the Apostle Peter, who assures us that "the angels desired to look into" these things —are deeply interested in them.—1 Pet. 1:12

As we have seen, the sentence upon mankind is an

Its Necessity—the Curse 413

absolutely just one and there would have been no room whatever for appeal from that sentence on the score of justice (it being admitted that Adam had a sufficiency of knowledge of his Creator to command his implicit obedience, and it being admitted also that it was but a just arrangement on God's part, that the life which would not be used in harmony with his righteous and benevolent arrangements should be forfeited, taken away). Nevertheless, we can readily see that God could have devised a different penalty in man's case, and that, too, without the violation of any principle of justice. We have proof of this in his dealing with the fallen angels. They were not put under a sentence of death; the penalty imposed upon them, on the contrary, was that they were **restrained**, and are still restrained, waiting for a final trial.—Jude 6

Similarly, God could have permitted man to live out these six thousand years, since his sin in Eden, without the impairment of his physical system, without putting him under sentence and power of death. Thus man, as well as the angels which kept not their first estate, might have been reserved alive unto the judgment of the great day, to have their cases finally disposed of. But God is not limited in his operations, and the same variety which we observe in nature, in that one flower differs from another flower in glory and beauty, and one creature differs from another creature, so, under what the apostle designates "the much diversified wisdom of God" (Eph. 3:10, Diaglott), God chooses one method of dealing with the angels who sinned, and another method of dealing with men who had become sinners. Divine wrath is manifested against both: a wrath of love and justice, which hates all sin, all evil, and will destroy it; but which will do all that can be done for such of the evil-doers as become loyal servants of righteousness, after having a large experience with sin and with righteousness, and their respective results.

In dealing with man God chose to exemplify the ultimate end of sin and sinners—destruction. This is testified in the various statements made to man, "The soul that sinneth it shall die"; "The wages of sin is death." That is to say, in these declarations made to man God is merely stating a general law, which ere long will be the absolute rule of all his dominion, —all creation, viz., that whatever is not perfect shall be destroyed, and that only which is perfect, **absolutely perfect, absolutely in harmony with the divine will and purpose, shall continue** to exist forever, a blessing to itself, an honor to the Creator, and a benefit to all his creatures.

But while man has been the illustration of the operation of this principle, so that every member of the human family has been cut off in death—"Death passed upon all"—nevertheless, it is not the divine purpose in thus making use of mankind as an illustration of the severity of divine justice, in the **extirpation of evil, to permit humanity to suffer on account of being thus used as an illustration.** On the contrary, it is the divine arrangement that mankind shall experience no less of divine mercy and favor and love than any other of God's creatures. Hence it is that in due time God provided redemption for all, fully adequate to the necessities of the case, that as by one man's (Adam's) disobedience the many became sinners, so by the obedience of one (Jesus) the many might become righteous.—Rom. 5:19

This does not say, nor does it mean, that the many must become righteous during this Gospel age or not at all: on the contrary, the Scriptural declaration is that it will be but a "little flock" that will become righteous during the present evil time—those only who are specially drawn of the Father and called to the high calling of joint-heirship with his Son. The residue of mankind will not even be called or drawn, until the Christ (head and body) has been lifted up both in sufferings and in glory, according to our Lord's own statement, "I, if I be lifted up, will draw all unto me." (John 6:44; 12:32) This universal drawing belongs to the coming Millennial age, not to the present nor to the past ages. It will not be the drawing of a few nor of a class, nor of a nation, as in the past, but the drawing of all mankind, redeemed with the precious blood.

Nevertheless, this drawing will not mean compulsion; for just as it is possible for the Father's drawing to be resisted in the present age, so that many are called but few will be chosen, so also it will be possible for the drawing of Christ to be resisted by the world of mankind in the next age. However, the Scriptures assure us that the way will be made so plain, and the conditions so reasonable, that only those who love sin, and deliberately choose it, after they have come to a knowledge of righteousness and of truth, will be amongst the resisters of that great Prophet, and be destroyed by him in the Second Death.—Acts 3:23

Viewing the divine dealings with mankind from the standpoint of the close of the Millennial age, we see that so far from the divine course working any unkindness toward mankind, the execution of the extreme penalty of the divine law against us, accompanied as it has been with the operation of divine mercy, through Christ, in ransom and restitution, has really been a great blessing. But this cannot be seen except from the one standpoint. From this standpoint we see not only the sorrow and trouble and pain, the dying and crying of the present time, the just penalty of transgression, its natural result, indeed, but we see also the redemption of man from sin and its curse, purchased by the Redeemer at Calvary, and to be accomplished by the same Redeemer subsequently—the Church being selected during this Gospel age, according to the divine program, to be his Bride and joint-heir in the Kingdom.

Severe as death, the penalty for Adam's sin, has been (including all the pain and sorrow and trouble of this dying state for the past six thousand years), we believe that man's portion has been more favorable than that of the angels who kept not their first estate, and who were not sentenced to death, and who, therefore, did not lose their vital energies in death, nor experience sickness or pain, but who have merely been restrained of their liberties, and of the fellowship of the holy. Had man been treated similarly to these fallen angels, and left in possession of his liberties in respect to the earth, etc., we can imagine what a terrible condition of things would have prevailed by the present time—how evil would have multiplied itself without restraints, how keenness and cunning in wrong doing would have increased the sorrows of earth. Even as it is, we can see that even the short lives of men suffice to develop a wonderful genius for selfishness, a wonderful wisdom for self-aggrandizement, and the oppression of fellow-creatures. When we consider that many of the millionaires of our day were poor boys, and that their accumulations of a hundred or two hundred millions of dollars were made in less than fifty years, what could we expect of such genius, if it had centuries for the scope of its operation? Carried to its legitimate result, it undoubtedly would have resulted in the enslavement and utter degradation, to bestiality, of a large proportion of the human family in the interest of the few master minds in cunning and avarice.

Viewing the matter from this standpoint, our hearts uplift in thankfulness to God that the form of the "curse" or sentence that came upon us was that which the Lord has permitted—dying thou shalt die. And if, in the meantime, our experiences, as a race, have been an object lesson, not only to ourselves, but to the holy angels and to the fallen angels, we may rejoice the more: and for aught we know it may be God's intention to use this one great lesson of the exceeding sinfulness of sin, and its unavoidable results, in other worlds of sentient beings not yet created. And who knows but that in the far distant future, instructors in righteousness for as yet uncreated billions will be drawn from among the worthy of earth's redeemed and restored race, who have had an actual experience with sin and who will be able to speak from experience, in guarding others against the least deflection from absolute obedience to the divine will.

An illustration of this principle, of overruling a disadvantage into a blessing to those who are used as an illustration, we see in Israel. As a nation, Israel was called out from the other nations, and used as a typical people. Their Law Covenant, while apparently an advantage, strictly speaking constituted for them a second trial, failure in which brought them under a second condemnation—apparently leaving them, as a people, more thoroughly condemned than the remainder of the world, whom God had already proposed (in his covenant with Abraham), should be **justified by faith** since none could be justified by works of Law. Israel's Covenant called for perfect works, and being unable through inherited weakness of the flesh to render perfect works, Israel fell under the "curse" or death-sentence of their own Covenant. Thus that Covenant which was ordained to life (which purported to give life everlasting) was found to be unto **death**. (Rom. 7:9-14) But although God thus used Israel as a typical people and as an illustration of the fact that no imperfect man can keep the **perfect** law of God, he did not permit this use of them, which involved their condemnation, to work their everlasting ruin; and consequently, when redeeming the remainder of mankind, his plan was so arranged that the same sacrifice by which all the race of Adam was redeemed by Christ, affected also the one specially favored nation, which under the Law Covenant was also the one specially condemned nation. (Rom. 2:11-13; 3:19-23) It was to this end that our Lord was born under the Law Covenant, in order that he might redeem those who were condemned under that law, with the same sacrifice by which he redeemed all the world of mankind, condemned originally in Adam.—Gal. 4:4, 5

We see then that the necessity for reconciliation between God and man, the necessity for their at-one-ment, lies in the fact that God himself is the source of life, and that if everlasting life be enjoyed by any of his creatures, it must be as his gift. "The gift of God is eternal life, through Jesus Christ our Lord."

(Rom. 6:23) According to the principles of the divine government and law, God cannot look upon sin with any degree of allowance (Hab. 1:13); he cannot condone sin, nor admit its necessity in any degree. Perfect himself, his decree is that none imperfect shall be recognized as his sons, for whom everlasting existence is provided. And hence, since man, through the fall, had not only come under a sentence of death, but additionally, had defiled, degraded, depraved himself, and largely obliterated the divine likeness from his mind and conscience, therefore the only hope for everlasting life lies in some power or way or agency through which two things can be accomplished: (1) The release of mankind from the **death sentence** inflicted by Justice; (2) the lifting up of mankind out of the degradation of sin and depravity to the conditions of absolute holiness and perfection from which he fell. If these two things can be effected, then there is hope. If they cannot both be effected, man has not the slightest hope of everlasting life. In vain do we look for help in the fallen human family, for although some are less fallen than others, less depraved, all have sinned, all have come short of the glory of God. If there were one righteous one, he might, indeed, give a ransom for his brother (for Adam and all condemned in Adam's transgression), and thus, under divine arrangement, become the savior (deliverer) of his race from the sentence; but none such could be found. "There is none righteous; no, not one."—Psa. 49:7; Rom. 3:10, 23

God, in his wisdom, had foreseen all this, and had provided for it all, before he began the creation of mankind, and in due time he manifested his plan for man's recovery from his blight of condemnation and depravity. When there was no eye to pity, and no arm to save, then God's arm brought salvation. The arm (power) of the Lord revealed, **stretched down from heaven for man's help out of the horrible pit** of death, and out of the miry clay of sin and depravity, was our Lord Jesus. (Psa. 40:2; Isa. 53:1) **Through** him God's declared purpose is—

Its Necessity—the Curse

(1) The ransom of mankind from the power of the grave, from the sentence of death, from the "curse," from the "wrath" that now rests upon the world. This ransom has been accomplished in the death of our Lord Jesus Christ: Divine Justice is fully met, and the whole world of mankind is reckonedly transferred to the Lord Jesus Christ, as his purchase, bought with the precious blood.

(2) He is now choosing out from the redeemed race the "little flock" of joint-heirs, who because of self-sacrificing devotion to him shall be **reckoned** as sharers in his sufferings and sacrifice, and be granted a share also in his heavenly glories and future work of blessing the world—the fruit of his sacrifice.

(3) The work of restitution is to be accomplished by this great Redeemer and his joint-heir, his Bride, the Church, during "the times of restitution of all things which God hath spoken by the mouth of all his holy prophets since the world began." (Acts 3: 19-21) And when the wilfully wicked, rejectors of the divine grace and mercy, under the terms of the New Covenant, shall have been destroyed by this great Mediator, Christ, and the remainder of the redeemed race shall be turned over to the Heavenly Father, perfect and complete, fully restored to his own likeness, and with increased knowledge of him and of righteousness and of sin—gained through the experiences of the present reign of sin, as well as under the reign of righteousness during the times of restitution—then the great work of Atonement will be complete. All who see this matter clearly can readily discern the necessity for the Atonement: that there can be no blessing of mankind except by bringing them into absolute harmony with their Creator; and that such a reconciliation necessitates first of all a redemption of the sinner—a payment of his penalty. For God must be just in justifying the sinners, else he never will justify them.—Rom. 3:26

In view of the foregoing we see clearly that the number atoned for by our Lord's sacrifice for sins—

the general lifting of the "curse" legally—gives no criterion by which we may judge the number who will by obedience of faith get actually free from sin and its curse and return to at-one-ment with the Father, by availing themselves of the opportunities opened to all by our dear Redeemer. There is no proposition on God's part, nor any reasonable ground for supposition on man's part, that divine favor and life everlasting through Christ will ever be attained by any except those who shall come into the fullest heart-harmony with God, and with all his laws of righteousness. We rejoice, however, that the knowledge of God's grace and other opportunities far better than are now enjoyed by the world shall in God's "due time" be extended to every creature.—1 Tim. 2:6

STUDY XV

"A RANSOM FOR ALL"
THE ONLY BASIS FOR AT-ONE-MENT

At-one-ment Impossible Without a Ransom—Secured but not Compelled—To be the Ransomer Became a Favor—The Significance of Ransom and Redeem—What Ransom was Paid for Man?—Justification by Faith thus Secured—"Ye are Bought with a Price."—By Whom?—Of Whom?—For what Purpose?—How Love Co-operated with Justice—The "Ransom for All" was not Taken Back—Fatherhood Rights of the First Adam Purchased by the Second Adam—Ransom not Pardon—Man's Death not a Ransom—False Reasoning of Universalist Theories—Justice not Obligated by the Ransom—The Only Name—The Mediator's Method Typed in Moses—Ransom, Substitution—Was a Different Plan Possible?

"There is one God, and one Mediator between God and men, the Man Christ Jesus, who gave himself a ransom for all, to be testified in due time."—1 Tim. 2:5, 6

AT-ONE-MENT between God and man was wholly dependent upon the presentation of an acceptable sacrifice for man's sins. Unless the divine sentence or "curse" could be lifted from mankind, it would stand as a perpetual embargo, to hinder man's recovery or restitution back to divine favor, fellowship and everlasting life. Under the divine law, the only word of God to man would be, You are a sinner; through your own wilful transgression in Eden you have brought your trouble upon yourself: I have pronounced the sentence of death against you justly, and I cannot remove that sentence without violating my own justice, the very foundation of my throne, my Kingdom. (Psa. 89:14) Hence your sentence must stand forever. It must be met by you unless an acceptable substitute takes your place under it.

We have seen clearly that the penalty or sentence against mankind was not eternal torture, but, as plainly and distinctly stated by the Creator to Adam, it was death. To suppose that it was any other penalty than death would be to suppose that God had dealt dishonestly with Adam and Eve in Eden—that he misinformed and deceived them. We have seen that a death sentence is a just sentence against sin— that life being a conditional grant, the Creator had full right to revoke it: but it requires no particular ability of mind to discern that an eternity of torture for Father Adam would not have been a just penalty for his partaking of the forbidden fruit—even attaching to that act of disobedience all the culpability of wilfulness and intelligence that can be imagined; much more, it would not have been just to have permitted such a sentence of eternal torture to be entailed upon the countless millions of Adam's posterity. But the death sentence, with all its terrible concomitants of sickness and pain and trouble, which came upon Father Adam, and which descended naturally through him to his offspring (inasmuch as an impure fountain cannot send forth a pure stream), all can see to be both reasonable and just—a sentence before which all mouths must be stopped; all must admit its justice—the goodness and the severity of God.

Knowing definitely the penalty pronounced against sin, we may easily see what Justice must require as a payment of that penalty, ere the "curse" could be lifted and the culprit be released from the great prison-house of death. (Isa. 61:1) As it was not because the entire race sinned that the sentence came, but because one man sinned, so that sentence of death fell directly upon Adam only, and only indirectly through him upon his race, by heredity—and in full accord with these facts Justice may demand only a corresponding price—Justice must, therefore, demand the life of another as instead of the life of

A Ransom for All

Adam, before releasing Adam and his race. And if this penalty were paid, the whole penalty would be paid—**one** sacrifice for all, even as **one** sin involved all. We have already seen that the perfect Adam, the transgressor, who was sentenced, was not an angel, nor an archangel, nor a god, but a man—in nature a little lower than that of angels. Strictest Justice, therefore, could demand as his substitute neither more nor less than one of Adam's own kind, under similar conditions to his, namely perfect, and free from divine condemnation. We have seen that none such could be found amongst men, all of whom were of the race of Adam, and therefore sharers, through heredity, of his penalty and degradation. Hence it was, that the necessity arose that one from the heavenly courts, and of a spiritual nature, should take upon him the human nature, and then give as substitute, himself, a **ransom** for Adam and for all who lost life through him.

Amongst the angels who had retained their first estate and loyalty to God, no doubt there might have been many found who would gladly have undertaken the accomplishment of the Father's will, and to become man's ransom price: but to do so would mean the greatest trial, the severest test to which loyalty to God could be exposed, and hence the one who would thus manifest his devotion and his loyalty and his faith would be worthy of having the very highest position amongst all the angelic sons of God, far above the angels and principalities and powers, and every name that is named. Moreover, it was a part of the divine purpose to make use of this opportunity to illustrate the fact that whoever seeks to exercise his own selfish ambitions (as Satan did), shall be degraded, abased, while, on the contrary, whoever shall most thoroughly humble himself, in obedience to the Heavenly Father's will and plan, shall be correspondingly exalted. God so arranged his plan as to make this feature a necessity; to the intent that in this manifestation of divine sympathy and love for the world, an opportunity might also be afforded for the manifestation of the love, humility and obedience of the Only Begotten of the

Father—his well-beloved Son, whom he delighted to honor.

As we have seen, our Lord Jesus (who, in his pre-human condition, we recognize as the archangel, the highest or chief messenger, the Logos, the Only Begotten of the Father, full of grace and truth) had up to this time been the agent of Jehovah in all the work of creation, and, as the first begotten, had been with the Father from before the creation of all others, and had known him intimately, had beheld his glory, and been the channel of his power. And inasmuch as he was already the first, the chief in the heavenly Kingdom, next to the Father, the apostle informs us that this work of redemption, this privilege of executing the divine will in respect to man was given to him as a mark of special confidence and as a favor because of the honors which according to divine law must attach to so great obedience, humility and self-sacrifice. (Matt. 23:12; James 4:10; 1 Pet. 5:6) With confidence in the Son and desiring his attainment of the high exaltation which would accrue as a result of that faithfulness, the Father gave the first opportunity to him, who had, in all the past, enjoyed pre-eminence in the divine plan, that thus he might continue to be the pre-eminent one— "that in all things he might have the pre-eminence: for it pleased the Father that in him all fullness should dwell. And having made peace through the blood of his cross, by him to reconcile all things unto himself—by him, I say, whether they be things in earth or things in heaven [fallen men and fallen angels, recovering and reconciling so many of each as, under fullest opportunity, will return to divine favor]."—Col. 1:18-20

The selection of a spirit being to become man's Redeemer does not imply that the sacrifice of a spirit being's existence was necessary as the redemption price of an earthly being's existence: quite the contrary. Divine Justice could no more accept the sacrifice of a spirit being for man than accept the sacrifice of bulls and goats as the ransom price. As the blood of bulls and goats could never take away sin, because they were of an inferior nature, so the death of angels or archangels could never have taken away Adam's sin, nor become a suitable atonement sacrifice for him, because these were not of his nature. It was man's life that had been forfeited through sin, and only a man's life could be accepted as the redemption price, the ransom price. It was for this cause that it was necessary that our Lord should leave the glory of his pre-human condition, and humble himself, and become a man, because only by becoming a man could he give the ransom price.

While the Scriptures point out that our Lord humbled himself in leaving the higher spiritual nature and in taking the lower human nature, they nowhere point this out as being our sin-offering. On the contrary he humbled himself thus, in order that he might become the sin-offering and pay our ransom price. The apostle distinctly points this out, saying, "Verily, he took not hold upon the nature of angels [as though referring to the angels which sinned] but he took hold on the seed of Abraham." Inasmuch as the children whom God had foreseen and purposed to redeem, and to deliver out of the bondage of sin and corruption, were partakers of flesh and blood, "he also himself took part of the same [flesh and blood, human nature]; that through death he might destroy him that hath the power of death, that is, the devil," and deliver them. (Heb. 2:14, 16) He states the matter most explicitly, saying, "As by a man came death, by a man also came the resurrection of the dead." (1 Cor. 15:21) The Apostle John bears similar testimony, saying, "The Word was made flesh." (John 1:14) To this agree also the words of our Lord Jesus, after he had come into the world and after he had reached manhood's estate; he said, "God sent not his Son into the world to condemn the world, but that the world through him might be saved." (John 3:17) He does not intimate that the world had yet been saved, or that anything had yet been done for the world's salvation, except the sending of the one who would redeem the world by the sacrifice of himself. The first step in the performance of his mission was, as our Lord declared—"The Son of Man came not to be ministered unto, but to minister [to serve others], and **to give his life a ransom for many.**" (Mark 10:45) Here we have proof positive that in the laying aside of the glory which he had with the Father before the world was, and exchanging the higher nature for the human nature, our Lord had not given his life as a ransom, but had merely made the preparation for that work which was immediately before him. This is further confirmed by the fact that it was as soon as he had reached manhood's estate, under the law, as soon as he was thirty years of age, he at once presented himself a living sacrifice, consecrating his life, laying it down, as represented in his symbolical immersion by John at Jordan.

There was fulfilled, as the apostle points out, the prophecy of old, "Lo I come (in the volume of the book it is written of me) to do thy will, O God." He had come to do the will of God, to offer the sacrifice for sins, and hence he had not previously offered it. In that act of his consecration he presented himself a living sacrifice to God's service, even unto death. Mark that at this particular point the apostle says he set aside the typical Law Covenant sacrifices that he might establish the second, the antitypical, the real sacrifice for sins, his own death (and his members) for the sealing of the New Covenant between God and men, by himself, the Mediator of the New Covenant. And our text tells us the same thing, that it was the "**man** Christ Jesus who gave **himself** a ransom for all"—not the prehuman **Logos**.

THE FIRST STEP IN THE PROGRAM

The apostle (Heb. 2:5-9) reviews the entire plan of God, and noting the divine promises of human restitution, quotes from the Prophet David (Psa. 8:4-8), that the divine plan ultimately is to have mankind perfect, as the lord of earth, controlling earth and its creatures, in harmony with the laws of the divine Creator, saying, "We see not yet all things put under him [man—as indicated in the prophecy]." We see not yet man in the image of God and lord of earth; but we do see the divine purposes to this end already begun. We see the first step in this program, viz., "We see Jesus, made a little lower than the angels for the suffering of death, crowned with glory and honor [the perfection of human nature] that he by the grace of God **should taste death for every man** [and thus make possible human restitution]." We see the work of man's salvation thus begun by Jehovah, in providing a suitable ransom price for our redemption, one equal in glory and honor and absolute human perfection with the first man, Adam; one who, to this end and for this purpose, had left the glories of a higher nature, and been made lower than the angels, although previously possessed of a higher nature than they. We see this one provided for the very purpose of "tasting death for every man." We see that he took the human nature **"for the suffering of death"**—the very penalty that was against our race. Seeing this, we can rejoice that the good purposes of our Heavenly Father for our ransom and restitution, and full reconciliation to himself, have been amply arranged for, and upon a plane of absolute justice, by which God can be just and yet be the justifier of them that believe in Jesus. Thus the sacrifice which our Lord Jesus gave for man's sin was not a spiritual one, which would not have been a proper, acceptable sacrifice because it would not have been "a **corresponding** price"—in every particular the exact ransom price for Adam.

THE SIGNIFICANCE OF "RANSOM" AND "REDEEM"

This brings us to the consideration of the word **ransom**, which in the New Testament has a very limited and very definite signification. It occurs only twice. Once in our Lord's own description of the work he was doing, and once in the apostle's description of that completed work—our text. The Greek word used by our Lord is **lutron-anti**, which signifies, "a price in offset, or a price to correspond." Thus our Lord said, "The Son of Man came . . . to give his life a ransom [**lutron-anti**—a price to correspond] for many." (Mark 10:45) The Apostle Paul uses the same words, but compounds them differently, **anti-lutron**, signifying, "a corresponding price," saying, "The man Christ Jesus, gave himself a ransom [**anti-lutron**—corresponding price] for all, to be testified in due time."—1 Tim. 2:6

There is no room for quibbling or disputing the meaning of these texts. Only by handling the Word of God deceitfully can any be blinded to the force and real meaning of this, the Lord's testimony to the work which has been accomplished by our great Mediator. And the more this thought of a ransom—a "**corresponding price**"—is considered, the more force does it seem to contain, and the more light does it shed upon the entire work of the Atonement. The thought, and the only thought, contained in it is that as Adam, through disobedience, forfeited his **being, his soul**, all his rights to life and to earth, so Christ Jesus our Lord, by his death, as a **corresponding price**, paid a full and exact offset for Father Adam's soul or being, and in consequence for all his posterity—every human soul—sharers in his fall and in his loss.—Rom. 5:12

This same thought is abundantly expressed in many other Scriptures, which speak of our Lord's work as that of redeeming, purchasing, etc. We have directed special attention to the word "ransom," **anti-lutron**, because it presents the thought in the purest and most unmistakable form. The words, "redeem," "redeemed," "redeemer," and "redemption," while they contain the thought of a price being paid, contain the additional thought of setting free, or liberating those for whom the price was paid. Hence these words, both in the English and in the original, are sometimes used in connection with the sacrifice, or giving of the price of redemption, and at other times used with reference to the setting at liberty of the redeemed ones, their deliverance. And the many foes of the doctrine of the **ransom,** of whom the chief is Satan, sometimes with great cunning attempt to divert the attention away from the price given for man's release from the curse of death, by pointing out those texts of Scripture in which the words "redeem" and "redemption" are applied merely as relating to the full deliverance of mankind from death. By calling attention to the deliverance, and "handling the Word of God deceitfully," they attempt to obscure the fact that the future deliverance, and all the blessings that now or in the future will come to mankind by divine grace, are of the Son, and through or by means of the **ransom-sacrifice** of himself, which he gave on our behalf, and which was "finished" at Calvary.—John 19:30

The translators of our Common Version English Bible unwittingly aided these opponents of the ransom, by using the word "redeem" to translate Greek words which have considerably different meanings. That the English reader may have this matter clearly before his mind, we will here cite all the various Greek words rendered "redeem," "redeemed" and "redemption," and following each will give the definition furnished by the learned lexicographer, Prof. Young, in his Analytical Concordance, as follows:—

The word "redeem" is sometimes used as the translation of the Greek word **agorazo.** This word is defined by Prof. Young to signify, "to acquire at the forum." Still more literally, it would signify, to purchase in the open market; for the root of the word, **agora,** signifies **market-place** and is so used repeatedly throughout the Scriptures: Matt. 20:3; Mark 12:38; Luke 7:32; Acts 16:19. The following are all the instances in which the word **agorazo** is translated "redeemed" in the New Testament:—

"Thou wast slain, and hast **redeemed** us to God by thy blood."—Rev. 5:9

"And no man could learn that song, but the hundred and forty and four thousand which were **redeemed** from the earth."—Rev. 14:3

"These were **redeemed** from amongst men, being the first fruit unto God and unto the Lamb."—Rev. 14:4

The thought in each of these cases is that of public purchase; and all the other uses of this word **agorazo**, throughout the New Testament, emphatically support a most commercial signification. The word occurs in the New Testament in all thirty-one times. In the above three instances it is rendered **redeemed**, in thirteen instances **bought**, in fifteen instances **buy**. We call especial attention to the signification of this word, because the tendency to deny that there was a purchase of our race effected by a **price** given for man's release from the "curse" is prevalent and a growing one—very subversive of the true "faith, once delivered to the saints."

Another word rendered "redeem," "redeemed," and "redemption," is related to the above, and formed out of it by the addition of a prefix, **ex**, which signifies **out of**—exagorazo. Prof. Young gives to this word the definition, "to acquire out of the forum." Still more literally, **to publicly purchase and take possession of.** The only uses of this word in the New Testament are as follows:

"Christ hath **redeemed** us from the curse of the Law, being made a curse for us." (Gal. 3:13) The apostle is here pointing out that Christians who had been Jews and had therefore been under the Jewish or Law Covenant, had not only been purchased from under its sentence, but were also released from its dominion. The word **agorazo** signifies the purchase, and the prefix **ex** signifies the release by that purchase, so that they were no longer under the dominion of the Law.

"God sent forth his son, made of a woman, under the Law, to **redeem** them that were under the Law [Covenant], that we might receive the adoption of sons." (Gal. 4:4, 5) This is a similar statement to the foregoing, and signifies the purchase of the Jewish people from under the dominion of the Law, and the liberation of believers from it, that they might become sons of God.—Compare John 1:12

A Ransom for All

"See that ye walk circumspectly, not as fools, but as wise, **redeeming** the time, because the days are evil." (Eph. 5:15, 16; Col. 4:5) This is a similar use of the word **exagorazo**: the Lord's people realize that they are in the midst of evil, the tendency of which is to absorb their energy, influence and time in things sinful or foolish, or at least unprofitable, as compared with the more weighty interests which lie closest to their hearts, as children of God. We are, therefore, to **purchase** and **to secure out** of the evil time, and apart from these unfavorable influences, as large a proportion of time as may be possible for devotion to higher interests—our own spiritual sustenance and strengthening, and for the assistance of others in spiritual things. Such purchase will cost us something of self-denial, of gratification of our own natural appetites and tendencies, and something also of the good opinion and fellowship of others, who will "think it strange" that we run not with them to the same excesses as formerly.—1 Pet. 4:4

Another Greek word is also rendered "redeemed," —namely **lutroo**. Prof. Young defines **lutroo** to signify "to loose by a price"—that is, to **set free by the payment of a price**. The basis or root of this word is **lutron**, which, as noted above with **anti**, used either as a prefix or a suffix, signifies a **corresponding price**.

This word, **lutroo**, occurs three times in the New Testament, as follows:—

"We trusted that it had been he which should have **redeemed** Israel." (Luke 24:21) The apostles were disappointed at our Lord's death, and declared this disappointment by saying that they had expected that the Lord would have set Israel at liberty from the Roman yoke, by the payment of a price. They had not yet been endued with the Holy Spirit, and did not understand the length and breadth, the height and depth of the **divine plan**, by which not only Israel but the whole world was **redeemed**, not only from the Roman yoke, but from Satan's yoke, and from the great prison-house of death, by the ransom price which our Lord gave and which was finished in death.

"Our Savior, Jesus Christ, who gave himself, that he might **redeem** us from all iniquity." (Titus 2:14) The price which our Lord gave on behalf of mankind is not only intended to secure to them an awakening from the tomb, in God's due time, during the Millennium, and an opportunity then to come into harmony with God on the terms of the New Covenant; but more than this, it means to those who hear the good tidings now, a message of present relief from the thraldom of iniquity—that we should no longer be servants of sin, but should become the servants of him who died for us, who bought us with his own precious blood.

"Ye know that ye were **redeemed,** not with corruptible things, as silver and gold, from your vain conversation, received by tradition from your fathers; but with the precious blood of Christ, as of a lamb without blemish and without spot." (1 Pet. 1:18, 19) The thought in this text is the same as in the preceding one. It relates not so much to our ultimate deliverance from death, in the resurrection, as to our present **loosing** from an evil course, vain conversation, foolish talking, and iniquity in general. This liberty was **purchased** for us by the blood of Christ, as well as the grander liberty of the resurrection, which is yet future. Without the payment of the ransom price, without the satisfaction of Justice, God could not accept us as sons, could not therefore deal with us as with sons, could not seal us as his sons with the spirit of adoption into his family, and hence these various agencies of his grace, which now are open to believers, and which are to us **the power of God** unto salvation, breaking in our hearts the power of sin, and establishing instead the mind or spirit of the Lord, as the ruling power, could not have come to us.

Another Greek word rendered "redemption" is **lutrosis.** Prof. Young gives as its definition, "a loosing"—literally, **setting free,** deliverance. This word does not contain the thought of a price being paid, and hence it should not have been rendered by our

A Ransom for All

English word, redemption, but rather by the word "deliverance." It occurs twice:—

"She, coming in that instant, gave thanks likewise unto the Lord, and spake of him [the babe Jesus] to all them that looked for **redemption [deliverance]** in Jerusalem." (Luke 2:38) Anna spoke to those who were looking for deliverance in Jerusalem—expecting freedom from the Roman yoke, but not necessarily understanding that the greater deliverance was to come by a payment of a ransom price.

"Christ being come an high priest . . . neither by the blood of goats and calves, but by his own blood, he entered in once into the holy place; having obtained eternal **redemption [deliverance]** for us." (Heb. 9:11, 12) The apostle is not referring to how our Lord obtained the eternal redemption of deliverance, and hence makes no reference here to the price paid: he refers merely to the present and future deliverance of God's people, and not to the method by which that deliverance was secured, prior to our Lord's entrance into the holy place—the sacrifice of himself as man's ransom price.

Another Greek word, translated "redeemed" in the New Testament, is **poieolutrosin**. Prof. Young defines its meaning to be, **"to make a loosing,"** i. e., **to set at liberty**, to deliver. It occurs but once.

"Blessed be the Lord God of Israel; for he hath visited and **redeemed** his people [literally, wrought redemption for his people]." (Luke 1:68) The preceding verse shows that this expression was a prophecy: things not completed are here mentioned as though they had been accomplished: the first step toward Israel's deliverance had been taken, and it was spoken of joyously as though the entire matter were already accomplished. This word does not contain the thought as to how the deliverance will be secured: other Scriptures show us that it is secured by the payment of a corresponding price, a ransom, and is to come through the setting up of the Kingdom of God. This word should not have been translated "redeemed" but rather **delivered**, as a

434 The Atonement Basis

guard against confusion of thought by the English reader.

Another Greek word, improperly rendered "redemption" is **apolutrosis.** It contains no thought respecting a purchase price, but simply signifies **deliverance,** setting free. Prof. Young defines its meaning to be **"a loosing away."** The word occurs ten times, and is only once properly translated "deliverance." Note the following:—

(1) "Then look up and lift up your heads, for your **redemption** [**deliverance**] draweth nigh." (Luke 21:28) There is no reference here to the ransom or the conditions precedent to the Church's deliverance, but merely to the deliverance itself.

(2) "Being justified freely by his grace, through the **redemption** [**deliverance**] that is in Christ Jesus (Rom. 3:24) The apostle does not in these words refer to the ransom, but merely to the deliverance which the Lord's people have, now reckonedly and by and by prospectively, in the resurrection. He is treating the matter from God's standpoint: believers are freely, unconditionally justified; aside from any works of merit on their part. This is accomplished through the **deliverance** which God has provided in Christ Jesus our Lord. In the following verse the apostle proceeds to show how this deliverance was effected, saying, "Whom God hath set forth to be a propitiation [literally, a mercy seat or channel of mercy] **through faith in his blood** [the sacrifice, the ransom price given for the sins of the whole world]."

(3) "Even we ourselves [the faithful Church] groan within ourselves, waiting for the adoption, to wit, the **redemption** [**deliverance**] of our body [the Church, the body of Christ, which is to be glorified with the head in due time]." (Rom. 8:23) Nothing in this statement has the slightest reference to the redemption accomplished at Calvary, the purchase-price: it refers purely and solely to the **deliverance** of the Church, which is to be a part of the result of the redemption finished at Calvary—the ransom.

(4) "Christ Jesus who of God is made unto us wisdom and righteousness and sanctification and **redemption [deliverance]**." (1 Cor. 1:30) Nothing here has any reference to the redemption-price paid at Calvary. The apostle is speaking, not of what our Lord did for us, but of what he is yet to do for us. He is our wisdom in that we are to lay aside our own wills, and accept his will, and thus have the spirit of a sound mind, and "walk in wisdom." He is our righteousness, in that, as our representative, he gave himself a **ransom for all,** and now in his righteousness represents all those who come unto the Father by him. He is our sanctification, in that, through his merit, we are accepted of the Father as (reckonedly perfect) living sacrifices, while really it is the power of Christ in us that enables us to present ourselves living sacrifices, and to walk in his footsteps, and to fulfil our covenant. He is our deliverance (mistranslated "redemption"), in that the fact that he lives, who, by the grace of God, bought us with his precious blood, is the guarantee that we shall live also; that he will, in due time, deliver from the bondage of corruption, death, his Church, which he purchased with his own blood. The deliverance, and not the purchase, is here referred to. But it is because he purchased that he has the right to be to any, wisdom, justification, sanctification, deliverance.

(5) "He hath made us accepted in the beloved, in whom we have **redemption [deliverance]** through his blood, the forgiveness of sins, according to the riches of his grace." (Eph. 1:7) The apostle does not here refer to the redemption purchase at Calvary. On the contrary, he is speaking of our acceptance with the Father, and declares that this acceptance with Jehovah is based upon something which he did for us in the Beloved One, our Lord Jesus, and through whose blood (the sacrifice, the ransom) we have **deliverance.** The construction of the sentence shows that the apostle means that our **deliverance** is from the sentence of sin, death, for he explains this **deliverance** as being "the forgiveness of sins." The sense of

the passage, then, is this: The Heavenly Father, who had already in his mind predestinated the adoption of a "little flock" to be sons on the plane of the divine nature, and joint-heirs with his first begotten and well-beloved Son, our Lord, took the steps of grace necessary to the accomplishment of this his purpose toward us. He made us accepted in the Beloved; for in the Beloved, through his blood, through his sacrifice, we have deliverance from the divine curse and wrath—the forgiveness of our sins, from which we are made free or justified.

(6) "The earnest of our inheritance unto the **redemption** [deliverance] of the purchased possession." (Eph. 1:14) The possession which Christ **purchased** by the sacrifice for sins as man's substitute includes mankind in general or so many as will accept the favor on the gospel conditions, as well as the Church, the Bride. The time for the deliverance is in the Millennial Kingdom and the Church is to be delivered first—"early in the morning." But the earth was part of man's original estate and was purchased by the same sacrifice once for all: hence it, too, is to be delivered from its share of the curse and shall become as the garden of the Lord—Paradise. The **purchase** is accomplished but the **deliverance** waits for God's "due time."

7) "In whom we have **redemption** [deliverance] through his blood, even the forgiveness of sins." (Col. 1:14) This statement is similar to the foregoing. We, the Church, already have **deliverance**, that is, the forgiveness of our sins, and hence harmony with the Father. The word "redemption" here has no reference to the sacrifice for sins, but merely to its effect upon us, **setting us free** from our sins. The apostle, however, does not ignore the sacrifice, but declares that our deliverance from the bondage and control of sin is through the efficacy of our Lord's blood—his death, his sacrifice for sins, the ransom paid.

(8) "Grieve not the Holy Spirit of God, whereby ye are sealed unto the day of **redemption** [deliver-

A Ransom for All

ance]." (Eph. 4:30) There is no reference here to the redemption sacrifice finished at Calvary. Yet not until that sacrifice was finished, and its merits presented in the holy of holies, and accepted by the Father, did the Holy Spirit come upon any to seal them as sons of God. But now these who have been sealed are to maintain this seal of sonship, this begetting of the divine nature, not to lose it. The sealing of the Spirit is the first-fruit of the Spirit, and is all that is communicated during this present life: for the full measure of the blessing of the divine nature we must wait until the time appointed of the Father, "the day of **deliverance**," the Millennial Day, in which day the Scriptures declare, concerning the Church, the Bride of Christ, "God shall help her early in the morning." (Psa. 46:5) Whoever loses the Holy Spirit and its seal will have neither part nor lot in the first resurrection, in the morning of "the day of [complete] deliverance" from the power of sin and death.

(9) "For this cause he is the mediator of the New Covenant, that by means of death for the **redemption** [**deliverance**] of the transgressions that were made under the first [previous] covenant, they which are called might receive the promise of eternal inheritance." (Heb. 9:15) Once more a faulty rendering partially obscures the meaning; but when the thought is seen to be **deliverance**, all is clear. To Israel our Lord's death meant more than to the Gentiles. It meant not only redemption from Adamic transgression, and its penalty, death, but it meant additionally to the Jew **deliverance** from the "curse" or penalty of the Law Covenant, which rested upon that nation, because of failure to comply with its terms. The Israelites were under the "curse" which came upon Adam, just the same as the remainder of mankind; but additionally they were under the "curse" of their Law Covenant, instituted through Moses, its mediator, at Sinai. It is to this double "curse" upon that people that reference is made in the hymn which says:

> "Cursed by the Law, and bruised by the fall,
> Christ hath redeemed us, once for all."

The Atonement Basis

(10) "Others were tortured, not accepting **deliverance**." (Heb. 11:35) This is the one instance in which the translators have properly rendered this word: they probably tried to render it "redemption," and found that it would make rather strange reading to say, "not accepting redemption," and then translated it properly—"deliverance."

In the Old Testament, the words, "redeem," "redeemed," "redeemer" and "redemption" are generally good translations of the original Hebrew words; for instance: **Gaal** signifies, to free—by avenging or repaying.—Young

"I know that my **Redeemer** liveth."—Job 19:25

"They remembered . . . the high God, their **Redeemer**."—Psa. 78:35

"Who **redeemeth** thy life from destruction."—Psa. 103:4

"One of his brethren may **redeem** him: either his uncle or his uncle's son may **redeem** him . . . or if he be able he may **redeem** himself."—Lev. 25:48, 49

"Ye have sold yourselves for naught and ye shall be **redeemed** without money."—Isa. 52:3; Compare 1 Pet. 1:18

"The **Redeemer** shall come to Zion."—Isa. 59:20

Our object in citing the instances in which **redemption** appears in our English New Testament, without the original Greek word containing a thought of a ransom-price, is to guard the reader against the deceptive methods of certain sophistical writers and teachers. Denying the **ransom**, denying that the world was **purchased** by our Lord's death, these are prone to cite passages where the word **redeem** is improperly used for **deliver**, and then give the inference that **deliver** is the only meaning of **redeem**, in every instance. In view of the carelessness of our translators the only safe and proper method to pursue in a case such as this where much depends on the exact meaning of a word, is to get at the original word and its meaning.

We have demonstrated that in many instances the Holy Spirit has expressed through the New Testament writers the thought of **purchase** of our race and of **corresponding price** paid, in the very strongest terms, interpretable only on the lines of **commercial transaction**, or the **substitution** of the purchase price for the thing bought. We have shown also that in other cases where the word used merely means **deliverance** nothing conflicts with the thought that such deliverance will be secured as a result of a **ransom** [**anti-lutron**, corresponding price], but that generally the context explicitly refers to the deliverance as being thus secured.

But while the Scriptures are thus explicit in their assurance that our Redeemer **bought** the world with his own life, "his own precious blood," it is merely in order to give God's people "full assurance of faith," letting them know that the remission of the death penalty is not a violation of God's justice but its satisfaction by his love. It also assures us of the **unchangeableness** of divine law, which could not be broken, but instead provided redemption at so great a cost. This assurance that God's love and justice operate in fullest harmony, gives us confidence that the same principles will continue to rule the universe forever—satisfies us that the "wrath," the "curse," will be lifted from all who come into harmony with God through Jesus the Mediator, and that all who do not avail themselves of this grace will be swallowed up of the Second Death—for "the wrath of God abideth on them."—Acts 3:23; John 3:36; Rev. 22:3

But so far as the redeemed are concerned it matters not how God's love and justice arranged the matter of our forgiveness, because to them it is a free gift, to be had only by accepting it as such. We cannot purchase it, nor can we compensate God for this "gift." The question then arises, If it is a "gift" to us, why should we trouble to investigate, or why should the Lord be particular to reveal the fact that this gift was secured to us at a **cost**, at a **price**, by the death of Christ? and why should the Scriptures so particularly point out to us that his death was the **exact** price, the **corresponding** price, that was due for our sins? We answer, that God thus explains to us the details of his operations on our behalf, to the intent that we may the better understand him and his laws, and their co-ordination and operation. He so explains, in order that we may understand that he is not abrogating or setting aside his own sentence against sin—that he is not declaring sin allowable, permissible, excusable. He wishes us to realize that his justice is absolute, and that there can be no conflict by which his love could dominate or overpower and overthrow the sentence of justice; that the only way that his just sentence against sin and **sinners could be set aside was by meeting the requirements of justice with a corresponding price**— "a ransom." Man had sinned, man had been sentenced to death, man had gone into death. There could be, therefore, no hope for man except as love and mercy might provide a substitute for father Adam. And a substitute, as we have seen, must be of the same nature as Adam, human nature; the substitute must be equally free from sin, free from the curse, free from wrath; similarly holy, similarly harmless, similarly separate from sin and sinners, similarly approved of God, as was Adam before his transgression.

We have seen that our Lord Jesus was made flesh —(not sinful flesh) but holy, harmless, separate from sinners.* We have seen that the man Christ Jesus was thus **a perfect man**, the counterpart of the first man, Adam, and thus we see that he was all ready to be our Redeemer, our ransom, to give his life and all human rights for the purchase, the redemption, of Adam and the race of Adam, which lost life and all human rights in him. We have seen that our Lord, "the man Christ Jesus," did consecrate, did sacrifice, did give up on man's behalf **all that he had.** This he clearly set forth in his teaching on this sub-

---

*Page 103.

ject. He represented himself as the man who found a treasure hidden in a field, and who went and **sold all that he had,** and bought that field. (Matt. 13:44) The field represents the world of mankind, as well as the earth itself. (Eph. 1:14) In this world of mankind our Lord saw a treasure—prophetically he saw the result of the redemptive work, the deliverance of many from the bondage of corruption into the full liberty of sons of God (the Church in this age, and the worthy of the world in the age to come). It was in view of this treasure that the field was bought. Speaking of the result of the ransom, and of the work of redemption, as it shall finally be accomplished by the close of the Millennial age, the Prophet speaking of our Lord says, "He shall see of the travail of his soul, and shall be satisfied." (Isa. 53:11) Our Lord was fully satisfied to give his life, and all he then had, to purchase the world.

WHAT RANSOM WAS PAID FOR MAN?

What our Lord did for us, what price he gave on our behalf, what he surrendered, or laid down in death, since it was a **corresponding price,** "a ransom for all," should correspond exactly to whatever was man's penalty. Our Lord did not go to everlasting torment; hence we have this indisputable testimony that everlasting torment is not the wages of sin prescribed by the great Judge, but merely a delusion, foisted upon mankind by the great Adversary, and those whom he has deluded. So surely as that which our Lord suffered in man's room and stead, as man's substitute, was the full penalty which men would otherwise have been obliged to suffer, so surely this is proof positive that no such punishment as eternal torment was ever threatened or inflicted or intended. Those who know the testimony of God's Word recognize its statements to be that "Christ **died** for our sins"; that he **"died** the just for the unjust, to bring us to God"; that "he is the propitiation [**hilasmos**—

satisfaction]* for our sins [the Church's sins], and not for ours only, but also for the sins of the whole world"; that "the Lord hath laid on him the iniquity of us all, and by his stripes [the things which he suffered in our stead—self-denial even unto **death**] we are healed." What harmony and consistency is seen in this Scriptural view of matters; and how utterly inconsistent are the unscriptural delusions of Satan, handed us by tradition and popularly received!— 1 Cor. 15:3; 1 Pet. 3:18; 1 John 2:2; Isa. 53:5, 6

"The wages of sin is **death**," "The soul that sinneth it shall **die**," say the Scriptures. (Rom. 6:23; Ezek. 18:4) And then they show us how completely this wage has been met for us, in the declaration, "**Christ died** for our sins, according to the Scriptures," and rose again for our justification. (1 Cor. 15:3; Rom. 4:25) His **death** was the **ransom price**, but his providing the ransom price did not give justification. First, our Lord must present that ransom price before the Father in our behalf; and this he did when "He ascended up on high," there to appear in the presence of God for us. He then and there imputed to the Church the merit of his ransom sacrifice. Then comes **justification** as a result, (1) of the ransom-sacrifice, and (2) its application for all men who will believe and obey him. Thus the resurrection and ascension of our dear Redeemer were necessary adjuncts to make his death-sacrifice available.

"Without the shedding of blood there is no remission [of sins]." (Heb. 9:22) Throughout the Law dis-

---

*Two Greek words are rendered "propitiation." **Hilasmos** is correctly rendered "propitiation" in two texts (1 John 2:2; 4:10), but **hilasterion** is incorrectly rendered "propitiation" in Rom. 3:25: it signifies **propitiatory**, i. e., place of satisfaction or propitiation. The "Mercy Seat" or covering of the Ark of the Covenant was the **place** of making satisfaction—the propitiatory or **hilasterion**; but the Priest in sprinkling the blood of atonement, the blood of the sin-offering, on the **hilasterion** accomplished **hilasmos**, i. e., he made satisfaction or propitiation for the sins of the people.

pensation God emphasized this feature of his arrangement by requiring the blood of bulls and of goats; not that these could ever take away sins, but that in due time they might be recognized as types or illustrations of better sacrifices, through which sins are blotted out and canceled. The expression, "shedding of blood," signifies simple death, life poured out, yet points to a sacrificial death, and not what is sometimes termed a natural death—though strictly speaking no death is natural. According to nature man was to live: death is the violation of the law of man's being, resulting from transgression, and its accompanying "curse" or sentence.

So far as Justice was concerned, the Jews might have put our Lord to death in any other form, and the requirements of Justice have been equally well met. The necessary thing was surrender of his innocent soul (being) as an off-set or in exchange for a guilty soul (being) whose existence was forfeited through transgression. Neither was it necessary, so far as the ransom feature was concerned, that our Lord's person should be wounded, and his blood literally shed or spilled on the ground. The penalty for sin was **death**, the cessation of being, and when that was accomplished the penalty was met. The requirement of the crucifixion and the pierced side were for other considerations.

The blood falling upon the earth, at the foot of the altar of sacrifice, represented that not only mankind had been purchased, but that the earth itself was included, and the blood was sprinkled upon it. The shame and ignominy of the public crucifixion, as a malefactor, was necessary, because our Heavenly Father had decided that the testing of the obedience of our Lord Jesus should be to the utmost; not only was he tested to see whether he would be willing to become a man, but additionally, whether he would be willing to **die as man's ransom-price** or substitute, and additionally, whether or not he would be willing to suffer the very extreme of ignominy, and thus prove to the last degree his worthiness of the greatest exaltation at his Father's hands.

The apostle presents the matter in this light, for after telling us of how he left the heavenly glory for our sakes, and became a man, he adds, "And being found in fashion as a man he humbled himself and became obedient unto death—**even the death** of the cross. Wherefore, God hath highly exalted him, and given him a name [title, honor, dignity] which is above every name"—the Father's name or title excepted.—Phil. 2:8, 9; compare 1 Cor. 15:27

Every reference of Scripture to **justification by faith**—that we are justified by the blood of Christ, etc., is a testimony corroborative of the foregoing—that "God was in Christ reconciling the world unto himself, not imputing their trespasses unto them," but imputing them unto "him who died for us and rose again." (2 Cor. 5:19, 21; 1 Thess. 4:14; 5:10) The guilt of the sinner was borne by the Redeemer, who gave the full corresponding price for our sins, that all seeking righteousness might be accepted as righteous, through the merits of his sacrifice. (Rom. 5:17-19) The fact that we needed to be **justified** or made right, proves that we were wrong, unrighteous, unjust in God's sight. The fact that men could not justify themselves by works was demonstrated by Israel under their Law Covenant, and proves that this wrong or sin was in the very natures of men; and this rendered it necessary that we should be redeemed and justified through the merit and sacrifice of another—a spotless Redeemer.

Justified signifies to be **made right;** but we are not made right or perfect **actually:** we are merely **reckoned** right or perfect because of our faith in and **acceptance of the righteousness of Christ and his sacrifice on our behalf. Everywhere throughout the** Scriptures this power of **justification** on the part of our Redeemer is attributed to his sacrifice on our behalf. That our own works could not justify us, or make us acceptable before God, see Gal. 2:16; Rom. 3:27, 28. That the Law could not justify those under **it,** see Gal. 5:4; Rom. 3:20. That faith in Christ's finished work alone justifies, see Gal. 2:17; 3:13, 14; Rom. 4:24, 25, etc.

Various Scriptures more or less distinctly speak of our being washed or cleansed or purified from sin. All such Scriptures are in support of the doctrine of the ransom, because it is distinctly stated in the same connection that the cleansing power is "the blood of Christ"—the merit of our Lord's sacrifice.— See 1 John 1:7; Rev. 1:5; 1 Cor. 6:11; 2 Pet. 2:22; Titus 3:5; Heb. 9:14; 1 Pet. 1:19

Justification is symbolically represented as a robe of righteousness, of pure linen, clean and white, by which the Lord covers the blemishes and imperfections of all whom he accepts through faith in his precious blood. All endeavors toward righteousness on our own part, aside from the merit of Christ, are likewise symbolically represented as "filthy rags" of our own righteousness. (Isa. 64:6) True, certain Scriptures refer to our efforts toward righteousness, by obedience to the divine commands, as a cleansing work, progressing throughout our entire Christian course, as the apostle expresses it, "Having our bodies washed with pure water," and cleansing of the Church by the "washing of water by the Word": and these are very proper presentations of the cleansing of our hearts, the "putting away of the filth of the flesh": and these Scriptures are very properly understood to refer to a daily and a life work. But all these cleansings of thoughts, words and acts—all these endeavors to bring our mortal bodies into closer conformity to the will of God in Christ, are based upon our previous acceptance of Christ and our justification through faith in his blood. The Scriptural thought is that from the time we consecrate ourselves to God, all our imperfections are covered from the Lord's sight through the merit of the ransom-sacrifice, provided by Jehovah's grace, and laid hold of and appropriated by faith. Since only that which is **perfect** could be acceptable of God, and since we, with all our efforts and washings, would still be imperfect, it is manifest that our acceptance with the Father is under the covering of the robe of Christ's righteousness, his perfection reckoned or applied or imputed to us. Thus we are first "accepted in the beloved" (Eph. 1:6); and then daily manifest our devotion to righteousness and our desire to please the Lord by efforts toward holiness.

How frequently the Scriptures refer to our Lord as our sin-offering, "the Lamb of God that taketh away the sin of the world!" (John 1:29) All the sacrifices of the Law, all the blood shed upon Jewish altars, pointed forward to this great sacrifice for sin slain on our behalf; for, as the apostle assures us, the blood of bulls and of goats could never take away sin—only the antitypical sacrifice could do this, "the precious blood." On this subject of the sacrifice for sins, as presented in the New Testament, see Heb. 9:12; 10:10; Eph. 5:2; 1 Cor. 5:7; 1 Pet. 2:22-24; 2 Cor. 5:21—Diaglott.

That this sacrifice was for us, the Church, and for all mankind, is likewise very clearly set forth in the Scriptures: "He, by the grace of God tasted death for every man," the just for the unjust, to bring us to God—to open up for us and for all mankind a way of return or reconciliation to harmony with the Heavenly Father, and thus indirectly to open up for us the way back to eternal life, the Father's favor or blessing or gift for all those who are truly his children. On this point see the following: 1 Thess. 5:10; Rom. 5:8; 1 Cor. 15:3; 2 Cor. 5:14, 15; John 10:15; 11:50-52; 1 Pet. 2:24; 3:18.

That it was the death of the man Christ Jesus, his "blood," that secured our release from sin and death, is most unequivocally stated in many Scriptures, and can only be repudiated by denying the inspiration of the Scriptures, or by "wresting the Scriptures," or by "handling the Word of God deceitfully." See 1 Pet. 1:2; Acts 4:12; 20:28; Rev. 5:9; 1:5; Rom. 5:9; Heb. 13:12.

"YE ARE BOUGHT WITH A PRICE" BY WHOM? OF WHOM? WHY? AND FOR WHAT PURPOSE?

"Ye are **bought** with a price; be not servants of men."—1 Cor. 7:23

A Ransom for All

"Thou hast redeemed [**bought**] us to God by thy blood."—Rev. 5:9

"There shall be false teachers among you, who shall privily bring in damnable heresies, even denying the Lord that **bought** them."—2 Pet. 2:1

The testimonies of Scripture, to the effect that man was "bought," are very unequivocal; and, as we have already shown, the Greek word from which they are translated is **agorazo**, which signifies a **public purchase**. The questions naturally arise, (1) By whom was man purchased? (2) Of whom was man purchased? (3) Why was man purchased? We consider these questions in their order.

(1) The Scriptures already cited clearly and unequivocally assert not only that mankind was purchased, but that the Lord Jesus Christ himself was the purchaser; and furthermore, these and other Scriptures assure us most distinctly that the purchase price was the precious blood of Christ—the sacrifice of his own life, the death of the man Christ Jesus, who gave himself a ransom [**anti-lutron**—a corresponding price] for all. Considering this question already indisputably proven, we proceed to the next.

(2) Of whom was man purchased? Opponents of the truth sneeringly inquire whether or not the Lord purchased us from the devil; and assert that there was no one else to whom the price could be paid: for according to the false reasoning of those who deny the **ransom**, God would not be a party to such a transaction. Their claim is that God was ever anxious for man's fellowship, and all along has done all in his power to effect man's reconciliation and recovery from sin and death. They reason therefore that God would not demand a ransom price, before permitting man's release. We reply, that such views are wholly contrary to the Scriptural teaching, which, while representing that God is love, and that he has sympathy for the sinner, declares also that God is just, and that man having been justly sentenced, cannot be justly released from that sentence in any other manner than by the payment of a ransom price for him.

The Atonement Basis

While the Scriptures declare that Satan is identified with the infliction of the penalty, death, saying, "As the children are partakers of flesh and blood [human nature], he likewise took part of the same, that through death he might destroy him that hath the power of death, that is, the devil," and elsewhere speak of Satan as being the "prince of this world," nevertheless they nowhere indicate that he has a title to rule authoritatively in the world. (Heb. 2:14; John 14:30) On the contrary, the Scriptures declare Satan to be the usurper, who, taking advantage of man's fallen condition, has blinded his mind toward God, and by deceiving man has enslaved him through ignorance, superstition and his own weaknesses. Satan's identity with sin constitutes his power of death. Had it not been for sin, Satan could have had no dominion over mankind. It was because of wilful sin that man was cast off from divine favor; but it was subsequently, when he did not wish to retain God in his thoughts, that God gave him over to a reprobate mind, etc. (Rom. 1:28) The highest authority, therefore, that Satan could claim in connection with the race would be the power of a usurper and the weakness of his slaves.

Moreover, since the divine sentence went forth, "Thou shalt surely die," Satan and any other agency of evil is **permitted** to co-operate in the carrying out of this divine decree. Thus does God sometimes cause the wrath of man and sometimes the wrath of evil spirit beings, to work out his wonderful plans, and unintentionally to praise him. (Psa. 76:10) But God has never recognized Satan as the owner of the race. The race was God's creation, and owed its all to him, but because of a failure to recognize him, and to render obedience, it came under the sentence, the curse, of divine law, as unworthy of life, and there it rests.

It was divine Justice which smote our first parents with the curse of death, and it is under the sentence of divine Justice that the race still remains dead. Nor can there be a hope of life for any, except through the redemption which is in Christ Jesus.

Since divine Justice was the Judge whose sentence forfeited man's life, therefore to divine Justice the ransom price must of necessity be paid, in order to secure the release of the culprit Adam, and his race sentenced in him.

Satan's power, though willingly exercised by him, could not be exercised were it not permitted by the great supreme Judge Jehovah, and Jehovah would not have permitted the great calamity of **death** to be inflicted upon mankind through Satan's agency or otherwise, except as a just penalty for sin—the penalty of Jehovah's violated law. Satan's power, like that of a hangman, is a delegated "power of death." The hangman is merely the servant of the law, to execute its penalties; and Satan, as the servant of the law laid down by the supreme Judge of all creation, is permitted and used for a time, as the executioner of the sentence pronounced: "The wages of sin is death," "dying thou shalt die."

If a prisoner's ransom or fine were to be paid, it would not be offered to the jailer or executioner, but to the Court whose sentence demanded it. So likewise the ransom for sin could not be paid to Satan (though to some extent he serves as an executioner of the penalty) but must be paid to the power which condemned sin, which decreed the penalty, and ordered the execution of the guilty.

Thus would reason answer us, that the **ransom-price for man's sin should be paid to "God, the Judge of all."** Now let us inquire, What say the Scriptures respecting the sacrifice of Christ, the offering which he made? Do they say that it was made to Satan or to Jehovah God? We answer that in all the types of the Jewish dispensation, which foreshadowed this better sacrifice, which does take away the sin of the world, the offerings were presented to God, at the hands of the priest, who typified our Lord Jesus. See Lev. 4:3, 4, 24, 27, 31, 34, 35; 5:11, 12; 9:2, 6, 7; Exod. 30:10; 2 Chron. 29:7-11, 20-24.

This answers our question emphatically, and we need no further testimony on the subject. But if further and direct testimony is desired, it is found in the words of the apostle, viz., "If the blood of bulls and of goats . . . sanctifieth to the purifying of the flesh, how much more shall the blood of Christ, who, through the eternal spirit, **offered himself without spot to God** . . . and for this cause he is the mediator of the New Covenant."—Heb. 9:13-15, 26; 7:27; 10: 4-10, 12, 20; Eph. 5:2; Titus 2:14; Gal. 1:4; 2:20; 1 John 3:16; John 1:29; 1 Pet. 1:19; 1 Cor. 10:20; Rom. 12:1

Thus we establish before our minds the scripturalness of this proposition, that God did require and did accept the death of Christ as man's ransom sacrifice.

(3) Why was man purchased?

Because in us, as fallen and imperfect creatures, the divine qualities of justice, wisdom, love and power are very imperfect: some find it more difficult than do others to grasp the reasonableness of the divine method of requiring a ransom, and accepting it. Those who cannot reason the matter out satisfactorily may very properly, and should, acknowledge and accept the testimony of the divine Word, irrespective of their ability to fully comprehend the why and the wherefore of it. This is the safe and proper course. Nevertheless, let us offer some suggestions which may help some to grasp the subject. As imperfect fallen creatures, in us these various qualities, wisdom, love, justice and power are continually in more or less antagonism with each other; but not so with our heavenly Father: in him each of these qualities is perfect, and in perfect accord with the others. There is no clash. Wisdom first surveyed the field, and laid out the best plan for man's salvation, with the full consent of divine justice, love and power. Under wisdom's direction, man was placed at once under a law, the penalty of which was the forfeiture of his existence, and all the train of woes accompanying death. Wisdom foreknew man's fall, through inexperience, but felt justified in view of the beneficial lessons, etc., in laying out the course of divine providence and dealings as revealed in the Scriptures.

A Ransom for All

As soon as man violated the divine law, Justice stepped forward, pronouncing him a rebel, who had come under the sentence of death, and drove him from Eden, from the source of subsistence previously arranged for him, and delivered him over to Satan, to be buffeted by evil circumstances, and to the intent that the full penalty of the violated law might be inflicted—"Dying thou shalt die." While this element of the divine character (Justice) was dealing with man, the Love element was not indifferent, but it was powerless, for two reasons: First, it could not oppose Justice, could not hinder the execution of the sentence, could not deliver man from the power of Justice, because it is the very foundation of the divine government; secondly, Love could not at that time interfere to relieve man, by paying the ransom-sacrifice for sin, because that would have been in opposition to the plan already marked out by infinite Wisdom. Thus divine Love and divine Power were held for the time, unable to relieve mankind, and compelled to assent to the Justice of his execution and to the Wisdom which permitted it to proceed through six thousand years of groanings, tribulation—death. In harmony with this, Love did not move to man's release, except to encourage and instruct him through promises and typical sacrifices, foreshadowing the method by which Love eventually, in Wisdom's due time, would accomplish man's rescue. Thus Love waited patiently for the auspicious moment when, under Wisdom's direction, it might act, and later might call to its aid divine Power.

That moment for Love to act finally came, in what the Scriptures term "the fullness of time" (Gal. 4:4), "in due time" (Rom. 5:6), when God sent forth his son as "the man Christ Jesus," that "he by the grace [favor, bounty, mercy] of God should taste death for every man." (1 Tim. 2:5; Heb. 2:9) Not until then was the divine Love manifested to mankind, although it had existed all along; as we read, **"Herein was manifested the Love of God,"** "in that while we were yet sinners, Christ died for us."—1 John 4:9; Rom. 5:8

By exercising itself in harmony with the law of God, and by meeting the requirements of that law, divine Love did not conflict with divine Justice. Love's method was not an attempt to overrule and oppose the sentence, nor to interfere with its full execution, but to provide a substitute, a ransom, for man. By meeting for man the death-penalty inflicted by Justice, Love brought release to mankind from the Adamic curse (death) which divine Justice had inflicted. This was divine Love's triumph, no less than the triumph of divine Justice. Love triumphed in offering the ransom-sacrifice, Jesus, to Justice—the element of God's character which enforces his righteous decrees and their penalties.

Nor is Love's triumph yet complete. It has accomplished the ransom, but its design is to accomplish more, viz., to effect a **restitution** for all of mankind, willing after experience to return to loyalty to God and his righteous law. But as Love waited more than four thousand years, under the direction of divine Wisdom, before bringing the ransom-sacrifice, so must it wait for nearly two thousand years more, after the ransom-price has been paid, before the great work of restitution shall even begin. (Acts 3:19-21) But Wisdom permits Love in the meantime to operate upon a special class, the "little flock," the elect of this Gospel age—to take out from amongst the redeemed "a people for his name"—Christ's Bride and joint-heir, the Church.

The necessity for the purchase of the race by Christ lay then in the fact that Father Adam had **sold** himself and his race into sin (and its wages or penalty, death), for the price of disobedience. (Rom. 7:14; 5:12) He needed to be **bought** back from the slavery of sin; and the payment of the ransom-price was necessary before any could be released from the sentence or start anew to prove themselves worthy of life everlasting.

But now let us take a still larger view of this purchase, and note that our Lord Jesus became not only theoretically but actually the owner, controller and father of the race, by reason of paying its ransom-price: in this **purchase** he took the place of Father

A Ransom for All

Adam, who had **sold** the race. As the race was **sold** by Adam through sin, in self-gratification, in disobedience to God, so the race was **bought** by the man Christ Jesus, by the sacrifice of himself in obedience to the Father's will—a corresponding price or ransom for Adam. The Scriptures present this thought, saying, "Christ both died and rose and revived—**that he might be Lord** both of the dead and the living." (Rom. 14:9) It was by virtue of our Lord's death that he became the master, ruler, father of the race, and obtained power to deal with the race as with his own children, freed from the curse of the divine sentence by his own sacrifice.

It is in this sense of the word that our Lord has become the second Adam—because he took the first Adam's position, as head of the race, by purchasing, redeeming it, with his own life. But as it was the **man** Christ Jesus who gave himself as the ransom-price, it could not be the man Christ Jesus who would be the father of the race. The **man** Christ Jesus laid down all that he had for the redemption of the **man** Adam and his race, a full corresponding price, a man for a man. The race of Adam not having been born at the time of his transgression, was not directly, but indirectly, sentenced, and consequently needed not to be directly, but indirectly purchased. An unborn seed in the loins of the man Christ Jesus became the offset or corresponding price for the seed of Adam unborn at the time of his transgression.

THE PRICE NOT TAKEN BACK

As we have already seen, the Scriptures clearly teach that our Lord was put to death in **flesh**, but was made alive **in spirit;** he was put to death **a man,** but was raised from the dead **a spirit being** of the highest order of the divine nature: having finished the work for which he had become a man, and having performed the service acceptably to the Father, he was raised from the dead to exceeding honor, and dignity, far above angels, principalities and powers, and every name that is named.

Nor could our Lord have been raised from the dead **a man,** and yet have left with Justice our ransom-price: in order to the release of Adam (and his condemned race) from the sentence and prison-house of death, it was necessary, not only that the **man** Christ Jesus should die, but just as necessary that the **man** Christ Jesus should never live again, should remain dead, should remain our ransom-price to all eternity.

For our Lord Jesus to have been raised a man would have implied two evils: (1) It would have implied the taking back of our ransom, which would have left us as much under sentence of death as before. (2) It would have implied to him an everlasting loss of the higher nature which he had left in order to become a man, and to be our Redeemer; and thus it would have implied that faithfulness to God on his part had resulted in his everlasting degradation to a lower nature. But no such absurdities and inconsistencies are involved in the divine arrangement. Our Lord humbled himself, and became **a** man, and as a man he gave up his life, the **ransom-price** for the fallen man; and as a reward for this faithfulness, the Heavenly Father not only restored him to conscious being, but gave him a nature not only higher than the human, but higher also than his own previous nature, making him partaker of the divine nature, with its superlative qualities and honors. In his present exalted condition death would be **impossible**—he is now immortal.

Since the man Jesus was the ransom-price, given for the purchase of Adam and his race, it could not be that the man Jesus is the Second Adam, the **new** father of the race instead of Adam; for the **man** Jesus is dead, forever dead, and could not be a father or life-giver to the world.

He who now owns, by purchase, the title of father to the human family, is the risen and glorified Jesus, partaker of the divine nature—this is the Second

A Ransom for All

Adam. As we have already seen,* our Lord Jesus in the flesh was not the Second Adam; he was not a father of a race, but merely came to purchase Adam and his race, and thus to become the father; and it took **all that he had** to effect the purchase, and nothing was left. This is the Scriptural thought, as presented by the apostle: "The first man is of the earth, earthy, the second man [the Second Adam] is the Lord from heaven [at his second presence, during the Millennium] . . . As we have borne the image of the earthly [Adam] we [the Church, joint-heirs with Christ, and sharers of the exceeding great and precious promises in the divine nature—Rom. 8: 17; 2 Pet. 1:4] shall also bear the image of the heavenly [—the Second Adam]." "And so it is written, the first man Adam was made a living soul; the last [second] Adam was made a **quickening spirit;** howbeit, that was not first which was spiritual, but that which was animal, and afterward that which is spiritual."—1 Cor. 15:45-48

Carrying further our question respecting why the race was bought, we have the apostle's testimony that by that purchase our Lord Jesus became (that is, acquired the right to become) the mediator of the New Covenant. (Heb. 8:6; 9:14-16) The New Covenant is an arrangement which God provides, by and through which he can have mercy upon the fallen race. The New Covenant could not go into effect without a mediator. The mediator must guarantee to God certain things on behalf of mankind. First of all he must redeem man, by paying the full ransom-price, and this sacrifice, which our Lord Jesus made, is therefore termed "the blood of the covenant," by which the covenant becomes effective, operative. Having purchased the world of mankind from under the condemnation which rested upon them, through sin, that he might seal the New Covenant and make it operative, the Mediator is fully prepared and fully authorized to do for the purchased race all that he can do by way of bringing them back to full human perfection, and into absolute har-

---

*Page 137

mony with God—that then he may present them blameless and irreprovable before the Father, in love, no longer needing the intervention of a special covenant of reconciliation, nor a mediatorship. But that work, so far from being yet accomplished, is only begun—hence the world has not yet been accepted by the Father, and it will involve all the restitution work of the Millennial age to fit and prepare the willing and obedient for the full harmony of complete reconciliation with the Father.

Meantime, during this Gospel age, a little handful of the redeemed race is called, and those who hear the divine call and approach the Father through faith in the Mediator and his work are **reckonedly** accepted as perfect, in order to permit them to present themselves, with their Redeemer, as living sacrifices in the service of the Father and his plan, and thus to develop in them the likeness of God's dear Son— to the intent that if willingly and gladly they suffer with him they may also be glorified with him by and by, and made associates and joint-heirs with him in the Millennial work of blessing the world under the terms of the New Covenant. These, be it remembered, are exceptions to the remainder of mankind: these, the "elect" of the Gospel age, are reckoned as the **"brethren"** of Christ, the "Bride" of Christ, the "Church which is his **Body**," but never called "children" of Christ. These are accepted of the Heavenly Father as sons, and begotten by the Word of truth and the spirit of that Word to the heavenly nature. These, as we have seen, may properly recognize Jehovah as their Father, because directly begotten of him, and thus these are "brethren" of Christ Jesus.—1 Pet. 1:3

For the world in general, however, the divine plan is somewhat different: instead of justifying them by faith, and then having them begotten to the divine nature, etc., they wait over until the Millennial age, and then, instead of being begotten of Jehovah to a new nature, they get back their old nature, the human nature, freed of its blemishes and corruption through sin. The hope of the world is **restitution** to

A Ransom for All

"that which was lost" in Eden. (Matt. 18:11; Acts 3: 19-21) God's provision for the world is just what we have seen in the ransom: the man Christ Jesus **laid down his human perfection, and all the** rights and privileges which that implied, to redeem for mankind "that which was lost"—the human perfection lost in Eden, the human dominion and all the rights and privileges of man, including his privilege of fellowship with God and everlasting life. These things which were purchased for mankind are the things which in due time are to be offered to all mankind under the New Covenant.

The fact that this Gospel age has been used of the Lord in selecting the "body of Christ," means to the world that instead of our Lord Jesus, the great Head of the Church, reserving to himself alone the office of **father** or life-giver to the world, he has associated with himself a "little flock," who have his own likeness, and who have participated in the sufferings of this present time, and who are to be sharers in the glory to come, and with him to constitute the great Prophet, the great Priest, the great King, the great Life-giver or Father to the world of mankind—to give life to whosoever will receive it, under the terms of the New Covenant. It is in harmony with this thought that the Scriptures declare one of our Lord's titles to be "the Everlasting Father." He has not yet fulfilled this office in any sense or degree. But he who bought the world at the cost of his own life has in his own power, by divine arrangement, the full right, title and authority to communicate to so many as will receive it, on his terms, all that was **lost** and all that was **bought** again of life and human rights and perfections, with an increase of knowledge.

Moreover, as being the legitimate father of the race and as giving them a life which had cost him his own, we find that the Scriptures imply that the race of mankind is fully in the hands of the Lord Jesus, to deal with them absolutely; and to judge of their worthiness or unworthiness of eternal life. This, which he will do for the world as its Father, during the next age, our Lord Jesus already does for his

Church, his spouse, his Bride, during this age; and herein the apostolic proposition is illustrated, that as the Heavenly Father is the head of Christ, so Christ is the head of the Church; as the husband, he is the head of the wife and of the family. Accordingly we read, "The Father judgeth no man, but hath committed all judgment unto the Son." (John 5:22) The betrothed Bride of Christ has no standing with the Father except in and through her beloved Bridegroom. Her requests are made in his name, through his merit, and must continue so to be made, until that which is perfect is come, when she shall be received into glory—the full liberty of the sons of God, through the first resurrection.

Similarly, the world of mankind, the children of Christ, must all report to him, as their Head, their Father, nor will they have any intercourse with the Heavenly Father, nor be recognized by him at all, until after the Millennial age shall have restored and brought back to perfection those who will avail themselves of those privileges. But at the close of the Millennial age, when our Lord Jesus shall deliver up the Kingdom to God, even the Father, then also shall they be introduced to and come under the direct control of the great, grand Father of all, Jehovah Almighty.—1 Cor. 15:24

From this standpoint may be seen why our Lord Jesus is called the Father of the redeemed and restored race, but was not recognized as the Father of Adam or his children previously, although he was the direct creator of Adam—as it is written, "Without him was not anything made that was made." The difference lies in the fact that in the original creation the **Logos** was the agent of Jehovah, and performed a work wholly without expense to himself; while as the Second Adam he will be giving to men life-rights at his own cost, bought with his own precious blood.

RANSOM NOT PARDON

The failure to discern the distinction between ransom and pardon has led to considerable confusion of thought on the subject. Christian people of general intelligence will quote texts relative to our being ransomed from the tomb, redeemed from death, bought with a price, even the precious blood of Christ, etc., and in the same breath they speak of the Father's gracious pardon of all offenses. Seemingly few think, though many must know, that pardon and ransom express exactly opposite thoughts.

The following primary definitions are from the Standard Dictionary:—

Redeem—To gain possession of by paying the price.

Ransom—The amount or consideration paid for the release of a person held in captivity, as a prisoner or slave.

Now contrast with these the signification of

Pardon—To remit the penalty of; to let pass.

Webster—"To refrain from exacting the penalty. In Law—To release from a punishment that has been imposed by sentence."

Notice here also the definition of another word which though closely related to **pardon** is not exactly the same, viz.—

Forgive—To release from punishment—to cease to cherish resentment towards.

"The law knows no forgiveness."

The most ordinary mind must discern that the thought expressed by "redeem" and "ransom" is opposed by and irreconcilable with the thought expressed by the word **pardon**. But since all of these words are used in the Scriptures in reference to God's dealings with fallen man, many Bible students think of them as used carelessly and synonymously in holy writ: and they then conclude that they may take their choice and either attach the definition of "pardon" to the words "ransom" and "redeem" or **vice versa** the definitions of "ransom" and "redeem" to the words "pardon" and "forgive." This procedure is far from "rightly dividing the word of truth:" it is confounding two separate and distinct matters, and the result is confusion. With many the difficulty seems to be that they do not want and therefore do not seek for the truth on the subject—fearing that their **no-ransom** theories would thereby be condemned.

Nothing can be clearer than that God did not **pardon** Adam's transgression and remit its penalty: the facts all about us, in the groaning and dying creation, no less than the testimony of God's Word concerning "wrath of God revealed"—the "curse" of death as the wages of original sin, all testify loudly that God did not pardon the world—did not remit its sin-penalty under which it has suffered for over six thousand years. He who confounds the **justification** of sinners through the merit of the **sin-sacrifice** of Christ, the sinner's substitute or ransomer, with **pardon** without payment, has not had his senses exercised properly. Had God **pardoned** Adam he would have restored him to the privileges of Eden and its life-sustaining orchard, and he would be living yet, and his numerous family would not have died for "one man's disobedience."

If at any time God were to come to man's rescue and **pardon** him, it would imply his full release from all the blight, disease, pain and death: it would mean full restitution to all that was lost. Evidently then God has not pardoned the original sin, but still holds the resentment of his holy law and sentence against the sinner. There is even no outward evidence to the world that they have been redeemed, ransomed. Only believers yet know of this and they receive it, not by sight, but by faith in the Lord's Word; its many declarations to this effect we have already cited. The sight-evidences proving the **ransom** will be discernible during the Millennium, when the work of restitution is under way—when the Redeemer begins the exercise of his purchased rights as the Restorer.

The words **forgive** and **pardon** are used not in respect to the world and its **original sin**, but in respect to those who through faith in the Redeemer and his work are reckoned as having passed from death unto life—from sentence to justification. The great Mediator who **bought them**, and who bought the charges which were against them, freely forgives them and starts them afresh on trial for life—under the spirit of the divine Law and not under its letter. And more than this forgiveness of the past, he continues to forgive them and to pardon all their offenses (which will not be wilful so long as they have his new spirit or mind—1 John 3:9; 5:18)—counting all such unwilful blemishes of thoughts, words and deeds as a part of the original sin and its depravity, still working in their flesh through heredity. Similarly the Heavenly Father is said to have **mercy** upon us, to **forgive** our trespasses, and to extend his **grace** (favor) to us; but the explanation is that all his grace is extended to us through our Lord Jesus' sacrifice: we are "justified freely by his grace **through the redemption** that is in Christ Jesus: whom God set forth to be a propitiation [satisfaction] through faith in his blood—to declare his righteousness for the remission [forgiveness] of sins." (Rom. 3:24, 25) Again, it is declared, "We have redemption through his blood, the forgiveness of sins, according to the riches of his grace."—Eph. 1:7; Col. 1:14

"We were reconciled to God by the death of his Son," i. e., God **ceased to resent our sins,** because our ransom price had been paid, as provided by himself, who so loved us that he gave his Son to redeem us. Thus, too, "God was in Christ reconciling the world to himself, **not imputing** their trespasses **unto them**" (but unto his beloved Son, who freely gave himself as our substitute). The sins were imputed to mankind until Jesus died; then God **forgave,** i. e., ceased to impute **to us** what had been paid by our Redeemer or Substitute. God did not **pardon,** i. e., **"refrain from exacting the penalty,"** but "laid upon him [our Redeemer] the iniquity of us all." (Isa. 53:6) "He bore [the penalty of] our sins in his own body on the tree." (1 Pet. 2:24) And thus we see how God forgave us freely **"for Christ's sake"**—because he paid the penalty which was the full satisfaction of justice.—1 John 1:7; 2:12; Eph. 4:32; Acts 4:12; 10:43; 13:38; Luke 24:47

Let it not be misunderstood that God **compelled** the just one to die for the unjust. Justice could not inflict the punishment of the guilty upon the innocent unless the innocent one **freely gave himself** as a substitute for the guilty. This our Lord Jesus did. The Scriptures declare that he laid down his life of himself; not for fear of divine wrath; not because compelled; but "for the joy that was set before him [the joy of obedience to the Father, the joy of redeeming and restoring mankind, and of bringing many sons to glory] he endured the cross."—Heb. 12:2

The Greek words (**apoluo, aphicmi** and **aphesis**) translated "forgiveness," "forgiven" and "forgive," in the New Testament, have the same significance as the corresponding English words: "To release from punishment, to cease to cherish resentment towards." But let us mark well that the meaning is not as some seem to infer—to send away **without an equivalent**, as the English word **pardon** would imply. It is not that God will let the sinner go unconditionally, but, as Scripturally declared, God will let go the prisoners out of the pit (out of death), because he has found a **ransom.** (Job 33:24) The man Christ Jesus **gave himself** a ransom (a corresponding price) for all. (1 Tim. 2:6) Therefore all that are in their graves (prisoners in the pit) shall hear his voice and come forth, in due time—when the Redeemer shall "take to himself his great power and reign."

Though the word **pardon** does not occur in the New Testament, a Greek word of nearly the same meaning does occur—**karazomai.** It signifies, **to forgive freely.** We will give some illustrations of the use of this word, from which it will be seen that it does not oppose but confirms the statement that our Father does not pardon, or **unconditionally** set sinners free from sin's penalty. The word **karazomai** occurs in all only twelve times, as follows:—"**Forgiving** one another . . . even as Christ **forgave** you" (Col. 3:13); "When they had nothing to pay he frankly **forgave** them both"; "He to whom he **forgave** most." —Luke 7:42, 43

A Ransom for All

Here are four instances in which free forgiveness or **pardon** is meant. But notice, it is not Jehovah, but Christ Jesus and the disciples who do the **free forgiving**. Our Lord Jesus was in the very act of paying the ransom price of Simon, Mary and others, and realizing that Justice would be satisfied by his act, he, as the **purchaser**, could freely forgive them. The very object of his purchasing sinners was, that he might **freely** release them from sin's condemnation. Had our Lord Jesus been unwilling to **pardon** those whom he had purchased with his own blood, had he still held against them the wages of Adam's sin, his sacrifice would have been **valueless** to them; it would have left all as they were—"cursed"—condemned. On the other hand, had the Father **pardoned** us, Christ's death would have been useless, valueless, as it would have accomplished nothing.

All will admit that God is just; and if so, he did not inflict too severe a penalty on man when he deprived him of life. Now if that penalty was just six thousand years ago, it is still a just penalty, and will be just for all coming time. If the penalty was too severe and God **pardons** the sinner (releases him from further continuance of the penalty) it proves either that God was at first unjust, or is so now. If it was right six thousand years ago to deprive mankind of life because of sin, it would always be wrong to restore the life unless the pronounced penalty were justly canceled by the payment of an equivalent price. And this could only be accomplished by the willing sacrifice of another being **of the same kind**, whose right to life was unforfeited, giving himself as a substitute or ransom.

> "Forever firm God's Justice stands,
> As mountains their foundations keep."

This very principle of justice which underlies all of our Father's doings, is the ground of our strong confidence in all his promises. The Scriptures declare that he is the same yesterday, today and forever, that with him is no variableness neither shadow of turning. (James 1:17) If he were so changeable as to condemn the race to death in Adam's day, and six thousand years after were to revoke his own decision, what assurance could we have that in six thousand years, more or less, he might not change again, and remand us to the prison-house of death by revoking the pardon of some or of all? As a race of sinners we have no foundation whatever for hope of a future everlasting life except in the fact that by God's grace Christ died for us and thus satisfied the claims of Justice against us.

So then, so far as Jehovah is concerned, we are **forgiven** through his own provision—through Christ. And so far as our relationship to the Lord Jesus, who **bought** us, is concerned, he freely **pardons** all who would come unto the Father by him. And so far as we are concerned, the results attained by God's plan are most favorable—to us it amounts to the same as though the Father had **pardoned** us unconditionally and without a ransom, except that a knowledge of the **fact** enables us to reason with God, and to see how, though our sins were as scarlet, we are made whiter than snow, and how God is just while justifying and releasing us. Thus God has furnished us a **sure** foundation for faith and trust.

DOES NOT DEATH CANCEL MAN'S DEBT?

When once it is recognized that "the wages of sin is death"—not eternal torment—there is with many a tendency toward false reasoning on this subject, which evidently is abetted by the great Adversary. This false reasoning proceeds to say, If the wages of sin is death, every man who dies pays the penalty of his sin: consequently, the argument is, there would be no necessity for a Redeemer and a ransom price— each one ransoming himself, redeeming himself by paying his own penalty. The argument is that Justice has no further claim upon man after death— having expended its force—having satisfied its own claims in his destruction; hence it is claimed that a resurrection of the dead would be next in order, and the proper thing. This view would make the divine requirement of a ransom-sacrifice for man's sin an injustice, a double payment of the penalty.

Whether this reasoning be true or false, it evidently is in violent conflict with the Scriptures, which declare, to the contrary, our need of a Savior, and that it was essential that he should give a ransom-price for us, before we could be released from the penalty of Adam's sin, and have any right to a future life. We have already referred to these Scriptures, and they are too numerous to be now repeated, hence we will confine ourselves to exposing the fallacy of the above claim; endeavoring to show that correct reasoning on the facts is in absolute accord with the Scriptural testimony, that the death of our Lord Jesus, as our ransom-price, was essential, that God might be just and yet be the justifier of him that believeth in Jesus, accepting him as his Redeemer.

Had the penalty against sin been merely **dying**— had the Lord said to Adam, Because of your sin you must experience the trying ordeal of **dying**! then, indeed, the penalty would be met by Adam and others **dying**. But such is not the penalty: the penalty is **death**, not **dying**; and death is the absence of life, destruction. Hence for man to pay his penalty would mean that he must stay **dead**, devoid of life forever. "The soul [being] that sinneth it shall die." As already pointed out, this destruction of the **soul** (being) according to the sentence would have been everlasting, except for the redemption accomplished by our Lord. It is in view of that redemption that death is turned into what is figuratively termed a "sleep"—in view of that redemption there will be an awakening from this sleep of death in due time, accomplished by the Redeemer, with the full consent of divine Justice, whose demands he met. Thus, as we have seen, had it not been for the redemption, Adamic death would have been what the Second Death is to be, viz., **"everlasting destruction from the presence of the Lord and from the glory of his power."** When once the proper view of the subject is obtained, there can be no further doubt in the mind of any reasonable person that paying the penalty of sin takes all that a man has, and leaves nothing either to suffer or enjoy. On the other hand, the more we investigate from this standpoint, the more clearly we may see the seriousness of the difficulty in which our race was involved under the divine sentence; and the more will we appreciate the necessity for the ransom. And seeing this feature of the subject clearly will show us clearly also that when our Lord Jesus did become our Redeemer, when he did give himself as our ransom-price, it meant to him what the original penalty would have meant to us, viz., that "the man Christ Jesus" suffered for us death, in the most absolute sense of the word, "everlasting destruction." Hence we know Christ no more after the flesh. The flesh, the human nature, was given as our ransom-price, and the fact that it was not taken back is our guarantee that all the blessed provisions of that ransom are available to the entire human family under the terms of the New Covenant—that all the perfections and rights which belonged to our dear Redeemer as a man were given in **exchange** for Adam's similar rights, which had been forfeited through disobedience; and that these, therefore, are to be given to all who will accept them upon the divine terms, during the "times of **restitution** of all things, which God hath spoken by the mouth of all his holy prophets since the world began."—Acts 3:19-21

"WHO WILL HAVE ALL MEN TO BE SAVED"

"Who will have all men to be saved and to come unto the knowledge of the truth."—1 Tim. 2:4

Another danger of false reasoning on the subject of the ransom besets the pathway of some. Many who at one time readily believed the testimony of men, without Scriptural evidence, to the effect that the wages of sin is eternal torment, and that all were sure to get that eternal torment except "the pure in heart," the "little flock," the "elect" Church, having once gotten free from that terrible delusion, are inclined to go to the opposite extreme, and to accept in some shape or form the doctrine of universal everlasting salvation.

The vast majority of those who take hold of this "Universalist" error deny the ransom **in toto;** but a few take hold of it because of **faith in the ransom**—whose operation, however, they fail to distinctly understand. This class is very apt to seize upon the Scripture above cited, and to satisfy themselves with the following process of reasoning: If God wills to have all men to be saved, that settles it; for the time is coming that his will shall be done on earth as in heaven. Therefore, say they, we perceive that the ransom given **for all** by the man Christ Jesus is to secure the will of God by securing the salvation of all. They proceed to entrench themselves in their error by saying, When we look at it, since God accepted the ransom-sacrifice of Jesus, he is bound **in justice** to save all the sinners, and to give back to them again the eternal life lost in Eden. We state their position as strongly as possible, to the intent that it may be answered to their satisfaction, and beyond all cavil.

The difficulty with this reasoning is that it is not sufficiently comprehensive. It takes hold of a few points of Scripture, and neglects many which should be granted a hearing, and whose testimony should have weight in reaching a conclusion. Besides, it only partially quotes, and misinterprets, the Scriptures supposed particularly to support it.

Our Heavenly Father declares, "I have no pleasure in the death of him that dieth, saith the Lord God: wherefore turn yourselves, and live ye." (Ezek. 18:32) This great favor of an offer of life through a Ransomer to the condemned world is not a new thing on our Heavenly Father's part. He changes not; he has always had this good will towards his creatures. He could have made them mere machines, intellectually and morally, without liberty to will or to do contrary to his good pleasure; but he chose not to make human machines, but to make beings in his own image, in his own likeness—with liberty of choice, freedom of will, to choose good or evil. He seeketh not such to worship him as could not do otherwise, nor such to worship him as would do so under constraint, but, as he declares, "He seeketh such to worship him as worship him in spirit and in truth" —voluntarily, from love and appreciation of his principles of righteousness, and of himself, which these represent.—John 4:23

Nevertheless, it was while God had this same good will toward men that he permitted Adam to take his own choice of obedience or disobedience, and when he chose the disobedience, this same God, who has no pleasure in the death of him that dieth, pronounced the penalty, and for six thousand years has enforced its execution. And now that he has provided a redemption in Christ Jesus, and an opportunity for every member of the human family to return to harmony with himself, and to obtain through Christ eternal life, he at the same time most unquestionably sets up **conditions** necessary to the obtaining of this eternal life. The terms of the New Covenant are a renewed heart and a right spirit toward God, and a full obedience to him. And the fulfilment of the requirements of this New Covenant is only possible through the help of the Mediator of that Covenant, and hence the declaration is that, He that hath the Son may have the life, and he who does not obtain an interest in the Son shall not see life, but the wrath of God abideth on him.—John 3:36

This is in perfect accord with the statement that God hath no pleasure in the death of him that dieth, and also in accord with the statement in the New Testament, that "God wills all men to be saved, and to come to a knowledge of the truth." Nevertheless, the Scriptures point out that those who reject the offers of divine mercy in Christ are thereby doing despite unto divine favor, and will surely die the Second Death, the wages or penalty of their choosing sin instead of righteousness.

Notice further: this text under consideration indicates merely that it is the will of God that all mankind should be saved from the ignorance and blindness and degradation which has come upon the race as a result of Adam's sin. There is no reference here to an **everlasting** salvation, but merely to a recovery from the loss sustained through Adam: and it should not be forgotten that father Adam did not lose **eternal** life, for although he had a perfect life, and was free from all elements of death, he was, nevertheless, placed in Eden **on probation,** to see whether, by obedience to God, he would develop a character in harmony with God, and so be accounted worthy of everlasting life. Consequently, when Adam and his race are redeemed from the curse of death, this redemption or salvation from the sentence of death does not entitle them to everlasting life, but merely entitles them to the favorable conditions of father Adam, and to a fresh trial as to worthiness for everlasting life.

This fresh trial secured for Adam and all his race will indeed be more favorable in some respects than was Adam's original trial, because of the large increase of knowledge. Man has had an opportunity to learn the exceeding sinfulness of sin, and will have an opportunity to learn the blessedness of righteousness and of God's grace in Christ. This knowledge will be of service to all who will use it, during the fresh trial for eternal life in the Millennial age— when for a thousand years the whole world of mankind shall be in judgment or trial for eternal life, before the great white throne.—Rev. 20:4

It is this salvation **from** the "curse," this recovery back **to** favorable opportunities of knowledge, that God wills; and on account of this he has appointed the Mediator between God and man, the man Christ Jesus, who gave himself a ransom for all, to be testified in due time.

This statement, that it is God's will that "all men should be saved" from the Adamic sentence, finds a parallel in the statement by the same apostle, in Rom. 11:26, "And so all Israel shall be saved." The thought in this last passage is not that all Israel shall be **saved eternally,** but merely that all Israel shall be **saved from their blindness**—in the sense of being recovered from blindness which came upon them as a people as a result of their national rejection of the Messiah. So the thought of the text is also limited and applies only to the Adamic catastrophe: "God wills that all men should be saved, not only from the just sentence which he pronounced and which cut short Adam's trial (this he has already accomplished in the death of his Son) but he also wills that all men shall be recovered from the ignorance and blindness with which Satan since the fall has darkened their minds: "The god of this world has blinded the minds of them which believe not, lest the light of the glorious gospel of Christ, who is the image of God, should shine unto them." (2 Cor. 4:4) God wills that all should be so saved from all the train of evils following Adam's sin and curse, that they may come to a knowledge of the truth. Why does he will this? To the intent that having a clear knowledge of the truth they may make the very best possible use of the new trial for life secured for them by their Redeemer's ransom-sacrifice. It is for the carrying out of this, God's will, that the Redeemer will inaugurate his Millennial Kingdom, which will first bind Satan (restrain all outside evil influences) and then release man from his blindness—as it is written, "the eyes of the blind shall be opened." (Isa. 35:5) For the same reason, viz., that the new trial shall be most favorable for man, it is the divine arrangement that its work shall be done gradually and require a thousand years.

JUSTICE NOT OBLIGATED BY THE RANSOM

The claim that God is now bound, by his own justice, to restore every man, is another mistake. On the contrary, we find that God has assumed no obligation: he has merely **sold** the race to the Lord Jesus Christ, who, as we have seen foregoing, "**bought us** with his own precious blood." The Heavenly Father has assumed no responsibilities for the race; he is not dealing with the race; he does not even propose that he will do the judging of them, to see whether or not they shall attain to worthiness of eternal life: on the contrary, we are assured that he has committed the whole matter to the Son, who **bought** the race, and hence is Lord of the race, its master, controller, owner, Judge, Prophet, Priest, King, and who, in harmony with the Father's plan, is arranging to identify with himself the elect Church of this Gospel age, for the great work of the world's enlightenment and the restitution of the obedient.

The fact that the Heavenly Father disposed of the entire race to our Lord Jesus does not imply any lack of interest on his part, but is so arranged in order to meet the requirements of his law. The divine laws are inflexible, and make no allowance for any degree of imperfection or sin; because those laws are arranged for perfect beings: for our Heavenly Father never created anything imperfect. Whatever there is of imperfection and sin has been of **depravity** subsequent to his creative operation. If he should admit of sin in mankind, and deal with imperfect man directly, it would mean (1) that all would quickly be sentenced as imperfect and unworthy, or (2) that God would pass over and fail to condemn our faults and condone our imperfections, which would be in violation of the laws of his empire. Hence it is for man's benefit as well as for the preservation of his own laws inviolate that the Father has turned the entire race over to the hands of Jesus, its Redeemer. Jesus can deal with the race so as to be **merciful** (not just) toward the imperfect ones seeking perfection, until he shall have brought them step by step, up, up, up to **perfection** at the close of the Millennium—when those who shall have obeyed the great Prophet will be ready to be transferred out of his Mediatorial hands into the Father's hands; having attained through Christ the perfection approved of the divine standard; while all others will be cut off in the Second Death. (Acts 3:23) It is in view of the fact that even with past sins blotted out our **present imperfections** would bring a fresh sentence of death if on trial before the Father's court of absolute justice, that the apostle, cautioning us against trifling with the opportunities afforded us in Christ, declares, "It is a fearful thing to fall into the hands of the living God." (Heb. 10:31) The divine arrangement for sinners knows no mercy except in and through Christ and his work of atonement and restitution, as the Mediator: outside this provision God's law is stern justice, with no allowances, ready to consume as a fire everything blemished.

Who cannot see that if God could deal with the sinners, and, condoning their sins, accept their best endeavors, though imperfect, there would have been no necessity for a Redeemer nor for a New Covenant in his blood? Moreover, every one of the holy angels might consistently, if they chose, say—God condoned one sin in the human family; he would be no less merciful toward us; hence if we desire to do so, we will be at liberty to commit one sin, and may rely upon divine mercy's forgiveness of it, and that God would not cast us off from his fellowship. And thus, to all eternity, there might be danger of sin on the part of those who had not already dabbled in it. Each one who would thus venture on divine mercy, overriding divine justice, and divine law, to the excusement of one sin, and be forgiven, would constitute another argument why every one of the holy angels should take a trial at sin, and experience divine forgiveness. Seeing this, it does not surprise us that God, in the interest of all his holy creatures, as well as for his own pleasure, decides that he will recognize nothing short of perfection in any creature, and makes **Justice** the foundation of his throne.— Psa. 89:14

"NO OTHER NAME—WHEREBY WE MUST BE SAVED"

From this standpoint, we see more clearly than ever before that all divine mercies toward the fallen race are extended in and through Christ—that the Heavenly Father extends no mercies personally, or independently of the Son, and that "there is no other name under heaven given amongst men whereby we must be saved." (Acts 4:12) We see too that the work of the Savior is not accomplished merely in purchasing the race, but that after purchasing them it is necessary that he should be the Great Physician, to heal them of sin-sickness, and to restore them to life and to all the perfections of their nature, and thus eventually, through the processes of restitution during the thousand years of his reign, to make ready as many as will obey him for presentation to the Father at the end of the Millennium, in absolute perfection.

Looking, then, to the Mediator, in whose hands has been placed "all power" to save, we inquire whether or not he proposes that those whom he redeemed shall all be eternally saved, or whether or not he has placed limitations upon the matter. We find that the Scriptures clearly state that there are limitations: for instance, when describing the Millennial age as the time when the Adamic curse shall be set aside, and be no longer in operation upon men, and when it shall no longer be the proverb, The fathers have eaten a sour grape and the children's teeth are set on edge; the declaration is that every man who then dies shall die for his own sin, and not for the sin of another. (Jer. 31:29, 30) We find the declaration also, that when the Lord is the ruler amongst the nations, "the evil-doer shall be cut off." (Psa. 37:9) We find that the Apostle Peter, after telling about these "times of restitution," the Millennial age, declares that then "it shall come to pass that whosoever will not hear [obey] that Prophet [the Christ glorified—head and body] shall be **cut off** from amongst his people"—the Second Death. (Acts 3: 19-23) Referring to this same type, another of the apostles declares: "He that despised Moses' law died without mercy. . . . Of how much sorer [severer] punishment suppose ye shall he be thought worthy, who hath trodden under foot the Son of God and hath counted the blood of the covenant wherewith he was sanctified [made acceptable to God, **justified**] an unholy [lit. common, ordinary] thing, and hath done despite unto the Spirit of [divine] grace? . . . It is a fearful thing to fall into the hands of the living God." "For if we sin wilfully, after that we have received the **knowledge of the truth** [the knowledge of God's grace in Christ, to which God wills that all shall come some time] there remaineth no more sacrifice for sins [the atonement for Adamic sin will not cover wilful sins against light and knowledge], but a certain fearful looking for of judgment [retribution] and fiery indignation which shall **devour** the adversaries."—Heb. 10:26-31

Here we are clearly shown that adversaries of the antitypical Moses (the glorified Christ) shall be devoured or destroyed in a still more severe manner than were those who opposed Moses. But if those who opposed Moses were punished with death, how can those who oppose Christ be more severely dealt with? We answer, that the death inflicted by Moses merely affected the remnant of Adamic life remaining, but could not affect the real being or soul which God purposed to **redeem** and did redeem by Christ's ransom-sacrifice. He, however, who after knowledge of his redemption refuses to obey the antitypical Moses, will be punished more severely in that he will not only lose a few years of his condemned life, but lose his soul, his being, his existence forever, and that without hope of recovery—for such, and all adversaries, will be devoured as stubble, as thorns and thistles, cumberers of the ground.

Similarly, throughout the entire New Testament, the testimony is conclusive that the law of God against sin will be radically enforced by the Mediator, and that the only deviations from its absolute rule will be allowances for the weaknesses and ignorance of the people; that as these weaknesses and ignorance are overcome during the Millennial age, by the process of restitution, the requirements of the law of Justice will become more and more exacting, until finally the judgment by which our Lord Jesus will in the end of the Millennial age test all who still remain will be no less severe, no less crucial, than that of the Heavenly Father: and under this trial all will fall into the Second Death who either practice sin or sympathize with it in any form or degree. Perfection having then been attained by the worthy of the race, through the processes of restitution, the

A Ransom for All

demands of Justice will be in full conformity to all the dictates of righteousness, in word, in deed and in thought.

We can see thus God's will shall be accomplished on earth as in heaven—remembering (1) that it is God's will that all should be recovered from the Adamic curse, and brought to a knowledge of the truth; (2) that it is the will of God that eternal life should be given to all the obedient; (3) that it is equally the will of God that all the disobedient "shall be **destroyed** from amongst the people." This feature of God's will shall be done on earth, also, and none can hinder it.

Some have assumed that since the ransom was provided to the intent that all mankind should be recovered out of the Adamic transgression, therefore an **instantaneous** restitution to full perfection of the human nature is to be expected for the world of mankind. But such an expectation is neither Scriptural nor reasonable. Nothing in the Scriptures intimates that the restitution work shall be an instantaneous one, but on the contrary, that it will be a gradual one. The inclination to look for instantaneous restitution to absolute perfection of the human nature is the result of false reasoning. It assumes that the race could not be properly on trial for eternal life, under equally favorable circumstances with father Adam, except by being made perfect, as he was, but we will demonstrate that this is incorrect— that they can receive a much more favorable trial while imperfect. It assumes that the weaknesses and imperfections common to all mankind through the fall would be insurmountable barriers, which would hinder the redeemed ones from rendering obedience to the divine law, but we shall see that God's provision abundantly meets the necessities of the case. We answer, that on the contrary, if mankind in general were placed back again, by an instantaneous restitution, to the perfection of human nature as enjoyed by Adam, it would mean:—

(1) That as **perfect beings** they should be required to obey the **perfect law** of God **perfectly;** and that

no excuse should be made for them, as none was made for father Adam. While a few of the race might pass such a trial favorably, because of present experience with sin, and the lessons learned thereunder, yet we are to remember that the majority of the race would be just as deficient in **knowledge** of sin and its penalty as was father Adam, because the majority of the race have died in infancy, and of the remainder a large proportion have died in comparative ignorance of the distinctions between right and wrong.

(2) Such a procedure would, to a large extent at least, make void the great lesson which God had been teaching the world for six thousand years, respecting the sinfulness of sin, the undesirability of sin; for the majority have thus far had comparatively little knowledge of righteousness. Their course of instruction will only be complete to mankind by the lessons on the opposite side of the question, the wisdom and profit of righteousness to be inculcated during the Millennial age.

(3) The race, if restored instantly, would be practically a new race, to which all experiences would be comparatively lost; because no member of it would be able to thoroughly identify himself, a perfect being, with perfect faculties and powers, with the being who now has such imperfect faculties and powers: and with infants, who had never come to a knowledge even of themselves, there could not be the slightest identification. So, if this were God's plan, he might just as well have created millions of human beings at first, in Eden, and have tried them all, as to adopt a plan which would place millions in a similar position, by restitution, with no benefit whatever from present experiences with sin.

(4) If each individual were thus instantaneously made perfect there would be no opportunity for the operation of the Church, with their Lord, as the seed of Abraham, to bless the world, to fulfil toward it the office of the "Royal Priesthood." (Gal. 3:16, 29) The divine provision for a "Royal Priesthood" implies weakness, imperfection, on the part of some whom the priests are to help and instruct, and from

whom they are to accept sacrifice and offerings for sin, and to whom they are to extend mercy and forgiveness of sins. There could be no room for such a priesthood, if the plan of God were one of instantaneous restitution at the second advent.

(5) If the restitution were to be an instantaneous work, why should a thousand years be appointed, as "times of restitution," when one year would be an abundance of time for an instantaneous restitution to human perfection and for a trial such as Adam passed through?

(6) If mankind were instantly brought to absolute perfection, it would imply that there would be no room for mercy on their account. There could be no plea for mercy for wilful, deliberate, intentional transgression. Furthermore, each individual who would transgress, would individually bring himself under the sentence of death, as a wilful sinner, and no redemption for these would be possible: unlike the case of Adam, where "by **one** man's disobedience" a whole race was involved, and another perfect man became the redeemer of that race. In this case each individual would be a personal transgressor, and come **personally** under the sentence of death. To release again from the penalty of even one transgression would require a life for a life for each individual transgressor: a million transgressors would require a million sacrificial deaths of the perfect and holy if their sins would be atoned for; but God having made a **full** provision for all in Christ, has made **no** provision for any further sacrifice for sins. Nor **could** these, after being once restored to perfection **by** Christ, claim anything further under the merit **of** his sacrifice, because they would have received **all** the gracious effects intended and secured by his ransom. There would remain to them no further share in the sacrifice for sins, if they had once experienced full restitution.

But now let us consider the reasonableness of the divine plan of a gradual restitution, progressing proportionately with man's growing at-one-ment with the Creator and his law—and the benefits of this plan to mankind.

(1) All are to be awakened from the Adamic death, as though from a sleep, by virtue of the ransom given: this will be the first step in restitution blessings. They will then be under the care, charge, supervision, of the Royal Priesthood, whose experience with sin, and with victory over sin, in this Gospel age, will well fit and prepare them to be patient and helpful toward those over whom they will reign, as Kings as well as Priests.—Rev. 5:10

The identity of the individual will be preserved, by reason of his being awakened to exactly the same conditions which he lost in death; and the various steps of his progression out of sin and the weaknesses of the present time will be most profitable lessons to him, as respects sin and as respects the benefits of righteousness. Thus, step by step, the great Redeemer will lift up toward perfection the world of mankind, which shall make progress toward perfection in proportion as it **wills** so to do; and those who will not progress, under all the knowledge and opportunities then accorded them, will, at the age of one hundred years, be cut off from the land of the living, in the Second Death, without hope of any future recovery or opportunity; because having had the opportunity in their hands, and having come to a considerable knowledge of right and wrong, they spurned the grace of God in Christ, in that they neglected the instructions of the great Prophet, and refused to make progress along the highway of holiness. (Isa. 65:20; 35:8) Nevertheless, as the Prophet points out, when dying at one hundred years of age, they may be considered merely as children, because all who will to make any progress might have continued to live at least until the end of the Millennial age.

(2) In taking these steps upward along the highway of holiness, during the Millennial age, the world, while still imperfect, will be to that extent still **covered by the merit of the ransom-sacrifice** while learning gradually valuable lessons, and cultivating

various fruits of the Spirit: and in the meantime breaks or blemishes, through indiscretion, or through attempts to try other methods, would still come in as part of their Adamic weakness, and to that extent be forgivable at the hands of the great Priest.

To claim that either physical perfection or perfection of knowledge is necessary to a trial for life or death everlasting, is to deny that the Church is now thus on trial: whereas all must concede the Scriptural declarations to the contrary. Nor will such perfections be essential to the world's trial. The world will indeed, as we, be brought first to a knowledge of God's grace in Christ before any trial can begin, and this God has promised they shall have. As a covering for their inherited weaknesses, they will have **the merit of Christ, the Mediator of the New Covenant, while attaining perfection**. Not until the end of Messiah's reign will the obedient attain to complete perfection.

(3) The Scriptures represent the Millennium as the Judgment Day for the world saying—"God hath appointed a day in the which he will judge the world in righteousness by that man [the Christ, head and body] whom he hath ordained." (Acts 17:31) If it were God's plan to coerce all the world or to everlastingly save every member of Adam's race, why call the coming age a Day of Judgment? Judgment signifies **trial, testing**, and this implies the rejection of the unfit as much as it implies the acceptance and blessing of those proved worthy. And the judgment is unto life or death everlasting.

Note our Lord's parable of the sheep and the goats, applicable not to the Gospel age, but to the world in the Millennium. It opens with "When the Son of Man shall come in all his glory"—and sit upon his glorious throne—a time when, according to his promise, the bride, the "elect" Church shall share his throne and glory—"then shall be gathered before him **all nations**," and he shall judge them, separating the sheep to the right hand of his favor and the goats to the left hand of disfavor. This separating and judging will occupy the entire Millennial age, and at its close the "sheep" will all be welcomed to the Father's favor—everlasting life, and the disobedient "goats," with Satan their leader, and all evil doers, shall be punished with "everlasting **destruction**," **everlasting** cutting off from life—symbolized by a lake of fire and brimstone—the Second Death.

The Scriptures represent the judgment of that great Millennial Judgment Day as before a great white throne of purity and justice, and portray the decision of the Judge to the effect that those who have, during that time, cultivated and developed the spirit of the Heavenly Father, the spirit of love, to perfection, shall be accounted as the Lord's people and be granted "the Kingdom prepared for them [the earthly Kingdom] from the foundation of the world.' Others, who during that favorable opportunity, shall fail to develop to the fullest extent the spirit of love as their character, in the likeness of the Lord, shall be accounted the Lord's opponents, and, with Satan, such shall be destroyed.—Compare Rev. 20: 9-13

RANSOM—SUBSTITUTION

The doctrine of substitution, clearly taught in the Scriptures, and firmly held for centuries by Christian people, is today giving way, because under clearer reasoning than in the past it is being generally discerned that if eternal torment be the wages of sin, and if our Lord Jesus were our substitute in the payment of our penalty, this would imply that, as our substitute, he must be eternally tormented, else we could not be set free from sin. This reasoning is sound enough: the difficulty is that the premise is a false one. Eternal torment is not the wages of sin, —not the penalty against man. Nevertheless, in the minds of many, there remains a general prejudice against the thought of **substitution**, even after seeing that the wages of sin is death, and that our Lord Jesus could be and was man's substitute in death, and suffered exactly what man was to suffer, in the

A Ransom for All

most positive and absolute sense. Many are prejudiced against this word, **substitution,** and inquire, Is the word, "substitution" used in the Scriptures? If not, why use it?

We answer that the word "substitution" is an English word and that no English words are used in the Scriptures, which were written in Greek and Hebrew. If, however, the translators of our English version had chosen so to do, they could, with perfect propriety, have used the word "substitution," because the Greek unquestionably contains the thought of substitution and substitute, in many places. The fact that the word does not occur is merely because the translators did not happen to use it; and inasmuch as we are seeking to impress the thought of the original Scriptures upon our minds, therefore it is proper that this word "substitute" should be impressed, because whatever is in opposition to the thought contained in the word **substitute** is equally in opposition to the thought contained in the word **ransom.** As we have already seen, the Scriptures abound with declarations that we were bought with the precious blood of Christ; that he released us by giving his own soul unto death to ransom ours. What is this but substitution?

When a thing is **bought,** that which is paid for the purchased thing is **substituted** for it. For instance, if we purchased a loaf of bread for a piece of money, we exchange the money for the bread, i. e., we substitute the money for the bread. If a farmer takes a sack of wheat to the mill, and receives therefor an equivalent value in flour, the wheat has become a substitute for the flour, and the flour a substitute for the wheat. The one is a **corresponding price,** a ransom, a substitute for the other. Thus it was that in the most absolute sense of the word, our Lord, the man Christ Jesus, gave himself into death, as a ransom, a substitute, in death for father Adam (and the race that had lost life in him)—a ransom for all, a substitute, a corresponding price. Indeed, the facts of this case are more exact than almost any other case that we could suppose, except it would be in an exchange of prisoners during war, when there is generally a great particularity to exchange private for private, colonel for colonel, general for general, a corresponding price being required on each side, man for man. The purchase of the bread with money is not so perfect an illustration; because the bread and the silver, although of the same **value**, are not of the same **kind**. In the case of man's redemption God required that there be absolute correspondence in nature, in perfection, in everything—a perfect substitute, a thoroughly corresponding price had to be paid, before the race could be liberated from the divine sentence.

One use of the word "substitute," common amongst men, has served to confuse the thought in this respect. In war time, when a draft becomes necessary, and a man is drafted for army service, he is sometimes permitted to find a substitute, who takes his place, serves in his stead, in the army—the man who provides the substitute being thereafter free from all obligations to military service. This particular use of the word "substitute" in connection with military matters, is harmonious enough in the sense that the man who is accepted by the government officer as a substitute for the one released must be up to the physical standards demanded at the time; secondly, he must be a man who has not himself been drafted, and who, therefore, is free to offer himself as a substitute. These features correspond to the case we are considering. Our Lord proposed to be the substitute in father Adam's place: he met all the requirements of the divine government, in that he was in every way qualified to be the substitute of Adam. He met also the requirement that he was not already under the sentence of death when he took our place and offered himself and was accepted. He had free life to give for Adam's forfeited life.

But here the correspondency between the two substitutions ends, because, in the case of the soldier, the draft or sentence was to participate in the war, and its difficulties, trials, etc., whereas, in the case

A Ransom for All

of Adam, the draft, the sentence was to death. The harmony between these two uses of the word "substitute" ends when the soldier is accepted and goes into the army-service—this corresponding to God's acceptance of the offering of our Lord Jesus and his start to go into death. Because the substituted soldier was accepted to the army, therefore the name of the drafted man was stricken off the lists of the drafted, as exempted; and when Christ entered death for Adam, Adam's name was stricken off the lists, so far as the divine condemnation was concerned. The parallel extends no further.

We doubtless do wisely not to unnecessarily obtrude this word "substitution" upon those who already are prejudiced, through a misunderstanding of the subject, and who, because of this prejudice, might be hindered from giving the subject a proper and thorough and unbiased consideration. Nevertheless, we should see to it especially in our own hearts that we are thoroughly loyal to the thought of substitution, which is the thought of the ransom. Whoever, after a proper understanding of the subject, does not believe that Christ was our substitute, is not exercising faith in the ransom, and is therefore lacking of the faith which justifies before God.

WAS NO OTHER PLAN OF SALVATION POSSIBLE?

Many, who see the subject of the ransom only imperfectly, are inclined to dispute the matter, and to say that they cannot see why God could not have saved the world in some other way than by the death of his Son, as man's substitute or ransom-price. We answer them, that they are taking an improper view of the matter. The question they should ask themselves is not whether God could have adopted some other way, but, did he adopt some other way, or did he adopt the plan of the ransom?

Unquestionably the divine wisdom could have adopted another plan of salvation for mankind, but we may just as positively set it down that no other plan could have been devised that would have been better, and so far as, our judgment and knowledge go, no other plan could have been devised, even by the Almighty, that would have been so good as the plan he has adopted, all the connecting circumstances, conditions and desired results being taken into consideration. The fact that God did adopt a different plan in dealing with the fallen angels proves, we may say, that he could have adopted a different plan in dealing with fallen man. He could have done with man as he did with the angels, but,* as we have seen, this would have been no more favorable, perhaps less desirable, in the judgment of many.

Even if we should suppose that a similar number of the human family would be blessed and ultimately restored by such a dealing on God's part, we would see other disadvantages in this method, viz., (1) how much more terrible would have been the moral degradation of our race, had it been left in possession of its complete mental and physical powers, and merely permitted to break down morally! How much of sin can be thoroughly learned in the short period of ten, twenty, fifty or a hundred years, and what depths of wickedness might have been explored and exploited had mankind continued to live with unimpaired powers for six thousand years, separated from God, but not condemned to death!

(2) Such a plan of salvation even if it should reach, eventually, as large a number as the plan God has adopted, would never have revealed to us to the same extent the qualities of the divine character. (a) We see God's Justice in the infliction of the death penalty, even upon those who "did not sin after the similitude of Adam's transgression," but who were merely born in sin, shapen in iniquity, brought forth sinners, by heredity. (Rom. 5:14, 12; Psa. 51:5) He has revealed to us thus, a justice which will by no means clear the guilty, and will recognize nothing short of absolute perfection. (b) He thus revealed

---

*See "Spiritualism" Price 5 cents.

to us a **love,** far greater than we could otherwise have conceived of—which followed us, and which laid hold upon us "while we were yet sinners," at the cost of the great ransom-price for our recovery. (c) The adoption of this plan of sentencing man to death, redeeming him from death, and subsequently, in due time, restoring him from death by a resurrection, furnishes an opportunity for the display of divine **power** far beyond anything connected with the work of creation, grand and wonderful as all that was; for unquestionably it requires a greater power to accomplish the divine promise of a resurrection of the millions of beings who have lived and who have died—to bring them forth, identically the same as they were before, even in their own consciousness —than was required for the creation of the one man. (d) This divine plan, when fully consummated, will show forth divine **wisdom** in a way in which no other plan could have shown it, so far as we are able to consider other plans. It will show how God knew the end from the beginning, and how he has been working all things according to the counsel of his own will, even while men and angels saw not the purpose and the intention of his operations, and even while the fallen angels and Satan supposed that they were frustrating the divine will. It will be demonstrated beyond peradventure that God is able to cause all things to work together for good, for the accomplishment of the divine purpose. In the end it will be demonstrated that the Word that goeth forth out of his mouth does not return unto him void, but accomplishes that which he pleases, and prospers in the thing whereunto he sent it.—Isa. 55:11

Furthermore, in adopting with man the plan pursued with the angels who sinned, or indeed in any other plan that we can conceive of, there could not have been so grand an opportunity for the election of the Gospel church to be the body of Christ; for there would not have been the same grand opportunity for the testing of the loyalty and obedience of the Logos to the Heavenly Father, and consequently of his exaltation to be a participator in the divine nature—nor an opportunity for a little flock of the redeemed to walk in his footsteps. And finally, we see that these lessons are not merely for humanity, but also for all the intelligent creatures of God, on every plane of being; and not only for a few centuries, but for all eternity.

"O the depth of the riches both of the wisdom and knowledge of God. How unsearchable are his decisions, and his ways past finding out. For who hath known the mind of the Lord, or who hath been his counselor? . . . For of him and through him and to him are all things: to whom be glory forever. Amen."—Rom. 11:33-36

STUDY XVI

THE MINISTRY OF RECONCILIATION OR AT-ONE-MENT

This Ministry Committed to the Royal Priesthood—Anointed to Preach of the At-one-ment—Why the Joyful News is not Appreciated—The Results of this Ministry—Persecution and Glory—How it Tests Fidelity—Only the Faithful may Share the Atonement Work Future.

"No man taketh this honor unto himself, but he that is called of God, as was Aaron. So also Christ glorified not himself to be made a high Priest."—Heb. 5:4, 5

THE MINISTRY of reconciliation or at-one-ment is participated in by the entire "Royal Priesthood" of which our Lord Jesus is the Chief Priest or High Priest. All the Priests share in the "better sacrifices" which have progressed throughout this Gospel age, and which will be finished with its close (Rom. 12:1): and all who thus share the sufferings of Christ shall likewise share his future glory as participators with him in the great and glorious ministry of reconciliation of the Millennial Kingdom.

As for these under-priests, they "were by nature children of wrath, even as others," and needed first to be reconciled or at-oned to God before they could be called of God to this priesthood—"for no man taketh this honor to himself, but [only] he that is called of God." It is not until after we have received the at-one-ment, at the hands of our Redeemer, the High Priest, that we are privileged to be reckoned as joint sacrificers, joint mediators, joint reconcilers, joint at-one-ers.

Whoever received the "spirit of adoption" which constitutes him a son of God and a priest, is forthwith impelled by that spirit to begin the ministry of reconciliation or at-one-ment each according to his several abilities and opportunities. Each realizes, as the High Priest did, the leadings of that Holy Spirit, saying, "The spirit of the Lord God is upon me, because he hath anointed me to preach the glad tidings to the meek [not now to the proud and arrogant and hard-hearted and profane], to bind up the broken hearted, and to proclaim the acceptable year of the Lord"—the period during which God is pleased to accept a little flock as living sacrifices, through the merit of the Redeemer.

The Apostle Paul as one of the under-priests felt the influence of this Spirit prompting him to engage in the work of telling all with whom he came in contact who had "ears to hear," of the "ransom for all," accomplished through our dear Redeemer's sacrifice; and to exhort all to be reconciled, at-oned, to God, and begin at once to walk in the paths of righteousness.

Note the apostle's statement of these matters in 2 Cor. 5:17-20

"If any man be in Christ he is a new creature: old things are passed away [old sins, ambitions, hopes, etc.]; behold all things are become new. And all [these new] things are of God, who hath reconciled us to himself by Jesus Christ, and hath given to us the ministry [service] of reconciliation [**kattalage**—the same word rendered "atonement" in Rom. 5:11]; to wit [namely], that God was in Christ reconciling [at-one-ing] the world unto himself, not imputing their trespasses unto them [because their penalty was borne by Christ. And [God] hath committed unto us [the royal priesthood] the word [message, good tidings] of reconciliation [at-one-ment]."

"Now then [because God has called us and given us as a priesthood this ministry or service in his name, and this message of favor to declare], we are ambassadors for Christ [our official head or High Priest, and the Father's representative] as though God were inviting by us, we in Christ's stead pray you—be ye reconciled [at-oned] to God."

This joyful message, which, rightly appreciated, should bring ready responses in every place and from every class, is generally rejected; and the Prophet speaking for the Royal Priesthood cries, "Who hath believed our report, and to whom is the Arm of Jehovah [Christ, the power of God unto salvation] revealed?" (Isa. 53:1; John 12:38) It is efficacious now toward the comparatively few only—even as many as the Lord our God calls to be of the Royal Priesthood; for no man taketh this honor to himself, but he that is called of God.

The reason for the general rejection of the message is evident: reconciliation, at-one-ment with God means opposition to sin: peace with God means a warfare against all the entrenched weakness and depraved desires of our fallen human nature: it means a complete **change or conversion** from the service of sin to the service of righteousness. Many who despise sin (in its grosser, viler forms at least) and who long for a reconciliation to God and an interest in the blessings which he bestows only on "the sons of God," make a start for righteousness by self-reform, only to find their own weaknesses too great for them to conquer, and that besides the whole world is arrayed on the side of sin. The only ones who can possibly get free from this slavery, wherein all were born, are those who, seeking deliverance, give heed to the Master's testimony: "No man cometh unto the Father but by me"—the one Mediator—"the Way, the Truth and the Life." Moreover, "the apostle informs us that the great Adversary, "the god of this world, hath blinded the minds" of the vast majority with falsehoods, so that they cannot appreciate the advantage contained in the offer of **at-one-ment** through the Redeemer.

Under these circumstances, the result of sin abounding, is it any wonder that to be true, faithful ambassadors for God, and in Christ's name and stead (as members of his body), means that the underpriests must follow in the footsteps of the High Priest —must suffer with him for **righteousness'** sake? The great High Priest who proclaimed "the word of reconciliation" most clearly, was despised and rejected and crucified by those who professed to love and follow righteousness. The apostles were similarly evil treated because of their faithfulness—their refusal to compromise the message, "the word of reconciliation."

"Ye shall be hated of all men for my sake," "they shall say all manner of evil against you falsely for my sake." Marvel not if the world hate you: ye know that it hated me before it hated you. These words by the great teacher were to be true "even unto the end of this age:" and they are as true today as ever. Whoever will faithfully **exercise** his ambassadorship, and not shun to declare the whole counsel of God, will speedily know something of the sufferings of Christ and can say truly—"The reproaches of them that reproached thee are fallen upon me."—Matt. 5:10-12; 10:22; Psa. 69:9; Rom. 15:3

And here again we behold the wonderful wisdom of the divine plan; for it is while performing his priestly ministry of "the word of reconciliation" to which the spirit of anointing impels, that each priest finds the necessity for offering up himself, a living sacrifice, holy and acceptable to God, and his reasonable service.—Rom. 12:1

Hence the measure of self-sacrifice and sufferings for Christ, endured by each of the consecrated, becomes a **measure** (from God's standpoint—for man cannot always discern it) of the faithfulness of each as ambassadors. Every priest who fails to suffer for Christ's sake, for the truth's sake, must therefore have been an unfaithful ambassador and minister of the New Covenant. And only to those now faithful as good soldiers of the cross will be granted the inestimable privilege of being participators with the great High Priest in the glorious at-one-ment work under the favorable conditions of the Millennial age. If we suffer with him we shall also reign with him. If we deny him, he will also [then] deny us.—Rom. 8:17; 2 Tim. 2:12, 13; Titus 1:16

Take heed that no man take thy crown.—Rev. 3:11

"Be thou faithful unto death and I will give thee a crown of life."—Rev. 2:10

INDEX

---- TO ----

SCRIPTURE CITATIONS

---- OF ----

SCRIPTURE STUDIES, SERIES V

GENESIS

1:2	175, 183
1:20, 21, 24	324
1:21, 24	334
1:30	325
1:31	22, 406
2:4	182
2:7	105, 319
2:17	22, 407
2:19	325, 334
3:17	22
3:22	340, 390
3:23	22
5:5	406
6:2, 4	104
6:17	174, 314
7:15	174, 314
7:22	314
7:21, 22	319
8:1, 21	174
9:3, 4	325
9:9, 10	325
9:10, 12, 15, 16	334
9:12	325
9:15	325
9:16	326
12:3	22
14:21	334
14:22	67
17:1	67
18:1	43
18:1, 2	94
18:2-4	73
18:18	22
19:1	73, 94
21:10	105
22:14	43
23:6	68
23:7, 12	73
24:47	99
26:35	174
27:29	73
30:8	69
31:29	69
35:20	356
36:6	334
37:35	355
42:38	355
44:29, 31	355
45:27	314
46:26, 27	100
50:5	356

EXODUS

1:5	100, 342
3:2	43
3:3-15	43
6:3	40, 65
7:1	68
15:8, 10	174
15:11	67
17:15	43
20:2-5	40
21:4	105
21:6	68
22:8, 9, 28	68
28:3	176
30:10	449
31:3, 4	176
35:30-35	176

LEVITICUS

4:3, 4, 24, 27, 31, 34, 35	449
4:27	334
5:11, 12	449
9:2, 6, 7	449
11:10	335
11:46	334
25:48, 49	438

NUMBERS

11:17-26	176
13:33	104
14:36, 37	104
16:22	314
16:30, 33	356
23:10	334
31:19	334
31:28	324
35:11, 15, 30	334

DEUTERONOMY

6:4, 5	41
10:20, 21	74
10:22	334
27:25	334
32:4	309, 406
32:22; 26-43	357

JOSHUA

20:3, 9	334

JUDGES

6:23, 24	43
13:9-11, 16	94
15:19	314
16:30	334

RUTH

4:1-10	153

1 SAMUEL

1:15	318
2:6	358
11:6	176
14:15	69
16:13, 14	176
24:8	73
25:23, 41	73

2 SAMUEL

9:6	73
14:4, 22, 33	73
22:6, 8-18	358

Index of Texts

1 KINGS

2:4	131
2:6, 9	358
8:19	100
11:9-13	132
20:32	334

1 CHRONICLES

28:5-7, 9	131

2 CHRONICLES

6:9	100
29:7-11, 20-24	449
34:28	348

JOB

2:1	105
7:9	358
7:21	359
10:19	348, 388
11:8	359
12:10	174, 314
14:4	97
14:13	346, 359, 410
14:14	346, 359, 383
14:15	346, 410
14:19-21	348
17:13-16	360
19:25	438
21:13	360
24:19	360
26:6	361
33:24	462
38:7	105

PSALMS

2:4-9	48
2:7	72
6:5	361
8:4-8	152, 301, 426
8:5	67, 390
9:17	361
16:7-11	52
16:10	348, 362
18:5	362
22:22	109
23:1	45
24:7-10	44
29:1	67
30:3	348, 363
30:5	345
31:5	315
31:17, 18	363
32:8	234
33:6, 9	182
36:6	69
37:7-11	240
37:9	473
37:9, 20	388
40:2	418
41:13	86
45:2-11	49
45:16	78, 142
46:5	437
46:9	372
49:7	96, 102, 418
49:14, 15	363
49:15	328, 348
50:1	67
51:5	409, 484
55:15	364
67	30
68:18	210
69:9	490
73:24	234
76:10	448
77:3, 6	318
78:35	438
82	69
82:6, 7	68, 69
83:18	65
86:6-8	67
86:13	365
88:3	365
88:5	348
89:14	421, 472
89:19	96
89:27	87
89:48	348, 365
90:1, 2	45
90:2	86
90:3	353
95:3	67
96:4	68
97:7	72
103:4	353, 438
105:18	334
106:48	86
110:1, 4, 5	49
110:3	92
115:6	174
116:3	366
131:2	334
132:11, 12	130
133:2	215
139:7, 8	366
139:14-16	404
141:7	366
145:20	392
148:8	174

PROVERBS

1:12	366
2:21, 22	30
5:5	367
7:27	367
8:22-30	93
9:18	367
11:13	318
14:10	334
15:11, 24	367
16:2, 18, 19	318
23:14	367
27:20	368
29:11	318
30:15, 16	368

ECCLESIASTES

3:19	174, 327, 389
3:19-21	315
6:9	318
7:8, 9	318
7:29	406
8:8	317
9:4-10	348
9:10	368
12:7	315, 317, 344

SOLOMON'S SONG

8:6	368

ISAIAH

1:5, 6	252
2:2-4	44
5:14	369
5:20	189
6:1	47, 48
6:3, 5, 8	48
7:2	174
8:13, 14, 16-18	49
8:20	167
9:6	46, 93, 141
9:7	46
11:1-10	52
11:2 3	169
12:2	65
14:4-8, 9, 11	369
14:12-14	80
14:14	113
19:10	334
25:6-9	45
26:4	65
26:14	348
26:19	345

Index of Texts

Reference	Page
28:15	369
28:17	193
28:18	370
35	23
35:5	470
35:8	240, 478
38:10	370
38:18	371
40:1, 2	357
40:3	43
40:9, 10, 11	46
42:1-8	41
42:8	41
43:3, 11	33
50:4-10	52
51:5-9	47
52:3	438
52:10	47
52:14, 15	158
53	47
53:1	418, 489
53:2, 3	156
53:4, 5	122
53:5, 6	442
53:6	461
53:9	348
53:10-12	23, 127, 328, 337
53:11	52, 92, 441
54:13	32, 50
55:11	35, 182, 485
57:9	371
59:15-20	47
59:16	96
59:20	438
60	23
60:16	33
61	23
61:1	91, 169, 378, 422
62:10	240
63:1	96
63:16	348
64:6	445
65:20	478
66:5	233

JEREMIAH

Reference	Page
6:16	62
15:16	225
22:24-30	132
23:5, 6	42
23:6	133
31:29, 30	309, 473
31:29-34	332
33:16	42
36:30	132

EZEKIEL

Reference	Page
18:2	309
18:4	442
18:2, 4, 20	331
18:20	330
18:4, 20	404
18:32	467
21:25-27	133
31:15-17	372
32:21	69, 372
32:27	372
37:5-10, 13, 14	316
47:9	335
48:35	43

DANIEL

Reference	Page
7:13	150
12:2	346
12:9, 10	219

HOSEA

Reference	Page
13:4	33
13:14	373

JOEL

Reference	Page
2:28	163, 217, 239
2:28, 29	164

AMOS

Reference	Page
9:2, 11-15	374

JONAH

Reference	Page
2:2	374

MICAH

Reference	Page
4:1-3	44
4:8	45, 152
5:2, 4	45

HABBAKUK

Reference	Page
1:13	418
2:5	374

MALACHI

Reference	Page
3:1	72
3:1-4	48
3:6	35

MATTHEW

Reference	Page
1:6, 16	129
2:20	335
4:1-11	110
5:5	255
5:25-34	125
5:6	403
5:10-12	490
5:11	191
5:14	264
5:14-16	293
6:10	45
6:23	264
6:25	335
6:34	171
7:7, 8	167
8:16, 17	106, 124
8:17	122
10:22	490
10:25	236
10:28	332
10:39	335
11:11	28
11:23	375
11:27	91
12:20	47
12:32	270
13:11	333
13:41	150
13:44	441
13:54	91
16:18	375
16:19	214
16:25	335
16:26	258
17:18	172
18:11	457
19:28	142
20:3	429
20:28	335
22:38	41
22:42-45	129
22:44, 45	49
23:2	351
23:12	424
23:34, 36, 38	48
24:24	116
24:27, 37	150
24:43	172
25:31	150
25:41, 46	30
26:28	28
26:67	52
27:26, 30	52
27:32	123
27:66	246
28:18	281

MARK

Reference	Page
3:4	335
3:24, 25	171
4:10	72, 74

Index of Texts

8:35-37 336	1:12 .. 28, 108, 209	8:28 51
8:38 ...... 150, 237	430	8:38 50
10:45 .. 336, 426, 428	1:12, 13 .. 143, 177	8:42 105
10:51 71	1:14 .. 93, 154, 297,	8:44 108
12:38 429	425	9:5 293
13:32 36	1:14, 33 212	10:10 336
14:24 28	1:18 .... 77, 93	10:11, 15, 17 .. 337
	1:29 ...... 446, 450	10:15 446
LUKE	3:3-8 177	10:20 196
1:28, 30, 42, 45-47 ..	3:6 175	10:25 36
103	3:8 174	10:26-28 386
1:35 .... 95, 103	3:13 150	10:28 44
1:46-55 133	3:13, 16 92	10:30 75
1:68 433	3:17 .... 36, 88, 425	10:34, 35 69
1:80 318	3:19, 20 161	10:36 89
2:29 70	3:31, 32 91	11:11 345
2:38 433	3:33 230	11:50-52 446
2:40, 52 52	3:34 184	12:25 337
2:49 89	3:36 .. 143, 386, 404,	12:31 113
3:15 157	439, 468	12:32 ...... 146, 414
3:31 129	4:10 442	12:34 150
3:38 .. 99, 105, 108,	4:14 386	12:38 ...... 47, 489
407	4:23 468	12:38, 41 47
4:18 ...... 169, 378	4:24 ...... 70, 310	12:50 36
4:22 154	5:9 172	13:13 134
6:9 336	5:13 38	13:38 337
6:19 125	5:17 395	14:6 28
7:32 429	5:19-23 53	14:7-10 76
7:42, 43 462	5:22 .. 48, 408, 458	14:16, 26 202
9:24, 56 336	5:23 .. 38, 49, 72, 83	14:17 170
10:12 171	5:25, 28, 29 346	14:18 203
10:15 376	5:26 .. 78, 389, 396	14:18, 23 204
11:13 222	5:27 48	14:24 50
12:22, 23 336	5:30 .... 36, 44	14:26 ...... 170, 267
13:23, 24, 25 .. 401	5:39 205	14:28 36
14:26 336	5:43 36	14:30 ...... 113, 448
16:15 236	6:27 ...... 196, 246	15:1 230
16:23 376	6:38, 39 60	15:2 206
17:33 336	6:38, 51 89	15:4 171
19:12 265	6:40, 54 386	15:13 337
20:1 172	6:44 ...... 146, 414	15:16 207
20:37, 38 352	6:45 50	15:19 ...... 109, 235
21:28 434	6:51 151	16:3 294
22:17 171	6:53 171	16:8 291
22:29 38	6:57 44	16:11 113
23:46 344	6:60-66 89	16:12, 15 239
24:21 431	6:62 150	16:13 ...... 265, 266
24:47 461	6:63 225	16:13, 14 170
24:49 36	6:70 207	16:23 74
	7:16-18 50	17:2, 3 386
JOHN	7:39 176	17:5 87
1:1 .. 43, 70, 86, 93	7:46 154	17:6, 14, 17 50
1:3 87	8:12 293	17:9, 20-23 75
1:9 401	8:14, 23, 42-58 .. 90	17:16 109
1:10, 14 89	8:15 110	17:17 243
		17:25 91
		19:5 154

Index of Texts

19:30	429	15:13-18	276
20:15	172	15:14	177
20:17	36, 143	15:18	35
20:21	36	15:26	337
		15:28	275
ACTS		16:6	276
1:7	36	16:9	277
2:1-4	209	16:16, 18	313
2:4	207, 268	16:19	429
2:27	348	17:11	205
2:27, 29, 31, 34	377	17:16	312
2:27-34	362	17:18	70
2:31, 32	349	17:29	71
2:32	213	17:31	479
2:33	211, 246	17:32	351
2:34	49	18:5, 25	312
2:37-41	214	19:12, 13, 15	313
3:15	213	19:20	70
3:19-21	23, 221, 360, 402, 419, 452, 457, 466	19:21	312
		20:10, 24	337
		20:23	277
		20:24	191
3:19-23	69, 140, 221, 306, 473	20:28	51, 278, 446
		21:10-14	278
3:22	402	21:11	277
3:22, 23	27, 144	23:5	68
3:23	20, 30, 193, 199, 219, 240, 333, 388, 415, 439, 471	23:8, 9	313
		27:10, 22	338
		ROMANS	
4:12	446, 461, 472	1:9	312
4:24	70	1:18	409
5:3, 4	269	1:20	71
5:9	270	1:23	397
5:19	277	1:28	448
5:31	35, 120	2:7	285, 390, 395, 397, 411
5:32	213		
6:15	162	2:11-13	417
7:59	344	3:10	102, 252
7:60	345	3:10, 23	96, 407, 418
8:13-21	207		
8:13-23	247	3:19-23	417
8:29	273	3:20	444
8:39	274	3:24	434
9:4	277	3:24, 25	461
10:19	274	3:26	17, 401, 419
10:36	134	3:27, 28	444
10:36, 40	136	4:17	353
10:39-41	213	4:24, 25	445
10:43	461	4:25	442
10:45	207	5:1	54
12:7	277	5:6	451
13:1	275	5:8	446, 451
13:2	274	5:8, 9	25, 446
13:31	213		
13:36	345	5:10, 12, 18, 19	25
13:38	461	5:11	488
14:2	335	5:12	309, 331, 428, 452
		5:12, 19	102
		5:12, 21	189
		5:14, 12	484
		5:15, 21	285
		5:17-19	444
		5:19	414
		6:8	411
		6:9	90
		6:16-23	185
		6:22	140
		6:23	285, 385, 387, 404, 418, 442
		7:9-14	417
		7:14	189, 452
		8:1-4	121
		8:4	110
		8:6	313
		8:9	109, 184, 244
		8:10	305
		8:14-16	163
		8:15	143
		8:15, 23	109
		8:16	226
		8:17	144, 233, 455, 490
		8:17, 18	294
		8:17-24	25
		8:19-21	288
		8:20, 21	189
		8:23	434
		8:23, 24	289
		8:23-25	27
		8:26, 27	287
		8:29	30, 137, 144, 395
		8:31	291
		8:31-34	197
		9:4, 29-33	177
		11:3	338
		11:8	199
		11:26	469
		11:26, 27	357
		11:26-29	377
		11:26-31	332
		11:33-36	486
		12:1	450, 487, 499
		12:3	185, 255
		12:11	259, 318
		14:9	18, 134, 453
		14:14	171
		15:3	490

Index of Texts

Reference	Page
15:4	268
16:4	338

1 CORINTHIANS

Reference	Page
1:2	243
1:27, 28	250
1:30	435
2:8	44
2:9, 10	164
2:9, 10, 11	201
2:10, 11	192
2:10, 13,	279
2:12	318
2:12-16	202
2:14	279
3:23	142
4:5	193
4:10	202
5:3	312
5:7	446
6:2	193, 364
6:11	241, 445
6:20	312
7:23	446
7:39	345
8:2	256
8:4, 6	54
8:6	45, 82, 143, 398
9:25	397
10:20	450
11:3	49, 55
11:5	171
11:31	171, 233
12:4-11	179
12:6, 7, 28	278
12:7	185
12:12, 27	215
12:13	214
12:25-28	245
12:28-31	284
12:31	180
13:1-3	247
13:4	200
13:5	171
13:8	179, 207
13:10	251
14:1, 22	180
14:12	174
15:3	127, 442, 446
15:6	345
15:8	277
15:12-54	348
15:13-18	345
15:14-18	344
15:17, 18	349
15:20	345
15:21	95, 425
15:22	102
15:24	458
15:24-28	30, 44, 47, 78, 142
15:25-28	40
15:27	79, 392, 394, 444
15:37, 38	344, 349
15:37-40	343
15:42-44, 49	396
15:42-44, 53, 54	78
15:42-45	316
15:44, 46	312
15:45-47	138
15:45-48	455
15:47	105, 137
15:48, 49	141
15:51	345
15:52	398
15:53, 54, 42, 50,	397
15:54, 55	373
15:55, 37, 38, 16-18	377
15:57	46
16:15	171
32 E	

2 CORINTHIANS

Reference	Page
1:21, 22	247
2:13	318
3:2	294
3:17	175, 298
4:4	19, 61, 113, 189, 218, 260, 364, 470
4:6	293
4:7	195, 245, 306
4:11	77
4:17	411
4:18	238
5:1	196
5:14, 15	446
5:16	110, 298
5:17-20	488
5:19, 21	444
5:21	446
8:9	87, 394
9:15	285
10:4	250
13:5	232

GALATIANS

Reference	Page
1:1	275
1:4	450
2:16	444
2:17	445
2:20	450
3:8, 16, 29	26
3:13	430
3:13, 14	445
3:16, 29	476
3:29	395, 403
4:4	105, 451
4:4, 5	417, 430
4:5	109, 177
4:23-31	105
5:4	444
5:16, 17	201
5:22, 23	180, 185
6:1	185, 313
6:8	386
6:10	117

EPHESIANS

Reference	Page
1:2-18	82
1:3	313
1:5	177
1:5, 11	109
1:6	446
1:7	435, 461
1:11	412
1:13, 14	246
1:14	153, 221, 436, 441
1:17, 18	186
1:17-19	147
1:17-22	39
1:19, 20	281
1:21	393
2:3	17, 108, 145
2:4-10	147
3:6	396
3:10	17, 413
3:19	224
4:8	210
4:11-13	284
4:16	171, 245
4:23	319
4:30	247, 264, 437
4:32	461
5:2	446, 450
5:8, 11, 13	293
5:15, 16	431
5:18-20	244
5:19	313
5:23	49
5:26	243
6:6	335
6:12	188, 189
6:24	397

PHILIPPIANS

Reference	Page
1:27	335
2:5	169

Index of Texts

2:6 79	3:16 77	4:15 110
2:8 51	4:10 33	4:15, 16 128
2:8, 9 ..... 394, 444	6:10 259	5:2 128
2:9 ... 83, 151, 298	6:12, 19 386	5:4, 5 487
2:9-11 37	6:15 ..... 71, 136	5:8 51
2:11 82	6:15, 16 78	5:8-10 120
2:14, 15 293	6:16 .... 392, 397	5:9 386
2:13 411	6:20 285	5:13, 14 238
2:30 338	6:20, 21 296	7:5, 10 100
3:8-11 338		7:22 28
3:10 230	## 2 TIMOTHY	7:25 ..... 96, 229
4:7 226	1:7 ... 196, 198, 249	7:25, 26 128
4:8 282	1:10 .. 383, 393, 397	7:26 ..... 97, 106
## COLOSSIANS	1:12 346	7:26, 28 95
	2:3, 4 250	7:27 450
1:9 313	2:12 ..... 146, 490	8:1 38
1:12 121	2:13 490	8:6 455
1:14 ..... 436, 461	2:25 284	8:11 20
1:15-18 86	3:12 ..... 191, 235	9:11, 12 433
1:18-20 424	3:17 .. 167, 179, 205	9:12 446
1:22 395		9:13-15, 26 450
1:24 .... 42, 146, 234	## TITUS	9:14 445
1:26 146	1:3 33	9:14-16 455
2:9 71	1:9, 13 284	9:15 437
2:10 79	1:16 490	9:15, 20 28
3:13 462	2:7 397	9:22 442
4:5 431	2:10 33	10:4-10, 12, 20, 450
## 1 THESSA-LONIANS	2:14 ... 30, 432, 450	10:10 446
	3:4-6 35	10:12 38
2:16 357	3:5 445	10:12, 13 49
4:13-15 346		10:22 ..... 226, 230
4:14 .... 328, 444	## HEBREWS	10:26-31 474
5:5 293	1:2-4 38	10:31 472
5:10 444	1:5, 6 72	10:38 350
5:19 264	1:8, 9 49	11 96
5:23 .... 242, 353	1:13 49	11:6 230
## 2 THESSA-LONIANS	2:1 .... 205, 245	11:10, 16 90
	2:3 393	11:32, 39, 40 .. 377
1:9 .. 20, 193, 330,	2:5-9 426	11:35 438
388, 392	2:7, 9 ...... 67, 82	11:39, 40 141,
2:3-7 286	2:9 ...... 105, 451	144, 403
## 1 TIMOTHY	2:9, 10 51	12:2 ... 39, 118, 462
	2:9, 16 151	12:3 ..... 159, 335
1:1 35	2:10 ...... 118, 395	12:3, 2 394
1:17 ..... 389, 398	2:10-13 144	12:7 231
2:3, 5 35	2:11 244	12:8 233
2:4 .... 20, 466	2:12 109	12:11 411
2:4-6 ...... 328, 401	2:13 49	12:22 90
2:5 .... 95, 451	2:14 ... 390, 392, 448	12:24 316
2:6 .... 17, 394, 420	2:14, 16 425	13:8 230
2:5, 6 .. 82, 83, 421	2:14-18 136	13:12 446
428, 462	2:16 138	13:14 90
3:2 284	2:17 107	13:17 284
2:14 .... 22, 408	2:17, 18 128	13:20 39
	2:18 52	

Index of Texts

JAMES

1:17	463
1:18	143
1:21	91
2:17	171
2:26	317
4:5	200
4:6	255
4:10	424

1 PETER

1:2	140, 147, 243, 446
1:3	105, 141, 143, 456
1:4	398
1:10-12	178
1:12	412
1:18	258, 438
1:18, 19	432
1:19	385, 445, 450
1:23	105, 398
2:2	238, 240
2:5	313, 375
2:9, 10	30
2:22-24	446, 461
2:23	191
3:4	312, 319, 398
3:7	262
3:18	84, 151, 442, 446
3:22	39
4:4	431
4:14	221, 237
5:2-4	284
5:5, 6	255
5:6	424
5:9	42

2 PETER

1:3, 4	71
1:4	69, 105, 146, 257, 388, 396, 410, 455
1:4-11	411
1:5-11	239
1:19	205
1:21	175, 178
2:1	70, 296, 447
2:4	104

2:18, 20	410
2:19	286
2:22	445
3:4	345
3:8	391

1 JOHN

1:1	85
1:3	284
1:7	445, 461
2:1	284
2:2	328, 442
2:8	284
2:12	461
2:18, 26, 27	286
2:20, 27	281
2:24	286
2:25	386
2:27	215
3:2	69, 175, 299, 349
3:5	97
3:7	284
3:9	461
3:13	284
3:16	338, 450
3:17, 18	349
4:1, 6	187
4:2	297, 298
4:2, 3	295
4:5, 6	199
4:6	284
4:9	88, 451
4:10	442
4:14	35
4:18	255
5:3	248
5:4	237
5:7	56
5:11, 12	386
5:16	172, 204
5:18	143, 235, 461

2 JOHN

7	295, 297, 298

JUDE

3:	62
4	70, 286
6	104, 413
20	294
25	33

REVELATION

1:1	36
1:5	136, 445, 446
1:17	93
1:18	378
2:8	93
2:10	490
2:17	247
2:20	171
3:11	490
3:12	43
3:14	87
3:21	38
5	36
5:9	429, 446, 447
5:9-12	395
5:9-13	37
5:10	478
5:12	120
6:8	378
6:10	71
7:4	395
7:9, 14	234
7:16	403
8:9	338
10:4	246
10:9	225
12:1	207
12:11	338
13:15	174
14:3	429
14:4	430
14:14	150
18:21	369
19:7	43
20:2	218
20:3	18, 20, 246
20:4	469
20:7-10	402
20:9-13	480
20:9, 14, 15	30
20:13	379
20:13, 14	380
21:2, 9	395
21:4	30
21:4, 6, 8	403
21:9	43
21:14	207
22:3	193, 405, 439
22:16	135
22:17	165, 208

The Divine Plan of the Ages

THE SATISFACTORY PROOF THAT

THE BIBLE is a divine revelation—reasonable and trustworthy, revealing a systematic plan, exemplifying justice, wisdom, and love.

The "key of knowledge" to the Scriptures, long lost, is found, and gives God's faithful people access to the "hidden mystery."—Luke 11:52; Col. 1:26

The Lord Jesus and his faithful followers are to be not only priests, but kings, and will reign over the earth.

This kingdom comes at Christ's second advent.

God's plan is to select and save the church in the Gospel age, and to use the church in blessing the world during the Millennium.

A ransom for all implies an opportunity to all for restitution.

The day of judgment is 1,000 years long, and will be the world's trial day.

"The narrow way" of self-sacrifice will cease at the end of this age.

"The highway" of righteousness will be open to all the redeemed race in the Millennium.—Isaiah 35:8, 9

"The kingdoms of this world" are but for an ordained period and must give place to the "kingdom of God."

These subjects and many others of deep interest to all are discussed fully and in language easy of comprehension in Volume I of the Scripture Study series.

354 PAGES—CLOTH BOUND—75 cents, POSTPAID

DAWN BIBLE STUDENTS ASSOCIATION
East Rutherford   New Jersey 07073

THINGS YOU WANT TO KNOW

The Time Is at Hand

VOLUME II

THERE ARE EVIDENCES THAT

SIX thousand years from Adam's fall into sin ended in A. D. 1874.

The date of our Lord's birth was October, 2 B. C.

The date of the annunciation to Mary was December 25, 3 B. C.

The date of our Lord's baptism was October, A. D. 29.

The date of our Lord's crucifixion was April, A. D. 33.

The "seventy weeks" of Israel's favor ended A. D. 36.

The Jewish age "harvest" was forty years, A. D. 30-70.

The Christian age "harvest" is its parallel.

The Jewish jubilees were typical of the "times of restitution of all things, which God hath spoken by the mouth of all his holy prophets since the world began."—Acts 3:19-21

The typical jubilees mark the date of their antitype.

The "times of the Gentiles" ended A. D. 1914.

The Jewish age, in its length, its ceremonies, etc., typified the realities of the Christian age and its length.

Elias, or "Elijah the prophet" was a type—now fulfilled.

The Antichrist foretold in the prophecies of the Bible has come!—What? When? Where?

These subjects and many others, deeply interesting to the "household of faith," and "meat in due season" to all who love and study God's Word, are discussed in this, the second volume of Studies in the Scriptures.

375 PAGES—CLOTH BOUND—75¢ POSTPAID

DAWN BIBLE STUDENTS ASSOCIATION
East Rutherford, N. J. 07073

THINGS YOU OUGHT TO KNOW

Thy Kingdom Come

VOLUME III

DO YOU KNOW THAT

WE ARE now living in the "time of the end" of this Gospel age?

This is the day of preparation for the Millennial age?

The present period of fear and distress was foretold by Jesus and the prophets and described as a "time of trouble such as never was since there was a nation"?

The "days of waiting" are ended, and the "cleansing of the sanctuary"—the church—the separating of its wheat and tares, is now in progress?

The time has now come for Israel to repossess the land of Palestine, hence the commercial interests of other nations will not long be permitted to interfere with this, the divine purpose?

The great pyramid in Egypt is a witness to all these events of the past and present—testifying in symbols? The pyramid's downward passage symbolizes the course of sin? Its first ascending passage symbolizes the Jewish age? Its grand gallery symbolizes the Gospel age? Its upper step symbolizes the present period of tribulation and coming anarchy—"judgments" upon Christendom? Its king's chamber symbolizes the divine nature, etc., of the overcoming church—The Christ, Head and body? Its antechamber symbolizes the correction in righteousness of the Spirit begotten, etc.? Its queen's chamber symbolizes those of Israel and the world who eventually attain restitution?

All these interesting topics, with ten pyramid illustrations, can be had in "Thy Kingdom Come."

500 PAGES—CLOTH BOUND—75¢ POSTPAID

DAWN BIBLE STUDENTS ASSOCIATION
East Rutherford, N. J. 07073

THINGS ALL NEED TO KNOW
The Battle of Armageddon

VOLUME IV

"THE WISE SHALL UNDERSTAND" THAT

THIS Gospel age is now closing with a "day of vengeance."

All political, social, financial, and religious systems will fall.

Our day is mentioned by the prophets as "the day of Jehovah," and is symbolically styled a "dark day," a "day of clouds," etc.

Its trouble is symbolically likened to a hurricane, to a flood, to a fire, etc., these strong figures being used to give an understanding, yet to hide the real nature of that "time of trouble such as never was since there was a nation."—Daniel 12:1

Preparations for this symbolic fire and tempest began many years ago, and the trouble is now well under way, and will continue to rage furiously and increase throughout the world.

It is a contest between masses and classes, which even now many see upon us, and are advocating various remedies.

All worldly schemes and panaceas will fail utterly. God's kingdom, the only hope for church and world, is sure.

Man's extremity will prove to be God's opportunity —in the establishment of God's kingdom—Christ's Millennial kingdom which will establish righteousness by force.—Revelation 2:26, 27; Daniel 2:34, 35, 44, 45

All these subjects are simply yet forcefully treated and Matthew 24th chapter elucidated in this, the fourth volume of "Studies in the Scriptures."

700 PAGES—CLOTH BOUND—$1.25, POSTPAID

DAWN BIBLE STUDENTS ASSOCIATION
East Rutherford, N. J. 07073

FOUNDATION OF CHRISTIANITY

The Atonement Between God and Man

VOLUME V

ALL SHOULD KNOW

ABOUT the great Mediator of the at-one-ment, our Lord Jesus Christ.

Respecting the necessity for the at-one-ment, and the necessity that the "only Begotten" must be "made flesh," and then die, and rise from the dead, in order to effect the at-one-ment.

Respecting the office and work of the Holy Spirit in connection with the at-one-ment.

About the important part of the at-one-ment not yet finished—which awaits the second coming of our Lord in his kingdom glory.

Respecting the central doctrine of at-one-ment, namely, the ransom—what it was—why it was, and is, the center, or hub, around which and into which all Bible doctrines fit.

How this doctrine is the test of the truth or falsity a guard against error in every form—especially the errors of modernism.

Respecting man, the subject of the great at-one-ment; his nature; his sin; his penalty; his deliverance through Christ; his future possibilities through acceptance of the at-one-ment.

All of these interesting and very important themes are lucidly discussed in simple language, and corroborated by 1,400 Scripture citations in this, the fifth volume of the Scripture Study series.

600 PAGES—CLOTH BOUND—$1.25, POSTPAID

DAWN BIBLE STUDENTS ASSOCIATION
East Rutherford, N. J. 07073

MANY CHRISTIANS IN PERPLEXITY

The New Creation

VOLUME VI

YOU OUGHT TO KNOW ABOUT

THE creative week of Genesis—its actual length—scientifically corroborated.

The true church of Christ, begotten of the Spirit as the new creation: the steps of grace divine—justification, sanctification, and deliverance in the first resurrection.

The duties and obligations of the new creation—toward the Lord, toward one another, toward earthly friends and neighbors, toward parents, children, husbands, wives, etc.

The Lord's memorial supper, or sacrament: what it is, and what it is not.

The many mistakes concerning baptism of nearly all denominations, as pointed out in this volume in kindly spirit, and about the true baptism, which is set forth in convincing style—indisputable, incontrovertible.

The foes and besetments of the new creation, and the scriptural method of overcoming them; also, the present and the future inheritance of the saints.

Satan, the devil, the archenemy of every consecrated follower of Jesus. Who created him, and his ultimate end. Satan's associates in deception, the fallen angels.

These subjects, and many others deeply interesting to all who love and study the Bible, are fully treated in this final volume of "Studies in the Scriptures."

725 PAGES—CLOTH BOUND—$1.25, POSTPAID

DAWN BIBLE STUDENTS ASSOCIATION
East Rutherford, N. J. 07073